Legal Research

DATE DUE

JE ꞏ04			

DEMCO 38-296

Paralegal Titles from Delmar Publishers

Legal Research, Steve Barber, Mark A. McCormick, 1996
Wills, Estates, and Trusts, Jay E. Gingrich, 1996
Criminal Law and Procedure, 2E, Daniel E. Hall, 1996
Introduction to Environmental Law, Harold Hickock, 1996
Civil Litigation, 2E, Peggy N. Kerley, Joanne Banker Hames, Paul A. Sukys, 1996
Client Accounting for the Law Office, Elaine M. Langston, 1996
Law Office Management, 2E, Jonathan S. Lynton, Terri Mick Lyndall, Donna
    Masinter, 1996
Foundations of Law: Cases, Commentary, and Ethics, 2E, Ransford C. Pyle, 1996
Administrative Law and Procedure, Elizabeth C. Richardson, 1996
Legal Research and Writing, David J. Smith, 1996

Legal Research and Writing, Carol M. Bast, 1995
Federal Taxation, Susan G. Covins, 1995
Everything You Need to Know About Being a Legal Assistant, Chere B. Estrin, 1995
Paralegals in New York Law, Eric M. Gansberg, 1995
Ballentine's Legal Dictionary and Thesaurus, Jonathan S. Lynton, 1995
Legal Terminology with Flashcards, Cathy J. Okrent, 1995
Wills, Trusts, and Estate Administration for Paralegals, Mark A. Stewart, 1995
The Law of Contracts and the Uniform Commercial Code, Pamela R. Tepper, 1995
Life Outside the Law Firm: Non-Traditional Careers for Paralegals, Karen
    Treffinger, 1995

An Introduction to Paralegal Studies, David G. Cooper, Michael J. Gibson, 1994
Administrative law, Daniel E. Hall, 1994
Ballentine's Law Dictionary: Legal Assistant Edition, Jack G. Handler, 1994
The Law of Real Property, Michael S. Kearns, 1994
Ballentine's Thesaurus for Legal Research and Writing, Jonathan S. Lynton, 1994
Ballentine's Thesaurus for Legal Research and Writing, Jonathan S. Lynton, Terri
    Mick Lyndall, 1994
Criminal Law for Paralegals, Daniel J. Markey, Jr., Mary Queen Donnelly, 1994
Family Law, Ransford C. Pyle, 1994
Paralegals in American Law: Introduction to Paralegalism, Angela Schneeman,
    1994
Intellectual Property, Richard Stim, 1994

Legal Writing for Paralegals, Steve Barber, 1993
Administration of Wills, Trusts, and Estates, Gordon W. Brown, 1993
Torts and Personal Injury Laws, William R. Buckley, 1993
Survey of Criminal Law, Daniel E. Hall, 1993
The Law of Corporations, Partnerships, and Sole Proprietorships, Angela
    Schneeman, 1993

Legal Research

Steve Barber

Mark A. McCormick

Delmar Publishers
I**T**P An International Thomson Publishing Company

Albany • Bonn • Boston • Cincinnati • Detroit • London • Madrid • Melbourne
Mexico City • New York • Pacific Grove • Paris • San Francisco • Singapore • Tokyo
Toronto • Washington

OTICE TO THE READER

of the products described herein or perform any independent analysis
rmation contained herein. Publisher does not assume, and expressly
le information other than that provided to it by the manufacturer.

The reader is expressly warned to consider and adopt all safety precautions that might be indicated by the activities herein and to avoid all potential hazards. By following the instructions contained herein, the reader willingly assumes all risks in connection with such instructions.

The publisher makes no representation or warranties of any kind, including but not limited to, the warranties of fitness for particular purpose or merchantability, nor are any such representations implied with respect to the material set forth herein, and the publisher takes no responsibility with respect to such material. The publisher shall not be liable for any special, consequential, or exemplary damages resulting, in whole or part, from the readers' use of, or reliance upon, this material.

Background by Jennifer McGlaughlin
Design by Douglas J. Hyldelund / Linda C. DeMasi

Delmar Staff
Acquisitions Editor: Christopher Anzalone
Developmental Editor: Jeffrey D. Litton
Project Editor: Eugenia L. Orlandi

Production Coordinator: Jennifer Gaines
Art & Design Coordinator: Douglas J. Hyldelund

Copyright © 1996
By Delmar Publishers and Lawyers Cooperative Publishing
divisions of International Thompson Publishing Inc.

The ITP logo is a trademark under license.

Printed in the United States of America

For more information, contact:

Delmar Publishers
3 Columbia Circle
Box 15015
Albany, New York 12212-5015

International Thomson Editores
Campos Eliseos 385, Piso 7
Col Polanco
11560 Mexico D F Mexico

International Thomson Publishing Europe
Berkshire House 168 - 173
High Holborn
London WC1V 7AA
England

International Thomson Publishing GmbH
Königswinterer Strasse 418
53227 Bonn
Germany

Thomas Nelson Australia
102 Dodds Street
South Melbourne, 3205
Victoria, Australia

International Thomson Publishing Asia
221 Henderson Road
#05 - 10 Henderson Building
Sinapore 0315

Nelson Canada
1120 Birchmount Road
Scarborough, Ontario
Canada M1K 5G4

International Thomson Publishing - Japan
Hirakawacho Kyowa Building, 3F
2-2-1 Hirakawacho
Chiyoda-ku, Tokyo 102
Japan

1 2 3 4 5 6 7 8 9 10 xxx 01 00 99 98 97 96 95

Library of Congress Cataloging-in-Publication Data

Barber, Steve, 1948–
    Legal research / Steve Barber
        p. cm.
        Includes index.
        ISBN 0-8273-7474-7
    1. Legal Research—United States. I. McCormick, Mark A., 1958–
. II. Title.
KF240.B267   1996
340'.0072073—dc20

95-21728
CIP

DEDICATION

Steve Barber dedicates this text to Mamie.

Mark McCormick dedicates this text to his boys, Jordan and Zachary,
who continually remind him of the joys of life.

Delmar Publishers' Online Services

To access Delmar on the World Wide Web, point your browser to:
http://www.delmar.com/delmar.html
To access through Gopher: gopher://gopher.delmar.com
(Delmar Online is part of "thomson.com", and Internet site with information on
more than 30 publishers of the International Thomson Publishing organization.)
For more information on our products and services:
email: info@delmar.com
or call 800-347-7707

CONTENTS

IIII CHAPTER 10 The Legal Research Process   281

IIII APPENDICES   A-1

IIII Glossary   G-1

IIII Index   I-1

DELMAR PUBLISHERS INC.

AND

LAWYERS COOPERATIVE PUBLISHING

ARE PLEASED TO ANNOUNCE THEIR PARTNERSHIP TO CO-PUBLISH COLLEGE TEXTBOOKS FOR PARALEGAL EDUCATION.

DELMAR, WITH OFFICES AT ALBANY, NEW YORK, IS A PROFESSIONAL EDUCATION PUBLISHER. DELMAR PUBLISHES QUALITY EDUCATIONAL TEXTBOOKS TO PREPARE AND SUPPORT INDIVIDUALS FOR LIFE SKILLS AND SPECIFIC OCCUPATIONS.

LAWYERS COOPERATIVE PUBLISHING (LCP), WITH OFFICES AT ROCHESTER, NEW YORK, HAS BEEN THE LEADING PUBLISHER OF ANALYTICAL LEGAL INFORMATION FOR OVER 100 YEARS. IT IS THE PUBLISHER OF SUCH RENOWNED LEGAL ENCYCLOPEDIAS AS **AMERICAN LAW REPORTS, AMERICAN JURISPRUDENCE, UNITED STATES CODE SERVICE, LAWYERS EDITION,** AS WELL AS OTHER MATERIAL, AND FEDERAL- AND STATE-SPECIFIC PUBLICATIONS. THESE PUBLICATIONS HAVE BEEN DESIGNED TO WORK TOGETHER IN THE DAY-TO-DAY PRACTICE OF LAW AS AN INTEGRATED SYSTEM IN WHAT IS CALLED THE "TOTAL CLIENT-SERVICE LIBRARY® (TCSL®). EACH LCP PUBLICATION IS COMPLETE WITHIN ITSELF AS TO SUBJECT COVERAGE. YET ALL HAVE COMMON FEATURES AND EXTENSIVE CROSS-REFERENCING TO PROVIDE LINKAGE FOR HIGHLY EFFICIENT LEGAL RESEARCH INTO VIRTUALLY ANY MATTER AN ATTORNEY MIGHT BE CALLED UPON TO HANDLE.

INFORMATION IN ALL PUBLICATIONS IS CAREFULLY AND CONSTANTLY MONITORED TO KEEP PACE WITH AND REFLECT EVENTS IN THE LAW AND IN SOCIETY. UPDATING AND SUPPLEMENTAL INFORMATION IS TIMELY AND PROVIDED CONVENIENTLY.

FOR FURTHER REFERENCE, SEE:

AMERICAN JURISPRUDENCE 2D: AN ENCYCLOPEDIC TEXT COVERAGE OF THE COMPLETE BODY OF STATE AND FEDERAL LAW.

AM JUR LEGAL FORMS 2D: A COMPILATION OF BUSINESS AND LEGAL FORMS DEALING WITH A VARIETY OF SUBJECT MATTERS.

AM JUR PLEADING AND PRACTICE FORMS, REV: MODEL PRACTICE FORMS FOR EVERY STAGE OF A LEGAL PROCEEDING.

AM JUR PROOF OF FACTS: A SERIES OF ARTICLES THAT GUIDE THE READER IN DETERMINING WHICH FACTS ARE ESSENTIAL TO A CASE AND HOW TO PROVE THEM.

AM JUR TRIALS: A SERIES OF ARTICLES DISCUSSING EVERY ASPECT OF PARTICULAR SETTLEMENTS AND TRIALS WRITTEN BY 180 CONSULTING SPECIALISTS.

UNITED STATES CODE SERVICE: A COMPLETE AND AUTHORITATIVE ANNOTATED FEDERAL CODE THAT FOLLOWS THE EXACT LANGUAGE OF THE STATUTES AT LARGE AND DIRECTS YOU TO THE COURT AND AGENCY DECISIONS CONSTRUING EACH PROVISION.

ALR AND ALR FEDERAL: SERIES OF ANNOTATIONS PROVIDING IN-DEPTH ANALYSES OF ALL THE CASE LAW ON PARTICULAR LEGAL ISSUES.

U.S. SUPREME COURT REPORTS, L ED 2D: EVERY REPORTED U.S. SUPREME COURT DECISION PLUS IN-DEPTH DISCUSSIONS OF LEADING ISSUES.

FEDERAL PROCEDURE, L ED: A COMPREHENSIVE, A-Z TREATISE ON FEDERAL PROCEDURE—CIVIL, CRIMINAL, AND ADMINISTRATIVE.

FEDERAL PROCEDURAL FORMS, L ED: STEP-BY-STEP GUIDANCE FOR DRAFTING FORMS FOR FEDERAL COURT OR FEDERAL AGENCY PROCEEDINGS.

FEDERAL RULES SERVICE, 2D AND 3D: REPORTS DECISIONS FROM ALL LEVELS OF THE FEDERAL SYSTEM INTERPRETING THE FEDERAL RULES OF CIVIL PROCEDURE AND THE FEDERAL RULES OF APPELLATE PROCEDURE.

FEDERAL RULES DIGEST, 3D: ORGANIZES HEADNOTES FOR THE DECISIONS REPORTED IN FEDERAL RULES SERVICE ACCORDING TO THE NUMBERING SYSTEMS OF THE FEDERAL RULES OF CIVIL PROCEDURE AND THE FEDERAL RULES OF APPELLATE PROCEDURE.

FEDERAL RULES OF EVIDENCE SERVICE: REPORTS DECISIONS FROM ALL LEVELS OF THE FEDERAL SYSTEM INTERPRETING THE FEDERAL RULES OF EVIDENCE.

FEDERAL RULES OF EVIDENCE NEWS

FEDERAL PROCEDURE RULES SERVICE

FEDERAL TRIAL HANDBOOK, 2D

FORM DRAFTING CHECKLISTS: AM JUR PRACTICE GUIDE

GOVERNMENT CONTRACTS: PROCEDURES AND FORMS

HOW TO GO DIRECTLY INTO YOUR OWN COMPUTERIZED SOLO PRACTICE WITHOUT MISSING A MEAL (OR A BYTE)

JONES ON EVIDENCE, CIVIL AND CRIMINAL, 7TH

LITIGATION CHECKLISTS: AM JUR PRACTICE GUIDE

MEDICAL LIBRARY, LAWYERS EDITION

MEDICAL MALPRACTICE—ALR CASES AND ANNOTATIONS

MODERN APPELLATE PRACTICE: FEDERAL AND STATE CIVIL APPEALS

MODERN CONSTITUTIONAL LAW

NEGOTIATION AND SETTLEMENT

PATTERN DEPOSITION CHECKLISTS, 2D

QUALITY OF LIFE DAMAGES: CRITICAL ISSUES AND PROOFS

SHEPARD'S CITATIONS FOR ALR

SUCCESSFUL TECHNIQUES FOR CIVIL TRIALS, 2D

STORIES ET CETERA—A COUNTRY LAWYER LOOKS AT LIFE AND THE LAW

SUMMARY OF AMERICAN LAW

THE TRIAL LAWYER'S BOOK: PREPARING AND WINNING CASES

TRIAL PRACTICE CHECKLISTS

2000 CLASSIC LEGAL QUOTATIONS

WILLISTON ON CONTRACTS, 3D AND 4TH

FEDERAL RULES OF EVIDENCE DIGEST: ORGANIZES HEADNOTES FOR THE DECISIONS REPORTED IN FEDERAL RULES OF EVIDENCE SERVICE ACCORDING TO THE NUMBERING SYSTEM OF THE FEDERAL RULES OF EVIDENCE.

ADMINISTRATIVE LAW: PRACTICE AND PROCEDURE

AGE DISCRIMINATION: CRITICAL ISSUES AND PROOFS

ALR CRITICAL ISSUES: DRUNK DRIVING PROSECUTIONS

ALR CRITICAL ISSUES: FREEDOM OF INFORMATION ACTS

ALR CRITICAL ISSUES: TRADEMARKS

ALR CRITICAL ISSUES: WRONGFUL DEATH

AMERICANS WITH DISABILITIES: PRACTICE AND COMPLI-
ANCE MANUAL

ATTORNEYS' FEES

BALLENTINE'S LAW DICTIONARY

CONSTITUTIONAL LAW DESKBOOK

CONSUMER AND BORROWER PROTECTION: AM JUR PRAC-
TICE GUIDE

CONSUMER CREDIT: ALR ANNOTATIONS

DAMAGES: ALR ANNOTATIONS

EMPLOYEE DISMISSAL: CRITICAL ISSUES AND PROOFS

ENVIRONMENTAL LAW: ALR ANNOTATIONS

EXPERT WITNESS CHECKLISTS

EXPERT WITNESSES IN CIVIL TRIALS

FORFEITURES: ALR ANNOTATIONS

FEDERAL LOCAL COURT RULES

FEDERAL LOCAL COURT FORMS

FEDERAL CRIMINAL LAW AND PROCEDURE: ALR ANNOTA-
TIONS

FEDERAL EVIDENCE

FEDERAL LITIGATION DESK SET: FORMS AND ANALYSIS

PREFACE

Mastering legal research is, without a doubt, a primary element in achieving success and growth in the legal profession. Although legal research is an essential component of any legal studies curriculum, most textbooks do not adequately prepare the student to consider the larger picture—resolving legal problems. Instead, they instruct the student only on how to research and employ individual sources of law in isolation. Rarely do they address the role of research in resolving legal issues as a whole.

Instructors should continually remind their students about the real implications of on-the-job failure. Poor legal research can contribute to losing a case, with the client losing money, resources, or even freedom. Such mishandling of a case can have profound consequences for the attorney or law firm. The client may have grounds to sue for legal malpractice, the reputation of the firm may be damaged, and the researcher will, in all likelihood, lose a job. Success, on the other hand, has its rewards. Protecting a client's interests, increasing firm prestige, and career advancement are all proper goals of any legal professional.

The purpose behind writing *Legal Research* is to provide a clear and compelling reason and templates on how to succeed at legal research, every time.

About the Textbook

Legal Research presents the legal process in ten chapters. Chapter 1 introduces the reader to the **legal process.** How to begin is an essential starting point. Chapter 2 discusses **statutes:** how to read them and how to research them. Chapter 3 explores **case law** with an overview of the anatomy of a typical case. The subject matter of Chapter 4 is three **case-finding tools:** digests, the A.L.R., and *Words and Phrases.* Chapter 5 discusses **secondary research aids** including encyclopedias, treatises, legal periodicals, restatements, and C.L.E. materials. In Chapter 6, additional methods of **researching statutory laws** are discussed. Chapter 7 is devoted to **computer-assisted legal research** (CALR). An exciting, and often neglected, aspect of CALR is the role of the **Internet** in resolving legal research problems. A significant portion of the chapter is devoted to this revolutionary new tool. Chapter 8 discusses the **updating and verifying of legal research.** The role and use of **shepardizing** is the main thrust of this chapter. Chapter 9 looks at how the researcher must consider various **practice aids** including form books, reference works, directories, and newspapers. Finally, in Chapter 10, the parts are assembled for another exploration of the **legal process.** This chapter explores matters such as the determination of facts and issues, decisions about legal authority and jurisdiction, how to find the law, how to verify results, and when to end the legal research.

Numerous special features and elements have been integrated throughout *Legal Research* to promote student understanding. All new terms are in **boldface** type. There are two glossaries for these new terms—a **running glossary** located in close proximity to the new term, and a more traditional **end-of-the-text glossary** that is alphabetized for quick reference. Glossary terms that correspond to *Ballentine's Legal Dictionary and Thesaurus* (Delmar/LCP, 1995) are indicated by a dagger (†) following the terms. **Step-by-step procedures** are found throughout the text to provide students with reminders and recommendations for resolving research barriers. **Tables** summarizing key points are included. **Flowcharts** provide visual references for the student. **Sidebars** round out the learning process with tips and suggestions for mastering the research process. Each chapter ends with a **bulleted summary, review questions**, and **research projects** to test and expand student understanding. *Legal Research* is full of **exhibits of statutes and cases** with explanatory information that will provide students with exposure to actual sources of law. And there are five **appendixes** to the text including a United States District Court opinion and an A.L.R. passage.

About the Appendix E Resource Manual

For each chapter of the text, the student Resource Manual presents a set of Test Your Knowledge Questions and Answers that will serve as a convenient aid for test review. The most important feature of the Resource Manual is the Legal Research Exercises for each chapter. The exercises are divided into five distinct groups, and generally are divided into separate geographic regions. These exercises will help students put into practice the legal research skills described in the text.

About the Instructor's Guide

For the instructor, we have published an accompanying Instructor's Guide with Testbank and a Computerized Testbank to assist in generating test questions. The Instructor's Guide includes **chapter learning objectives, lecture material, teaching suggestions**, and **answers** to the Legal Research Exercises for each chapter. With the realization that preparing for a legal research course is very difficult and time-consuming, we have put together instructor material that will enrich and enliven lectures and reduce the burdens of "prepping."

An excellent resource that should be part of every paralegal's library is the *Ballentine's Legal Dictionary and Thesaurus* (Delmar/LCP, 1995), which was the source for most of the legal terms included in this text.

About the Authors

Steve Barber earned his Juris Doctor degree from Indiana University School of Law, where he was inducted into the Order of the Coif. He is an adjunct instructor in the Paralegal Program at the University of Evansville (Indiana) where he has taught legal research and legal writing since 1976. An attorney in private practice in Evansville, Mr. Barber has published various law-related articles as well as a companion textbook *Legal Writing for Paralegals* (Delmar Publishers/South-Western Publishing, 1993).

Mark A. McCormick earned his Bachelor of Arts degree from Davidson College and his Juris Doctor degree from New York University School of Law. He is currently associate professor of Paralegal Studies and Coordinator of the Paralegal Studies Program at the Community College of Philadelphia. He has ten years of experience in paralegal education, specializing primarily in legal research and writing. He is also a member of the Pennsylvania bar and maintains a private law practice in Philadelphia.

ACKNOWLEDGMENTS

Steve Barber thanks his office staff, especially Janet Williams, Jo Jackson, Heather McGillem and Jason Hamilton for their untold hours on this project. He also would like to acknowledge the assistance of Helen Reed, both in her capacity as a reviewer for this book and as the law librarian who contributed numerous materials for this text. Finally, he would like to thank Barry Corrado for his early direction of this project.

Many friends and colleagues provided Mark McCormick with support, encouragement, and guidance in this project, most notably Anthony J. D'Angelo, Thomas E. Hora, Aram L. Terzian, Sharon Thompson, Alan LaPayover, Esther Bruce Kirk, Andrew L. Gangolf III, Charlotte Carter, and Stephen Housewright. He also wishes to acknowledge the invaluable assistance of Joan Johnson, Executive Director of the Educational Resources Center at the Community College of Philadelphia and all of her staff as well as the law librarians at the Theodore F. Jenkins Memorial Law Library in Philadelphia.

We would also like to thank the following reviewers for their valuable insight and suggestions.

Nancy L. Hart
Midland College
Midland, TX

Judy Gibbs
Avila College
Kansas City, MO

Anne M. Dodds
Carrington, Coleman, Sloman & Blumenthal
Dallas, TX

Joyce Wang Birdoff
Nassau Community College
Garden City, NY

Helen Reed
William H. Miller Law Library
Evansville, IN

Steve Barber
Mark McCormick

IIII
CHAPTER 1

INTRODUCTION TO THE LEGAL RESEARCH PROCESS

Legal research may be the most important skill taught in a legal studies curriculum. Mastering legal research techniques enables paralegals to do most of the job duties expected of them in a law office. If paralegals can use the law library, they can read the law, draft a simple contract or lease, draft a complaint for filing in court, or prepare to interview a witness. The importance of these skills to a practicing paralegal is shown by a study conducted by the United States Department of Labor. The study found that a paralegal is expected to be able to research cases, statutes, and other legal rules. Although a paralegal's work must be supervised, the more familiar the paralegal is with the legal research process, the more productive the paralegal will become. A legal professional soon discovers that learning about the legal research process means learning the tools of the legal trade.

The Law Library

Many law offices have their own law library. Sometimes these libraries are quite simple, while others can cost hundreds of thousands of dollars each year to maintain. A local unit of government (a city or county) or a bar association may maintain a law library. Law schools maintain extensive law libraries, sometimes with thousands or even millions of books. When you understand the legal research process and become familiar with the different sets of legal books, you will feel comfortable in any law library—whatever its size.

Using a law library is not like using the public library, although as you become more familiar with the common techniques of legal research, you will begin to see some similarities and differences in the two processes. For instance, most students begin research in a library by resorting to a card catalog or to a computerized version of a card catalog, while most legal professionals bypass the card catalog system in the research of law. On the other hand, many students research magazines through the *Reader's Guide to Periodical Literature*, and legal professionals can research periodicals through a similar method.

As you begin to learn about legal research, you should walk through a law library to acquaint yourself with the many sets of law books it contains. You will find that the law is not contained in any one book, or even in any one set of books. You will notice that in addition to books of law, there are sets of books that explain the law, such as legal encyclopedias and legal treatises. You will not become a good researcher simply by reading about the legal research process. As you begin to learn about the process, you should spend more time in the law library and practice your skills. The more legal research you do, the more competent you will become.

What Is Law?

Laws are the rules laid down by the different branches of government. There are many different government bodies that make laws. Basically, laws in the United States are made by legislatures, by courts, by administrative agencies, and by cities or counties.

The United States Congress and state legislatures enact bills that are presented to the executive (President or Governor) for approval. If approval is not provided, the executive can reject, or veto, the bill. The legislature can override a veto, in which case the bill becomes a law, or statute. Both federal and state courts will decide **cases**. The court rulings in these cases become precedents guiding future decisions on similar issues. A case is also law. Administrative agencies enact **regulations**, which are laws designed to control or govern behavior. Regulations are a growing source of law in the United States. Some administrative agencies also render decisions and opinions, or even issue orders. A city or town will enact **ordinances**, which are statutes (laws) or regulations enacted by the city or town. Ordinances are also law.

There are some conventional distinctions in legal research. Laws are classified as substantive or procedural, as binding or persuasive, and as primary or secondary. There are federal and state laws, and there are official and unofficial sources. Let us look at some of these distinctions.

Substantive and Procedural Laws

Substantive laws govern conduct and relationships. **Procedural laws**, such as agency and court rules, deal with methods of enforcing

--------------------------------- LEGAL TERMS ---------------------------------

law† The entire body of rules of conduct created by government and enforced by the authority of government.

case† A contested question in a court of justice, a lawsuit; the written opinion of a judge or court deciding or commenting on a lawsuit.

regulation† A rule having the force of law, promulgated by an administrative agency; a rule of conduct established by a person or body in authority for the governance of those over whom they have authority.

ordinance† A law of a municipal corporation; a local law enacted by a city council, town council, board of supervisors, or the like.

substantive law† Area of the law that defines right conduct, as opposed to procedural law, which governs the process by which rights are adjudicated.

procedural law† The law governing the manner in which rights are enforced; the law prescribing the procedure to be followed in a case. Also called adjective law, procedural law dictates *how* rights are *presented* for interpretation and enforcement, as distinguished from substantive law, which *creates* legal rights.

substantive rights. For instance, in criminal law, the statute outlining the elements of an offense (such as a description of what constitutes murder or arson) is substantive law, while the statute describing the sentencing process (such as a description of a presentence report made by the probation officer or a requirement that a victim must be notified of the sentencing date) is procedural law. Procedural rules tell how to practice before a court or administrative agency.

Official and Unofficial Sources

An **official source** is the source in which the government requires that the law be published. An **unofficial source** is one containing legal material that is published by a private publisher. When a case is decided, the opinion is issued by the court in a slip opinion. In some states, that slip opinion is required by law to be published by a government printer in a set of books called a **reporter.** The slip opinion is also sent to private publishers such as West Publishing Company and Lawyers Cooperative Publishing. These companies may publish the same case in their unofficial reporters. The same case might be published in both an official reporter and several unofficial reporters. Some states no longer publish official reporters but rely instead on the private publishers' unofficial reporters.

Primary and Secondary Sources

In legal research, a source that contains actual law—such as a case, statute, ordinance, or regulation—is referred to as a **primary source.** Not all books in a law library, however, contain laws; some books contain information interpreting or explaining the laws. Works that write about or explain primary sources are called **secondary sources.** A legal encyclopedia or treatise is a secondary source.

In addition to primary and secondary source materials, there are books and indexes intended to help you find cases and other laws. These finding aids contain neither law nor explanations of law. To

---------------------------------- LEGAL TERMS ----------------------------------

offical source Publications in which the government requires that the law be published.

unofficial source Publications of legal material produced by private publishers.

reporters† Sets of books containing official, published reports of cases.

primary source Actual law, such as a case, statute, ordinance, or regulation, as opposed to a secondary source that interprets or explains the law.

secondary source† Publications that do not contain the law itself, but simply comment upon or summarize the law.

understand why finding aids are necessary, consider the fact that over four million cases have been decided in the United States. Suppose one of these cases is the case you need to answer a legal problem. A finding aid, for example, a digest, would help you pinpoint the case. After you find a case that answers a legal problem, you may want to see if that case has been overruled by cases decided more recently, in which case a finding aid such as a Shepard's citator would facilitate your search.

Binding and Persuasive Authority

The law is not uniform throughout the United States. New York laws are different from California laws. Federal law is different from state law. Early in the research process, you must identify what jurisdiction's law will answer your legal question. You will need to research New York law if the problem involves a New York situation. If the problem arises over a federal matter, then you will direct your research to federal statutes. You will look at the law that is binding on the parties. In dealing with court cases, a **binding authority** means a case decided by an equal or higher ranking court in the same jurisdiction.

Sometimes you may find no relevant authority from a specific jurisdiction on a particular question. Then you might look to cases from other jurisdictions to see how the question is answered. When you use legal authority from another jurisdiction, it is not binding authority, but it may be persuasive authority. In other words, a court in Pennsylvania may consider a decision by a court in New Jersey as persuasive, but the Pennsylvania court is not necessarily bound by it. **Persuasive authority** is authority that is not binding on the resolution of a problem. A case from another jurisdiction is just one example of a persuasive authority. Another example is a decision by a lower court in the same jurisdiction, which decision is not binding on higher courts in the same jurisdiction.

There are other forms of persuasive authority. For example, a book or article about the law may be cited as authority, and a court can choose whether to adopt that reasoning or analysis or reject that approach.

LEGAL TERMS

binding authority† Previous decisions of a higher court or statutes that a judge must follow in reaching a decision in a case.

persuasive authority Authority that is neither binding authority nor precedent, but which a court may use to support its decision if it chooses.†

Federal and State Laws

One reason law libraries contain such extensive sets of books is the multiple sources for state and federal laws. Each state has its own laws—its own case law, statutes, and regulations. In addition, the federal government has its own body of case law, statutes, and regulations. The legal system in the United States consists of fifty different sets of state laws plus federal laws, agency regulations, and ordinances made by local units of government. Because of these separate systems, any particular legal problem may be governed by more than one set of laws.

The Primary Sources of Law

Because there are multiple jurisdictions and sources of law in the United States, you must check many different sets of books to find the law. Every day statutes are passed by federal and state legislatures, ordinances are passed by cities and counties, regulations are proposed and enacted by federal and state agencies, and cases are decided by federal and state courts. The law changes constantly. Let us look at the various primary sources of law in the United States.

Constitutions

A **constitution** is a document that establishes the framework for a government. A constitution provides for the organization of the government, develops the basic rules of the government, and prescribes the relationship between the government and its citizens. A constitution also defines the relationship between the institutions of government. A constitution is the highest form of law in a democracy. No law can conflict with the United States Constitution.

A constitution prescribes how power is to be exercised in a given jurisdiction. It sets up the branches of government. For instance, the United States Constitution outlines the three branches of government: the legislative, the executive, and the judicial. A constitution also gives rights to the citizens of a country. The **Bill of Rights** contained in the Amendments to the federal Constitution provides for the rights of individuals. (See Figure 1–1.) Many significant issues such as slavery, abortion, and prohibition are constitutional questions. A legal

───────────────── LEGAL TERMS ─────────────────

constitution† The system of fundamental principles by which a nation, state, or corporation is governed. A nation's laws must conform to its constitution.

researcher should learn to identify basic constitutional issues. If a question involves a constitutional concern, the researcher should begin research by reading the relevant constitutional provisions.

FIGURE 1–1
The First
Amendment
of the
Constitution of
the United
States

Amendment 1

Freedom of religion, speech, and the press; rights of assembly and petition

Congress shall make no law respecting an establishment of religion, or prohibiting the free exercise thereof; or abridging the freedom of speech, or of the press; or the right of the people peaceably to assemble, and to petition the government for a redress of grievances.

In the United States, because there is a federal government as well as fifty state governments, there is a federal constitution as well as a constitution for each of the fifty states.

Federal Constitution

The **Constitution of the United States** (reprinted in its entirety in Appendix D) sets up our government. It tells us how laws are made, who commands the armed forces, and how taxes are levied. It provides checks and balances between the branches of government. Under the United States Constitution, three branches of government enact, interpret, and enforce laws: the legislative branch (Congress) has the power to pass bills; the executive branch administers and enforces the laws; and the judicial branch (the courts) resolves disputes about the interpretation of the laws. The Constitution also contains the Bill of Rights, which grants certain rights to American citizens. The United States Constitution is the supreme law in our country and is binding on all citizens of the United States. No law can conflict with its provisions.

———————————————————— LEGAL TERMS ————————————————————

Bill of Rights† The first ten amendments to the United States Constitution, which set forth the fundamental rights of American citizens.

Constitution of the United States† The fundamental document of American government, as adopted by the people of the United States through their representatives in the Constitutional Convention of 1787, as ratified by the states, together with the amendments to that Constitution.

The United States Constitution establishes the federal system of government, which means there is a national government as well as state governments, all of which enact laws. The relationship between the federal system and the state systems is defined by the United States Constitution.

State Constitutions

Each state has its own constitution. A **state constitution** functions at the state level in the same manner in which the federal Constitution functions at the national level. A state constitution sets up the framework for a state government. It defines the powers of the governor, the state legislature, and the state courts, as well as the relationship between the state government and the citizens of that state. A state constitution, like the Bill of Rights in the United States Constitution, also provides rights to citizens of that state.

Each state constitution is unique. However, no state constitution can contradict the United States Constitution. A state constitution is the highest law of the state, and no state law can conflict with that state's constitution. A state constitution is binding on all activity within that state's jurisdiction. Figure 1–2 contains several state constitutional provisions according rights to Indiana residents.

Statutes

The legislature is a body of elected officials who enact written laws in the form of **statutes.** In a law library, these statutes are found in sets of books called session laws or in sets of books called **codes.** Session laws place statutes in chronological order. A statute passed immediately before another statute will be placed immediately before that statute in the session laws. A code, on the other hand, puts statutes in subject categories. In other words, all divorce laws are put together and all civil rights laws are put together regardless of when these statutes were enacted.

LEGAL TERMS

state constitution The constitution of a state, as opposed to the United States Constitution, that establishes the framework for the state government.

statute† A law enacted by a legislature; an act.

code† The published statutes of a jurisdiction, arranged in systematic form.

FIGURE 1–2
An Indiana
constitutional
provision

BILL OF RIGHTS   Art. 1, § 10

§ 2. Natural right to worship

Section 2. All people shall be secured in the natural right to worship *ALMIGHTY GOD*, according to the dictates of their own consciences. *(History: As Amended November 6, 1984).*

§ 3. Freedom of religious opinions and rights of conscience

Section 3. No law shall, in any case whatever, control the free exercise and enjoyment of religious opinions, or interfere with the rights of conscience.

§ 4. Freedom of religion

Section 4. No preference shall be given, by law, to any creed, religious society, or mode of worship; and no person shall be compelled to attend, erect, or support, any place of worship, or to maintain any ministry, against his consent.

(History: As Amended November 6, 1984).

Federal Statutes

Federal statutes are passed by the United States Congress, which consists of the Senate and the House of Representatives. Federal statutes pertain to national concerns such as bankruptcy, civil rights, commerce, Social Security, and federal taxes. Figure 1–3 is an excerpt from a federal statute dealing with discrimination in employment. A federal statute cannot conflict with the United States Constitution. In addition, no state statute can conflict with a federal statute.

----------------------- LEGAL TERMS -----------------------
federal statutes Laws enacted by the United States Congress that pertain to national concerns.

FIGURE 1–3
An excerpt from a
federal statute
dealing with
discrimination in
employment

> **§ 623. Prohibition of age discrimination**
>
> **(a) Employer practices.** It shall be unlawful for an employer—
>   (1) to fail or refuse to hire or to discharge any individual or otherwise
>   discriminate against any individual with respect to his compensation,
>   terms, conditions, or privileges of employment, because of such individu-
>   al's age;
>   (2) to limit, segregate, or classify his employees in any way which would
>   deprive or tend to deprive any individual of employment opportunities
>   or otherwise adversely affect his status as an employee, because of such
>   individual's age; or
>   (3) to reduce the wage rate of any employee in order to comply with
>   this Act.

State Statutes

State statutes are passed by state legislatures and deal with state concerns. They only affect people in the state in which they are passed. State statutes deal with issues such as products liability, commercial law, workers' compensation, divorce, real property, and medical malpractice. A state statute is only applicable to disputes arising in that state's jurisdiction. A state statute is not considered to be of even persuasive weight outside that state's territory. Figure 1–4 is an excerpt from a divorce statute in Illinois.

Cases

In a **common law** system (that is, one in which laws are made by courts on a case-by-case basis) like the United States, a previously decided case is accorded precedential treatment. The common law tradition is based on the doctrine of **stare decisis**. Literally, stare decisis means "to stand by things decided." In other words, the stare decisis doctrine says that lower courts are bound by previously decided cases. A **precedent** is a source of law when a similar question is presented in a later case. Stare decisis is based

---

————————————————————————— LEGAL TERMS —————————————————————————

state statutes Laws enacted by state legislatures that pertain to state concerns.

common law† Law found in the decisions of the courts rather than in statutes; judge-made law.

stare decisis† Means "standing by the decision." *Stare decisis* is the doctrine that judicial decisions stand as precedents for cases arising in the future.

precedent† Prior decisions of the same court, or a higher court, which a judge must follow in deciding a subsequent case presenting similar facts and the same legal problem, even though different parties are involved and many years have elapsed.

5/401. Dissolution of marriage

§ 401. Dissolution of marriage. (a) The court shall enter a judgment of dissolution of marriage if at the time the action was commenced one of the spouses was a resident of this State or was stationed in this State while a member of the armed services, and the residence or military presence had been maintained for 90 days next preceding the commencement of the action or the making of the finding; provided, however, that a finding of residence of a party in any judgment entered under this Act from January 1, 1982 through June 30, 1982 shall satisfy the former domicile requirements of this Act; and if one of the following grounds for dissolution has been proved:

(1) That, without cause or provocation by the petitioner: the respondent was at the time of such marriage, and continues to be naturally impotent; the respondent had a wife or husband living at the time of the marriage; the respondent had committed adultery subsequent to the marriage; the respondent has wilfully deserted or absented himself or herself from the petitioner for the space of one year, including any period during which litigation may have pended between the spouses for dissolution of marriage or legal separation; the respondent has been guilty of habitual drunkenness for the space of 2 years; the respondent has been guilty of gross and confirmed habits caused by the excessive use of addictive drugs for the space of 2 years, or has attempted the life of the other by poison or other means showing malice, or has been guilty of extreme and repeated physical or mental cruelty, or has been convicted of a felony or other infamous crime; or the respondent has infected the other with a communicable venereal disease. "Excessive use of addictive drugs", as used in this Section, refers to use of an addictive drug by a person when using the drug becomes a controlling or a dominant purpose of his life; or

(2) That the spouses have lived separate and apart for a continuous period in excess of 2 years and irreconcilable differences have caused the irretrievable breakdown of the marriage and the court determines that efforts at reconciliation have failed or that future attempts at reconciliation would be impracticable and not in the best interests of the family. If the spouses have lived separate and apart for a continuous period of not less than 6 months next preceding the entry of the judgment dissolving the marriage, as evidenced by testimony or affidavits of the spouses, the requirement of living separate and apart for a continuous period in excess of 2 years may be waived upon written stipulation of both spouses filed with the court. At any time after the parties cease to cohabit, the following periods shall be included in the period of separation:

(A) any period of cohabitation during which the parties attempted in good faith to reconcile and participated in marriage counseling under the guidance of any of the following: a psychiatrist, a clinical psychologist, a clinical social worker, a marriage and family therapist, a person authorized to provide counseling in accordance with the prescriptions of any religious denomination, or a person regularly engaged in providing family or marriage counseling; and

(B) any period of cohabitation under written agreement of the parties to attempt to reconcile.

FIGURE 1–4   An excerpt from an Illinois divorce statute

on the concepts of fairness, equality, and predictability. After a case is decided, it will stand as law in future controversies between other parties. Parties can consult previous cases to make decisions about whether their actions are legal. A precedent can be changed when it no longer can be justified by contemporary legal standards.

A legal researcher must learn how to locate and read court cases for law. Cases resolve legal issues. In one case, parties may dispute ten different legal issues, and the court may resolve all these issues in its decision. In such a case, the court has, in effect, made or applied law on ten different points. The legal principles decided by the court are called its holdings, or the *ratio decidendi* of the case. A court also may make statements that are not necessary to its decision but that are instructive of the court's predisposition on an issue. These statements are called obiter dicta, which literally means "remarks by the way."

Remember that a case precedent can be law just as a statute is law. Cases are found in sets of books called reporters. With over four million cases in the United States, each of which contain holdings on as many as three or four principles of law, the task of the legal researcher is to find that one legal principle in that one case that matches and answers the legal problem being researched. (Appendix A contains a copy of *United States v. Sproed,* 628 F. Supp. 1234 (D. Ore. 1986).)

Courts are organized in a hierarchical manner. The lowest level courts are called **trial courts.** These are the courts where a judge or jury first hears evidence and resolves disputes for parties. Trial courts generally do not issue decisions for publication, although the federal district courts sometimes do send their opinions for publication.

If a party does not agree with a judgment of a trial court, that party may appeal the case to a higher court called an **appellate court.** The party taking the appeal is called an **appellant,** and the party defending the appeal is called an **appellee.** Appellate courts are sometimes divided into districts or circuits, usually on a territorial basis. The parties generally are not permitted to introduce evidence to an appellate court. Instead, the appellate court reviews a transcript of the evidence from the trial court and briefs filed by the

---

LEGAL TERMS

trial court† A court that hears and determines a case initially, as opposed to an appellate court; a court of general jurisdiction.

appellate court† A higher court to which an appeal is taken from a lower court.

appellant† A party who appeals from a lower court to a higher court.

appellee† A party against whom a case is appealed from a lower court to a higher court.

parties. A **brief** is a written argument to a court. When the appellate court decides a case, it writes a slip opinion that may be sent for publication in a reporter. There are different sets of reporters for cases from different jurisdictions.

A party who loses a case in an appellate court may appeal to an even higher appellate court. This higher court also may issue an opinion that will *affirm, reverse,* or *remand* the case.

Federal Cases

The federal court system is maintained separately from the state court systems. The trial courts in the federal system are referred to as **District Courts.** In Indiana, for example, there is a Northern and a Southern District Court. A party who disagrees with a judgment of a District Court may appeal the case to an appellate court. In the federal system, the appellate courts that review the actions of the District Court are called the Court of Appeals of the United States (formerly the **Circuit Courts of Appeal**). There are thirteen Circuit Courts of Appeal, including eleven numbered circuits, the District of Columbia Circuit, and the Federal Circuit. Figure 1–5 is a map of the Circuit Courts of Appeal. If a party is dissatisfied with a decision in the Circuit Court, the party may appeal to the United States Supreme Court. Decisions of District Courts, Circuit Courts of Appeal, and the United States Supreme Court are precedents for later decisions.

State Cases

The typical state court structure mirrors that of the federal system. (See Figure 1–6.) The lowest level courts are called trial courts and may include juvenile, probate, misdemeanor, and small claims courts. These courts may be called circuit, superior, or district courts, depending on the state involved. Trial court decisions normally are not published. Appeals in a typical state system are made to a court of appeals, and the highest appeals court in most states is called the state supreme court.

--------------------------------- LEGAL TERMS ---------------------------------

brief† A written statement submitted to a court for the purpose of persuading it of the correctness of one's position. A brief argues the facts of the case and the applicable law, supported by citations of authority.

District Courts of the United States† Officially termed United States District Courts, the courts or original jurisdiction for both criminal prosecutions and civil cases arising under federal statutes, cases involving federal constitutional questions, and suits by and against citizens of different states. Each state and territory, and the District of Columbia, has at least one federal judicial district.

Circuit Court of Appeals† The former name of the intermediate federal appellate courts, now called the Court of Appeals of the United States.

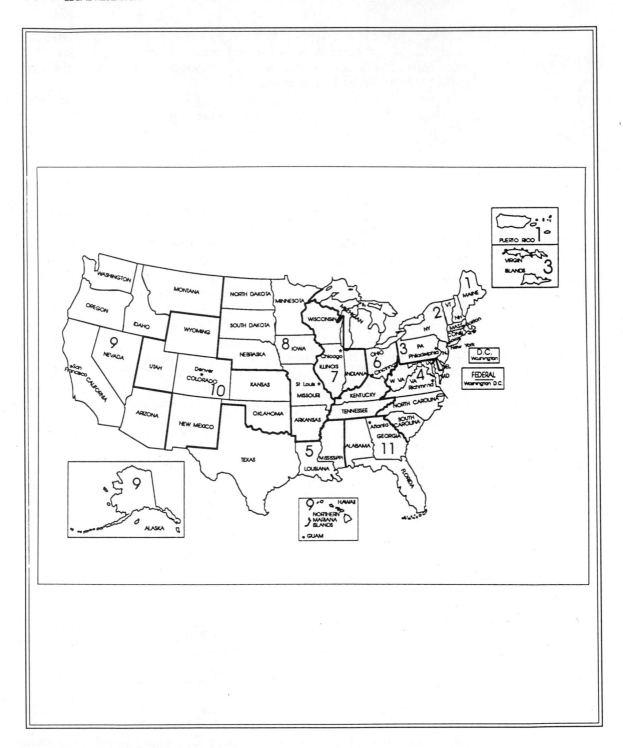

FIGURE 1-5   A map representing the United States Circuit Courts of Appeal

FIGURE 1–6
The typical state
court structure

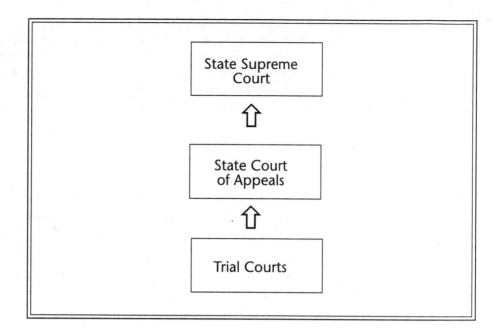

However, in some states, the highest court may not be called the supreme court. For instance, in New York, the trial court is referred to as the Supreme Court and the highest appellate court is called the Court of Appeals. Decisions of appellate level courts are sent for publication and become precedents to be followed in future cases. A party still dissatisfied with a decision of a state's highest court may be able to appeal in some circumstances to the United States Supreme Court.

Court Rules

Court rules govern practice and procedure for the parties who come before the courts. There are general court rules that apply across the board to similar courts. For instance, the Federal Rules of Civil Procedure apply to all of the federal District Courts, while the Federal Rules of Appellate Procedure apply to all of the federal Circuit Courts of Appeal. The United States Supreme Court has adopted rules applicable to that Court. Some courts have their own particular rules. For instance, the Southern District of Indiana has local rules governing practice and procedure for parties who practice before that court. So a party with a procedural question would need to consult both the Federal Rules of

Civil Procedure and the Local Rules of the Southern District of Indiana. Figure 1–7 is a rule from the Federal Rules of Civil Procedure.

Each state court system has its own set of rules governing the practice in that state's courts. Most states have modeled their trial court rules on the Federal Rules of Civil Procedure. However, it is essential to consult the particular rules applicable to the court in which you are practicing, since these rules may be different from the federal rules.

FIGURE 1–7
A rule from the
*Federal Rules of
Civil Procedure*

TRIAL RULE 64.   SEIZURE OF PERSON OR PROPERTY

(A) Ancillary Remedies to Assist in Enforcement of Judgment. At the commencement of and during the course of an action, all remedies providing for seizure of person or property for the purpose of securing satisfaction of the judgment ultimately to be entered in the action are available under the circumstances and in the manner provided by law and existing at the time the remedy is sought.

The remedies thus available include, without limitation, arrest, attachment, attachment and garnishment, lis pendens notice, ejectment, replevin, sequestration, and other corresponding or equivalent legal or equitable remedies, however designated and regardless of whether by existing procedure the remedy is ancillary to an action or must be obtained by an independent action. Such remedies are subject to the provisions of this rule, and, except as herein otherwise provided, the action in which any of the foregoing remedies is used shall be commenced and prosecuted pursuant to these rules.

There are also rules governing evidence and ethics. Any litigation paralegal who will be working on a court matter should first consult all the relevant rules that apply to that court.

Regulations

Since the Great Depression of 1929, there has been an ever increasing reliance upon administrative agencies. During the Depression era, Congress attempted to deal with the economic upheaval by delegating broad authority to agencies, in the hope that these agencies would gain expertise in their particular areas. An **administrative agency** is an entity established by law to administer a statutory program.

───────────── LEGAL TERMS ─────────────

administrative agency†   A private organization or unit of government organized to provide a particular service or type of service.

There are two broad categories of administrative agencies—independent agencies and executive agencies. An **independent agency** is established by Congress and is given powers to act without political interference from the traditional branches of government. The Social Security Administration and the Federal Reserve Board are examples of independent agencies. The heads of these agencies are appointed for fixed terms and may be removed from office only for cause. An **executive agency** is an agency that is set up as part of the executive branch. The head of such an agency serves at the discretion of the President. The Department of Justice and the Department of Defense are two examples of executive agencies.

Administrative agencies pass regulations that define and clarify the role of the agency. Regulations are found in **registers** in chronological order and in **administrative codes** by subject matter. A regulation cannot conflict with the grant of power given to the agency by statutes. If a regulation does conflict with a statute, it is invalid. Figure 1–8 is an excerpt from a federal OSHA regulation that prescribes standards for ensuring a safe workplace for employees.

States and local units of government, such as cities and counties, also have administrative agencies. Figure 1–9 is a chart that describes examples of federal, state, and local administrative agencies and their functions.

Administrative Decisions

Administrative agencies may be authorized to decide disputes or to issue orders in administrative proceedings. An administrative hearing officer may take evidence and issue decisions much like a judge in a court proceeding. These decisions are called **administrative decisions** and are sometimes published in the *Code of Federal Regulations* (CFR). These decisions may have precedential value, like court decisions. At other times, administrative agencies may render formal or informal

---
LEGAL TERMS
---

independent agency An administrative agency established by Congress that is given powers to act without political interference from the traditional branches of government.

executive agency An administrative agency that is set up as part of the executive branch of government.

register† A book of records, particularly official records or public records; an official list; a registry.

administrative codes The published regulations of administrative agencies, arranged by subject matter.

administrative decision† The conclusion of a hearing officer in an administrative agency proceeding.

Occupational Safety and Health Admin., Labor   **§ 1910.243**

§ 1910.242 **Hand and portable powered tools and equipment, general.**

(a) *General requirements.* Each employer shall be responsible for the safe condition of tools and equipment used by employees, including tools and equipment which may be furnished by employees.

(b) *Compressed air used for cleaning.* Compressed air shall not be used for cleaning purposes except where reduced to less than 30 p.s.i. and then only with effective chip guarding and personal protective equipment.

§ 1910.243 **Guarding of portable powered tools.**

(a) *Portable powered tool*—(1) *Portable circular saws.* (i) All portable, power-driven circular saws having a blade diameter greater than 2 in. shall be equipped with guards above and below the base plate or shoe. The upper guard shall cover the saw to the depth of the teeth, except for the minimum arc required to permit the base to be tilted for bevel cuts. The lower guard shall cover the saw to the depth of the teeth, except for the minimum arc required to allow proper retraction and contact with the work. When the tool is withdrawn from the work, the lower guard shall automatically and instantly return to covering position.

(ii) Paragraph (a)(1)(i) of this section does not apply to circular saws used in the meat industry for meat cutting purposes.

(2) *Switches and controls.* (i) All hand-held powered circular saws having a blade diameter greater than 2 inches, electric, hydraulic or pneumatic chain saws, and percussion tools without positive accessory holding means shall be equipped with a constant pressure switch or control that will shut off the power when the pressure is released. All hand-held gasoline powered chain saws shall be equipped with a constant pressure throttle control that will shut off the power to the saw chain when the pressure is released.

(ii) All hand-held powered drills, tappers, fastener drivers, horizontal, vertical, and angle grinders with wheels greater than 2 inches in diameter, disc sanders with discs greater than 2 inches in diameter, belt sanders, reciprocating saws, saber, scroll, and jig saws with blade shanks greater than a nominal one-fourth inch, and other similarly operating powered tools shall be equipped with a constant pressure switch or control, and may have a lock-on control provided that turnoff can be accomplished by a single motion of the same finger or fingers that turn it on.

(iii) (*a*) All other hand-held powered tools, such as, but not limited to, platen sanders, grinders with wheels 2 inches in diameter or less, disc sanders with discs 2 inches in diameter or less, routers, planers, laminate trimmers, nibblers, shears, saber, scroll, and jig saws with blade shanks a nominal one-fourth of an inch wide or less, may be equipped with either a positive "on-off" control, or other controls as described by paragraph (a)(2)(i) and (ii) of this section.

(*b*) Saber, scroll, and jig saws with nonstandard blade holders may use blades with shanks which are nonuniform in width, provided the narrowest portion of the blade shank is an integral part in mounting the blade.

(*c*) Blade shank width shall be measured at the narrowest portion of the blade shank when saber, scroll, and jig saws have nonstandard blade holders.

(*d*) *Nominal* in this subparagraph means ±0.05 inch.

(iv) The operating control on hand-held power tools shall be so located as to minimize the possibility of its accidental operation, if such accidental operation would constitute a hazard to employees.

(v) This subparagraph does not apply to concrete vibrators, concrete breakers, powered tampers, jack hammers, rock drills, garden appliances, household and kitchen appliances, personal care appliances, medical or dental equipment, or to fixed machinery.

(3) *Portable belt sanding machines.* Belt sanding machines shall be provided with guards at each nip point where the sanding belt runs onto a pulley. These guards shall effectively prevent the hands or fingers of the operator from coming in contact with the nip points. The unused run of the sanding belt shall be guarded against accidental contact.

FIGURE 1–8   An excerpt from a federal regulation explaining OSHA standards to ensure a safe workplace

FIGURE 1-9
Examples of
federal, state, and
local
administrative
agencies

FEDERAL AGENCIES

Federal Aviation Administration (FAA)	Determines flight safety procedures Investigates crash sites Certifies pilots
Environmental Protection Agency (EPA)	Determines levels and monitors pollution emission for industry Monitors air quality in metropolitan areas
Food and Drug Administration (FDA)	Approves new drugs Regulates manufacture of drugs and cosmetics Issues recalls on contaminated foods

STATE AGENCIES

Bureau of Motor Vehicles	Issues vehicle and driver's licenses Maintains records of title and registration Issues parking permits for handicapped individuals
Department of Transportation	Constructs, reconstructs, improves, maintains, and repairs highways
Alcoholic Beverage Commission	Issues liquor licenses Regulates manufacture of alcohol and alcoholic beverages Regulates advertising of alcoholic beverages

LOCAL AGENCIES

Building Commission	Issues building permits Inspects new construction Condemns dangerous structures
Health Department	Records vital statistics (birth and death) Controls communicable disease Regulates immunizations
Division of Parks and Recreation	Constructs, manages, and maintains public parks playgrounds, swimming pools, recreation centers, and recreation programs

administrative opinions to parties about the consequences of their actions. For instance, the Internal Revenue Service may issue an opinion about whether a party can claim a certain deduction or exemption. An agency also may make **administrative rulings** about matters of general concern.

Municipal Charters and Ordinances

Local units of government, such as cities, will have **municipal charters** to organize the institutions of that unit of government. These charters perform a function similar to that of a constitution at the state or federal level.

Even local units of government such as cities and counties pass laws. These laws are called ordinances. Ordinances deal with the particular concerns of the city or county. For example, there might be ordinances on zoning, building permits, building restrictions, and barking dogs. Figure 1–10 is an excerpt from a New York city ordinance dealing with summer camps.

FIGURE 1–10
An excerpt from a New York City ordinance

CHAPTER 2

SUMMER CAMPS FOR CHILDREN

§ 18–201 **Summer camps for children.**

§ 18-201 **Summer camps for children.** a. The board of estimate, within the amounts appropriated therefor, is authorized to establish camps in spaces provided therefor in parks adjacent to the city under the jurisdiction and control of the state council of parks, recreation and historic preservation. Such camps shall be used to furnish free instruction and maintenance of children between the ages of six and sixteen years and shall be under the jurisdiction of such agency as may be designated by the board.

b. Such agency shall provide opportunity for children to receive instruction which shall not exceed ten hours per week in camp sanitation, elementary hygiene, first aid to the injured, life saving, swimming and physical training and such other similar subjects as it may deem proper. Such agency shall prescribe rules and regulations for admission to such camps and the conduct and discipline thereof.

c. Such camps shall be operated between July first and August thirty-first of each year. Children shall be entitled to free instruction and maintenance in any such camp for a period of only two weeks during any one year.

d. Such agency shall make an annual report to the mayor on or before the fifteenth day of February of matters relating to carrying out the provisions of this section.

--------- LEGAL TERMS ---------

administrative opinion A formal or informal opinion statement made by an administrative agency to parties regarding the consequences of the parties' actions.

administrative ruling† A determination made by a hearing officer during the course of an administrative agency hearing.

municipal charter† The basic law of a local unit of government, such as a city or town.

Other Primary Sources

Law is made in a variety of ways other than those already discussed. Executive orders and proclamations and treaties and compacts between states are examples. An executive order may direct the activities of a government official or an agency. A proclamation may declare a certain day in honor of some individual or group. A compact between states may describe the rights of states with respect to a river that forms the boundary between them. Laws affect a wide gamut of activity. Figure 1–11 is a chart of the primary sources of law in the United States.

Beginning the Legal Research Process

There are many approaches to legal research. There is no correct approach, nor even a preferred approach in many cases. Each research situation is different. Some researchers will have a working familiarity with the area of law being researched, while others will have no background in the particular area. Their approaches may be different.

The ultimate goal of any researcher presented with a question of law is to find the primary source material applicable to that question as efficiently as possible. Different legal publishers have devised various techniques for finding and explaining the law. These companies provide competing ways to answer legal questions. Every private publisher attempts to present the most efficient way to locate and to understand the law. When presented with the task of finding a particular case, one researcher may start with a digest (Chapter 4), another with an encyclopedia (Chapter 5), and a third with a treatise (Chapter 5). Although some legal research techniques are unique, many are similar to techniques you already use.

There are two threshold questions every researcher must answer before proceeding with any legal research. First, what is the source authority? Is it a constitutional provision, statute, regulation, court rule, case, or some other authority? Second, what jurisdiction's law will determine the outcome of the case? Answering these questions will frame the research project and save many hours of research time. For example, it does not make sense to look for Kansas statutes when researching an Ohio law problem. Nor does it make sense to look through regulatory authority when the answer to the query is in the case law.

Once the two threshold questions are answered, it should be fairly easy to select the appropriate finding tools to locate the primary authority. The paralegal should remember that every legal research system is designed to either find or explain primary authority. Most systems begin with the use of some sort of index, and most systems have a means to update the search so the researcher can find the most current laws.

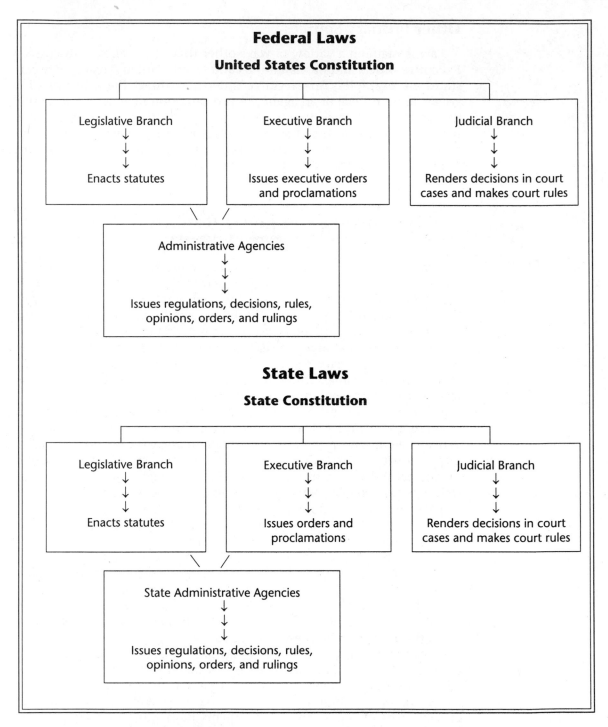

FIGURE 1–11   An illustration of the primary sources of law in the United States at both the federal and state levels

Using Legal Indexes

After answering the two threshold questions, the next step is to select key words for providing access to the indexes to the various research tools. It is helpful at the outset to recognize that legal indexes are not much different from other indexes. Virtually every text contains a table of contents (a topical outline) in the front of the book and a subject-matter or descriptive-word index at the end of the book. Although the indexing elements in legal texts may bear different names or may not appear in the traditional front-back locations, law books are indexed in a similar manner. Most have both the topical (table of contents) and the descriptive-word (subject) index. Once paralegals understand this basic fact, they feel more comfortable with the indexing used by most legal resources.

An index is especially important to legal research because so much law is collected chronologically. For example, reporters collect cases by the date they are decided. A case decided on May 17 is put before a case decided on May 18. A researcher needs a tool by which to pinpoint a particular case in these reporters.

An Example of Using a Legal Index

To research any legal problem, the paralegal must look under the right words in the indexes. A good way to penetrate a legal index is to use the **TAPP rule.** TAPP is an acronym for Things, Actions, Persons, and Places. Using the TAPP rule, the researcher can categorize the facts into terms the publisher might have used to index the legal problem.

Let us consider a hypothetical case to see how the TAPP rule works:

> A client's child, age 15, is bitten by a neighbor's dog while crossing the neighbor's backyard in Evansville, Indiana. The dog has never bitten anyone before, but it has snarled and snapped at others. The lawyer for whom you work is concerned because in some states, an owner is not liable unless the dog has bitten someone before. (The dog gets one free bite.) She wants you to research Indiana law on this subject: Is Indiana a one-bite or a two-bite state?

Using the TAPP rules, you begin by identifying what *thing* is involved. In this case, it is a "dog," an "animal" or a "pet." The second fact to identify in using the TAPP rule is the *action* involved. This case would be a negligence or tort action. When thinking of the action, consider also what relief is sought (for example, money damages) or what defense to the action is involved (for example, waiver, contributory

──────────────── LEGAL TERMS ────────────────

TAPP rule   A method for categorizing facts based on the acronym TAPP, which refers to Things, Actions, Persons, and Places.

negligence, incurred risk). *Persons* refers to the legal relationship of the parties, such as landlord-tenant, assignor-assignee, lawyer-client, bailor-bailee. In our hypothetical, one person is the dog owner, or landlord, and the person bitten may be a trespasser, a licensee, or an invitee. *Places* refers to the location where the wrong or offense took place. Did it occur in a supermarket, on a sidewalk, in an alley, or in a home? In this case, the place is a backyard. So in working with the hypothetical problem, a researcher would search the legal index for words such as "dog," "pet," "negligence," and "trespasser."

Use the TAPP rule to rethink any factual problem. This rule helps you think in concrete rather than abstract terms. It works as a means to penetrate most legal indexes because legal indexes are prepared with the TAPP rule in mind.

Before beginning your research, it is important to remember that all legal systems have some indexing means to access the legal information from the system. Every time you use a new legal finding tool, determine what indexing method accesses the information from the system. Then you will understand how that research tool works.

Using Secondary Sources

Lawyers are given in-depth training in certain basic areas such as torts, civil procedure, contracts, property, and constitutional law. Many paralegals lack the training necessary for researching some legal problems. To overcome this deficiency, paralegals must acquaint themselves with the general legal principles relating to their research project before they begin the research.

In order to resolve or address a legal problem, the researcher usually begins by locating general legal principles, then gradually narrows the search by locating more specific principles. The researcher is always looking for primary authority. To acquaint yourself with the necessary background principles, start with a secondary source, such as an encyclopedia. If you understand the legal issue and are fairly certain the source authority is a case, go directly to a digest. Similarly, if you understand the legal issue and are fairly certain the source authority is a statute, go directly to an annotated code.

There are times when paralegals must do basic research to understand how to proceed with a problem. In such situations, there are secondary sources designed to provide the elementary knowledge that is needed. Some secondary sources are written by well-recognized authorities in a particular area of the law. These works can provide more than just background—they can provide a sophisticated interpretation of the law. Such works can be persuasive with the courts.

Sometimes one secondary source is more accurate than another. Do not hesitate to use several techniques to verify your conclusion. The fact that a particular tool seems to answer your question should not stop you from verifying the answer with an alternative tool. No single tool works best in every situation. Knowing which tool to start with is something you will learn through experience. You should read the primary authority also to determine whether more research is needed to find a more complete answer.

Using Updating Aids

Sometimes the only law applicable to a particular situation is a case decided over one hundred years ago or a statute passed many decades ago. At other times, though, new statutes have amended or repealed old laws and new cases have overturned old cases. That is why it is absolutely critical that the legal researcher find the most current law. Reading a statute that has been repealed will not provide the right answer. Relying upon a case that has been overturned by a more recent case will lead to embarrassing results.

Legal publishers use several different methods to keep the researcher abreast of changes in the law. Some publishers issue pocket parts or supplements. A **pocket part** is simply a pamphlet designed to fit in a pocket holder in the back of a book. Periodically (usually annually) the publisher sends a new set of pocket supplements to subscribers to update the pocket supplements from the previous period. Some publishers use replacement pamphlets instead of pocket supplements or use the pamphlets along with pocket supplements. Other publishers use a looseleaf system. In sets of books where a **looseleaf system** is used, pages with new information replace pages with outdated information. **Replacement volumes** are sometimes provided by publishers—the publisher sends new volumes to subscribers, and the old volumes are discarded.

As you use sets of law books and other legal research tools, notice the updating techniques employed by the publishers. Failure to use the available updating materials is a common mistake of paralegals. Do not fall into that trap. Legal research must be continually updated. If a paralegal fails to provide the most up-to-date authority, the client may be given the wrong advice. Although attorneys supervise the research, they often assume paralegals have updated any research. A paralegal

-- LEGAL TERMS --

pocket part   A pamphlet designed to fit in a pocket holder in the back of a book that enables publishers to update volumes without replacing the whole book.

looseleaf system   A method used by publishers for updating looseleaf volumes by which pages with new information replace pages with outdated information.

replacement volume   A book produced by a legal publisher and sent to subscribers to replace a different version of the same book that now has outdated information.

can lose a job and an attorney can even be sued for malpractice by a client who receives wrong advice and relies upon it.

The amount of law in a law library is staggering. No legal professional knows even a small fraction of that law. Legal research skills provide the ability to pinpoint a particular law when it is needed. Sometimes your research will lead you to a statute, and then to a regulation that clarifies the statute, and then to a case that interprets both the statute and the regulation, and finally to another case that overrules this case. The making of law is a process that is ever changing. You must continue to research until you are satisfied that you have found the current law.

Using Legal Citations

Whether preparing a term paper in high school or a thesis for a PhD degree, there are certain conventional rules that apply for citing to a newspaper, a magazine, or a book. The typical citation includes a title, publisher, and date. Legal researchers also use citations. A legal **citation** is a shorthand reference to a legal authority that is used by legal professionals for referencing cases, statutes, regulations, or any other legal authorities. It is critical that the paralegal learn how to read and write legal citations. Good form in using legal citations also reflects a degree of professionalism.

Let us look at several examples:

Citation to a case

Roe v. Wade, 410 U.S. 113 (1973)

Roe refers to the appellant and *Wade* refers to the appellee. Notice that the title uses only last names, and only the name of one party appellant and one party appellee. The first number refers to the volume in a set of reporters—in this case, volume 410 of a set of books called the *United States Reports*. The *United States Reports* is an official publication. The last number, 113, refers to the page on which this case begins in volume 410. The date is when this case was decided.

Citation to a statute

42 U.S.C. § 1983 (1970)

The number 42 references the title and 1983 the section of the *United States Code*. The symbol § is used to indicate "section."

LEGAL TERMS

citation† Reference to authority (a case, article, or other text) on a point of law, by name, volume, and page or section of the court report or other book in which it appears.

Citation to a regulation

47 C.F.R. § 73.609 (1980)

The number 47 references the title and 73.609 the section of the *Code of Federal Regulations.*

SIDEBAR

For a more extensive discussion of legal citations, study *A Uniform System of Citation*, 15th ed. (The Harvard Law Review Association, 1991). This work is sometimes referred to as the "Bluebook" or the "Harvard Citator." Proper citations will make your work appear more professional.

A **parallel citation** is a citation to an alternative source for the same authority. Some cases are reported in both official and unofficial publications. For instance, *Roe v. Wade* is reported in an unofficial reporter published by West Publishing Company called the *Supreme Court Reporter* (S. Ct.) and an unofficial reporter published by Lawyers Cooperative Publishing Company called *United States Supreme Court Reports—Lawyer's Edition* (L. Ed.). A parallel citation of *Roe v. Wade* would read:

Roe v. Wade, 410 U.S. 113, 93 S. Ct. 705, 35 L. Ed. 2d 147 (1973).

The number before each reporter abbreviation is the volume number, and the number after each reporter abbreviation is the beginning page reference.

Using Computers and Other Media

Traditionally, all legal research was done through books. Today, paralegals find law in many different media. For instance, by using a computer, a legal researcher might locate law found on software or on a compact disc. Another researcher might use a modem with a computer to contact an on-line computer service such as LEXIS or WESTLAW, which will permit the researcher to research almost any area of the law. Other laws, such as old cases, may be stored on microfilm or ultrafiche.

Computers are changing the way legal professionals approach research. Twenty years ago, computer-assisted legal research was too expensive for most law firms, and much of the material was not available via this medium. Now computers have become a daily part of

---
LEGAL TERMS
---

parallel citation† A citation to a court opinion or decision that is printed in two or more reporters.

the legal research process. Most lawyers understand the importance of computerized research, but some remain intimidated by the process itself. Many paralegals who become expert at computer-assisted research find themselves a valuable asset to a law firm. In any case, the successful paralegal must master both the traditional and the modern approaches to legal research.

Legal professionals also learn about the law through publications such as magazines, newspapers, and journals. As shown in Chapter 5, legal professionals can subscribe to magazines and newspapers that cover only legal topics and events.

Nonlegal Research

Legal professionals must be able to research more than just law. If a legal problem concerns negligence in the design of a bridge or malpractice committed in a surgical procedure, a legal professional may need to make an extensive search of engineering or medical texts. However, there are various legal publications that can be used by legal professionals to acquaint themselves with many of these situations. Some of these research methods are discussed in Chapter 9.

On-line computer services have provided new opportunities for legal professionals to conduct nonlegal research. Chapter 7 discusses some of these techniques.

Summary

- There are multiple jurisdictions in the United States (federal, state, county, municipal) that have various types of laws (constitutions, statutes, cases, ordinances).

- The highest source of law in the United States is the United States Constitution. Each state also has a constitution that establishes the framework for that state's laws.

- Federal and state legislatures pass laws that are found in sets of books called session laws and codes.

- Court cases are grounded on the stare decisis principle by which lower level courts must adhere to precedents set by higher level courts.

- The court system in the United States is hierarchical. The lowest level courts are called trial courts and intermediate level courts are called appellate courts. The highest court in the United States is called the Supreme Court. The highest court in many (but not all) states is also referred to as the supreme court.

- Before beginning any research query, the researcher should determine the source authority and what jurisdiction's law will decide the issue.
- The TAPP rule is used as a method to access information from a legal index.
- A primary source is the law. Something written about that law is a secondary source.
- Learning about updating processes (pocket parts, pamphlets, page or volume replacement) is an important part of the legal research process.
- Computers introduce new methods for researching law.

Review Questions

1. What is the difference between a primary source and a secondary source? Which is more important? Explain.

2. List the different sources of law in the United States.

3. Why is it important to keep legal research current?

4. What are the different media used by legal professionals to research law?

5. What is the difference between a binding authority and a persuasive authority?

6. Define stare decisis. Why is it an important concept to our legal system?

7. Explain how and when to use the TAPP rule.

8. What are the two threshold questions that should be asked at the outset of any research project?

Research Projects

1. Go to your local law library and make a report on the various sources of law found there. Are there any sources of law that you cannot locate there?

2. While at your local law library, locate the following:

    a. Your state constitution

    b. Your county ordinances

    c. Your city ordinances

||||

CHAPTER 2

THE LEGISLATIVE PROCESS—HOW LAWS ARE REPORTED

Because there are so many sources of law, there is no one set of books that contains all the laws of the United States. Thus, a legal researcher looking up a New York City ordinance will use a different set of books than a researcher looking up a California statute. A legal researcher locating a federal statute will use a different set of books than a researcher locating a federal regulation. The first step in mastering the legal research process is simply learning to identify which sets of books are used for each particular source of law. Some sources of law are located in the same set, but even when sources are in different sets, the researcher often uses similar techniques for locating them. This chapter covers constitutions, statutes, regulations, and ordinances, all of which are researched with basically the same methods. Research of case law, which requires a different method, is covered in a later chapter. Figure 2–1 illustrates the primary sources covered in this chapter and their relationship to each other. Each of these sources is a primary authority.

FIGURE 2–1
Primary sources of law and their relationship to each other

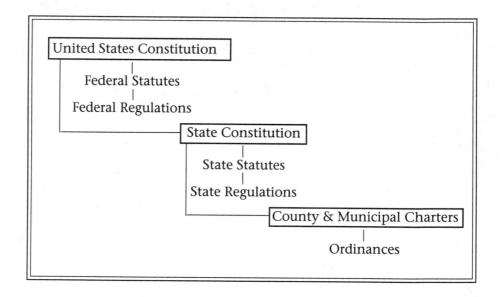

Researching Statutes

To understand how to research statutory law, it is helpful to begin with the differences between session laws, codes, compilations, and annotated codes. Figure 2–2 is a chart briefly summarizing the differences between these various methods used to report statutes.

FIGURE 2–2
A summary
of differences
between
various
methods
used to
report
statutes

Slip Laws . . . . Texts of single statutes

Session Laws . . . . Arrange slip laws in
chronological order

Compilations. . . . . Arrange the law by subject
matter

Codes. . . . . Official arrangements of law
by subject matter

Annotated Codes. . . . . Unofficial publications of
codes with reference
citations

Session Laws

When a statute (sometimes called an act or a public law) is enacted
by a legislature, it is sent to a publisher to be printed. Each statute may
be separately published as a slip law. At the federal level, a slip law is
identified by its public law number. Federal slip laws can be found at
libraries that are depositories for the United States Government
Printing Office. Except when the statute is not available in any other
form, slip laws are rarely used for legal research purposes.

Slip laws are sent by the legislature to the official printer, which
typically publishes these slip laws in chronological order. A statute
passed on May 17, 1994, will be placed before a statute passed on May
18, 1994. Statutes collected by an official publisher in chronological
order are called **session laws**. Federal session laws are published in the
Statutes at Large. Laws passed during each session of Congress are
published in separate volumes of the *Statutes at Large.* The statutes are
arranged in chronological order. There are subject indexes in each
volume as well as tables identifying how each public law affects other
public laws.

---------------------------------- LEGAL TERMS ----------------------------------

session laws† The collected statutes enacted during a session of a legislature,
arranged in chronological order.

Statutes at Large† An official publication of the federal government, issued after
each session of Congress, which includes all statutes enacted by the Congress and all
congressional resolutions and treaties, as well as presidential proclamations and
proposed or ratified amendments to the Constitution.

It is usually impractical to use session laws for legal research purposes. To illustrate why this is so, consider the research of a law relating to marijuana use. The state may have first proscribed the use of marijuana in the 1800s. However, through the years there may have been amendments or modifications to that statute. The original statute might even have been repealed and replaced with an entirely different statute. Related statutes also may have been passed. The legislature may have tinkered with the statute every year for the past five years. A legal researcher who used session laws to research this question would have to check in *each* year's collection to trace the evolution of that statute—a daunting task.

Compilations

Sometimes a private group or publisher will sort through all the statutes to find those statutes on a particular topic and then publish this collection as a **compilation.** For instance, the publisher might find all the divorce or estate statutes in a certain state. Hence, compilations are arranged by subject matter rather than chronologically. The disadvantage of using a compilation is that the legal researcher does not know how carefully these statutes were compiled. There may have been errors in or omissions from the compilation. When you use a compilation, you trust that the compiler accurately found all the applicable laws on the subject. Compilations are unofficial sources for statutes.

Codes

Neither session laws nor compilations are effective research tools. Researching statutory law by using session laws is too laborious, and compilations may be incomplete. Many statutes simply have not been compiled. That is why codes were developed. Codes are official compilations of statutes. The legislature sorts through all the laws and then groups the statutes by subject matter—all laws dealing with divorce are grouped in one chapter or title, and all laws dealing with criminal law are grouped in another chapter or title. The legislature then enacts this compilation into law. In other words, the legislature performs the same task a private publisher performs in preparing a compilation. The difference is that the code contains all the laws having general application to the public and this code itself becomes law.

--------------------------------------- LEGAL TERMS ---------------------------------------

compilation†   A collection of statutes or data.

Every six years the *United States Code* (U.S.C.), the code of all federal statutes, is revised. In the years between revisions there are cumulative supplements issued containing the new laws for that period. The U.S.C. is divided into fifty titles. Each title has a separate topic. Figure 2–3 is a breakdown of the various titles. The U.S.C. is **presumptive evidence** of the law rather than **positive law.** A court will accept or presume that the code contains the exact language of the law *unless* the court is shown that there is a difference between the code and the session law. If there is a difference, then the positive law (the session law) will overcome the presumptive law (the code).

Annotated Codes

After a statute is passed, it may be interpreted by court decisions. There may be amendments or changes to that statute as the legislature tinkers with the meaning of the statute. Scholars may write books or articles about the statute. These court decisions, amendments, and scholarly articles are all pertinent to understanding the meaning of the statute. An **annotated code** is a code published by a private publisher using the same format as the code but including historical references about the statute, annotations of court cases that have interpreted each statute section, and references to secondary sources that have discussed the statute. In an annotated code, the legal researcher will find not only all the information included in the code but also other information that will round out the legal research process. An annotated code provides references to almost all the pertinent information about a statute in a single set of books. Perhaps the most important research rule to remember is that if you are searching for law in the form of a statute, use an annotated code.

The search of an annotated code can be accomplished in several media, including on-line with a computer, on compact discs, and in book form. There are both federal and state annotated codes. At the federal level, there are two annotated versions of the U.S.C.: the

---

LEGAL TERMS

United States Code (U.S.C.)† The official codification of the statutes enacted by Congress.

presumptive evidence† Evidence that the law regards as proof unless it is rebutted; probable evidence.

positive law† Legislation, as opposed to natural law or moral law; unquestionable as evidence, as opposed to presumptive or probable evidence.

annotated codes† Books or volumes that contain both statutes and commentaries upon the statutes.

TITLES OF UNITED STATES CODE

*1. General Provisions.

2. The Congress.

*3. The President.

*4. Flag and Seal, Seat of Government, and the States.

*5. Government Organization and Employees; and Appendix.

†6. [Surety Bonds.]

7. Agriculture.

8. Aliens and Nationality.

*9. Arbitration.

*10. Armed Forces; and Appendix.

*11. Bankruptcy; and Appendix.

12. Banks and Banking.

*13. Census.

*14. Coast Guard.

15. Commerce and Trade.

16. Conservation.

*17. Copyrights.

*18. Crimes and Criminal Procedure; and Appendix.

19. Customs Duties.

20. Education.

21. Food and Drugs.

22. Foreign Relations and Intercourse.

*23. Highways.

24. Hospitals and Asylums.

25. Indians.

26. Internal Revenue Code; and Appendix.

27. Intoxicating Liquors.

*28. Judiciary and Judicial Procedure; and Appendix.

29. Labor.

30. Mineral Lands and Mining.

*31. Money and Finance.

*32. National Guard.

33. Navigation and Navigable Waters.

‡34. [Navy.]

*35. Patents.

36. Patriotic Societies and Observances.

*37. Pay and Allowances of the Uniformed Services.

*38. Veterans' Benefits; and Appendix.

*39. Postal Service.

40. Public Buildings, Property, and Works.

41. Public Contracts.

42. The Public Health and Welfare.

43. Public Lands.

*44. Public Printing and Documents.

45. Railroads.

*46. Shipping; and Appendix.

47. Telegraphs, Telephones, and Radiotelegraphs.

48. Territories and Insular Possessions.

*49. Transportation; and Appendix.

50. War and National Defense; and Appendi:

FIGURE 2–3   Titles of *United States Code*

United States Code Annotated **(U.S.C.A.)**, published by West Publishing Company, and the *United States Code Services* **(U.S.C.S.)**, published by Lawyers Cooperative Publishing Company.

Figure 2–4 is a statute from the U.S.C.S. dealing with the mutilation of United States coins. The text of this statute is, of course, no different from the text as you find it in the U.S.C. or in the *Statutes at Large*. However, the material found after each individual statute has been added by the publisher and illustrates the difference between a code and an annotated code. For instance, there is the historical information (Figure 2–4), the "Cross References" to other laws (Figure 2–5), the "Research Guide" (Figure 2–5) that directs the researcher to other Lawyers Cooperative sources that relate to this statute, and the "Interpretive Notes and Decisions" (Figure 2–5). The "Interpretive Notes and Decisions" section references cases that have interpreted or applied this statute.

The U.S.C.A. has similar features. (See Figures 2–6 and 2–7.) In the U.S.C.A., there are also "Historical Note" sections (Figure 2–6), a "Cross Reference" section (Figure 2–7), a "Library References" section (Figure 2–7), and a "Notes of Decisions" section (Figure 2–7). Under some statutes, the "Library References" section in the U.S.C.A. and the "Research Guide" section in the U.S.C.S. cover multiple pages. The "Notes of Decisions" section in the U.S.C.A. can fill a volume for a single statute.

Most states also have an annotated code that can be used for searching that state's statutes. A paralegal is expected to locate statutes, so you should familiarize yourself with the annotated version of the code in your state.

Using a Code or Annotated Code

Most of a paralegal's research of statutes is done with annotated codes. In fact, a paralegal who can master the use of an annotated code will be able to do almost any constitutional or statutory research. There are five steps to follow in researching any statute:

Step 1 - Identify the applicable annotated code.
Step 2 - Locate the appropriate statute by using an index or table.
Step 3 - Read the statute.

LEGAL TERMS

United States Code Annotated (U.S.C.A.) An annotated version of the United States Code published by West Publishing Company.

United States Code Services (U.S.C.S.) An annotated version of the *United States Code* published by Lawyers Cooperative Publishing Company.

CHAPTER 17.   COINS AND CURRENCY

Section
331.   Mutilation, diminution, and falsification of coins
332.   Debasement of coins; alteration of official scales, or embezzle-
         ment of metals
333.   Mutilation of national bank obligations
334.   Issuance of Federal Reserve or national bank notes
335.   Circulation of obligations of expired corporations
336.   Issuance of circulating obligations of less than $1
337.   Coins as security for loans

HISTORY; ANCILLARY LAWS AND DIRECTIVES
Amendments:
1965. Act July 23, 1965, P. L. 89-81, Title II, § 212(b), 79 Stat. 257,
amended the analysis of this chapter by adding item 337.

§ 331.   Mutilation, diminution, and falsification of coins

Whoever fraudulently alters, defaces, mutilates, impairs, diminishes, falsifies, scales, or lightens any of the coins coined at the mints of the United States, or any foreign coins which are by law made current or are in actual use or circulation as money within the United States; or

Whoever fraudulently possesses, passes, utters, publishes, or sells, or attempts to pass, utter, publish, or sell, or brings into the United States, any such coin, knowing the same to be altered, defaced, mutilated, impaired, diminished, falsified, scaled, or lightened—

Shall be fined not more than $2,000 or imprisoned not more than five years, or both.
(June 25, 1948, ch 645, § 1, 62 Stat. 700; July 16, 1951, ch 226, § 1, 65 Stat. 121.)

HISTORY; ANCILLARY LAWS AND DIRECTIVES
Prior law and revision:
This section is based on Act March 4, 1909, ch 321, § 165, 35 Stat. 1119 (former 18 U.S.C. § 279).

Mandatory punishment provision was rephrased in alternative because the court has this discretion by making use of its power to suspend sentence under former 18 USCS § 3651.

Reference to persons causing or procuring was omitted as unnecessary in view of definition of "principal" in former 18 USCS § 2.

Changes were also made in phraseology.

Amendments:
1951. Act July 16, 1951 inserted "alters,", substituted "any of the" for "the gold or silver", and deleted "gold or silver" following "foreign" in the first paragraph and inserted "altered" in the second paragraph.

FIGURE 2–4   The historical record of statutes as found in U.S.C.S.

18 USCS § 331   CRIMES & CRIMINAL PROCEDURE

CROSS REFERENCES

Forfeiture of counterfeit paraphernalia, 18 USCS § 492.
This section is referred to in 18 USCS §§ 14, 492.

RESEARCH GUIDE

Am Jur:
54 Am Jur 2d, Money § 21.

INTERPRETIVE NOTES AND DECISIONS

1. Purpose
2. Construction, generally
3. Relationship with other laws
4. Intent
5. Alteration of value of coin
6. Evidence

1. Purpose

By enacting portion of predecessor of 18 USCS § 331 regarding coins of foreign countries made current, Congress intended to protect foreign coins which had become legal tender in United States. Tyson v United States (1960, CA10 Okla) 285 F2d 19.

2. Construction, generally

Since coin had not been made current, possession of Mexican cinco centavo (5 cent) coins which had been fraudulently altered, defaced, mutilated, impaired, diminished, falsified, scaled, and lightened did not constitute offense under 18 USCS § 331. Tyson v United States (1960, CA10 Okla) 285 F2d 19.

3. Relationship with other laws

Although violation of 18 USCS § 331 for mutilating or defacing coin occurred when coin was made into blank, at which time it was no longer coin at all, counterfeiting within meaning of 18 USCS § 485 took place when blank was restruck with counterfeit dies, and United States could charge defendants with violation of either § 331 or § 485, or both, as it saw fit. United States v Wilson (1971, CA5 Tex) 451 F2d 209, cert den (1972) 405 US 1032, 31 L Ed 2d 490, 92 S Ct 1298.

4. Intent

"Fraudulent alteration," prohibited by 18 USCS § 331, includes any alteration, whether or not affecting legal tender value or utility of coin, which is made with intent to defraud United States, any person or group of persons or organizations. Barnett v United States (1967, CA5 Miss) 384 F2d 848, reh den (1968, CA5 Miss) 391 F2d 931.

If defendants' acts were done inadvertently, mistakenly, or in good faith without intention to defraud, defendants must be acquitted of charges under 18 USCS § 331. United States v Sheiner (1967, SD NY) 273 F Supp 977, affd (1969, CA2 NY) 410 F2d 337, cert den (1969) 396 US 825, 24 L Ed 2d 76, 90 S Ct 68 and cert den (1969) 396 US 859, 24 L Ed 2d 110, 90 S Ct 127.

5. Alteration of value of coin

Alteration of legal tender value or utility of coin is not required for crime arising under 18 USCS § 331. Barnett v United States (1967, CA5 Miss) 384 F2d 848, reh den (1968, CA5 Miss) 391 F2d 931.

Silver coins were counterfeited where they were punched and mutilated and appreciable amount of silver removed from them and hole plugged up with substance other than silver; but they were not counterfeited where they were punched with sharp instrument changing their shape but leaving all silver in them. United States v Lissner (1882, CC Mass) 12 F 840.

6. Evidence

In prosecution under 18 USCS § 331, government's expert witness description of technical operation of mint as factual basis from which to determine source of alterations was opinion based on factual presentation, and admissible. United States v Sheiner (1969, CA2 NY) 410 F2d 337, cert den (1969) 396 US 825, 24 L Ed 2d 76, 90 S Ct 68 and cert den (1969) 396 US 859, 24 L Ed 2d 110, 90 S Ct 127.

§ 332.   Debasement of coins; alteration of official scales, or embezzlement of metals

If any of the gold or silver coins struck or coined at any of the mints of the United States shall be debased, or made worse as to the proportion of fine gold or fine silver therein contained, or shall be of less weight or value than the same ought to be, pursuant to law, or if any of the scales or weights used

FIGURE 2–5   An example of Cross References, Research Guide, and Interpretive Notes and Decisions found in U.S.C.S.

18 § 292   CRIMES   Part 1

The words "or both" are substituted for "or by both such fine and imprisonment".

Minor changes in phraseology are made to conform to the style of title 18.

Library References

United States ☞123.

C.J.S. United States § 173.

CHAPTER 17—COINS AND CURRENCY

Sec.
331. Mutilation, diminution, and falsification of coins.
332. Debasement of coins; alteration of official scales, or embezzlement of metals.
333. Mutilation of national bank obligations.
334. Issuance of Federal Reserve or national bank notes.
335. Circulation of obligations of expired corporations.
336. Issuance of circulating obligations of less than $1.
337. Coins as security for loans.

Historical Note

1965 Amendment. Pub.L. 89-81, Title II, § 212(b), July 23, 1965, 79 Stat. 257, added item 337.

§ 331. Mutilation, diminution, and falsification of coins

Whoever fraudulently alters, defaces, mutilates, impairs, diminishes, falsifies, scales, or lightens any of the coins coined at the mints of the United States, or any foreign coins which are by law made current or are in actual use or circulation as money within, the United States; or

Whoever fraudulently possesses, passes, utters, publishes, or sells, or attempts to pass, utter, publish, or sell, or brings into the United States, any such coin, knowing the same to be altered, defaced, mutilated, impaired, diminished, falsified, scaled, or lightened—

Shall be fined not more than $2,000 or imprisoned not more than five years, or both.

June 25, 1948, c. 645, 62 Stat. 700; July 16, 1951, c. 226, § 1, 65 Stat. 121.

Historical and Revision Notes

Reviser's Note. Based on Title 18, U.S.C., 1940 ed., § 279 (Mar. 4, 1909, c. 321, § 165, 35 Stat. 1119 [derived from R.S. § 5459; Mar. 3, 1897, c. 377, 29 Stat. 625]).

Mandatory punishment provision was rephrased in the alternative.

Reference to persons causing or procuring was omitted as unnecessary in view of definition of "principal" in section 2 of this title.

Changes were also made in phraseology. 80th Congress House Report No. 304.

1951 Amendment. Act July 16, 1951, made section applicable to minor coins (5-cent and 1-cent pieces), and to fraudulent alteration of coins.

Canal Zone. Applicability of section to Canal Zone, see section 14 of this title.

492

FIGURE 2–6   The Historical Note found in U.S.C.A. (Reprinted by permission of West Publishing Company.)

Ch. 17   COINS AND CURRENCY   18 § 331

Cross References

Forfeiture of counterfeit paraphernalia, see section 492 of this title.

Library References

United States ⊂⇒34.   C.J.S. United States § 125.

Notes of Decisions

"By law made current" 2
Evidence 6
Intent 3
Mutilation 4
Purpose 1
Value of coins 5

---

1. Purpose

In enacting this section forbidding fraudulent alteration, defacement and other acts on foreign coins by law made current, the congressional intent was to protect foreign coins which at the time were legal tender in the United States. Tyson v. U. S., C.A.Okl.1960, 285 F.2d 19.

2. "By law made current"

Where Mexican Cinco Centavo (5 cents) coins had not been made current in United States by United States law, the possession of fraudulently altered Centavo coins was not a violation of this section which in effect forbids fraudulent alteration, defacement and other acts on foreign coins by law of Congress made current in United States. Tyson v. U. S., C.A.Okl. 1960, 285 F.2d 19.

In this section forbidding fraudulent alteration, defacement and other acts on foreign coins "by law made current", the quoted words mean by law of Congress made current in United States; the 1951 Amendment did not change this meaning. Id.

3. Intent

Within this section prohibiting fraudulent alteration of any coin of United States, "fraudulent alteration" includes any alteration whether or not affecting legal tender value or utility of coin if alteration is made with intent to defraud United States or any person or group of persons or organizations. Barnett v. U. S., C.A.Miss.1967, 384 F.2d 848, rehearing denied 391 F.2d 931.

Attempt to use altered coins to deceive those purchasing them for their value as collectors' items was sufficient fraudu-lent intent within this section prohibiting fraudulently altering coins. Id.

If defendants' acts were done inadvert-ently, mistakenly or in good faith with-out intention to defraud, then defendants must be acquitted of charges of mail fraud, wire fraud, fraudulent possession and sale of altered coins and conspiracy. U. S. v. Sheiner, D.C.N.Y.1967, 273 F. Supp. 977.

Essential elements for conviction of fraudulent possession and sale of altered coins are criminal intent and guilty knowledge. Id.

If defendants acted willfully and pur-posefully with an evil intent, or with reckless disregard to the truth, then they would be chargeable with knowledge and criminal intent requisite to conviction for mail fraud, wire fraud, fraudulent pos-session and sale of altered coins and conspiracy. Id.

4. Mutilation

Where a coin regularly coined at the mint was afterwards punched and muti-lated, and an appreciable amount of sil-ver removed from it, and the hole plugged up with base metal, or with any substance other than silver, it was an act of counterfeiting; but otherwise where the hole was punched with a sharp instrument, leaving all the silver in the coin, though crowding it into a different shape. U. S. v. Lissner, C.C. Mass.1882, 12 F. 840.

5. Value of coins

Defendants who altered mint marks and dates on United States coins which were sold as rare collectors' items violat-ed this section prohibiting fraudulently altering coins, even though alterations did not in any way affect value of coins as currency and were not intended to do so. Barnett v. U. S., C.A.Miss.1967, 384 F.2d 848, rehearing denied 391 F.2d 931.

6. Evidence

That coins found in possession of de-fendants had been altered was admissi-ble to show intent, purpose or motive, in

493

FIGURE 2–7   An example of Cross References, Library References, and Notes of Decisions found in U.S.C.A. (Reprinted by permission of West Publishing Company.)

Step 4   -   Scan the annotated materials to see if there are cases or articles that should be read.

Step 5   -   Examine the updating sources such as pocket parts, supplemental pamphlets, or Shepard's citations.

If you must use a code rather than a annotated code, follow the same steps except skip step 4.

Step 1—Identify the applicable annotated code. State statutes are found in separate annotated codes. New York statutes are found in a separate annotated code from California statutes. In researching federal statutes, use the U.S.C.A. or the U.S.C.S. When researching a state statute, use an annotated code from that state.

Step 2—Locate the appropriate statute by using an index or table. Occasionally you will begin your research with a citation to a particular statute. Your supervisor may tell you to look up 42 U.S.C. § 2000(e)-2(a), in which case you will merely pull the volume containing title 42 of the *United States Code* and turn to section 2000(e)-2(a). You will find a statute that reads:

Employer Practices

(a)   It shall be an unlawful employment practice for an employer—

(1)   to fail or refuse to hire or to discharge any individual or otherwise to discriminate against any individual with respect to his compensation, terms, conditions, or privileges of employment, because of such individual's race, color, religion, sex, or national origin; or

(2)   to limit, segregate, or classify his employees or applicants for employment in any way which would deprive or tend to deprive any individual of employment opportunities or otherwise adversely affect his status as an employee, because of such individual's race, color, religion, sex, or national origin.

The federal code is referenced by a title number and by a section number. State codes may follow the same technique, although some state codes use a more detailed numbering method.

At other times, you may begin your research with a session law citation, a public law number, or a compilation citation. Then you will use the tables in the annotated codes to convert such citations to code citations.

However, in most research situations, the paralegal is merely given a fact situation and asked to look up an applicable statute. There are three alternative methods to use in this situation:

(1) Descriptive word index method
(2) Topical approach
(3) Popular name table approach

The descriptive word index method is usually the most beneficial.

Descriptive Word Index Method. Most codes or annotated codes have detailed, multivolumed descriptive word indexes at the end of the set. In order to use the index, the paralegal must be able to match the vocabulary of the researched problem with the vocabulary terms in the index. You must formulate and reformulate the terms you are searching by expanding your vocabulary or by searching for more precise terms. You may need to expand or narrow your search vocabulary by using a legal dictionary, a nonlegal dictionary, a thesaurus, or the TAPP method discussed in Chapter 1. Let us work through an example.

Assume you are asked to research a problem concerning the age categories protected under the federal age discrimination laws. Your first step would be to go to the descriptive word index. Whether you use the U.S.C., the U.S.C.A., or the U.S.C.S., the descriptive word index will be found at the end of the set. You could look under "age," "discrimination," or "employment" in the index. (Figure 2–8 is an excerpt from the U.S.C.S. descriptive word index.) Once you have located the appropriate reference, you would find a title and section number and could look up the statute in the main volume. Paralegals begin most research of codes with use of a descriptive word index.

Topical Approach. Conventional textbooks contain descriptive word indexes in the back and tables of contents in the front. When you review a table of contents, you are using a topical approach. The U.S.C. is categorized into fifty titles. If you know what title to look under, you may opt to use the topical approach to find the specific statute. Each U.S.C. title is divided into chapters and subchapters, and the beginning of each U.S.C. volume contains a table of titles and chapters. A review of the chapter listings will reveal the relevant chapter number. For example, using the topical approach to research the age discrimination problem, you can scan the applicable U.S.C.A. chapter and sections table in Figure 2–9 to find a citation.

The topical approach is useful when you have enough information to identify the right title. The more experience you have in a particular area of the law, the more the topical approach can be used to pinpoint the correct section of the code.

Popular Name Table Approach. On occasion you may know a popular name for a statute. For example, you may have heard of the Clean Air Act or the Children's Justice Act. The U.S.C. as well as both annotated codes contain popular name tables. You can find the volume containing the "Popular Name" table and check alphabetically for the

UNITED STATES CODE SERVICE

AFRICAN DEVELOPMENT FUND —Cont'd

Rank of Governor, 22 § 290g-1
Regional integration, promotion, 22 § 2293
Removal of actions, 22 § 290g-6
Repayments, appropriations, 22 § 290g-4
Review of contribution and voting structure with other donors, 22 § 290g-10
SADCC project support, 22 § 2293
Secretary of Treasury, performance of functions and delegation of Presidential functions respecting, 22 § 286b note, 2381 note
Service of process, 22 § 290g-6
Short title of Act, 22 § 290g note
Taxation of salaries and emoluments paid to United States citizens, 22 § 290g-7
Types of assistance, 22 § 2293
Venue, 22 § 290g-6
Voluntary organizations, 22 § 2293
Voting structure, 22 § 290g-10

AFRICAN ELEPHANT CONSERVATION ACT

Generally, 16 § 4201 et seq.
African Elephant Conservation Assistance, 16 § 4211 to 4213
Annual reports, 16 § 4213
Appropriations, authorization, 16 § 4245
Certification under Pelly Amendment, 16 § 4242
CITES
- CITES Ivory Control System, defined, 16 § 4244
- defined, 16 § 4244
- effectiveness, 16 § 4243
Confiscated ivory, 16 § 4222
Congress, 16 § 4202
Conservation Fund, 16 § 4212
Convention on International Trade in Endangered Species of Wild Fauna and Flora. CITES, supra
Definitions
- African elephant, 16 § 4244
- CITES, 16 § 4244
- CITES Ivory Control System, 16 § 4244
- fund, 16 § 4244
Endangered Species Act of 1973, 16 § 4241
Finances. Funds, infra
Fines, penalties, and forfeitures, 16 § 4224
Forfeitures, fines, and penalties, 16 § 4224
Funds
- African Elephant Conservation Fund, 16 § 4212
- defined, 16 § 4244
Ivory producing countries, 16 § 4222
Moratoria and prohibited acts, 16 § 4221 to 4225
Pelly Amendment, certification, 16 § 4242
Penalties, fines, and forfeitures, 16 § 4224
Relationship to Endangered Species Act of 1973, 16 § 4241
Reports, 16 § 4213
Review of African elephant conservation programs, 16 § 4221
Rewards, 16 § 4225
Sport-hunted trophies, 16 § 4222
Statement of policy, 16 § 4203
Statement of purpose, 16 § 4201

AFRICAN FAMINE RELIEF AND RECOVERY ACT OF 1985

Generally, 22 § 2292q et seq.

AFRICAN NATIONAL CONGRESS

Anti-apartheid program
- policy towards, 22 § 5012
- reports, 22 § 5101

AFRO-AMERICAN HISTORY AND CULTURE COMMISSION

National Afro-American History and Culture Commission (this index)

AFTERCARE

Defined, 18 § 3621

AFTERCARE SERVICES

Indians, alcohol and substance abuse, 25 § 1665c

AFTER NOTICE AND A HEARING

Definitions, 11 § 102(1)

AFTER-SCHOOL SERVICES

Child care and development block grant, 42 § 9858f
School lunch program, 42 § 1766a

AGASSIZ WILDERNESS

Designation, Agassiz National Wildlife Refuge, 16 § 1132 note

AGATE FOSSIL BEDS NATIONAL MONUMENT

Establishment, 16 § 431 note

AGE

Person. Age of Person (this index)
Property. Age of Property (this index)

AGE DISCRIMINATION

Generally, 29 § 621 et seq.
Administration, 29 § 625
Administrative rulings, reliance in future, 29 § 626
Advertisement or notice indicating preference, printing or publication, 29 § 623
Age Discrimination Act of 1975, 42 § 6101 et seq.
Age Discrimination Claims Act of 1988, 29 § 626, 626 note
Age Discrimination in Employment Act Amendments of 1978, 29 § 621 et seq.
Age Discrimination in Employment Act Amendments of 1986, 29 § 621, 623, 630, 631
Age Discrimination in Employment Act of 1967, generally, 29 § 621 et seq.
Appeal and review, discrimination in federally assisted programs, 42 § 6105
Appropriations, authorization, 29 § 634
Arbitration, mediation or conciliation, 29 § 626
Benefit plans, 29 § 623
Bona fide executives, 29 § 631

AGE DISCRIMINATION—Cont'd

Bona fide occupational qualification, 29 § 623, 633a
Cessation or reduction of benefit accrual, 29 § 623
Civil actions, 29 § 626, 633a
Civil Service Commission, enforcement, 5 § 903 note; 29 § 633a; 42 § 2000e-4 note
Collective bargaining, 29 § 623 note
College or university, tenured employee, 29 § 631
Commerce, defined, 29 § 630
Conciliation, conference, and persuasion, 29 § 626
Congressional statement of findings and purpose, 29 § 621
Criminal penalties, 29 § 629
Damages, 29 § 626
Definitions
- commerce, 29 § 630
- employee, 29 § 630
- employer, 29 § 630
- employment agency, 29 § 630
- firefighter, 29 § 630
- industry affecting commerce, 29 § 630
- labor organization, 29 § 630
- law enforcement officer, 29 § 630
- person, 29 § 630
- state, 29 § 630
Discharge or discipline for good cause, 29 § 623
Discipline for good cause, 29 § 623
Distribution of benefits after attainment of normal retirement age, 29 § 623
Duty of government agency or official, 29 § 633a
Education and research program, 29 § 622
Employee, defined, 29 § 630
Employee benefit plans, 29 § 623
Employee pension benefit plans, 29 § 623
Employer, defined, 29 § 630
Employer practices prohibited, 29 § 623
Employment agencies, 29 § 623, 630
Employment agency, defined, 29 § 630
Enforcement, 5 § 903 note; 29 § 626
Equal Employment Opportunity Commission, 5 § 903 note; 29 § 622 et seq.; 42 § 2000e note
Exemptions from rules and regulations, 29 § 628, 633a
Fair labor standards, prohibition of age discrimination, 29 § 626
Federal agencies affected, 29 § 633a
Federal government employment, 29 § 631, 633a
Federally assisted programs. Age Discrimination in Federally Assisted Programs (this index)
Federal-State relationship, 29 § 633
Filing of charge with Secretary, 29 § 626
Firefighters, 29 § 623, 630
Foreign practices, 29 § 623
Forty years old, individuals at least that age, 29 § 631
Future reliance on administrative rulings, 29 § 626
Government contracts, contractors and subcontractors, nondiscrimination, 5 § 3301 note

References to Code are to Title and Section

FIGURE 2–8   An excerpt from U.S.C.S. descriptive word index

CHAPTER 14—AGE DISCRIMINATION IN EMPLOYMENT

Sec.
621. Congressional statement of findings and purpose.
622. Education and research program; recommendation to Congress.
→ 623. Prohibition of age discrimination.

 (a) Employer practices.
 (b) Employment agency practices.
 (c) Labor organization practices.
 (d) Opposition to unlawful practices; participation in investigations, proceedings, or litigation.
 (e) Printing or publication of notice or advertisement indicating preference, limitation, etc.
 (f) Lawful practices; age an occupational qualification; other reasonable factors; laws of foreign workplace; seniority system; employee benefit plans; discharge or discipline for good cause.
 (g) Entitlement to coverage under group health plan.
 (g)[1] Practices of foreign corporations controlled by American employers; foreign persons not controlled by American employers; factors determining control.

624. Study by Secretary of Labor; reports to President and Congress; scope of study; implementation of study; transmittal date of reports.
625. Administration.

 (a) Delegation of functions; appointment of personnel; technical assistance.
 (b) Cooperation with other agencies, employers, labor organizations, and employment agencies.

626. Recordkeeping, investigation, and enforcement.

 (a) Attendance of witnesses; investigations, inspections, records, and homework regulations.
 (b) Enforcement; prohibition of age discrimination under fair labor standards; unpaid minimum wages and unpaid overtime compensation; liquidated damages; judicial relief; conciliation, conference, and persuasion.
 (c) Civil actions; persons aggrieved; jurisdiction; judicial relief; termination of individual action upon commencement of action by Commission; jury trial.
 (d) Filing of charge with Commission; timeliness; conciliation, conference, and persuasion.
 (e) Statute of limitations; reliance in future on administrative ruling, etc.; tolling.

3

FIGURE 2–9 Using the topic approach to legal research (Reprinted by permission of West Publishing Company.)

popular name. The table will provide a citation to a title and section of the code. Figure 2–10 is an excerpt from the U.S.C.A. popular name table that references the Children's Justice Act.

Step 3—Read the statute. A statute is primary authority. It is the law. Paralegals too often rely upon interpretations of statutes found in secondary sources and pay too little attention to the literal words of the statute. Read the statute. Most statutes include a title of the code, headings, a purpose section, definitions, the substantive provisions, and remedies. You will have to study in detail the operative provisions of the statute to discern its meaning. Check the definitions and read them along with the operative provisions. Check the effective date of the statute. Some statutes only pertain to conduct that happened before or after a certain date. Read every word of the statute and assume that every word was intentionally put into the statute.

Reading statutes takes practice. If you cannot understand the statute, read it through quickly. Then go back and read it again line by line. Refer to the titles and headings. Some statutes are easier to read than others. If you are still having trouble, go to step 4 and then repeat step 3.

Step 4—Scan the annotated materials to see if there are cases or articles that should be read. The unique feature of the annotated code is that it provides references to historical information such as earlier amendments to the statute, citations to case law, and references to secondary sources. In other words, the annotations provide you with background information and references to encyclopedias, legal articles, and other materials that will enable you to complete an exhaustive research. Rarely will you research a legal question without carefully looking through the annotated materials for more information.

Historical Information

The statute you are reading may have been amended or changed many times over the years. Most annotated codes provide you with a detailed history of the statute, usually found immediately after the statute. (See Figure 2–11.) At times you can glean the intent of the legislature from the changes made in a law.

Cross References

The annotated code also may refer you to related or similar statutes relevant to your inquiry. By using this information, you may be able to locate other statutes that might affect your analysis.

POPULAR NAME TABLE 912

Children With Disabilities Temporary Care Reauthorization Act of 1989
Pub.L. 101–127, Oct. 25, 1989, 103 Stat. 770 (42 §§ 5117 notes, 5117a, 5117a note, 5117c, 5117d)

Childrens Bicycle Helmet Safety Act of 1994
Pub.L. 103–267, Title II, June 16, 1994, 108 Stat. 726 (15 §§ 6001, 6001 note, 6002 to 6006)

Children's Bureau Act
Apr. 9, 1912, ch. 73, 37 Stat. 79

Children's Justice Act
Pub.L. 99–401, Title I, Aug. 27, 1986, 100 Stat. 903 (42 §§ 290dd–3, 290ee–3, 5101, 5101 notes, 5103, 5105, 10601, 10603, 10603a)

Children's Justice and Assistance Act of 1986
Pub.L. 99–401, Aug. 27, 1986, 100 Stat. 903 (42 §§ 290dd–3, 290ee–3, 5101, 5101 notes, 5103, 5105, 5117, 5117 notes, 5117a to 5117d, 10601, 10603, 10603a)

Children's Nutrition Assistance Act of 1992
Pub.L. 102–512, Oct. 24, 1992, 106 Stat. 3363 (42 §§ 1771 notes, 1769, 1769 note, 1776, 1786, 1786 notes)

Children's Television Act of 1990
Pub.L. 101–437, Oct. 18, 1990, 104 Stat. 996 (47 §§ 303a, 303a note, 303b, 393a, prec. 394, 394, 394 note, prec. 395, prec. 396, prec. 397, 397, 609 notes)
Pub.L. 102–356, § 15, Aug. 26, 1992, 106 Stat. 954 (47 § 303b)
Pub.L. 103–414, Title III, § 303(c), Oct. 25, 1994, 108 Stat. 4296 (47 § 303(f))

China Aid Act
Feb. 7, 1942, ch. 47, 56 Stat. 82

China Aid Act of 1948
Apr. 3, 1948, ch. 169, Title IV, 62 Stat. 158

China Appropriation Act
Feb. 12, 1942, ch. 71, 56 Stat. 89

China Area Aid Act of 1950
June 5, 1950, ch. 220, Title II, 64 Stat. 202

China Trade Act (Corporations Act)
June 6, 1932, ch. 209, §§ 261 to 264, 47 Stat. 232

China Trade Act, 1922
Sept. 19, 1922, ch. 346, 42 Stat. 849 (15 §§ 141 to 162)
Feb. 26, 1925, ch. 345, 43 Stat. 995 to 997 (15 §§ 144, 146, 147, 149, 150, 160, 162)
Oct. 15, 1970, Pub. L. 91–452, Title II, § 217, 84 Stat. 929 (15 § 155)

Chinese Student Protection Act of 1992
Pub.L. 102–404, Oct. 9, 1992, 106 Stat. 1969 (8 § 1255 notes)

Choctaw-Chickasaw-Cherokee Boundary Dispute Act
Pub. L. 93–195, Dec. 20, 1973, 87 Stat. 769

Choctaw-Chickasaw Supplemental Agreement
July 1, 1902, ch. 1362, 32 Stat. 641 (16 § 151)

Choice in Public Housing Management Act of 1992
Pub.L. 102–550, Title I, Subtitle B, § 121(b), Oct. 28, 1992, 106 Stat. 3701 (42 § 1437w)

Christopher Columbus Fellowship Act
Pub.L. 102–281, Title IV, Subtitle B, May 13, 1992, 106 Stat. 142 to 145 (20 §§ 5701, 5701 note, 5702 to 5708)

Christopher Columbus Quincentenary Coin Act
Pub.L. 102–281, Title IV, Subtitle A, May 13, 1992, 106 Stat. 139 to 142 (31 § 5112 note)

Christopher Columbus Quincentenary Jubilee Act
Pub.L. 98–375, Aug. 7, 1984, 98 Stat. 1257
Pub.L. 100–94, Aug. 18, 1987, 101 Stat. 700

Chrysler Corporation Loan Guarantee Act of 1979
Pub. L. 96–185, Jan. 7, 1980, 93 Stat. 1324 (15 §§ 631 note, 1861 to 1875, 2003, 2512)

FIGURE 2–10 An excerpt from the U.S.C.A. Popular Name Table (Reprinted by permission of West Publishing Company.)

§ 700. Desecration of the flag of the United States; penalties

(a)(1) Whoever knowingly mutilates, defaces, physically defiles, burns, maintains on the floor or ground, or tramples upon any flag of the United States shall be fined under this title or imprisoned for not more than one year, or both.

(2) This subsection does not prohibit any conduct consisting of the disposal of a flag when it has become worn or soiled.

(b) As used in this section, the term "flag of the United States" means any flag of the United States, or any part thereof, made of any substance, of any size, in a form that is commonly displayed.

(c) Nothing in this section shall be construed as indicating an intent on the part of Congress to deprive any State, territory, possession, or the Commonwealth of Puerto Rico of jurisdiction over any offense over which it would have jurisdiction in the absence of this section.

(d)(1) An appeal may be taken directly to the Supreme Court of the United States from any interlocutory or final judgment, decree, or order issued by a United States district court ruling upon the constitutionality of subsection (a).

(2) The Supreme Court shall, if it has not previously ruled on the question, accept jurisdiction over the appeal and advance on the docket and expedite to the greatest extent possible.

(As amended Oct. 28, 1989, P. L. 101-131, §§ 2, 3, 103 Stat. 777.)

[HISTORY; ANCILLARY LAWS AND DIRECTIVES]

Amendments:

1989. Act Oct. 28, 1989 substituted subsecs. (a) and (b) for ones which read:

"(a) Whoever knowingly casts contempt upon any flag of the United States by publicly mutilating, defacing, defiling, burning, or trampling upon it shall be fined not more than $1,000 or imprisoned for not more than one year, or both.

"(b) The term 'flag of the United States' as used in this section, shall include any flag, standard, colors, ensign, or any picture or representation of either, or of any part or parts of either, made of any substance or represented on any substance, of any size evidently purporting to be either of said flag, standard, colors, or ensign of the United States of America, or a picture or a representation of either, upon which shall be shown the colors, the stars and the stripes, in any number of either thereof, or of any part or parts of either, by which the average person seeing the same without deliberation may believe the same to represent the flag, standards, colors, or ensign of the United States of America.".

Such Act further added subsec. (d).

Short title:

Act Oct. 28, 1989, P. L. 101-131, § 1, 103 Stat. 777, provides: "This Act [adding this note and amending this section] may be cited as the 'Flag Protection Act of 1989'.".

RESEARCH GUIDE

Am Jur:

16 Am Jur 2d, Constitutional Law § 287.

Annotations:

Supreme Court's views as to constitutionality of laws prohibiting, or of criminal convictions for, desecration, defiance, disrepect, or misuse of American flag. 105 L Ed 2d 809.

FIGURE 2–11 An excerpt from U.S.C.S. Crimes and Criminal Procedure illustrating the history of a statute

SIDEBAR

In the text of many materials published by Lawyers Cooperative Publishing, the publisher provides references solely to related materials published by Lawyers Cooperative under the caption "References to Total Client Service Library." West Publishing Company likewise provides "Library References" to other West publications in its annotated codes.

Case Digests

Sometimes disputes arise about the meaning of a statute. When such a dispute goes to court, the case will decide the proper interpretation of the statute. Statutes may be applied by many different court cases. Annotated codes digest these cases, categorize them by subject matter, and may provide an index for them. (See Figure 2–12.)

Figure 2–13 is an excerpt from a page of the U.S.C.A. with digested cases on the age discrimination statute. You can read these digest notes to find citations to cases analogous to the client's situation. Each digest contains summaries of these cases prepared by legal editors. As with other summaries, they may be incomplete or even inaccurate. Always read the actual cases and do not rely on the case summaries.

Secondary Sources

The major publishers such as West and Lawyers Cooperative publish various secondary materials to help explain the law. As previously noted, these publishers reference other sources they have published that might apply to your research in the annotated materials. Figure 2–14 is an example of such a reference in the U.S.C.S. You will need to read any related statutes to ensure you have a thorough understanding of the impact of the law before your legal research task will be fully completed.

Step 5—Examine the updating sources such as pocket parts, supplemental pamphlets, or Shepard's citations.   Law changes every day. Congress passes new laws, repeals laws, and changes the meaning of laws with amendments to existing statutes. Courts interpret and reinterpret statutes. Some courts have conflicting interpretations of the wording of a statute. Law is never static. The researcher must always look for these changes. It is quite embarrassing to be told by a judge or an opposing party that the law upon which you are relying has been changed or repealed.

Annotated codes are usually updated by pocket parts (paperback supplements inserted into the back of the book) and by pamphlets when the pocket parts become too bulky to fit in the back of the book. Always update your research by checking for pocket part information.

§ 360b. New animal drugs

(a) **Unsafe new animal drugs and animal feed containing such drugs; conditions of safety; exemption of drugs for research.** (1) A new animal drug shall, with respect to any particular use or intended use of such drug, be deemed unsafe for the purposes of section 501(a)(5) and section 402(a)(2)(D) [21 USCS §§ 351(a)(5), 342(a)(2)(D)] unless—

(A) there is in effect an approval of an application filed pursuant to subsection (b) of this section with respect to such use or intended use of such drug,

(B) such drug, its labeling, and such use conform to such approved application, and

(C) in the case of a new animal drug subject to subsection (n) of this section and not exempted therefrom by regulations it is from a batch with respect to which a certificate or release issued pursuant to subsection (n) is in effect with respect to such drug.

INTERPRETIVE NOTES AND DECISIONS

Index for cases →

1. Generally
2. Approval of application
3. Withdrawal of approval
4. Service of orders
5. Hearings
6. Evidence

1. Generally

Agency's interpretation of relevant statute is entitled to even greater deference where agency has participated in drafting it. International Nutrition, Inc. v United States Dept. of Health & Human Services (1982, CA8) 676 F2d 338.

New drug is deemed to be unsafe unless there is in effect approval of new drug application file pursuant to 21 USCS § 360b with respect to use or intended use of such drug, or notice of claimed investigational exemption under § 360b(j) is on file for drug in question. United States v Articles of Animal Drug etc. (1981, DC Neb) 528 F Supp 202.

2. Approval of application

FDA's policy to deny approval of supplemental animal drug application was arbitrary and capricious where based on rationale that additional suppliers of drug would cause increase in potential risk of human exposure to drug residues, not that changes would affect quality of new animal drug in such way as to call into question drug safety. Rhodia, Inc., Hess & Clark Div. v Food & Drug Administration (1979) 197 App DC 219, 608 F2d 1376.

3. Withdrawal of approval

Commissioner was fully authorized to withdraw approval of New Animal Drug Application where holder failed to comply with regulatory provisions and failed to fully exhaust administrative remedies, nor was petitioner entitled to hearing before Commissioner on question of whether product constituted new animal drug. Agri-Tech, Inc. v Richardson (1973, CA8) 482 F2d 1148.

Under 21 USCS § 360b, Food and Drug Administration can remove new animal drug from market when new evidence indicates violation of Delaney Clause, which clause prohibits approval of carcinogenic drug. Hess & Clark, Div. of Rhodia, Inc. v Food & Drug Administration (1974) 161 App DC 395, 495 F2d 975.

4. Service of orders

Notice given by Food and Drug Administration concerning withdrawal of new animal drug application must contain enough information to provide adverse party a genuine opportunity to identify material issues of fact; this is needful to provide "due notice and opportunity for hearing" required by 21 USCS § 360b. Hess & Clark, Div. of Rhodia, Inc. v Food & Drug Administration (1974) 161 App DC 395, 495 F2d 975.

5. Hearings

No hearing was required by regulations under 21 USCS § 360b(e) prior to removal of approval of new drug application, where new evidence submitted by manufacturer did not warrant reconsideration of post-approval demonstrated harmful effect of drug. Diamond Laboratories, Inc. v Richardson (1972, CA8) 452 F2d 803.

FIGURE 2–12 An excerpt of case digest material—index for cases

29 § 631   LABOR   Ch. 14

Retroactive effect   3
State regulation or control   4

_____

1. Constitutionality

Change of mandatory retirement age by overriding federal law was a benefit to city employees' retirement system members in that it permitted them to continue working until age 70; thus, such modification did not impair any contractual right of members. Michael v. Majority of Bd. of Trustees of New York City Emp. Retirement System, 1981, 437 N.Y.S.2d 977, 80 A.D.2d 147 appeal dismissed 55 N.Y.2d 1036, 449 N.Y.S.2d 1031, 434 N.E.2d 1082, appeal denied 57 N.Y.2d 603, 454 N.Y.S.2d 1027, 440 N.E.2d 798.

2. Construction

Provisions of this section should not be construed so as to expose an employer to risk of liability for having failed to use a diplomat's circumlocution in putting relevant questions to job applicants. Olsen v. Southern Pac. Transp. Co., D.C.Cal.1979, 480 F.Supp. 773, affirmed 654 F.2d 733.

3. Retroactive effect

Reference in section 623(f)(2) of this title, which provides that no seniority system or employee benefit plan shall require or permit involuntary requirement of any individual prior to specified age limit, and which. was effective as of Apr. 6, 1978, to subsec. (a) of this section, which raised the age limit for workers protected by this chapter from 65 to 70, but which had an effective date of Jan. 1, 1979, did not make subsec. (a) of this section effective on the effective date of section 623(f)(2) of this title. McDonnell v. Gannett News Service, Inc., D.C.Del.1981, 518 F.Supp. 1326.

4. State regulation or control

To extent that 1978 amendments to this chapter conflict with existing state mandatory retirement statutes, supremacy clause U.S. C.A. Const. Art. 6, cl. 2, dictates that federal law will prevail. Orzel v. City of Wauwatosa Fire Dept., C.A.Wis.1983, 697 F.2d 743, certiorari denied 104 S.Ct. 484, 78 L.Ed.2d 68.

Maine antiage discrimination statute, 5 M.R.S.A. § 4572, does not specifically limit its protection to a particular age group; it is age-neutral, and thus it does not extend protection only to persons within age group protected by this chapter. Maine Human Rights Com'n on Behalf and Use of Trudel v. Kennebec Water Power Co., Me.1983, 468 A.2d 307.

5. Persons within section—Generally

Since former employee's cause of action under this section accrued prior to effective date of amendment to this section raising upper age limitation to 70, his cause of action was governed by prior age 65 limitation, thus precluding his claim for reinstatement. Tribble v. Westinghouse Elec. Corp., D.C.Mo. 1980, 508 F.Supp. 14, affirmed 669 F.2d 1193, certiorari denied 103 S.Ct. 1767, 460 U.S. 1080, 76 L.Ed.2d 342.

Where plaintiff, claiming that university policy with respect to retirement was in violation of Constitution and this chapter, was 67 at time of his retirement, and where he was retired on June 30, 1977, before 1978 amendment of this chapter took effect and increased protected age to age 70, this chapter bore no relevance to case. Mittelstaedt v. Board of Trustees of University of Arkansas, D.C.Ark. 1980, 487 F.Supp. 960.

A 32-year-old plaintiff does not have a cause of action for age discrimination under this chapter. Kodish v. United Airlines, Inc., D.C.Colo.1979, 463 F.Supp. 1245, affirmed 628 F.2d 1301.

This section limiting applicability of prohibitions to individuals at least 40 years of age but less than 65 [now 70] years of age excluded plaintiffs, whose candidacies for union offices were barred because they both would become 65 before end of the nominating period, from protection of this chapter, and, even if plaintiff were not excluded, they would not be entitled to relief because the alleged age discrimination involved was not arbitrary. Hart v. United Steelworkers of America, AFL–CIO–CLC, D.C.Pa.1972, 350 F.Supp. 294, vacated on other grounds 482 F.2d 282.

Justice of district court who was required to retire at age 70 under article of Constitution was not entitled to relief under this chapter since this chapter applies only to individuals under age 70. Grinnell v. State, 1981, 435 A.2d 523, 121 N.H. 823.

Where worker was 70 years of age at time of his injury, he was not within affected class for purposes of standing to challenge age/wage-loss provision of West's F.S.A. § 440.15 as being in contravention of this section. Patrick v. Palm Aire Const. of Sarasota, Inc., Fla.App. 1 Dist.1983, 431 So.2d 304, review dismissed 441 So.2d 632.

6. —— Bona fide executive employees

High salary and title of chief labor counsel did not automatically remove attorney from coverage of Age Discrimination in Employment Act under "bona fide executive * * *

186

_____

FIGURE 2–13   An excerpt of digested cases from U.S.C.A. (Reprinted by permission of West Publishing Company.)

RESEARCH GUIDE

Federal Procedure L Ed:

6 Fed Proc L Ed, Civil Rights §§ 11:132, 230.

6A Fed Proc L Ed, Class Actions § 12:5.

12 Fed Proc L Ed, Evidence § 33:262.

21 Fed Proc L Ed, Job Discrimination § 50:306.

23 Fed Proc L Ed, Labor and Labor Relations § 52:702.

29 Fed Proc L Ed, Removal of Actions § 69:4.

32 Fed Proc L Ed, Transportation § 76:223.

33 Fed Proc L Ed, Veterans and Veterans' Affairs § 79:105.

Am Jur:

15 Am Jur 2d, Civil Rights §§ 3, 137, 147, 186, 226, 247, 248, 499–501, 504, 510.

45A Am Jur 2d, Job Discrimination §§ 98, 106, 873, 1337, 1346.

45B Am Jur 2d, Job Discrimination §§ 2076, 2081, 2084, 2100, 2108-2111, 2157, 2178, 2246.

60A Am Jur 2d, Pensions and Retirement Funds § 420.

Am Jur Trials:

21 Am Jur Trials, Employment Discrimination Action Under Federal Civil Rights Acts, p. 1.

Age Discrimination in Employment Actions under ADEA, 29 Am Jur Trials, p. 1.

Am Jur Proof of Facts:

15 Am Jur Proof of Facts, Age as Bona Fide Occupational Qualification under ADEA, p. 481.

FIGURE 2–14   An excerpt from U.S.C.S. Research Guide

Supplementary statutory research can also be done using computers and Shepard's. Computer research techniques are discussed in Chapter 7, and shepardizing is discussed in Chapter 8.

Choosing Between the U.S.C.A and the U.S.C.S.

Most legal practitioners develop a preference for either the U.S.C.A. or the U.S.C.S. Although each publisher touts the advantages of its version over the other, as a practical matter, there are more similarities than differences between these volumes. Both follow the title and section format used in the U.S.C. In fact, the U.S.C.A. prints the statutes exactly as found in the U.S.C. The U.S.C.S. prints the statutes as found in the U.S.C. except when Lawyers Cooperative Publishing identifies differences between the U.S.C. and the *Statutes at Large*. When there are such differences, the U.S.C.S. copies the material from the *Statutes at Large* rather than from the U.S.C. Both the U.S.C.A. and the U.S.C.S. provide historical references detailing legislative history about particular statutes. Both also provide annotated references to cases that cite each statute.

The U.S.C.A. provides fewer references to regulatory materials than does the U.S.C.S. The U.S.C.A. provides more case coverage, but the U.S.C.S. provides more selective case coverage. West's system is to provide detail in the U.S.C.A. and let the researcher make the choice. Lawyers Cooperative Publishing provides examples in the U.S.C.S. so that the researcher will not bog down in detail. Both methods have benefits and disadvantages. The U.S.C.S. also provides some uncodified laws that are not in the U.S.C.A. and information such as presidential proclamations and treaties. Both sets provide the full text of the United States Constitution, of court rules, and of the Federal Rules of Evidence.

Both the U.S.C.S. and the U.S.C.A. are updated by annual pocket parts. The U.S.C.A. is further updated by quarterly noncumulative supplementary pamphlets. In addition to pocket parts, the U.S.C.S. is updated by quarterly pamphlets called the *Cumulative Later Case and Statutory Service* (*C.L.C.S.S.*) and by monthly pamphlets called the *U.S.C.S. Advance* that contain new public laws without annotations. The U.S.C. is updated quite slowly, so both the U.S.C.A. and the U.S.C.S. are clearly superior to the U.S.C. in this regard.

The main difference between the U.S.C.A. and the U.S.C.S. is the scope of the annotated materials furnished to the researcher. Lawyers Cooperative Publishing provides references in the U.S.C.S. to Lawyers Cooperative materials such as *American Law Reports* (A.L.R.) annotations and *American Jurisprudence Second* (Am. Jur. 2d), the legal encyclopedia published by Lawyers Cooperative Publishing. The U.S.C.A. provides references to West research materials such as the West key numbers (discussed in the next chapter) and *Corpus Juris Secundum* (C.J.S.), the encyclopedia published by West Publishing Company.

At times you may use both the U.S.C.S. and the U.S.C.A. Both publications are superior to the U.S.C. except, perhaps, in a few situations in which the researcher is using on-line computer techniques.

Choosing a State Code

Many states have session laws, compilations, codes, and annotated codes. Always choose an annotated code, if available, for your state statutory research.

Researching Constitutions

The federal Constitution is the basis of all law in the United States, and every paralegal should be able to research the text of that document.

In addition to the federal Constitution, each state has a constitution. The Pennsylvania constitution, for example, may have some similarities to the federal Constitution, but it has unique features as well. The Pennsylvania constitution is different from New York's constitution. The technique for researching a state constitution, however, is the same in most cases as that used in researching the statutory law for that jurisdiction. Constitutions are usually researched through an annotated code. For example, the United States Constitution is researched by using either the U.S.C.A. or the U.S.C.S., using the same techniques used in researching statutory law:

Step 1 - Identify whether to use a state constitution or the federal Constitution, and then select the applicable annotated code.

Step 2 - Locate the appropriate constitutional provision by using an index.

Step 3 - Read the constitutional provision.

Step 4 - Scan the annotated materials to see if there are cases or articles that should be read.

Step 5 - Examine the updating sources such as pocket parts or supplemental pamphlets.

If you are researching the federal Constitution, you will usually use the U.S.C.A. or the U.S.C.S. If you are researching a state constitution, you will find it in the annotated code for that state. The legal researcher typically finds the citation for the particular constitutional provision by using the same descriptive word index used for statutory research.

Constitutional provisions are usually more general than statutory provisions so that they can have wide application. For instance, you will find terms such as "equal protection," "due process," and "free exercise of religion." Although you may think you have a good grasp of these terms, often they have been exhaustively defined and applied in court cases to a variety of problems. To assist the researcher in understanding the subtle interpretations of these constitutional provisions, each particular provision is followed by annotated references in a format similar to that used for statutes (Figure 2–15). These annotated materials provide citations to cases that will help expand your understanding of the constitutional provision being researched. There are also historical references and citations to secondary sources. Review these annotated materials carefully.

The final step is to examine the pocket parts or supplemental pamphlets to update your research, just as you must do for statutory research. Pocket parts and other supplements may provide references to recent cases that have interpreted the constitutional provision and other current information.

To illustrate how to research a constitutional issue, suppose you were asked by an attorney to find the United States constitutional provision that deals with the right to trial by jury in a civil case. Using the descriptive word index in the U.S.C.S., you could find the entries shown in Figure 2–16. Then you would simply look up the citation in the U.S.C.S. or the U.S.C.A. (See Figure 2–17.)

Researching Rules and Regulations

No area of the law has burgeoned more in the past fifty years than administrative law. Although administrative agencies have existed since the founding of this nation, the number of agencies multiplied with the spread of the 1929 Great Depression—when Congress could not devise solutions to the economic difficulties, it turned to administrative agencies to provide expertise in solving the problems. When Congress establishes an administrative agency, it sets standards within which the agency must operate and delegates to the agency power to make law. An administrative agency makes law by rules, regulations, and decisions. An administrative agency issues orders and renders opinions.

Sec. 7, Cl. 3. Approval or veto of Resolutions, orders, or votes—Passage over veto.

Every Order, Resolution, or Vote to which the Concurrence of the Senate and House of Representatives may be necessary (except on a question of adjournment) shall be presented to the President of the United States; and before the Same shall take Effect, shall be approved by him, or being disapproved by him, shall be repassed by two thirds of the Senate and House of Representatives, according to the Rules and Limitations prescribed in the Case of a Bill.

RESEARCH GUIDE

Law Review Articles:
Black, Some Thoughts On The Veto. 40 Law & Contemp Prob (2) 87.
Gewirtz, The Courts, Congress, and Executive Policy-Making. 40 Law & Comt Prob (3) 46.
Kennedey, Congress, the President, and the Pocket Veto. 63 Va L Rev 355.

INTERPRETIVE NOTES AND DECISIONS

1. Generally
2. "Single-house veto"
3. Miscellaneous

1. Generally

Joint resolution takes effect on approval of President, and when so approved has all characteristics and effects of act of Congress which becomes law when approved by President. United States ex rel. Levey v Stockslager (1889) 129 US 470, 32 L Ed 785, 9 S Ct 382.

Procedural steps set forth in Article I, section 7, of Constitution for enactment of legislation do not exclude other forms of congressional action. 43 Op Atty Gen No. 10.

2. "Single-house veto"

Legislative veto provision in 8 USCS § 1254(c)(2), which authorizes one House of Congress to invalidate decision of executive branch allowing particular deportable alien to remain in United States, is unconstitutional,

85

FIGURE 2–15   An excerpt of annotated references for a constitutional provision from U.S.C.S.

UNITED STATES CODE SERVICE

JURISDICTION—Cont'd
Yosemite National Park
- administrative site for park, transfer of jurisdiction, 16 § 47-1
- exclusive jurisdiction of United States, 16 § 57

JURISDICTIONAL AMOUNT
Generally, 28 § 1332 et seq.
Arbitration, Convention on Recognition and Enforcement of Foreign Arbitral Awards, 9 § 203
Courts of Appeals, 28 § 2108
District courts, 28 § 1331 et seq.
Evidence, 28 § 2108
Investment dispute settlement, 22 § 1650a
Medicare, Provider Reimbursement Review Board, 42 § 1395oo
Removal, 28 § 1445
Water pollution prevention and control, actions involving interstate compacts, 33 § 466g-1

JURY AND JURY TRIAL
Generally, 28 § 1861 et seq.
Additional acts and matters
generally, 28 § 1870, 1871
- jurors, 18 § 3321
Admiralty cases, 28 § 1873
Adverse affect upon deliberations, 28 § 1866
Affidavits, 28 § 1866
Age of person
- discrimination actions, 29 § 626
- requirement for service, 28 § 1865
Alphabetical list, 28 § 1864, 1865
Arbitration, 9 § 4
Armed Forces members serving on state and local juries, 10 § 982
Assignment, 28 § 1863, 1866
Attachment and garnishment, 28 § 2713
Attendance fees, 28 § 1871
Attorney General of United States, 18 § 3331, 6003; 28 § 515, 591 note, 594, 1867
Attorneys' fees, 28 § 1875
Aviation, issue of fact, 49 Appx § 1473
Bailiffs, 28 § 524, 755
Bankruptcy
generally, 28 § 1411
- bankruptcy rules and official forms, contempt proceedings, Rule 9020
- grand jury investigations, 18 § 3057
Bribery and graft, 18 § 201
Canal Zone (this index)
Capital offenses and punishment
- hearing before court or jury to determine whether sentence of death is justified, 18 § 3593
- protection of jurors, Federal Death Penalty Act of 1994, 18 § 1503, 3432
Certificates and certification
generally, 28 § 1871
- Grand Jury (this index)
Challenges, 18 § 3321; 28 § 1866, 1867, 1870
Chief judge of district court, 28 § 1863 et seq.
Citizenship requirement for service, 28 § 1865

JURY AND JURY TRIAL—Cont'd
Civil penalty, discharge of employee for jury service, 28 § 1875
Civil Rights and Discrimination (this index)
Classified Information Procedures Act, security procedures, 18 Appx § 9 note
Clerks of courts, 28 § 1863 et seq.
Coasting trade, 28 § 1873
Commission, 28 § 1863 to 1868
Commissioners, Judicial Conference of United States, 28 § 1863
Communist party membership, determination of, 50 § 844
Composition, affecting composition on or before refilled compliance of master jury wheel, 28 § 1863 note
Conditions, ineligibility for service, 28 § 1865
Congress, 2 § 30a, 130b
Constitution of United States, guaranty of jury trial, US Const Art 3 sec 2 cl 3; 6th Amend; 7th Amend
Contempt, 18 § 3691, 3692
Conviction of juror, 28 § 1861, 1869
Costs of action, 28 § 1824, 1863, 1864, 1871
Court of International Trade (this index)
Covenants, jury trial in action to recover forfeiture, 28 § 1874
Crimes and offenses, generally, 28 § 1865, 1869
Dangerous special offenders sentencing, 18 § 3575
Date. Time or date, infra
Death penalty. Capital offenses and punishment, supra
Declaration of policy, 28 § 1861
Decrees. Judgments and decrees, infra
Deputy clerks of district courts, 28 § 1866
Disclosure, names drawn, 28 § 1863, 1864, 1867
Discrimination. Civil Rights and Discrimination (this index)
Dismissal of indictment, 28 § 1867
Disqualification from service, 28 § 1863, 1865, 1866
Disruption of proceedings, 28 § 1866
District courts, 18 § 3006A; 28 § 1363, 1411, 1863 et seq.
District of Columbia (this index)
Division, defined, 28 § 1869
Drawing names from master jury wheel, 28 § 1864, 1866
Drug abuse prevention and control, 21 § 882
Economic matters, 28 § 1862, 1867, 1869
Effective date, plan for random selection, 28 § 1863
Egg products inspection, 21 § 1049
Eligibility. Qualifications, infra
Employment. Labor and employment, infra
English language, 28 § 1865, 1869
Evidence, 28 § 1865, 1867
Examination, plan for random selection, 28 § 1863
Exclusions and exemptions, 18 § 243; 28 § 1862 to 1869
Federal Unemployment Tax Act, approval of State laws, 26 § 3304 note
Fees
generally, 28 § 1824

JURY AND JURY TRIAL—Cont'd
Fees—Cont'd
- attorneys' fees, 28 § 1875
- clerks of courts, attendance fees of jurors, 28 § 1871
- dual pay and dual employment, fees for jury and witness service, 5 § 5537
- grand jury, 28 § 1864, 1871, 1875
Ferries, payment of toll charges, 28 § 1871
Fines, penalties, and forfeitures, 19 § 1305; 28 § 1864, 1866, 1867, 1874, 1875
First-class mail, service of summons for jury service, 28 § 1866
Forfeiture of obscene imported article, jury trial in proceedings for, 19 § 1305
Form for juror qualification. Qualification form, infra
Government officers and employees. Public Officers and Employees (this index)
Grand Jury (this index)
Grounds for excuse or exemption from service, 28 § 1863
Groups of persons or occupational classes excused or exempt from service, 28 § 1863
Guam, 28 § 1861 et seq.
Hardship as excuse from service, 28 § 1863, 1866, 1869
Impartial service, 28 § 1866
Improvement, Jury System Improvement Act of 1978, 28 § 1363, 1364, 1861 note, 1863 et seq.
Inconvenience, 28 § 1863, 1866, 1869
Injuring juror, 18 § 2516
Inspection, 21 § 467b, 673, 1049; 28 § 1867, 1868
Instructions or directions
- juror qualification form, 28 § 1864
- jury instructions. Instructions to Jury (this index)
Interception of wire or oral communications, 18 § 2516
Interim travel allowances, 28 § 1871
Internal revenue taxes, 28 § 2402
Internal security, determination of communist party membership, 50 § 844
Intimidation, 18 § 1503, 1507
Judgments and decrees
generally, 28 § 1864, 1866
- Grand Jury (this index)
Judicial Conference of United States (this index)
Judicial Council, 28 § 1863, 1866
Judicial districts, 28 § 1863 note
Jurisdiction, 18 § 3333; 28 § 1363, 1863
Jury System Improvement Act of 1978, 28 § 1363, 1861 note, 1863 et seq.
Jury wheel, 28 § 1863 to 1869
Labor and employment
- age discrimination actions, 29 § 626
- discharge of employee for jury service, civil penalty, 28 § 1875
- dual employment, fees for jury and witness service, 5 § 5537
- Federal Unemployment Tax Act, approval of State laws, 26 § 3304 note
- labor disputes, 18 § 3692
- protection of juror's employment, 28 § 1875
- Public Officers and Employees (this index)

References to Code are to Title and Section

FIGURE 2–16   An excerpt from U.S.C.S. descriptive word index

TRIAL BY JURY

Art III, § 2, cl 3

In connection with certiorari petition seeking United States Supreme Court's review of state court decision, record must clearly indicate that claim under federal statute or United States Constitution was presented in state court and that court was apprised of nature or substance of federal claim at time and in manner required by state law before Supreme Court takes jurisdiction. Webb v Webb (1981) 451 US 493, 68 L Ed 2d 392, 101 S Ct 1889.

Annotations:

What judgment or decree of state court in civil cases is final for purpose of review by United States Supreme Court under 28 USCS § 1257 and similar predecessors. 29 L Ed 2d 872.

Noncompliance with state procedural rule as constituting "adequate state ground" for denial of relief so as to preclude Supreme Court review of federal question. 24 L Ed 2d 837.

Sec. 2, Cl. 3. Trial by jury.

The Trial of all Crimes, except in Cases of Impeachment, shall be by Jury; and such Trial shall be held in the State where the said Crimes shall have been committed; but when not committed within any State, the Trial shall be at such Place or Places as the Congress may by Law have directed.

CROSS REFERENCES

Accused's right to trial by impartial jury in state and district in which crime is committed, USCS Constitution, Amendment 6.

Right of trial by jury in civil cases, USCS Constitution, Amendment 7.

Venue and change of venue in federal criminal trials, generally, USCS Rules of Criminal Procedure, Rules 18-22.

Procedure for jury trial in federal criminal case, generally, USCS Rules of Criminal Procedure, Rule 23.

RESEARCH GUIDE

Federal Procedure L Ed:

Contempt, Fed Proc, L Ed, § 17:19.

Criminal Procedure, Fed Proc, L Ed, §§ 22:53, 59, 66, 775.

Postal Service, Fed Proc, L Ed, § 63:322.

Am Jur:

21 Am Jur 2d, Criminal Law §§ 361-393, 395-402.

47 Am Jur 2d, Jury §§ 7 et seq.

Annotations:

Distinction between "petty" and "serious" offenses for purposes of federal constitutional right to trial by jury—Supreme Court cases. 26 L Ed 2d 916.

Validity and construction of Federal Criminal Procedure Rule 23, dealing with trial by jury or by the court. 13 L Ed 2d 1119.

Right to jury trial for offense punishable by fine exceeding $500 as affected by definition of petty offenses in 18 USCS § 1(3). 40 ALR Fed 876.

Alternate jurors in federal trials under Rule 24(c) of Federal Rules of Criminal Procedure or Rule 47(b) of Federal Rules of Civil Procedure. 10 ALR Fed 185.

Propriety and prejudicial effect of court-authorized separation of jury in federal criminal case. 4 ALR Fed 310.

671

FIGURE 2–17   An excerpt from U.S.C.S. article III, section 2, clause 3, Trial by Jury

Agency rules establish procedures governing practice before the agency, and **agency regulations** define the scope of the agency's discretion. Administrative agencies also make agency decisions, performing a quasi-judicial function much like a court. Agency actions must be consistent with the statutes Congress passed to set up that agency. If the agency action is not consistent with its statutory mandate, it may be challenged in a court proceeding by an affected party.

Today federal and state agencies affect virtually every aspect of life in the United States. There is, for example, the Social Security Administration, the Environmental Protection Agency, and the National Labor Relations Board. State agencies regulate the licensing of a myriad of occupations ranging from the practice of law to barbers, and they control a gamut of activities ranging from land use control to welfare. Regulatory agencies monitor the activities of business and administrative claims (such as Social Security benefits, railroad retirement benefits, and veterans' benefits). Agencies investigate matters, hold hearings, and handle appeals. The actions of some agencies can be challenged in court, while the actions of other agencies are final.

The statutes that grant power to an agency usually are written quite broadly. For instance, the Social Security Administration is empowered to grant disability benefits to those who are unable to engage in "substantial, gainful employment." This is a broad standard. This agency must then decide which individuals meet this standard. It will promulgate criteria that individuals must meet. Figure 2–18 is a regulation setting forth the medical criteria required of an individual with a heart condition to meet the disability standard. Since administrative law is now so ingrained in our society, every paralegal must know how to research agency rules, regulations, and procedures.

How Rules and Regulations Are Enacted

Both federal and state agencies promulgate rules and regulations. Typically, these rules and regulations are collected chronologically or by subject matter. For instance, at the federal level, regulations are kept chronologically in the *Federal Register* and by subject matter in the *Code of Federal Regulations.*

LEGAL TERMS

agency rules Rules established by an administrative agency that govern practice before that agency.

agency regulations Regulations promulgated by an administrative agency that define the scope of that agency's discretion.

4.01 CATEGORY OF IMPAIRMENTS, CARDIOVASCULAR SYSTEM

4.02   *Congestive heart failure (manifested by evidence of vascular congestion such as hepatomegaly, peripheral or pulmonary edema).* With:

A. Persistent congestive heart failure on clinical examination despite prescribed therapy; or

B. Persistent left ventricular enlargement and hypertrophy documented by both:

   1. Extension of the cardiac shadow (left ventricle) to the vertebral column on a left lateral chest roentgenogram; and

   2. ECG showing QRS duration less than 0.12 second with S_{v1} plus R_{v5} (or R_{v6}) of 35 mm. or greater *and* ST segment depressed more than 0.5 mm. *and* low, diphasic or inverted T waves in leads with tall R waves, or

C. Persistent "mitral" type heart involvement documented by left atrial enlargement shown by double shadow on PA chest roentgenogram (or characteristic distortion of barium-filled esophagus) and either;

   1. ECG showing QRS duration less than 0.12 second with S_{v1} plus R_{v5} (or R_{v6}) of 35 mm. or greater *and* ST segment depressed more than 0.5 mm. *and* low, diphasic or inverted T waves in leads with tall R waves, or

   2. ECG evidence of right ventricular hypertrophy with R wave of 5.0 mm. or greater in lead V_1 *and* progressive decrease in R/S amplitude from lead V_1 to V_5 or V_6; or

D. Cor pulmonale (non-acute) documented by both:

   1. Right ventricular enlargement (or prominence of the right out-flow tract) on chest roentgenogram or fluoroscopy; and

FIGURE 2–18   An excerpt from a regulation setting forth disability standards

Federal Register

In the 1930s, a dispute over the interpretation of a federal regulation was pending in the United States Supreme Court when it was discovered that the regulation had been repealed. As a result of this situation, Congress passed the Federal Register Act of 1935. This law requires that all proposed federal regulations must be published in the *Federal Register* before the regulation can be promulgated. This requirement gives the public an opportunity to comment to the agency about proposals and places the public on notice of a change in the law. Then, when the regulation has been promulgated, it is again published in the *Federal Register*. The *Federal Register* collects regulations alphabetically by agency, and then chronologically. The *Federal Register*, therefore, is similar to the session laws used to research statutes. Just as session laws usually are not used as a primary means to locate statutes, the *Federal Register* usually is not used as a primary means for locating regulations. For that purpose, researchers use the *Code of Federal Regulations*.

Code of Federal Regulations

The *Code of Federal Regulations* (C.F.R.) is similar to the U.S.C. except it contains regulations rather than statutes. The C.F.R. is organized by titles following substantially the same format as that found in the fifty titles of the U.S.C. The C.F.R. is broken down further into chapters, subchapters, parts, and sections. The C.F.R. is printed by the government in pamphlet form and updated on an annual basis. Each year part of the set is replaced in January, another part in April, another in July, and the remainder in October. As a result, the old pamphlets that become outdated are replaced.

The process for researching regulations is similar to that involved in researching statutes:

Step 1 - Identify the set of books that contains the regulation applicable to your research.

Step 2 - Use an index or table to find the regulation.

──────────────── LEGAL TERMS ────────────────

Federal Register† An official publication, printed daily, containing regulations and proposed regulations issued by administrative agencies, as well as other rulemaking and other official business of the executive branch of government. All regulations are ultimately published in the Code of Federal Regulations.

Code of Federal Regulations (C.F.R.)† An arrangement, by subject matter, of the rules and regulations issued by federal administrative agencies.

Step 3   -   Read the regulation as well as the applicable statute dealing with the problem.

Step 4   -   Update your research.

Although these steps are similar to those used for statutes and constitutions, there are some unique features.

Step 1:   Identify the set of books that contains the regulation applicable to your research.   When researching the federal regulations, use the C.F.R. If you are aware of a recently enacted regulation not found in the C.F.R., refer to the *Federal Register*. Most states also publish administrative codes. If you are researching, for example, a Pennsylvania regulation, you would look in the Pennsylvania Administrative Code.

Step 2: Use an index or table to find the regulation. The C.F.R. has an index at the end of the set called the "Index and Finding Aids." Even though the quality of this index has improved in recent years, even the ablest researcher sometimes will have difficulty finding specific regulations. As with most legal research, perseverance and the ability to improvise usually results in the right information.

Several techniques are used in the "Index and Finding Aids" section. The first is the descriptive word index. The problem with this approach is that the index is not very thorough, and it references a part rather than a specific section of the C.F.R. Another technique used in the "Index and Finding Aids" is the outline or table of contents. This approach means the researcher must examine pages of headings looking for a specific point. (See Figure 2–19.) However, since the C.F.R. parallels the U.S.C., if a researcher is familiar with the U.S.C. title that pertains to the researched matter, the researcher can find that title and scan it to find the relevant regulation. The third technique used in the "Index and Finding Aids" volume of the C.F.R. is the parallel table of authorities and rules, a table that matches U.S.C. statute citations with C.F.R. regulation citations. (See Figure 2–20.)

If the researcher using these C.F.R. indexing methods is unsuccessful, the researcher can make a computer search, use a looseleaf service, or look for a citation in an annotated code or a secondary source book. There are also private indexes such as the *C.I.S. Index to the Code of Federal Regulations* published by the Congressional Information Service.

Step 3: Read the regulations as well as the applicable statutes dealing with the problem. After locating a citation, the next step is to read the regulations. If you use an index to the C.F.R., remember that it directs you to a part, but not to a specific section. You must scan the referenced part for all specific regulations that might affect the analysis.

List of CFR Titles, Chapters, Subchapters, and Parts

TITLE 1—GENERAL PROVISIONS—Continued

455	National Capital Planning Commission (Privacy Act regulations).
456	National Capital Planning Commission (Freedom of Information Act regulations).
457	Enforcement of nondiscrimination on the basis of handicap in programs or activities conducted by the National Capital Planning Commission.
462	Federal Home Loan Mortgage Corporation (Book-entry regulations).
500	Enforcement of nondiscrimination on the basis of handicap in programs or activities conducted by the National Commission for Employment Policy.

TITLE 2—[RESERVED]

TITLE 3—THE PRESIDENT

PRESIDENTIAL DOCUMENTS
 Proclamations.
 Executive orders.
 Presidential documents other than proclamations and Executive orders.

Chapter I—Executive Office of the President (Parts 100–199)

Part
100	Standards of conduct.
101	Public information provisions of the Administrative Procedures Act.
102	Enforcement of nondiscrimination on the basis of handicap in programs or activities conducted by the Executive Office of the President.

TITLE 4—ACCOUNTS

Chapter I—General Accounting Office (Parts 1–99)

SUBCHAPTER A—PERSONNEL SYSTEM

Part
2	Purpose and general provision.
3	Employment.
4	Employee performance and utilization.
5	Compensation.
6	Attendance and leave.
7	Personnel relations and services.
8	Insurance and annuities.
9	Senior Executive Service.
11	Recognition of attorneys and other representatives.

SUBCHAPTER B—GENERAL PROCEDURES

21	Bid protest regulations.
25	Conduct in the General Accounting Office building and on its grounds.
27	General Accounting Office Personnel Appeals Board; organization.
28	General Accounting Office Personnel Appeals Board; procedures applicable to claims concerning employment practices at the General Accounting Office.
29	General Accounting Office Personnel Appeals Board; procedures applicable to claims concerning employment practices at the Architect of the Capitol.

SUBCHAPTER C—CLAIMS; GENERAL

30	Scope of subchapter.
31	Claims against the United States; general procedure.
32	Review and reconsideration of General Accounting Office claims settlements.
33	Deceased civilian officers and employees; procedures for settlement of accounts.
34	Deceased members of the Armed Forces and National Guard; procedures for settlement of accounts.
35	Deceased public creditors generally, claim settlement procedures.
36	Incompetent public creditors; procedures for settlement of accounts.

SUBCHAPTER D—TRANSPORTATION

51	Determinations.
52	Uniform standards and procedures for transportation transactions.
53	Review of General Services Administration transportation settlement actions.

FIGURE 2–19   An excerpt from C.F.R. "Index and Finding Aids"

CFR Index

FIGURE 2–20   A parallel Table of Authorities and Rules

Some regulations are written in detail and with technical terminology. As with statutes, you may need to read and reread the regulations, as well as related regulations, to grasp the correct meaning.

As noted above, agencies can promulgate only regulations that fit within statutory standards set by Congress. The regulations cannot be broader in scope than the statutes allow. Accordingly, a researcher should become familiar with the statute that authorized the promulgation of the regulation being researched, which means the researcher should check the statute in the U.S.C.A. or the U.S.C.S. along with reading the regulation in the C.F.R. This process should be followed in researching both federal and state regulations.

Step 4: Update your research. The C.F.R. is updated annually with replacement volumes, and outdated volumes are discarded. So the regulations found in the C.F.R. are fairly current. However, new regulations are enacted and others are repealed on a regular basis. Research in the C.F.R. can be updated with the *LSA—List of C.F.R. Sections Affected.* This pamphlet, which is published to be used along with the C.F.R., contains tables showing regulations that have been affected since the publication of the C.F.R. (See Figure 2–21.) The *LSA—List of C.F.R. Sections Affected* cumulates changes from the preceding month, but there is still a gap during which changes might have been made. To update the research in the *LSA—List of C.F.R. Sections Affected,* turn to the most recent issue of the *Federal Register* and the last issue of the preceding month. Each of these issues will have a C.F.R. Parts Affected table similar to that found in the *LSA—List of C.F.R. Sections Affected.*

Two alternative approaches to updating regulations (computers and Shepard's) are discussed in later chapters.

Researching Ordinances

The federal and state governments derive their power from constitutions. Cities and counties typically derive their power from charters. These charters authorize cities and counties to make laws called ordinances. Ordinances, which are statutes or regulations enacted by a city government, deal with matters such as building permits, licensing of merchants, zoning, and animal control. Local ordinances are typically published at the local level and can be located by contacting a county or city clerk. If there is a local law library, you will usually find a copy of the applicable ordinances there.

Although some ordinances are kept chronologically, in most instances ordinances are arranged by subject matter. Some ordinances

22   **LSA—LIST OF CFR SECTIONS AFFECTED**

CHANGES JANUARY 4, 1993 THROUGH DECEMBER 30, 1993

TITLE 5   Chapter VI—Con.   Page

1633.71 Removed	31332
1633.72 Removed	31332
1633.73 Removed	31332
1633.74 Removed	31332
1633.75 Removed	31332
1633.76 Removed	31332
1633.77 Removed	31332
1633.78 Removed	31332
1633.79 Removed	31332
1633.80 Removed	31332
1633.81 Removed	31332
1633.82 Removed	31332
1633.83 Removed	31332
1633.200—1633.236 (Subpart B) Removed	31332
1633.250—1633.257 (Subpart C) Undesignated center headings removed	31332
1633.250 Removed	31332
1633.251 Removed	31332
1633.252 (a), (c), (f) and (g) removed; (b), (d) and (e) redesignated as (a), (b) and (c)	31332
1633.253 Removed	31332
1633.254 Removed	31332
1633.255 Removed	31332
1633.256 Removed	31332
1633.257 Removed	31332
1636 Added	57696
1636.170 (c) revised	57697
1650 Authority citation revised	45381
1650.2 Amended	45381
1650.4 Heading revised	45381
1650.5 Revised	45381

Chapter XI—United States Retirement Home (Parts 2100—2199)

Chapter XI Removed; new Chapter XI heading added.....68505

Chapter XIV—Federal Labor Relations Authority, General Counsel of the Federal Labor Relations Authority and Federal Service Impasses Panel (Parts 2400—2499)

2429.24 (a) revised	53105
2471.2 Revised	53105
2471.4 Revised	53105
2472.5 Revised	53105
Chapter XIV Appendix A revised	13695

Chapter XVI—Office of Government Ethics (Parts 2600—2699)

Page

2600 Authority citation revised	69176
2634.203 (c)(1) revised; interim	38912
2634.601 (a) revised; interim	38912
2634.704 (f) added; interim	38912
2634.903 (a) revised; (b)(2)(ii) amended; (b)(2)(iii) added; interim	38912
2634.907 (a)(1) and (2) revised	63024
2636.305 (b) heading revised	69176
2637 Authority citation revised	69176
2638.203 (b)(3) and (4) amended	69176
2638.204 (a) and (b) amended	69176
2641 Appendix B amended	33755

Chapter XXII—Federal Deposit Insurance Corporation (Part 3202)

Chapter XXII Established; interim......39627

Chapter XXVI— Department of Defense (Part 3601)

Chapter XXVI Established; interim......47622

Chapter XXXIII—Overseas Private Investment Corporation (Part 4301)

Chapter XXXIII Established; interim......33320

Chapter XL—Interstate Commerce Commission (Part 5001)

Chapter XL Established......41990

Chapter XLI—Commodity Futures Trading Commission (Part 5101)

Chapter XLI Established......52638

Chapter XLVI—Postal Rate Commission (Part 5601)

Chapter XLVI Established; interim......42840

FIGURE 2–21   An excerpt from *LSA—List of C.F.R. Sections Affected* with dates

are updated in a looseleaf fashion by replacing outdated pages with newer pages. There is usually an index provided for these ordinances. Ordinances can be researched by the same methods used to research statutes: first, find the primary source material containing the ordinances for the unit of government with which you are concerned; second, use a topical or descriptive word approach to find a citation to an ordinance; third, read the ordinance; and fourth, update your research by referring to any pocket parts or other supplemental materials.

Each local governmental agency has a different way of recording its ordinances. The researcher must become familiar with how ordinances are organized in a specific locality.

Further Research Is Critical

Locating and reading constitutional provisions, statutes, regulations, and ordinances is only part of the legal research process. After locating and reading this law, the researcher may still have questions about how narrowly or broadly to read the law, whether the law is even applicable to the researched question, and what particular words mean. Cases may answer some of these questions; therefore, a researcher needs to locate and read all relevant cases. Scholars may have written books and articles suggesting answers to these questions—the researcher needs to locate and read these books and articles. Finding the primary authority is only the beginning of the research process.

Summary

- Statutes are first reported as slip laws. These slip laws are arranged chronologically in sets of books called session laws. The legislature may arrange these laws by subject matter in a code. Annotated codes, published by private publishers, add information to the code such as historical information about the statute and references to cases that refer to the statute.

- The session laws are positive law. Codes, on the other hand, are presumptive evidence of the law. This presumption can be overcome with proof that there is a difference between the law as it is found in the code and as it is found in the session laws.

- At the federal level, there are two annotated codes: *United States Code Annotated* (U.S.C.A.), published by West Publishing Company, and the *United States Code Services* (U.S.C.S.), published by Lawyers Cooperative

Publishing. Most states have an annotated code containing the statutes for that state.

- There are more similarities than differences between the U.S.C.A. and the U.S.C.S. Often the choice of which set to use is determined by what set is available.

- Constitutions are frequently researched through annotated codes, using many of the same methods as those used in researching statutes.

- The *Federal Register* collects regulations alphabetically by agency, and then chronologically. The *Code of Federal Regulations*, on the other hand, is organized by subject matter and follows substantially the same format as the *United States Code* (U.S.C.).

- Ordinances are laws enacted by a local unit of government and are usually published by a private publisher.

Review Questions

1. Explain the difference between session laws, compilations, codes, and annotated codes. Which of these is usually preferred in doing day-to-day research?

2. What is the difference between a statute, a regulation, and an ordinance?

3. What are the steps in researching a constitutional provision, a statute, a regulation, and an ordinance? Compare the similarities and differences.

4. What is the function of the *Federal Register?*

5. Is a code presumptive or positive law? Explain the difference.

6. How does a researcher update a search of federal regulations?

7. In researching a statute, what is the difference between using a descriptive word method, a topical approach, and a popular name table approach?

8. After locating a statute in a code, what is the procedure for updating that search?

Research Projects

1. Using either the U.S.C.A. or the U.S.C.S., find the statute that defines what is protected by the Americans with Disabilities Act. Are there regulations that pertain to this law? Can you find any laws in your state that provide similar protections? Does your city or county have any ordinances that provide protection to people with handicaps? Provide citations for all of your answers.

2. Using either the U.S.C.A. or the U.S.C.S., locate the volume or volumes that concern the Fourteenth Amendment to the United States Constitution. How is this volume or volumes updated? Using a state annotated code, see if your state has constitutional provisions similar to the equal protection clause of the Fourteenth Amendment.

‖‖‖

CHAPTER 3

REPORTING CASE LAW

CHAPTER OUTLINE

Courts make law through written decisions. Although not all of these decisions are published, case law takes a substantial amount of space in most law libraries. Consider that the federal judiciary consists of eighty-nine district courts, located in all fifty states, plus other district courts located in the territories of the United States, thirteen circuit courts of appeal, and the United States Supreme Court. There are also the United States Claims Court, the United States Tax Court, the United States Court of Military Appeals, the United States Court of International Trade, the United States Court of Veterans Appeals, and bankruptcy courts. These are just the federal courts. Each state has its own court system. Many cases from these courts are published almost daily, adding to this ever expanding body of case law.

Case Features

Cases vary in length. A case might be less than a page or more than a hundred pages. There is no fixed format for any case. However, almost all cases contain the following features: description of the procedural posture, a statement of the facts, a statement of the issues, a holding, legal reasoning to support the holding, and a disposition.

Procedural Posture

The **procedural posture** is the present status of the case. Decisions can be made at different stages of a case. For example, a case is commenced with the filing of a complaint. The complaint may not state a legal claim, and the court may dismiss the complaint. The case would end at that stage. On the other hand, the court might grant a motion for **summary judgment.** A summary judgment motion is filed when a party believes there are no genuine issues of material fact. If a court grants a motion for summary judgment, the case can end at that stage. During the course of a case, one party may request information from another party as part of the **discovery** process, and the court may issue an opinion ruling on the request. Or a court may be asked to

---

LEGAL TERMS

procedural posture The present status (or stage) of a case.

summary judgment† A method of disposing of an action without further proceedings.

discovery† A means for providing a party, in advance of trial, with access to facts that are within the knowledge of the other side, to enable the party to better try his or her case.

grant an **injunction.** An injunction is an order of a court that commands of prohibits a course of conduct. A preliminary injunction may issue at an early stage of a case, and a permanent injunction may issue at the conclusion of a case. Any of these decisions may be appealed to a higher court. The appellate court can then reverse or remand the case back to the lower court for a new decision. It is always important to note the procedural posture, or stage, of the case.

Statement of the Facts

Most decisions contain a detailed **statement of the facts** of the case. A statement of the facts is a listing of the events that led to the legal dispute prompting litigation. Courts elaborately describe the facts because factual differences between cases may determine the way in which the court rules. Courts often try to ascertain if the differences between the facts of the current case and those of a precedent should change the outcome of the case.

Statement of the Issues

The court also identifies **legal issues.** These issues are the legal questions the court must resolve. A legal issue is often framed in the form of a question. There may be only one issue, or there may be several.

The Holding

A **holding,** or *ratio decidendi*, is the rule of law that determines the result of a case. Sometimes the court plainly states the holding. At other times, the court does not spell out its holding, and the holding will be inferred from the court's reasoning. As a result, legal professionals reading the same case may disagree on how broad or how narrow the holding should be interpreted.

--- LEGAL TERMS ---

injunction† A court order that commands or prohibits some act or course of conduct.

statement of the facts   A listing of the events that led to a legal dispute prompting litigation.

legal issue† A question arising in a case with respect to the law to be applied or the meaning of the law.

holding† The proposition of law for which a case stands; the "bottom line" of a judicial decision.

Sometimes the court writes statements more broadly than necessary for the decision. Statements made in a case not necessary to the case are not binding on later court cases, although such statements may be persuasive. Such a statement is called **obiter dictum.**

When some legal professionals may read a holding in a case quite narrowly and others may read the same language quite broadly, new disputes may arise. Discerning the *ratio decidendi* of a case can be a subjective process. Yet, the holding is the law of the case. The legal professional must be able to distill the holding from the rest of the case.

The Legal Reasoning

A case also contains the legal reasoning used to reach the particular result. Explaining the reasoning is a way to ensure that cases are decided in an impartial manner and helps to predict how future cases will be resolved. Courts include citations to other laws relied upon or to other cases that were read and used in the analysis.

The Disposition

Finally, the case contains the action taken by the court. An appellate court might **affirm** a case (uphold the decision of the lower court), **reverse** a case, or **remand** a case for new proceedings. A trial court may dismiss a case, enter an order or injunction, rule on a motion, or decide the merits of the case in the written decision.

Function of Case Law

The primary function of the court system is to resolve disputes for parties who are unable to resolve disputes themselves. For centuries, courts have been deciding disputes and, in that process, have recorded their decisions as precedents to be consulted by other courts in

---

LEGAL TERMS

obiter dictum† Means "A comment in passing."

affirm† In the case of an appellate court, to uphold the decision or judgment of the lower court after an appeal.

reverse† To overthrow, vacate, annul, nullify, transpose, disaffirm ("to reverse a prior decision").

remand† The return of a case by an appellate court to the trial court for further proceedings, for a new trial, or for entry of judgment in accordance with an order of the appellate court.

resolving future controversies. The English system began recording court decisions as part of the stare decisis process. Since the American system is basically derived from the English system, courts in this country follow the stare decisis doctrine. Reporting of court decisions allows courts to use prior court precedents as guides for resolving future cases.

Stare decisis provides predictability and uniformity to the legal system. It ensures that parties with the same problems are treated equally and fairly. Stare decisis also provides stability to the system. However, the stare decisis doctrine is flexible in that courts can change a precedent if the precedent was wrongly decided or if changes in society warrant a change in the law.

How Courts Make Law

Courts make substantive law in a variety of situations. The common law that was adopted in most states is continually evolving. Courts decide new common law problems. In cases involving common law issues, the legal researcher must be able to search for precedents. A precedent may be a case decided in the 1700s or a case decided yesterday.

But courts do more than merely decide common law issues. They also apply and interpret other laws such as constitutions, statutes, regulations, and ordinances. A court may interpret a word or phrase in a statute or in an ordinance, or the court may decide the relationship of laws. In the latter situation, a court may hold that a statute conflicts with the constitution and, hence, is unconstitutional. Prior court decisions may have already decided whether a particular statute is constitutional or unconstitutional. Or a court may need to decide whether a regulation is in conflict with a statute, and other courts may have already decided how that regulation should be applied. So the legal professional needs to be able to locate the precedents.

In addition to resolving substantive issues, courts also decide procedural issues—for instance, how a case is to be handled. Issues concerning pleadings and motions, the process of discovering information about the case from opposing parties, what evidence is admissible, and what instructions will be read to a jury are all procedural issues that may arise in a case. Most courts have adopted rules of procedure and rules of evidence that deal with such issues. When such rules have been adopted, courts interpret a rule if the parties to a lawsuit have different interpretations of that rule. Courts make rules of law as they decide these procedural issues.

Sometimes, despite a thorough search, there will be no precedents on point. In that situation, the researcher must locate similar cases and try to reason how existing precedent should be used to deal with the new problem. At other times, the researcher may discover several lines of precedents that conflict. A court confronted with different lines of parallel authority will need to choose between them.

In feudal England, manors had different customs and traditions, so different manors could reach a variety of results in legal disputes that involved the same subject matter. In the United States, the states have different laws, so different courts will reach a variety of results even when the disputes are the same. Courts in the same **jurisdiction** (a geographic area in which a court has power to hear disputes) may even reach opposite conclusions. For instance, many states have different appellate districts or divisions. One district may reach a conclusion opposite from that of another district when deciding a case with the same facts. At the federal level, there are different circuit courts of appeals, and it is not unusual for these circuits to reach different conclusions with the same facts. In these situations, a higher court (a state supreme court or the United States Supreme Court) must clarify and resolve the differences.

Hence, the legal researcher may need to search for a precedent on a common law issue or a precedent dealing with the interpretation of a constitutional provision, a statute, a regulation, or an ordinance. Almost every research project requires a search for applicable case law. The legal researcher is always looking for binding precedent or, where there is none, the most analogous persuasive precedent applicable to the question in dispute. The legal researcher searches for precedents that cover a wide variety of legal issues.

How Cases Are Reported

Cases are reported in sets of books called *reporters*. There are different sets of reporters for different courts. For example, cases decided by the United States Supreme Court are found in one reporter, while cases decided by the United States Circuit Courts of Appeals or cases decided by the federal District Courts are found in others. State court decisions are found in different sets of books from federal cases. Cases from different states may be in different reporters.

LEGAL TERMS

jurisdiction† The right of a court to adjudicate lawsuits of a certain kind; the right of a court to determine a particular case; the power of a court to hear cases only within a specific territorial area.

Not all cases are published. In most states, trial court decisions are not published. In a few states (New York and New Jersey, for instance), a few selected trial court cases are reported. In the federal system, the federal District Courts (which are trial courts) report some of their decisions. Usually only district court cases of national importance or general interest are published.

Even the courts of appeals may not publish all the cases they decide. For example, cases dealing with issues that have been decided previously may not be published. In the federal system, many courts have rules dealing with the manner in which published and unpublished cases can be used as precedents. Figure 3–1 is an example of a local rule from the Ninth Circuit Court of Appeals.

FIGURE 3–1
U.S.C.S. Rules of Court, Court of Appeals, Ninth Circuit, Rule 36-2 on which cases can be used as precedents

> **Circuit Rule 36-2.   Criteria for Publication**
> A written, reasoned disposition shall be designated as an OPINION only if it:
> (a) Establishes, alters, modifies or clarifies a rule of law, or
> (b) Calls attention to a rule of law which appears to have been generally overlooked, or
> (c) Criticizes existing law, or
> (d) Involves a legal or factual issue of unique interest or substantial public importance, or
> (e) Is a disposition of a case in which there is a published opinion by a lower court or administrative agency, unless the panel determines that publication is unnecessary for clarifying the panel's disposition of the case, or
> (f) Is a disposition of a case following a reversal or remand by the United States Supreme Court, or
> (g) Is accompanied by a separate concurring or dissenting expression, and the author of such separate expression requests publication of the disposition of the Court and the separate expression.

Slip Opinions

In deciding a case, a court first issues a **slip opinion**. A slip opinion is merely a copy of the court's decision. This slip opinion is sent to the parties in the case and a copy is kept in the court's records in the court clerk's office. Some courts have an official publisher; however, it is becoming the practice of some courts to rely solely upon private publishing companies to report their cases. If a court has a designated official reporter, then a copy of the slip opinion is sent to that publisher for printing. Private publishers also receive copies of the slip opinion.

Advance Sheets

Cases are reported in chronological order in reporters. When there are enough cases to fill one volume, the book is printed and sent to

--- LEGAL TERMS ---

slip opinion†   A single judicial decision published shortly after it has been issued by the court and well before it is incorporated into a reporter.

subscribers. Because there may be a lag period between the time the case is decided and the time the volume is completed, some publishers send subscribers a partial set of the cases in a soft bound pamphlet called an **advance sheet**. Advance sheets contain the text of the most recent cases in the same format as that used in the reporters. When there are enough advance sheets to fill a new volume, the publisher sends the new volume to subscribers, and any advance sheets covering the same cases are discarded. Advance sheets enable the legal researcher to stay more up-to-date, and some include a section informing subscribers of other cases across the country that are of particular interest. (See Figure 3–2.) Some advance sheets also include tables of cases reported in the advance sheets and tables of statutes cited in the advance sheets.

Cases are found first in slip opinions, then in advance sheets, and finally in sets of bound reporters. The same case may be published in several different reporters and may also be found on-line on a computer, on ultrafiche, or on CD-ROM. Let us look at the different sets of books that report federal and state cases.

Reporting Federal Cases

Let us look again at the federal court system, which consists of the United States Supreme Court, the federal Circuit Courts of Appeal, and the federal District Courts. There are different reporters for each of these courts.

Federal District Courts

The trial courts in the federal system are called the federal District Courts. These are the courts that hear the disputes of the parties and determine (either by a jury, a master, or a judge) questions of fact. Each state has at least one District Court. California, which has the most districts, has four District Courts—a Southern District, a Northern District, an Eastern District, and a Central District. Basically, federal District Courts hear cases involving federal questions or hear cases where the parties are from different states and the amount in controversy is in excess of $50,000. A decision by a federal District Court is not binding on other District Courts or on any of the federal appellate courts. So District Court decisions are persuasive authority.

LEGAL TERMS

---

advance sheets† Printed copies of judicial opinions published in looseleaf form shortly after the opinions are issued. These published opinions are later collected and published in bound form with the other reported cases which are issued over a longer period of time.

JUDICIAL HIGHLIGHTS

Full Text Via WEST*fax:* 1-800-562-2329

---

his heel. He also suffered a back injury that might result in paralysis to both of his arms, which would leave him a quadriplegic. Because was a paraplegic, he did not feel the same type of pain in his heel that a non-paralyzed person would. However, the feelings of pain in his neck and arms were unaffected by his paraplegia.—This decision may not yet be released for publication.—*Domangue v. Mr. Gatti's, Inc.*, 1995 WL 377587 (La.App. 1 Cir.) (Opinion by Judge Melvin A. Shortess).

An award of **$150,000** in punitive damages under the Americans with Disabilities Act for the wrongful firing of an employee with cancer was not excessive. The sizeable award was necessary to punish and deter a corporation with over 300 employees and gross yearly revenues of several million dollars. The award was three times the amount of compensatory damages, and was not "out-of-line with prior awards. *U.S. E.E.O.C. v. AIC Security Investigations, Ltd.*, 55 F.3d 1276 (C.A.7-Ill. 1995) (Opinion by Circuit Judge Michael S. Kanne).

OTHER RECENT DECISIONS OF INTEREST:

Antitrust: judge exceeded power in review of Microsoft consent decree. *U.S. v. Microsoft Corp.*, 1995 WL 357850 (C.A.D.C.).

Business Regulation: nude dancing ordinance could regulate conduct occurring within 1,000 feet of bars. *Dodger's Bar & Grill, Inc. v. Johnson County Bd. of County Com'rs*, 1995 WL 349013 (D.Kan.).

Civil Procedure: qualified immunity summary judgment was not immediately appealable collateral order. *Winfrey v. School Bd. of Dade County, Fla.*, 1995 WL 396649 (C.A.11-Fla.).

Civil Rights: while architect had standing to challenge California's public utilities "set aside" law. *Bras v. California Public Utilities Com'n*, 1995 WL 390732 (C.A.9-Cal.).

Commercial Law: New York's ticket scalping statute held constitutional. *People v. Concert Connection, Ltd.*, 1995 WL 367287 (N.Y.A.D. 2 Dept.).

Education: statute requiring school closures on Good Friday violated First Amendment. *Metzl v. Leininger*, 1995 WL 364017 (C.A.7-Ill.).

Environmental Law: no right to jury trial in contribution suit under CERCLA. *Hatco Corp. v. W.R. Grace & Co.—Conn.*, 1995 WL 396749 (C.A.3-N.J.).

Family Law: custody dispute arbitrable under Uniform Arbitration Act. *Dick v. Dick*, 1995 WL 310841 (Mich.App.).

Labor and Employment: public employer's use of prescription reports to learn of employee's HIV status violated right to privacy. *Doe v. Southeastern Pennsylvania Transp. Authority*, 1995 WL 334290 (E.D.Pa.) (WESTLAW only).

Legal Services: malpractice plaintiff was prevailing party entitled to costs despite offset reducing award to $0. *Hoitt v. Hall*, 1995 WL 398958 (Me.).

FIGURE 3–2   An advance sheet from West Publishing Company (Reprinted by permission of West Publishing Company.)

Most decisions of the federal District Courts are not reported in any media, and there is no official reporter for those cases. West Publishing, however, does publish cases it deems of material interest in a reporter called the *Federal Supplement*. The *Federal Supplement* reports District Court cases decided since 1932. (Cases prior to 1932 were published in the *Federal Reporter* or *Federal Cases*. See next section, below.) Cases are reported in chronological order in the *Federal Supplement*, and each volume is consecutively numbered. Subscribers routinely receive advance sheets to update the *Federal Supplement*. A citation to a *Federal Supplement* case includes the names of the parties, the District Court making the decision, a date, and a volume and page reference:

> *Roe v. Wade*, 314 F. Supp. 1217 (N.D. Tex. 1970)

Federal Circuit Courts of Appeals

If a party disagrees with a decision of a District Court, the party can appeal to the federal Circuit Courts of Appeals. The thirteen Circuit Courts of Appeals consist of eleven regional circuits, a circuit for the District of Columbia, and a federal Circuit Court of Appeals. The federal circuit handles appeals only in special types of cases.

Proceedings in appellate courts are altogether different from proceedings in trial courts. In the appellate court, parties file written arguments about whether there have been errors of law committed by the trial court. The parties may present an oral argument, but no new evidence is taken during the appeal. Although a circuit consists of twenty or more judges, usually a panel of three judges decides the case at the federal Circuit Court of Appeals level. As with the federal District Court cases, there is no official reporter for reporting Circuit Courts of Appeals decisions; a decision of the panel, if published, is found in the *Federal Reporter* from West Publishing Company. The *Federal Reporter* is abbreviated in citation format as "F."

Like the *Federal Supplement*, the *Federal Reporter* volumes are consecutively numbered. However, when volume 300 of this set was reached, West Publishing started renumbering with the next volume in the set as Volume 1 of a new series. This second series of the *Federal Reporter* is abbreviated "F.2d" in case citations. There is now a third series, which is abbreviated as "F.3d" in citations. The first series covers cases from 1880 through 1924, the second series covers cases decided from 1924 to 1993, and the third series began after publication of volume 999 of the second series in October 1993. The following is a citation to a federal circuit court case:

> *Grove Fresh Distrib. v. New England Apple Prod.*, 969 F.2d 552
> (7th Cir. 1992)

West's *Federal Supplement* was not published until 1932, so older District Court cases decided between 1880 and 1932 are also collected in the *Federal Reporter*.

Prior to 1880, there was no uniform publisher for federal cases in either the District Courts or the Circuit Courts of Appeals. Almost every court had its own publisher, which made research of federal cases quite difficult. To remedy this situation, West Publishing collected district and circuit court decisions decided between 1789 and 1880 from these varied sources and published them in a set of books called *Federal Cases* (abbreviated "Fed. Cas."). These cases were arranged alphabetically by case name rather than chronologically.

United States Supreme Court

The highest court in the United States is the United States Supreme Court. The Supreme Court has authority over all other courts in the United States involving any federal constitutional or statutory issues. The official reporter for the United States Supreme Court is a set of books called the *United States Reports* (abbreviated as "U.S."). Remember that an official reporter is where the court is required to publish its cases. All Supreme Court cases are now published in the *United States Reports*. Early Supreme Court cases were published by private publishers in reporters that used the name of the publisher. Here is a list of these publishers:

Reporter	Volumes
Dallas	4
Cranch	9
Wheaton	12
Peters	16
Howard	24
Black	2
Wallace	23

Each of these cases was given a *United States Reports* citation when this set was commissioned. If the citation is to one of the earlier cases, it will look like this:

Marbury v. Madison, 5 U.S. (1 Cranch) 137 (1803)

A citation to a United States Supreme Court decision is usually made only to the *United States Reports*. Here is an example:

Roe v. Wade, 410 U.S. 113 (1973)

Both West Publishing and Lawyers Cooperative publish the Supreme Court decisions in different reporters. The West Publishing reporter is called the *Supreme Court Reporter* (abbreviated "S. Ct.") and the Lawyers

Cooperative reporter is called the *United States Supreme Court Reports—Lawyer's Edition* (abbreviated "L. Ed.") and is known simply as the *Lawyer's Edition*.

SIDEBAR

Lawyer's Edition includes some articles on selected cases with legal analysis called annotations. These articles from volumes 1 through 31 of the *Lawyer's Edition* are updated in a separate volume called *Lawyer's Edition (2d Series) Later Case Service*. Later volumes are updated by pocket parts.

Because the *United States Reports*, the *Supreme Court Reporter,* and the *Lawyer's Edition* report the same cases, a citation to all three of these sets is called a parallel citation. A complete parallel citation to a Supreme Court case looks like this:

> *Roe v. Wade,* 410 U.S. 113, 93 S. Ct. 705, 3 L. Ed. 2d 147 (1973).

The advantage of using a parallel citation is that it provides easy access for the reader who subscribes to a reporter other than the official reporter.

Because legal professionals are usually expected to cite to the *United States Reports* even if they are using the *Supreme Court Reporter* or the *Lawyer's Edition*, both West Publishing and Lawyers Cooperative use a method called **star pagination.** Star pagination is simply the placement of a star or other mark on the page of an unofficial reporter to show where text pages change in the official reporter. Star pagination is used because the pages in the unofficial reporters are printed differently from and do not correspond with those in the official reporters. Hence, if a reader finds a quotation while reading the *Supreme Court Reporter*, star pagination permits the reader to tell what page that quotation is on in the *United States Reports*. Figure 3–3 illustrates this method.

Some citations to the *Lawyer's Edition* reporter will have a "2d" after the L. Ed. abbreviation. This "2d" indicates that the citation is to the second series. Like the *Federal Reporter*, the *Lawyer's Edition* set begins with volume 1 of the second series after volume 100 of the first series.

LEGAL TERMS

star pagination The placement of a star or other mark on the page of an unofficial reporter to show where text pages change in the official reporter.

431 U.S. 774   WARD v. ILLINOIS   2089

Cite as 97 S.Ct. 2085 (1977)

→ |₇₇₂ *DeVilbiss*, 41 |Ill.2d 135, 142, 242 N.E.2d 761, 765 (1968); [4] cf. *City of Chicago v. Geraci*, 46 Ill.2d 576, 582–583, 264 N.E.2d 153, 157 (1970).[5] The construction of the statute in *Sikora* gives detailed meaning to the Illinois law, is binding on us, and makes plain that § 11–20 reaches the kind of sexu-

→ |₇₇₃ al materials which we now |have before us. If Ward cannot be convicted for selling these materials, it is for other reasons and not because the Illinois statute is vague and gave him no notice that the statute purports to ban the kind of materials he sold. The statute is not vague as applied to Ward's conduct.

[2] Second, Ward appears to assert that sado-masochistic materials may not be constitutionally proscribed because they are not expressly included within the examples of the kinds of sexually explicit representations that *Miller* used to explicate the aspect of its obscenity definition dealing with patently offensive depictions of specifically defined sexual conduct. But those specifics were offered merely as "examples," 413 U.S., at 25, 93 S.Ct., at 2615; and, as later pointed out in *Hamling v. United States*, 418 U.S. 87, 114, 94 S.Ct. 2887, 2906, 41 L.Ed.2d 590 (1974), they "were not intended to be exhaustive". Furthermore, there was no suggestion in *Miller* that we intended to extend constitutional protection to the kind of flagellatory materials that were among those held obscene in *Mishkin v. New York*, 383 U.S. 502, 505–510, 86 S.Ct. 958, 961–964,

16 L.Ed.2d 56 (1966). If the *Mishkin* publications remain unprotected, surely those before us today deal with a category of sexual conduct which, if obscenely described, may be proscribed by state law.

[3] The third claim is simply that these materials are not obscene when examined under the three-part test of *Miller*. This argument is also foreclosed by *Mishkin v. New York, supra*, which came down the same day as *Memoirs v. Massachusetts*, 383 U.S. 413, 86 S.Ct. 975, 16 L.Ed.2d 1 (1966), and which employed the obscenity criteria announced by the latter case. See *Marks v. United States*, 430 U.S. 188, 194, 97 S.Ct. 990, 994, 51 L.Ed.2d 260 (1977). The courts below examined the materials and found them obscene under the Illinois statute, which, as we shall see, *infra*, at 2090–2091, conforms to the standards set out in *Miller*, except that it retains the stricter *Memoirs* formulation of the "redeeming social value" factor. We have found no reason to differ with the Illinois courts.

[4] Fourth, even assuming that the Illinois statute had been |construed to overcome the vagueness challenge in this case and even assuming that the materials at issue here are not protected under *Miller*, there remains the claim that Illinois has failed to conform to the *Miller* requirement that a state obscenity law, as written or authoritatively construed, must state specifically the kinds of sexual conduct the description or representation of which the

FIGURE 3–3   Star pagination in *Ward v. Illinois,* 97 S. Ct. 2089 (1977) (Reprinted by permission of West Publishing Company.)

SIDEBAR A paralegal must distinguish between a citation to a first series edition and a citation to a second series edition. Publishers use different series numbers to identify the volume numbers of law books. A paralegal should be careful to include the series reference in any citation. Some sets may have a third (3d), fourth (4th), or even fifth (5th) series.

Advance sheets are published for both the *Lawyer's Edition* and the *Supreme Court Reporter*. For researchers who desire even quicker access to Supreme Court information, two publishers print Supreme Court decisions in a weekly looseleaf service. Both the *United States Law Week*, published by the Bureau of National Affairs, Inc., and the *United States Supreme Court Bulletin*, published by Commerce Clearing House, Inc., provide subscribers with decisions from the Supreme Court. The *United States Supreme Court Bulletin* reports many of the decisions in abbreviated form, although some of the more important decisions are printed in full. These services include summaries from the oral arguments made by counsel and other information about pending cases. Even quicker access to Supreme Court cases can be achieved through an on-line search by computer (see Chapter 7).

Figure 3–4 is a diagram of the federal court system with sample citations from the applicable reporters.

State Court Systems

The typical state court system generally mirrors the federal court system. (See Figure 3–4.) The state court system usually includes a supreme court, appellate courts, and trial courts.

A few states publish a small number of trial court cases, but most state trial court decisions are not reported. Trial courts handle probate, small claims, misdemeanor, and juvenile matters. Trial courts handle both civil and criminal trials. Although these state trial courts may issue written orders or decisions, the cases usually are not published except for a few selected decisions in states such as New Jersey, California, and New York.

Official State Court Reporters

Just as in the federal system, parties who disagree with a state trial court decision can appeal the case to a higher state appellate court, and then to a state supreme court. These decisions by state appellate courts and state supreme courts usually are first published in slip opinion form and then sent to an official publisher. Statutes designate the official reporter. These state courts also send their decisions to private publishers, so in some states, the cases are reported in both official and unofficial reporters.

FIGURE 3–4
Diagram of the
federal and state
court systems
with sample
citations

U.S. COURT SYSTEM WITH SAMPLE CITATIONS

<u>Federal System:</u>	<u>Sample Citations:</u>
Court	
United States Supreme Court	*Jones v. Smith,* 50 U.S. 44 (1962)
↑	
United States Court of Appeals	*Smith v. Jones,* 52 F.2d 38 (7th Cir. 1961)
↑	
United States District Court	*Smith v. Jones,* 44 F. Supp. 650 (S.D. Ill. 1960)

<u>Typical State Court System:</u>	<u>Sample Citations:</u>
Court	
State Supreme Court	*Jones v. Smith,* 150 Ill. 820, 68 N.E.2d 250 (1961)
↑	
Court of Appeals	*Smith v. Jones,* 140 Ill. App. 22, 66 N.E.2d 55 (1960)
↑	
Trial Courts (could be a circuit, municipal, criminal, superior, small claims, family, juvenile, or probate court to name just a few)	Cases not reported

---

*The highest court in a state is usually referred to as the Supreme Court, although in several states it is referred to as the Court of Appeals (Maryland and New York), in several states as the Supreme Judicial Court (Maine and Massachusetts), and as the Supreme Court of Appeal in West Virginia.

Source: S. Barber, *Legal Writing for Paralegals* 29 (1993).

West Publishing Company is the main publisher of state court decisions. In fact, many states have abandoned publishing cases in an official reporter, relying instead upon West Publishing to publish these decisions. In states with official reporters, there may be separate reporters for the intermediate appellate court decisions and for the decisions of the highest courts in those states.

West's National Reporter System

West Publishing publishes cases for the federal courts in the *Federal Supplement*, *Federal Reporter*, and the *Supreme Court Reporter*. West publishes the cases for each of the fifty states in its regional reporters.

West Regional Reporters

West's National Reporter System groups states with similar economic and geographic systems together. For example, the Northeastern region consists of New York, Massachusetts, Ohio, Indiana, and Illinois. Any reported cases from these states are published in the *Northeastern Reporter*. There are seven regions: Atlantic, Northeastern, Northwestern, Pacific, Southeastern, Southern, and Southwestern. Figure 3–5 is a chart showing the various regional reporters and the states covered by each region. Although West Publishing's rationale was to group states with similar economic interests, it is doubtful whether these distinctions are meaningful today. Nonetheless, West continues to use the original regional groupings.

Cases are printed in the regional reporters by state and in chronological order. In any volume of the *Northeastern Reporter*, for example, Massachusetts or New York cases will be grouped in chronological order. Each regional reporter is updated frequently with advance sheets of new cases from its specific region. These regional reporters typically publish the entire text of the court's decisions, so the legal researcher will find the same case as that found in an official reporter.

West's State Reporters

The expense of maintaining a set of regional reporters has grown with the increased volume of case law. A legal professional practicing in New York usually does not need to know the law of another state.

FIGURE 3–5
Regional
reporters
published by
West Publishing
Company
and the
states they
cover

WEST'S NATIONAL REPORTER SYSTEM

Regional Reporter	Jurisdiction Included
Atlantic	Connecticut, Delaware, District of Columbia, Maine, Maryland, New Hampshire, New Jersey, Pennsylvania, Rhode Island, Vermont
Northeastern	Illinois, Indiana, Massachusetts, New York, Ohio
Northwestern	Iowa, Michigan, Minnesota, Nebraska, North Dakota, South Dakota, Wisconsin
Pacific	Alaska, Arizona, California, Colorado, Hawaii, Idaho, Kansas, Montana, Nevada, New Mexico, Oklahoma, Oregon, Utah, Washington, Wyoming
Southeastern	Georgia, North Carolina, South Carolina, Virginia, West Virginia
Southwestern	Arkansas, Kentucky, Missouri, Tennessee, Texas
Southern	Alabama, Florida, Louisiana, Mississippi

Source: S. Barber, *Legal Writing for Paralegals* 31 (1993).

Because of the huge numbers of reported cases in New York, West Publishing collects the New York cases, including some trial court decisions, in a set of reporters called the *New York Supplement*. West also continues to print some New York cases in the *Northeastern Reporter*. West Publishing handles California cases in a similar manner by publishing the *California Reporter*; and for Illinois, the company publishes *West's Illinois Decisions*.

In recent years, West has begun to publish many state versions of regional reporters. A Florida professional, for instance, might subscribe only to the *Florida Reporter*, rather than to the *Southern Reporter*. Such a subscriber will receive only the Florida cases from the *Southern Reporter*, which means there may be gaps in pagination. For example, the book may skip pages 101 through 405 because the publisher has removed the non-Florida cases. The advance sheets for this set also contain only the Florida decisions. These Florida cases, however, are identical to what the researcher would find by going directly to the *Southern Reporter*. West state reporters have replaced official reporters in many states where an official version is no longer published.

Specialized Reporters

Perhaps the most important change in the practice of law in the past twenty years in the United States, next to the growth of the paralegal profession, is the move toward legal specialties. Although lawyers are not permitted in most states to advertise specialties, as a practical matter, as the law becomes more complex, lawyers have limited their practice to certain areas of law. Some lawyers, for example, practice mostly bankruptcy law. Other lawyers practice only labor law. To accommodate this trend, publishers are providing legal professionals with reporters that contain only cases concerned with a particular legal topic. For example, West Publishing Company publishes a *Bankruptcy Reporter* that collects cases from the United States bankruptcy courts and other courts that deal with bankruptcy issues. Other specialized reporters include the *Social Security Reporter*, the *Military Justice Reporter*, and the *Education Reporter*. This trend started when West Publishing published a set of books called the *Federal Rules Decisions* (abbreviated F.R.D.), which contained selected cases and articles dealing with federal procedural issues. Figure 3–6 is a chart showing the specialized reporters published by West Publishing.

FIGURE 3–6
Specialized reporters published by West Publishing Company

WEST'S SPECIALIZED REPORTERS	
Bankruptcy Reporter (B.R.)	Collects cases from U.S. Bankruptcy Courts, as well as other federal cases (district, court of appeals, and Supreme Court) dealing with bankruptcy
Federal Rules Decisions (F.R.D.)	Collects U.S. District Court decisions involving the federal Rules of Civil Procedure and Rules of Criminal Procedure not published in the F. Supp.
Military Justice Reporter (M.J.)	Collects decisions from U.S. Court of Military Appeals and Courts of Military Review
United States Claims Court Reporter (Cl. Ct.)	Collects decisions from U.S. Claims Court, U.S. Court of Appeals, and U.S. Supreme Court
Veterans Appeals Reporter (Vet. App.)	Collects decisions of the U.S. Court of Veterans Appeals

West Publishing includes the same headnote information before each case in these specialized reporters that is found in its other reporters. Figure 3–7 is a copy of a bankruptcy court decision. Each of these specialized sets have consecutively numbered volumes, and the cases are found chronologically.

Other Private Publishers

Other private publishers also report cases, yet none of these companies has been as successful as West Publishing. The chief rival of West Publishing is Lawyers Cooperative Publishing, which publishes Supreme Court cases in the *United States Supreme Court Reports—Lawyer's Edition*. Lawyers Cooperative also publishes representative cases in its *American Law Reports* (A.L.R.) system, which is discussed in Chapter 4.

Editorial Features of a Case

Publishers include more information in a reporter than just the actual text of the case. A paralegal must be able to distinguish these special features from the text of the case. Only the text of the case is law. Let us look at the editorial features in a typical case.

Caption

A case first has a **caption.** A caption contains the name of the parties, the name of court deciding the case, the docket number (the number assigned to the case by the court), and the dates the case was argued and decided. In a caption in a trial court, the plaintiff is usually named first and the defendant second. If the case is on appeal, the appellant may be listed first and the appellee next. (See Figure 3–8.)

───────────────── LEGAL TERMS ─────────────────

caption The heading of a case that contains information such as the parties' names, the court, and the date.

ation Agencies is not in itself sufficient to effect termination. It states in pertinent part that "You are hereby notified that written notice of *proposed termination or modification* of the existing collective bargaining agreements was served upon the other party to this contract and that no agreement has been reached." [emphasis added] Similarly, the letter from the Bakers Local stated an intention to "reopen" the Agreement. The parties continued to negotiate after the termination dates in the Agreements. All of this evidence can be construed as evidence of an intention by the unions to modify the Agreements. A notice to terminate must be clear and explicit. *International Union of Operating Engineers, Local No. 181 v. Dahlem Const. Co.,* 193 F.2d 470, 475 (6th Cir.1951). *See also Chattanooga Mailers v. Chattanooga News–Free Press,* 524 F.2d 1305, 1311 (6th Cir.1975). A notice of modification does not effect termination. *Id.*

The case of *In re Sullivan Motor Delivery, Inc.,* 56 B.R. 28 (Bankr.E.D.Wis.1985), on which the debtor relies, is either distinguishable on its facts or wrongly decided, and this court declines to follow it in this case. The debtor has not met its burden of proving that the Agreements terminated prepetition. The court, therefore, denies the debtor's motion, and determines that the Agreements were in full force and effect when the bankruptcy petition was filed.

The attorneys for the unions are to jointly submit an order under Rule 4 of the Local Rules of Bankruptcy Practice.

In re Walter Wayne REISHER a/k/a Bummy Reisher, Lois Marie Reisher t/a Reisher's Duraclean Service, Debtors.

Walter Wayne REISHER a/k/a Bummy Reisher, Lois Marie Reisher t/a Reisher's Duraclean Service, Movants,

v.

INTERNAL REVENUE SERVICE, Respondent.

Bankruptcy No. I–86–00366.
No. 1–92–0347 Adv.

United States Bankruptcy Court, M.D. Pennsylvania.

Oct. 30, 1992.

Chapter 11 debtor brought postconfirmation action against creditor for violation of automatic stay. The Bankruptcy Court, Robert J. Woodside, Chief Judge, held that, where Chapter 11 plan confirmation order provided for discharge at completion of plan, and thus automatic stay remained in effect until completion of plan, creditors were required to obtain relief from stay in order to collect plan payment defaults.

Order denied.

1. Bankruptcy ⟜3570
In case of conflict, language of confirmation order prevails over language of Chapter 11 plan.

2. Bankruptcy ⟜3570

FIGURE 3–7   An excerpt from *In re Reisher,* 149 B.R. 372 (Bankr. M.D. Pa. 1992), a bankruptcy court decision (Reprinted by permission of West Publishing Company.)

FIGURE 3–8
An example of a caption (Reprinted by permission of West Publishing Company.)

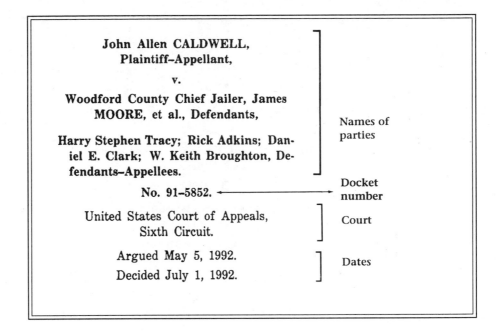

John Allen CALDWELL, Plaintiff–Appellant,

v.

Woodford County Chief Jailer, James MOORE, et al., Defendants,

Harry Stephen Tracy; Rick Adkins; Daniel E. Clark; W. Keith Broughton, Defendants–Appellees.

Names of parties

No. 91–5852.

Docket number

United States Court of Appeals, Sixth Circuit.

Court

Argued May 5, 1992.
Decided July 1, 1992.

Dates

Syllabus

Following the caption may be a **case syllabus** prepared by the editor of the reporter. (See Figure 3–9.) This syllabus is not an actual part of the case but is merely a short summary of the facts, issues, and disposition of the case. This summary is often incomplete and should never be quoted; it merely provides a quick snapshot of the case.

Names of Participating Judges or Justices

Next, the opinion identifies the name of the judge or justices who participated in the decision. More than one judge may decide a case. For example, the United States Supreme Court consists of nine justices. A simple majority of five justices is all that is necessary to reach a result in a case. Law is made by those in the majority.

At times, the justices may reach the same result but for different reasons. In such cases, the justices may write separate concurring opinions. Other justices may reach an opposite conclusion. If such a justice is in the minority, the justice may write a dissenting opinion. A paralegal should be careful, in reading a case, to distinguish between a majority, a dissenting opinion, and a concurring opinion.

─────────────── LEGAL TERMS ───────────────

case syllabus A short summary of the facts, issues, and disposition of a case that is written by the editor of the reporter in which the case appears.

The PEOPLE, Plaintiff and Respondent,

v.

Reggie Roschi JOHNSON, Defendant and Appellant.

Cr. 21982.

Supreme Court of California, In Bank.

Dec. 17, 1981.

Defendant was convicted in the Superior Court, Contra Costa County, William R. Channell, J., of assault with intent to murder, intentional infliction of great bodily injury and was found to have used a firearm in commission of an offense, and he appealed. The Court of Appeal, White, P. J., 171 Cal.Rptr. 471, affirmed in part and reversed in part, and defendant appealed. The Supreme Court, Richardson, J., held that trial court committed prejudicial error in instructing jury that finding of implied malice could support conviction for assault with intent to commit murder.

Reversed and remanded.

Case syllabus

1. Homicide ⊕310(1)

In prosecution for assault with intent to commit murder, trial court committed prejudicial error in instructing jury that finding of implied malice could support conviction. West's Ann.Penal Code § 217 (Repealed).

FIGURE 3–9   An example of a case syllabus (Reprinted by permission of West Publishing Company.)

Names of Counsel

The opinion usually identifies counsel involved in the case. This information is useful if the paralegal wants to contact the attorney who handled the case for information about that case.

Headnotes

Before the text of a case, many publishers include headnotes. A **headnote** is a summary of a legal point from the case. Many official as well as unofficial reporters include headnotes. Because they are prepared by a publisher and not by a court, these headnotes are not part of the case. They should never be cited or quoted. The headnotes may be numbered consecutively, with these same numbers inserted in the body of the case so the reader can quickly locate the part of the case that deals with any particular headnote point. (See Figure 3–10.)

Both West Publishing Company and Lawyers Cooperative Publishing assign topic headings and subtopic references to headnotes. Let us examine West's key numbering system to understand why this is done. West has created an outline of most case law principles. Each outline point is assigned a topic reference, as well as a subtopic reference called a "key number." For example, two topics are contracts and torts. When a new case is received by West Publishing, its staff carefully reads the case and each legal point or principle discussed in the case is summarized. These summaries are the headnotes that are published at the beginning of the case. Then the editorial staff checks the West outline (called a digest) for the topic and subtopic reference most analogous to the summary and assigns it that topic and key number reference. (See Figure 3–11.) This system of cataloging each point of law distinguishes the West system from the official reporters and other private publishers. Because there are over 40,000 subtopics to choose from in the West key number system, the West system is quite thorough.

Lawyers Cooperative Publishing also prepares headnotes for its cases and assigns a topic reference and subtopic number to them. This topic reference and subtopic number do not correspond with the topic and key number references used by West Publishing.

LEGAL TERMS

headnote† A summary statement that appears at the beginning of a reported case to indicate the points decided by the case.

DIVERSIFIED
COMMUNICATIONS, INC.

v.

Ivan GODARD, d/b/a "The
Back Forty".

Supreme Judicial Court of Maine.

Argued Sept. 6, 1988.
Decided Oct. 19, 1988.

Summary judgment was granted to plaintiff on matters defendant was deemed to have admitted by failing to file timely response to requests for admission, by the District Court, Bangor, Cox, J., and the Superior Court, Penobscot County, Browne, J., affirmed. On defendant's appeal, the Supreme Judicial Court, Hornby, J., held that responses to requests for admissions not served until day of hearing on plaintiff's motion for summary judgment were properly deemed admitted.

Affirmed.

1. Pretrial Procedure ☞479

Matters referred to in plaintiff's requests for admissions were properly deemed admitted where responses were not served within thirty days as required by rule and, indeed, were not served until day of hearing on plaintiff's motion for summary judgment. Rules Civ.Proc., Rule 36.

2. Pretrial Procedure ☞474

Fact that some of the requests for admissions went to ultimate issue, involved matters that were contested in answers to interrogatories or otherwise, entailed legal conclusions, or were inadmissible at trial did not make them invalid, and opposing party should have filed objections rather than failing to answer the requests. Rules Civ.Proc., Rule 36(a).

3. Pretrial Procedure ☞483

On proper motion, trial court can permit withdrawal or amendment of deemed admissions if there is no showing of prejudice to other party. Rules Civ.Proc., Rule 36(b).

Stuart M. Cohen, Jay Otis (orally), Cohen & Cohen, Bangor, for plaintiff.

Ivan Godard, Deer Isle, pro se, (orally).

Before McKUSICK, C.J., and ROBERTS, WATHEN, GLASSMAN, CLIFFORD and HORNBY, JJ.

HORNBY, Justice.

The defendant appeals the Superior Court's (Penobscot County; Browne, J.) affirmance of the District Court's (Bangor; Cox, J.) grant of summary judgment to the plaintiff. The District Court based its award of summary judgment upon matters the defendant was deemed to have admitted by failing to file a timely response to requests for admissions. We affirm.

[1,2] The District Court's finding that the plaintiff properly served the requests for admissions upon the defendant is not clearly erroneous. Responses were not served within the 30 days required by M.R. Civ.P. 36 and indeed were not served until the day of the hearing on the plaintiff's motion for summary judgment. As a result, the matters were properly deemed admitted under the Rule. Contrary to the defendant's argument, the fact that some of the requests went to the ultimate issue, involved matters that were contested in answers to interrogatories or otherwise, entailed legal conclusions or were inadmissible at trial did not make them invalid. The defendant should have filed objections rather than failed to answer the requests. See Rule 36(a).

[3] Although the District Court could on motion have permitted withdrawal or amendment of the deemed admissions if there were no showing of prejudice to the plaintiff, see Rule 36(b), the defendant made no such motion. Since the District Court was therefore never asked to exercise the discretion it possesses under the Rule, we have no occasion to review whether there was an abuse of discretion.

The entry is:

JUDGMENT AFFIRMED.

FIGURE 3–10   An example of case head notes and numbers (Reprinted by permsission of West Publishing Company.)

UNION CAMP CORPORATION,
Plaintiff,

v.

CONTINENTAL CASUALTY
COMPANY, Defendant.

No. CV476–167.

United States District Court,
S. D. Georgia,
Savannah Division.

June 27, 1978.

Insured employer brought action against insurer seeking to recover for losses arising out of settlement of employment discrimination suit brought against employer. The District Court, Lawrence, J., held that policy insuring employer against losses resulting from racially discriminatory practices was not violative of public policy.

Motion to dismiss denied.

Topic ⟶ **1. Insurance** ⟜124 ⟵ Key number reference

An insurance policy that is clear and unambiguous and is neither illegal nor against public policy should be enforced by the courts.

2. Contracts ⟜108(1)

Exercise of freedom of contract is not lightly to be interfered with, and it is only in clear cases that contracts will be held void as against public policy.

FIGURE 3–11   An example of topic and key number references (Reprinted by permission of West Publishing Company.)

SIDEBAR Remember that the headnotes are merely summaries. A paralegal should always read the text of the decision, and not depend just on the headnotes. Headnotes can be incomplete and even inaccurate.

Briefs of Counsel

Lawyers Cooperative Publishing prepares excerpts from the briefs filed in the case by counsel. A brief is a written argument filed with the court. This feature is unique to the reporters published by Lawyers Cooperative Publishing.

Locating Case Law

Constitutions and statutes can be researched directly using an annotated code. Regulations can be researched directly using the *Code of Federal Regulations* (C.F.R.). However, a legal researcher cannot effectively locate cases by using only a reporter. Citations to cases must be accessed by using other tools such as a digest, an encyclopedia, or an *American Law Reports* (A.L.R.) volume—tools that will be discussed in the next two chapters.

Summary

- The standard features of a case consist of the procedural posture, a statement of the facts, a statement of the issues, a holding, legal reasoning to support the holding, and a disposition.

- When a case is first decided, the court issues a slip opinion that is sent to the parties. The sets of books in which cases are reported are called reporters. Because there may be a lag time between the time the case is decided and the time there are enough cases to complete the volume, the publisher may send its subscribers an advance sheet.

- Current federal District Court decisions are published in the *Federal Supplement*. Current federal Circuit Courts of Appeals decisions are published in the *Federal Reporter*.

- If different book publishers report the same case, a case citation to each of the reporters is called a parallel citation.

- United States Supreme Court decisions are reported officially in the *United States Reports*. West publishes an unofficial reporter for these decisions called the *Supreme Court Reporter*. Lawyers Cooperative also publishes an unofficial reporter for these decisions called the *United States Supreme Court Reports—Lawyer's Edition*.

- West Publishing has grouped the states into seven regions and publishes a reporter for each region. West Publishing also publishes state versions of these regional reporters.

Review Questions

1. Describe the federal judiciary. For each court that you identify, provide the reporter or reporters that cover that court.

2. Describe your state's judiciary. For each court that you identify, provide the reporter or reporters that cover that court.

3. What are the different features of a case?

4. What is the *ratio decidendi* of a case? Compare the *ratio decidendi* to obiter dictum.

5. What is an advance sheet?

6. What is a parallel citation? Give an example of a parallel citation.

7. What is the difference between an official and unofficial reporter?

8. Describe West's national reporter system.

9. What is a key number?

Research Projects

1. Paralegal and law students are often advised to "brief" a case to help the student understand what he or she has read. Briefing a case means that the student prepares a one- or two-page summary of the case that includes the case features set out in this chapter: a description of the procedural posture, a statement of the facts, a statement of the issues, a holding, the legal reasoning, and the disposition. Brief *Evans v. General Motors*, 359 F.2d 822 (7th Cir. 1966). Then brief *Larsen v. General Motors Corp.*, 391 F.2d 495 (8th Cir. 1968). Explain why these cases reached different results. Which court do you agree with?

2. *Irvin v. Dowd* is a case that went to the United States Supreme Court on two separate occasions. It went through appeals in state court and in federal court. Make a report on every written decision published about this case.

IIII
CHAPTER 4

CASE FINDING METHODS—THE MAIN TOOLS

CHAPTER OUTLINE

Legal professionals are able to locate case law effectively today only because law has been so carefully classified. Without methods for classifying legal concepts, a legal researcher would never be able to find a particular case dealing with a particular point of law. However, because of the precise classification systems available to the legal researcher, a researcher can effectively pinpoint a case decided yesterday or a case decided two hundred years ago. There are several different systems used to locate legal principles among the millions of cases already decided. This chapter discusses three case-finding methods that are designed to find only case law. They are digests, *American Law Reports* (A.L.R.), and *Words and Phrases*.

DIGESTS

A **digest** is a research tool used specifically for finding case citations. A digest contains an outline of legal principles. A researcher who is searching for a legal principle dealing with a criminal question will look under one part of the outline, and a researcher who is searching for a legal principle dealing with an evidence question will look under another part of the outline. When the researcher locates the applicable outline entry, case summaries with case citations will be found under that entry.

Perhaps the most apt way to describe how to use a digest is to compare the digest with a department store catalog. To order merchandise, a customer looks through the catalog for a merchandise order number. In a digest, the researcher searches for a citation number so the researcher can look up a particular case. In a department store catalog, there are indexes that are used to direct the user to exact pages of the catalog. In digests, the researcher can use indexes to find the exact part of the outline to search. In a merchandise catalog, there is a description or even a picture for each catalog item. In a digest, there is a written summary for each case principle. And just as there are different merchandise catalogs (such as seed catalogs, clothing catalogs, wine catalogs, etc.), there are different digests. There is a digest for finding federal cases, another digest for finding Georgia cases and even a digest for finding cases from every jurisdiction. The paralegal who begins using any digest soon learns that the digest is merely a catalog for finding case citations. Figure 4–1 is a chart showing the various digests available.

LEGAL TERMS

digest† A series of volumes containing summaries of cases organized by legal topics, subject areas, and so on. Digists are essential for legal research.

FIGURE 4–1
Guidelines for selecting the appropriate digest

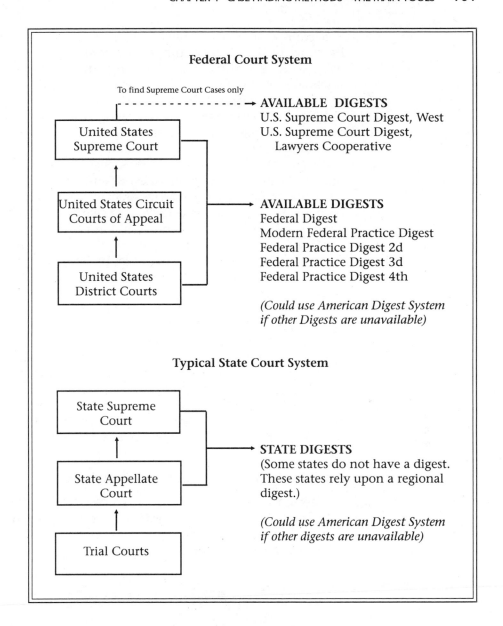

Federal Court System

To find Supreme Court Cases only

AVAILABLE DIGESTS
U.S. Supreme Court Digest, West
U.S. Supreme Court Digest,
　Lawyers Cooperative

United States
Supreme Court

United States Circuit
Courts of Appeal

United States
District Courts

AVAILABLE DIGESTS
Federal Digest
Modern Federal Practice Digest
Federal Practice Digest 2d
Federal Practice Digest 3d
Federal Practice Digest 4th

*(Could use American Digest System
if other Digests are unavailable)*

Typical State Court System

State Supreme
Court

State Appellate
Court

Trial Courts

STATE DIGESTS
*(Some states do not have a digest.
These states rely upon a regional
digest.)*

*(Could use American Digest System
if other digests are unavailable)*

How Digests Function

Digests typically have several common features. First, digests contain outlines of the different legal principles. Publishers develop their own outlines. The most frequently used digests are those published by West Publishing; they have comprehensive outlines covering almost all legal principles.

Second, digests have indexes or other means for accessing particular headings in the digest outlines. As a result, a legal researcher does not need to look under all the headings of the outline every time the researcher uses the digest. The index will promptly lead the researcher to the exact reference. These indexes are necessary because digest outlines are so extensive. Consider, for instance, the fact that the West outline encompasses more than 400,000 entries.

Third, digests insert case summaries with case citations under appropriate headings of the outlines. A legal researcher can scan these case summaries until a citation for a case (or cases) dealing with the legal question being researched is located. When the researcher finds a case summary that appears on point, he or she can write down that citation and look up the case in the appropriate reporter. A case is on point if it has the same or similar facts and legal issues as the facts and legal issues of the researched problem.

Finally, there must be a method for updating digests because new cases will be decided after the original digests are published. Digests are updated by pocket parts, by separate pamphlets, or by volume replacement.

In using any digest, a researcher usually first looks in the index to find an appropriate outline heading. Then the researcher looks under a specific topic and key number and scans the case summaries. Once the researcher locates appropriate cases and writes down the citations, the researcher locates these cases in the reporters, using an updating method to check to see whether there are any more recent cases involving the same legal principles.

Let us examine these features of a digest in more detail by examining the digest system published by West Publishing Company, since these digests are most frequently used in legal research.

A Digest Is an Outline of Legal Principles

The most basic characteristic of any digest is the outline of legal principles. The West digest system contains an outline of all case law principles that has more than 400,000 subheadings and 400 topics. There are seven main headings:

- Persons
- Property
- Contracts
- Torts
- Crimes
- Remedies
- Government

There are topics such as negligence, false imprisonment, nuisance, and waste. The main topics are arranged alphabetically, and under each main topic there are multiple subtopics. (See Figure 4–2.) Notice that each subtopic is assigned a number, which is referred to as a headnote number or a key number. Once a researcher locates a specific topic and key number, the researcher merely has to look alphabetically for the topic and then turn to that headnote in that volume.

Main heading ⟶ **HOSPITALS**

SUBJECTS INCLUDED

Institutions for cure or relief of sick, wounded, or infirm persons, whether founded or maintained by private means, or in part or wholly by government

Establishment, maintenance, regulation, and management of such institutions

Rights, duties, powers, and liabilities of managers and other officers, etc., thereof

SUBJECTS EXCLUDED AND COVERED BY OTHER TOPICS

Charities, hospitals as, see CHARITIES

Mental hospitals and institutions, see MENTAL HEALTH

Municipalities' powers to establish, maintain, etc., see MUNICIPAL CORPORA-TIONS

Rest or nursing homes and other custodial institutions for the afflicted and unfortunate, see ASYLUMS

For detailed references to other topics, see Descriptive-Word Index

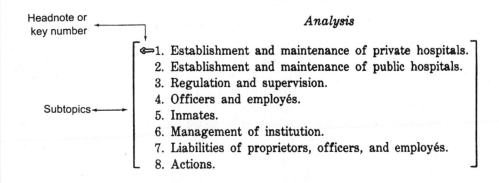

Analysis

Headnote or key number ⟶

1. Establishment and maintenance of private hospitals.
2. Establishment and maintenance of public hospitals.
3. Regulation and supervision.
4. Officers and employés.
Subtopics ⟶ 5. Inmates.
6. Management of institution.
7. Liabilities of proprietors, officers, and employés.
8. Actions.

FIGURE 4–2   Main topic with several subtopics (Reprinted by permission of West Publishing Company.)

A Digest Has Finding Aids for Accessing Case Summaries

To look for a case in the digest, the researcher needs a reference to a specific topic *and* to a specific key number

Often the researcher will not know what topic applies, and rarely will the researcher have any reference to a specific key number. Because the digest outline is so large, it is usually necessary to pinpoint the exact topic and headnote reference by consulting an index. Researchers rely upon several different methods to access topic and key number references.

Descriptive Word Indexes

The most commonly used method for locating a particular topic and key number is the descriptive word index. This index is usually found in separate volumes at the end of the digest set. The index is organized so that the researcher can use common words to find the exact topic and key number reference. The index works well with the TAPP rule discussed in Chapter 1.

Suppose a person trips on a sidewalk crack. After the accident, the owner fixes that crack. Under the law in most jurisdictions, repairs made after an accident cannot be used as evidence. The reason for this rule is that the law wants to encourage parties to make repairs so other accidents will not happen. However, what if the owner testifies in court that the sidewalk was safe? Can the injured party impeach that witness with evidence that the party fixed the sidewalk immediately after the accident?

A researcher might begin a digest search of this problem in the descriptive word index by looking under terms such as "sidewalk," "repairs," "negligence," "witness," "impeach," and "evidence." Figure 4–3 is a page from a digest descriptive word index. Notice that the researcher is directed to two topics: Negligence 131 and Witnesses 331$^1/2$. "Negligence" and "Witnesses" are the topic references, and 131 and 331$^1/2$ are the key number references. Now the researcher merely has to pick out the volumes from the set that cover these topics, open the volumes to the topics, and look under the correct key numbers. (Figure 4–4 shows cases that can be located under Negligence 131.)

The Table of Contents under Each Topic

Sometimes the researcher will know the exact topic, but not the exact subtopic. Topics are arranged alphabetically, so the researcher will find topics beginning with "A" in the first volume and topics beginning with the last letters of the alphabet in the last volume. Each digest volume has on its spine the first and last topic covered in that volume. When a researcher opens a volume to a particular topic, the

36-7th D—653

REPAIRS

RENUNCIATION
Legacy—
Revocation of renunciation in proceeding to enforce internal revenue tax liens. **Int Rev 1721**
Right, intent to renounce. **Aband 5**
Surviving joint tenant. **Joint Ten 5, 6**
Trusts—
Beneficiary's renunciation of income—
Trusts 39
Wills 717
Income by life beneficiary. **Trusts 39**
United States citizenship. **Citiz 13**
Wills—
Abandonment of bequest. **Wills 717, 719**
Charitable devise, effect of renunciation by general assembly and county commissioners. **Char 49**
Decree for distribution on widow's renunciation—
Construction and operation. **Ex & Ad 315(5)**
Sale for assignment of dower to widow who renounces will. **Dower 101**

RENVOI DOCTRINE
Conflict of laws. **Action 17**

REOPENING
Grandfather proceedings by Interstate Commerce Commission. **Commerce 85.29(5)**

REOPENING CASE
Administrative proceeding for suspension or removal of public officer. **Offic 72(1)**
Arrangement proceeding in bankruptcy. **Bankr 968**
Claim against state. **States 184.29**
Court of Claims. **States 184.5**
Estate by common law wife. **Witn 139(11)**
Further evidence—
Admiralty proceeding. **Adm 82**
Discretion of court. **Crim Law 686(1, 2)**
Plaintiff's motion. **Trial 66**
Homicide. **Crim Law 686(2)**
Juvenile court. **Infants 16.12**
Rebuttal, discretion of trial court. **Trial 62(3), 66**
Suspension of deportation proceedings. **Aliens 54(1)**

REOPENING ORDER
Fixing amount of estate tax. **Tax 900 (3)**

REPAIR SHOP
Automobile repair shop—
Minimum wages and maximum hours—
Retail or services establishment exemption. **Labor 1212**
Injuries to invitee, proprietor not required to render safe repair shop to which invitee went for his own pleasure or curiosity. **Neglig 32(1)**
Zoning—
Evidence in proceeding to procure permit. **Zoning 435**

REPAIRMEN
Air conditioner—
Electric shock injuries, indemnity to tenant store operator. **Judgm 185.3(14)**
Automobile repairman—
Common carriers certificate—
Towing one truck over highways. **Autos 76**
Hotel room occupant, permission to enter room. **Inn 6**
Telephone service—
Agents, service of process. **Tel 39**
Entering premises, causing customer fright and emotional upset. **Tel 283**

REPAIRS
Agent's undertaking to have repairs made—
Action for accounting between principal and agent. **Princ & A 78 (6)**
Construction of agent's authority as between principal and agent. **Princ & A 51**
Aircraft—
Penalty liability of repair station. **Aviation 252**
Alimony, fire damage to former wife's home, payment as alimony. **Divorce 231**
Attorney fees—
Diversity action under Outer Continental Shelf Lands Acts. **Courts 359**
Quantum meruit actions. **Damag 71**
Automobile accident while road testing, permission, questions for jury. **Garn 171**
Automobile insurance, extent and liability of insurer. **Insurance 506(2)**
Automobiles, road testing, implied permission. **Garn 171**
Bailee, hired property. **Ballm 11**
Bailee's duty. **Ballm 14(1)**
Bailee's liability. **Ballm 32**
Bailment, duties of bailor. **Ballm 9**
Bridges, liability of sureties for county commissioners' negligent failure to repair. **Counties 96**
Building, interpleader against contractor, laborers and materialmen. **Interpl 11**
Building code, nonfireproof buildings. **Mun Corp 628**
Building permit, police power. **Mun Corp 621**
Buildings—
Duty of care by building contractor in making repairs. **Neglig 2**
Evidence—
Action to recover amount due under contract for repair work. **Contracts 350(1)**
Terms of contract in action for amount due for repairs. **Contracts 350(2)**
Express contract as affecting right of recovery on implied promise to pay for repair. **Work & Lab 10**
Liability of building contractor for negligence of subcontractor. **Mast & S 315**
Mutual promises as consideration for agreement to repair. **Contracts 58**
Proof of substantial performance necessary in action for amount due under contract for repair work. **Contracts 346(2)**
Satisfaction of party as test of performance of contract for repair work. **Contracts 282**
Certificate after completion of work as to articles and materials—
Evidence admissible under general denial. **Contracts 346(9)**
Pleading as release. **Release 45**
Chimney—
Fake chimney repair racket. **False Pret 49(1)**
Community property—
Credit to husband in suit by beneficiaries of wife's will. **Hus & W 274(4)**
Contracts—
Burden of proof in action for breach. **Contracts 348**
Implied contract to pay for work. **Work & Lab 4(2)**
Revocation of offer. **Contracts 19**
Deeds, conditions subsequent, forfeiture for failure to keep house in repair. **Deeds 167**
Drains, mandamus to compel public board to keep drains in repair. **Mand 94**
Dwellings, permits, police power. **Mun Corp 621**
Easements, evidence, adverse claim. **Ease 6**

REPAIRS—Cont'd
Evidence—
Action for breach of contract for repair of building. **Contracts 350 (1)**
Agent's apparent authority to order work. **Princ & A 123(3)**
Easement by prescription, adverse claim. **Ease 6**
Subsequent repairs, impeaching witness—
Neglig 131 ⟶ Key number references
Witn 331½
Gas appliances, landlord's duty. **Land & Ten 162**
Highways—
Authority and duty to make—
County. **Highways 187(2)**
Contracts—
County. **Highways 105(1)**
Contributory negligence of user of highway under repair. **Autos 204, 245(67)**
County contract. **Highways 105(1)**
Diversion of funds for improving and constructing roads to repair of roads. **High 149**
Injunction. **Inj 88**
Injuries from failure to make—
Counties, liability. **High 105 (2), 189, 198, 203**
Guard rails after notice. **Autos 278**
Negligence of county in failing to maintain highway. **Highways 208(1)**
Liability of contractor repairing highway for motor vehicle accident. **Autos 290**
Mandamus to command repairs—
High 17
Mand 94
Mandamus to compel. **Mand 94**
Pedestrian's fall crossing roadway being resurfaced—
Damag 130(1)
Indem 13(2)
Tort liability, immunity of county—
Counties 141
Highways 187(2)
Town's payment for repairs. **Towns 49**
Tractor making U turn, collision, contributory negligence. **Autos 244(41)**
Husband and wife—
House occupied by wife, jurisdiction to order repair. **Hus & W 308**
Separate maintenance, household repairs. **Hus & W 299(1)**
Implied promise to pay for. **Work & Lab 4(2)**
Injunction. **Inj 219, 223, 231**
Insurance—
Breach of insurer's obligation to return vehicle of which possession was taken to repair damage. **Insurance 595**
Contract to repair fixtures as. **Insurance 2**
Damages for insurer's failure to repair. **Insurance 595, 661, 666, 669(1)**
Election to restore, repair or take property. **Insurance 595**
Buildings under construction, description. **Insurance 163(1)**
Marine insurance. **Insurance 483**
Leased premises—
Action for breach of covenant to surrender premises in good repair. **Land & Ten 160(4)**
Apartment building, window screen defects, occupant's duty. **Land & Ten 169(11)**
Condemnation of premises on landlord's failure to repair as ejection by paramount title. **Land & Ten 174**
Covenant. **Land & Ten 152, 152(1)**
Nature and form of remedy for breach. **Land & Ten 154(1)**
Covenant of landlord to repair as contract to indemnify tenant. **Indem (1)**

FIGURE 4–3 Research using a digest descriptive word index (Reprinted by permission of West Publishing Company.)

make material difference.—Weiss v. Sears, Roebuck & Co., 186 N.E.2d 797.

Admissibility or non-admissibility of evidence of condition which allegedly caused accident depends almost entirely on nature of specific thing or condition whose existence is in issue and particular circumstances affecting it.—Id.

Ill.App. 1963. Evidence depicting manufacturing processes in 1959 of plant which made cable, which was purchased in 1956 and which broke in 1957 resulting in injuries and deaths when platform of hoist fell, was admissible in contesting charge against manufacturer that its 1956 operations were negligent and evidence was not incompetent because jury might draw improper inference that, since processes had remained unchanged for three years, no changes were required and manufacturer had therefore not been negligent in 1956.—Nelson v. Union Wire Rope Corp., 187 N.E.2d 425.

Ky. It is within trial court's discretion whether to admit testimony with reference to the condition of a certain object or thing prior or subsequent to date of injury suffered because of the object or thing.—Darnell v. Beard, 296 S.W.2d 743.

Ky. 1965. Evidence of condition of stair several weeks after customer's fall was properly excluded in action for injuries sustained in fall where it was not proved that condition of stair was unchanged in intervening period.—Hannin v. Driver, 394 S. W.2d 750.

Md. In action for injuries to pedestrian on sidewalk on storeowners' property, wherein a civil engineer testified that almost three years after alleged accident, he made inspection of premises where alleged accident occurred, objection to question as to what engineer found in connection with sidewalk as he observed it from engineering standpoint and based upon his experience in erecting buildings and sidewalks was properly sustained in view of general nature of question, and in view of absence of evidence that condition of sidewalk was the same at time of alleged accident as it was when inspected by engineer.—Nocar v. Greenberg, 124 A.2d 757.

Mass. In action for injuries sustained by seventy-three year old woman when she fell (at night) over retaining wall in parking area of shopping center, evidence as to lighting in parking area five years after accident would not be admissible, unless it appeared that there had been no change in illumination in intervening period.—Underhill v. Shactman, 151 N. E.2d 287.

Mass. In action for injuries sustained by plaintiff when she tripped on floor outlet cover which was allegedly raised on one side, there was implicit in defendant's employees' testimony that no change had been made in cover between time of accident on Saturday and the following Tuesday and that it had been in same position on Tuesday as it had been on day of accident, assertion that witnesses had, in such period, seen no one move cover and, accordingly, it was error to strike plaintiff's husband's testimony that cover had, on Monday, been in position similar to that claimed by his wife and that it looked as though screw threads on its perimeter had crossed with those of receiving orifice.—Cobb v. Worcester County Elec. Co., 154 N.E.2d 900.

In action for injuries sustained by plaintiff when she tripped on floor outlet cover which was allegedly raised on one side, plaintiff's husband's testimony that, when he observed cover on Monday following Saturday on which accident occurred, it appeared that screw threads on its perimeter were crossed with those of receiving orifice would have been relevant, if offered for that purpose, to show that cover had been in a wedged position of some firmness and thus rebut testimony for defendant, indicating that it was not physically possible for cover to be and remain in position asserted.—Id.

Mich. In action for personal injuries sustained by customer who slipped on wet stairs, there was no error in excluding pictures of stairs taken after later addition of nonskid stripping.—Mandjiak v. Meijer's Super Markets, Inc., 110 N.W.2d 802.

Mo. 1964. Testimony of condition of lawnmower blade more than two years after accident was inadmissible as too remote, absent showing that mower was in same condition at both times.—Phillips v. Shaw, 381 S.W.2d 768.

Nev. 1962. Improvement of safety devices is not indicative of negligence but merely of a desire to prevent future injury to person or property.—Alamo Airways, Inc. v. Benum, 374 P.2d 684.

N.C. In action by pedestrian against store operator for injuries received when operator's advertising sign fell on pedestrian after unknown motorist, who was in parking lot for store customers, backed into the sign, exclusion of police officer's testimony that the sign was not anchored when he saw it after the accident was not error.—Johnson v. Meyer's Co., 98 S.E.2d 315.

N.C. In action for injuries sustained by customer who allegedly fell on wet floor of store on rainy day, testimony of man in charge of ambulance relative to condition of floor 15 to 20 minutes after accident was competent and should not have been excluded where there was no evidence of increased use of aisle by customers after customer's fall, and, in view of fact that such testimony was corroborative of plaintiff's testimony as to water on floor and of circumstance that it had been raining all morning, testimony was admissible as substantive evidence and weight thereof was for jury.—Powell v. Deifells, Inc., 112 S.E.2d 56.

Pa. 1963. Testimony of plaintiff's wife, who visited sidewalk where plaintiff fell several days later, as to her impression of condition of pavement was inadmissible when there was no indication that conditions existing several days later were the same as at time of accident.—Puskarich v. Trustees of Zembo Temple of Ancient Arabic Order of Nobles of Mystic Shrine, 194 A.2d 208.

Pa. 1965. When testimony concerning observations made subsequent to accident is admitted to prove existence of condition at time of accident, with or without additional proof of no change in condition, defendant may attempt to diminish its probative value.—Brandon v. Peoples Natural Gas Co., 207 A.2d 843.

Pa.Super. Testimony as to physical conditions should be limited to those at or about the time of the event in question, unless it is shown that they remained static for the time testified to until the happening of the event, and this is especially true where testimony is that of a police officer.—Robinson v. Brown, 171 A.2d 865.

Pa.Super. If condition causing accident is not shown to be static, testimony as to condition is limited to what existed at or about time of accident, but if there is no change in condition, evidence as to condition either before or after accident is admissible to show condition at time of accident.—Nelson v. Facciolo, 179 A.2d 258.

Admission of testimony of witness, whose first knowledge of outside steps of defendant's apartment came to her about month after accident, was not improper where it appeared that physical condition of steps or bush overhanging rail of steps had not changed between time plaintiff fell on them and time when witness first observed condition.—Id.

Pa.Com.Pl. The general rule is that where there is no change in the condition of an appliance or premises or scene of the accident, evidence as to the condition of such appliance or place, either before or after the accident, is relevant and admissible to show its condition at the time of such event, provided it relates directly to the issue and is not too remote in time.—Townsend v. Wildman, 47 Del. Co. 322.

Tex.Civ.App. Although evidence of change of conditions or repairs made by defendant is inadmissible on issue of negligence, changes may be shown to test witness' credibility or powers of observation or in connection with pictures to show whether specific condition existed at time of accident.—Texas & N. O. R. Co. v. Broadway, 345 S.W.2d 814.

Wash. 1965. Evidence of subsequent conduct is inadmissible only when it has no probative value on issues before the court.—Golden Gate Hop Ranch, Inc. v. Velsicol Chemical Corp., 403 P.2d 351.

Admission in evidence in action against chemical manufacturer for hop crop damage resulting from application of chemical, that manufacturer made application for label clearance for use of the chemical on hop crops after correspondence with plaintiff's representative was discretionary in view of fact that taken in conjunction with evidence that label clearance is required by the federal government, it showed that manufacturer was aware of a possible danger and was aware or should have been aware that no clearance had been obtained to recommend the product for use on hops.—Id.

☞130(2). Criminal proceedings against defendant or his servants

Ohio App. 1963.· An arrest and forfeiture of bond are not admissible in negligence action.—Hannah v. Ike Topper Structural Steel Co., 201 N.E.2d 63.

☞131. — Precautions against recurrence of injury

C.A.Conn. 1965. Under Connecticut law, evidence as to remedial measures taken after accident is excluded on basis of policy to encourage repairs.—Stephan v. Marlin Firearms Co., 353 F.2d 819.

C.A.La. 1963. Evidence of subsequent improvements after accident are not admissible.—Eastern Air Lines, Inc. v. American Cyanamid Co., 321 F.2d 683.

C.A.Mich. 1962. Evidence of plaintiff, suing manufacturer for injuries sustained while using manufacturer's washing machine, offered to show that after accident manufacturer changed machine's design by installing braking device which brought spinning tub to stop when machine was shut off and by installing locking device that prevented top cover from being opened until tub had ceased rotating was properly excluded.—Cox v. General Elec. Co., 302 F.2d 389.

C.A.Mont. Evidence of repairs made after an accident is inadmissible to show failure of due care on part of defendant.—Johnson v. U. S., 270 F.2d 488.

C.A.N.J. 1964. Exception to general rule that evidence of subsequent repairs and precautions is inadmissible exists when evidence is introduced to show that defendant had con-

FIGURE 4–4   The next step is to actually look up the subtopic in the digest (Reprinted by permission of West Publishing Company.)

HOMICIDE

SUBJECTS INCLUDED

Killing a human being, aiding in, attempting or soliciting such killing, and assaults with intent to kill

Nature and elements of murder, manslaughter, and of degrees thereof, and of attempts and assaults with intent to commit such offenses

Nature and extent of criminal responsibility therefor and grounds of defense, more particularly justification or excuse

Prosecution and punishment of such acts as public offenses, and review therein

SUBJECTS EXCLUDED AND COVERED BY OTHER TOPICS

Automobiles, homicide by, see AUTOMOBILES

Bail, right to, see BAIL

Civil liability for wrongful death or assault, see ASSAULT AND BATTERY, DEATH

Conspiracy to kill, see CONSPIRACY

Killing one's self, see SUICIDE

For detailed references to other topics, see Descriptive-Word Index

---

Analysis

I. THE HOMICIDE, ☞1–6.

II. MURDER, ☞7–30(3).

III. MANSLAUGHTER, ☞31–83.

IV. ASSAULT WITH INTENT TO KILL, ☞84–100.

V. EXCUSABLE OR JUSTIFIABLE HOMICIDE, ☞101–126.

VI. INDICTMENT AND INFORMATION, ☞127–142(10).

VII. EVIDENCE, ☞143–257(8).
    (A) PRESUMPTIONS AND BURDEN OF PROOF, ☞143–152½.
    (B) ADMISSIBILITY IN GENERAL, ☞153–199.
    (C) DYING DECLARATIONS, ☞200–221.
    (D) PROCEEDINGS AT INQUEST, ☞222–227.
    (E) WEIGHT AND SUFFICIENCY, ☞228–257.

VIII. TRIAL, ☞258–315.
    (A) CONDUCT IN GENERAL, ☞258–267.
    (B) QUESTIONS FOR JURY, ☞268–282½.
    (C) INSTRUCTIONS, ☞284–311.
    (D) VERDICT, ☞312–315.

IX. NEW TRIAL, ☞316–321.

X. APPEAL AND ERROR, ☞322–349.

FIGURE 4–5   Topical index of subtopics in a digest (Reprinted by permission of West Publishing Company.)

Thus, if the researcher knows that a principle falls under a certain topic, the researcher can scan the contents of that topic to find the applicable headnote references. For example, in looking for cases dealing with whether evidence of postaccident repairs to the sidewalk can be used to impeach a witness, the researcher might know that this is a negligence question and begin by looking directly under the negligence topic, rather than beginning with the descriptive word index. The researcher would find a detailed outline for the negligence topic with subtopic numbers (see Figure 4–6) and, by perusing these entries, would find headnote 131. Notice, however, that the researcher would not find the Witnesses reference found in the descriptive word index by using this approach.

Case Headnotes

Sometimes the legal professional will find a key number in a case from a West reporter or in some other secondary source with references to key numbers. Look at Figure 3–10 in Chapter 3. For each headnote summary, there is a topic and a key number. Remember that the topic and key numbering system are the same in every West digest; therefore, once the researcher has located the West key number in any source, he or she can use the reference in any West digest.

SIDEBAR

Because the same key number system is used in every West digest, it is important that you retain any references you locate for later research purposes.

Table of Cases

Occasionally, the legal researcher may remember the name of a case but have no citation for that case. West digests have tables of cases that list cases by the names of the parties. The cases are listed by the plaintiff's name, although most of the digests also have a defendant-plaintiff table of cases that lists the cases by the defendant's name as well. The researcher can find topic and key number references for cases in these tables. (See Figure 4–7.) The tables also provide the history of cases as they are affected by subsequent cases.

Words and Phrases

West digests contain a section of words and phrases. Whenever a particular word or phrase has been defined in a court case, that word or phrase will be listed alphabetically in this section. (See Figure 4–8.)

32–8th D—5

NEGLIGENCE

IV. ACTIONS.—Cont'd

(B) EVIDENCE.—Cont'd

1. PRESUMPTIONS AND BURDEN OF PROOF—Cont'd

121.2. —— Happening of accident or injury; res ipsa loquitur.—Cont'd
- (8). —— Management and control.
- (9). Operation and effect of doctrine.
- (10). —— Burden of proof or going forward, effect on.
- (11). —— Sufficiency and effect of rebuttal evidence.
- (12). Application of doctrine; effect of pleadings.

121.3. —— Particular defects or occurrences, res ipsa loquitur.
121.4. —— Spread of fire.
121.5. —— Cause of injury.
122. Contributory negligence.
- (1). In general.
- (2). As affected by plaintiff's evidence.
- (3). As affected by pleadings.
- (4). Use by defendant of testimony offered by plaintiff.
- (5). Instincts of self-preservation.
- (6). Children.

2. ADMISSIBILITY.

124. In general.
- (1). In general.
- (2). Requirements of statutes and ordinances.
- (3). Custom and usage.

125. Similar facts or transactions; prior accidents.
126. Relation of defendant to cause of injury.
- (1). In general.
- (2). Knowledge of defect or danger.

127. Conditions preceding injury.
128. Precautions against injury.
129. Occurrence and circumstances of injury.
130. Conditions after injury.
- (1). In general.
- (2). Criminal proceedings against defendant or his servants.

131. Precautions against recurrence of injury.
132. Contributory negligence or other fault of person injured.
- (1). In general.
- (2). Children.
- (3). Habits and reputation.
- (4). Similar matters and transactions.
- (5). Imputed negligence.

3. WEIGHT AND SUFFICIENCY.

134. In general.
- (1). Negligence of defendant in general.
- (2). Direct or circumstantial evidence.
- (3). Liability for injuries to licensees and trespassers.
- (4). Machinery and other instrumentalities.
- (5). Buildings.
- (6). —— Elevators, hoistways, and shafts.
- (7). Knowledge by defendant of defect or danger.
- (8). Precautions against injury.
- (9). Violation of statute or ordinance.
- (10). Relation of defendant to cause of injury.
- (11). Proximate cause of injury.

135. Contributory negligence.
- (1). In general.
- (2). Degree of proof.
- (3). Direct or circumstantial evidence.
- (4). Duty to observe defects and precautions against known dangers.
- (5). Proximate cause of injury.
- (6). Injury avoidable notwithstanding contributory negligence.
- (7). Children and others under disability.
- (8). Imputed negligence.
- (9). Comparative negligence.

(C) TRIAL, JUDGMENT, AND REVIEW.

136. Questions for jury.
- (1). Taking case from jury in general.
- (2). Questions of law or fact in general.
- (3). Mixed questions of law and fact.
- (4). Injuries occurring in another state.
- (5). Sufficiency of evidence to raise question for jury in general.
- (6). Existence of defect or happening of accident.
- (7). Weight of evidence and credibility of witnesses.
- (8). Uncontroverted evidence.
- (9). Inferences or conclusions from evidence.
- (10). Conflicting evidence or disputed facts.
- (11). On findings of fact.
- (12). Presumptions and burden of proof.
- (13). Persons liable.
- (14). Negligence in general.
- (15). Liability as to licensees and trespassers.
- (16). Knowledge of defect or danger.
- (17). Fires.
- (18). Defective or dangerous instrumentalities and operations.
- (19). Machinery and places attractive to children.
- (20). Places abutting on or near highway or path.
- (21). Piling of material.
- (22). Buildings and structures.
- (23). Elevators, hoistways, and shafts.
- (24). Precautions against injury.
- (25). Proximate cause of injury.
- (26). Contributory negligence.
- (27). —— Duty to observe defects and precautions against known dangers.
- (28). —— Acts in emergencies and danger incurred to save life.
- (29). —— Children and others under disability.
- (30). —— Imputed negligence.
- (31). —— Effect of contributory negligence.
- (32). —— Injury avoidable notwithstanding contributory negligence.

137. Instructions.
138. —— In general.
- (1). Form and sufficiency in general.
- (2). Presumptions and burden of proof.
- (3). Applicability to pleadings and issues.
- (4). —— Contributory negligence.

139. —— Negligence.
- (1). Nature, definition, and effect of negligence.
- (2). Degrees of care.
- (3). Willful, wanton, or reckless acts or conduct.

FIGURE 4–6 A digest outline of topics with subtopic numbers (Reprinted by permission of West Publishing Company.)

PEOPLE

TABLE OF CASES

References are to Digest Topics and Key Numbers

1138

577.10(10), 577.11(6), 577.15(3), 577.16(3), 1144.7, 1166(7).

People v. Schmidt, MichApp, 492 NW2d 509, 196 MichApp 104.—Autos 336, 355(8), 356; Crim Law 862.

People v. Schoenneman, IllApp 2 Dist, 177 IllDec 349, 603 NE2d 130, 237 IllApp3d 1.—Crim Law 1144.13(3), 1159.2(1), 1159.2(7); Licens 42(4); Sales 197.

People v. Schollaert, MichApp, 486 NW2d 312.—Crim Law 351(2), 407(1), 720(1); Homic 22(2), 22(3), 147, 232, 282, 354(1); Searches 40, 114.

People v. Schuett, Colo, 833 P2d 44.—Crim Law 1030(1), 1038.1(6); Kidnap 1; Statut 181(1), 181(2), 188, 241(1).

People v. Schulz, CalApp 4 Dist, 7 CalRptr2d 269, 5 CA4th 563.—Const Law 270(1); Crim Law 586, 1083, 1208.6(5); Double J 30, 95.

People v. Schwarz, NYAD 2 Dept, 584 NYS2d 101.—Infants 69(1), 69(4), 69(8).

People v. Scott, Ill, 171 IllDec 365, 594 NE2d 217, 148 Ill2d 479.—Arrest 63.5(2), 63.5(4), 63.5(5); Const Law 268.2(2); Crim Law 30, 48, 354, 412.2(5), 414, 438(5), 438(6), 438(7), 470(2), 486(5), 486(6), 531(3), 673(2), 719(1), 730(3), 736(2), 772(1), 778(1), 778(7), 804(9), 824(8), 878(2), 986.6(3), 1035(6), 1036.1(3), 1036.1(6), 1036.6, 1037.1(2), 1038.1(1), 1137(2), 1137(6), 1158(4), 1166(12), 1169.1(2), 1169.3, 1169.9, 1172.2, 1172.7, 1172.8, 1177, 1208.1(4), 1208.3(5), 1213.1; Evid 560; Homic 357(4), 357(10); Ind & Inf 191(4); Judgm 751; Jury 131(17); Mental H 434.

People v. Scott, NY, 583 NYS2d 920, 79 NY2d 474, 593 NE2d 1328.—Courts 97(1), 97(5); Searches 26, 27, 79, 120.

People v. Scott, NYAD 2 Dept, 584 NYS2d 103.—Crim Law 1026.10(1).

People v. Scott, NYAD 2 Dept, 582 NYS2d 238.—Crim Law 412.1(4), 414, 854(7).

People v. Seabourn, CalApp 5 Dist, 11 CalRptr2d 641, 9 CA4th 187.—Crim Law 772(4), 1172.1(3).

People v. Seawright, IllApp 1 Dist, 171 IllDec 183, 593 NE2d 1003, 228 IllApp3d 939.—Arrest 68(3); Crim Law 349, 359, 361(4), 394.5(3), 394.6(2), 394.6(5), 412(1), 412.1(1), 412.1(3), 412.1(4), 413(1), 414, 419(1.5), 632(5), 736(2), 805(1), 829(13), 864, 1136, 1158(2), 1158(4), 1159.3(2), 1159.4(2), 1169.1(9); Homic 169(8), 234(10); Ind & Inf 121.5.

People v. Secore, NYAD 4 Dept, 591 NYS2d 126.—Crim Law 438(5), 438(7), 531(2).

People v. Segool, NYJustCt, 583 NYS2d 891.—Crim Law 29(9).

People v. Seigler, ColoApp, 832 P2d 980, cert gr.—Const Law 268(11); Crim Law 438.1, 778(5), 1030(2); Judges 49(2), 51(3), 51(4).

People v. Seiver, NYAD 2 Dept, 590 NYS2d 248.—Crim Law 366(6), 419(4); Infants 20.

People v. Sellers, IllApp 3 Dist, 178 IllDec 470, 604 NE2d 993, 237 IllApp3d 545.—Drugs & N 188(4.1), 189(2); Searches 121.1, 200.

People v. Serrano, NYAD 1 Dept, 583 NYS2d 245.—Crim Law 627.5(5), 627.6(6).

People v. Serrano, CalApp 2 Dist, 15 CalRptr2d 305, 11 CA4th 1672.—Const Law 258(2); Crim Law 13.1(1); Extort 27; False Imp 43; Kidnap 2; Statut 181(1).

People v. Sesmas, IllApp 3 Dist, 169 IllDec 414, 591 NE2d 918.—Autos 349.5(2); Const Law 270(1); Crim Law 1158(2), 1158(4), 1168(2); Drugs & N 43, 119, 184(2); Searches 165, 181, 183, 184, 186.

People v. Sevier, IllApp 1 Dist, 174 IllDec 336, 598 NE2d 968, 230 IllApp3d 1071.—Arrest 63.4(2), 63.4(7), 63.4(15), 68.5(7); Crim Law 394.6(4), 394.6(5), 412(6), 412.1(1), 414, 428, 519(1), 535(2), 662.9, 662.10, 662.11, 878(4), 1158(2), 1158(4); Infants 68.4.

People v. Sevilla, NYAD 1 Dept, 581 NYS2d 682.—Arrest 63.5(5), 63.5(9).

People v. Seymour, NYAD 1 Dept, 588 NYS2d 551.—Crim Law 366(6), 1169.1(9); Homic 235, 236(1).

People v. Shafer, MichApp, 491 NW2d 266, 195 MichApp 596.—Crim Law 982.7.

People v. Shannon, NYAD 1 Dept, 582 NYS2d 425.—Crim Law 1036.1(7); Homic 162, 254; Rob 24.1(3); Weap 17(4).

People v. Sharkey, NYAD 1 Dept, 588 NYS2d 149.—Rob 24.1(4); Witn 337(27).

People v. Sharlow, NYAD 2 Dept, 585 NYS2d 799.—Crim Law 636(3), 829(11).

People v. Sharp, MichApp, 481 NW2d 773, 192 MichApp 501.—Assault 100; Crim Law 1042, 1134(3), 1208.9(3).

People v. Sheffield, NYAD 2 Dept, 586 NYS2d 17.—Crim Law 339.11(2), 1168(2).

People v. Shelato, IllApp 4 Dist, 170 IllDec 149, 592 NE2d 585.—Assault 48.

People v. Shepley, NYAD 2 Dept, 587 NYS2d 368.—Arrest 63.5(6); Searches 66.

People v. Sherk, NYCity Ct, 584 NYS2d 266.—Crim Law 273(2), 274(3).

People v. Shine, NYAD 4 Dept, 590 NYS2d 965.—Const Law 257.5; Crim Law 36.6, 394.1(2).

People v. Shlimon, IllApp 1 Dist, 173 IllDec 754, 597 NE2d 728.—Crim Law 317, 339.5, 371(12), 374, 641.13(1), 641.13(2), 661, 698(1), 723(1), 1030(1), 1037.1(2), 1144.13(3), 1159.2(7), 1169.11, 1208.2; Homic 234(6), 354(1).

People v. Shoals, CalApp 6 Dist, 10 CalRptr2d 296, 8 CA4th 475.—Const Law 269; Crim Law 641.10(2), 641.13(1), 641.13(6), 713, 728(2), 781(8), 829(11), 938(2), 938(5), 945(2), 1166.11(5), 1202.5; Disorderly H 17, 20.

People v. Shuman, IllApp 3 Dist, 168 IllDec 777, 590 NE2d 99.—Crim Law 273.1(4), 998(5), 1181.5(8), 1184(4).

People v. Silva, IllApp 1 Dist, 172 IllDec 615, 595 NE2d 1285.—Crim Law 338(7), 369.2(1), 662.8, 723(1), 1035(10), 1038.1(4), 1169.1(1), 1171.1(3), 1171.1(6), 1171.2; Homic 340(1).

People v. Simac, IllApp 2 Dist, 177 IllDec 316, 603 NE2d 97, 236 IllApp3d 1096.—Contempt 2, 10, 60(3), 63(4), 66(1).

People v. Simmonds, NYAD 2 Dept, 582 NYS2d 236.—Crim Law 339.8(3), 339.8(4), 1036.1(7), 1072.

People v. Simmons, NY, 584 NYS2d 423, 79 NY2d 1013, 594 NE2d 917.—Jury 33(5.1).

People v. Simmons, NYAD 1 Dept, 588 NYS2d 32.—Crim Law 1038.2, 1169.5(2); Rob 11, 24.3.

People v. Simmons, NYAD 3 Dept, 583 NYS2d 46.—Crim Law 625.10(3), 641.4(1), 641.4(4), 641.4(5), 641.7(1); Jury 29(6).

People v. Simon, NYAD 2 Dept, 590 NYS2d 533.—Gr Jury 35; Ind & Inf 125(45).

People v. Sims, IllApp 3 Dist, 174 IllDec 591, 599 NE2d 137.—Crim Law 986.2(1), 1042, 1044.1(1), 1126, 1147, 1208.2.

People v. Sims, NYAD 1 Dept, 586 NYS2d 103.—Searches 175.

People v. Singh, NYAD 2 Dept, 589 NYS2d 897.—Crim Law 273.1(2), 1026.10(2.1).

People v. Singh, NYAD 2 Dept, 588 NYS2d 573.—Crim Law 412(3), 469, 474.3(3), 474.4(2), 474.4(4), 1169.11, 1169.12, 1170.9(1), 1170.9(5); Witn 270(2).

People v. Singletary, IllApp 3 Dist, 178 IllDec 486, 604 NE2d 1009, 237 IllApp3d 503.—Crim Law 37(2.1), 37(4), 37(8), 569, 739.1(1), 1159.2(7), 1159.2(9), 1159.4(2).

People v. Sinnott, IllApp 4 Dist, 168 IllDec 865, 590 NE2d 502, 226 IllApp3d 923.—Const Law 42.2(1), 270(1); Crim Law 641.12(1), 795(1), 824(1), 824(3), 1042, 1064(6); Drugs & N 133; Fines 1½.

People v. Sioba, NYAD 1 Dept, 589 NYS2d 164.—Crim Law 394.6(4), 394.6(5), 700(5), 1158(4).

People v. Sito, NYAD 2 Dept, 581 NYS2d 867.—Crim Law 1077.3.

People v. Sizemore, IllApp 4 Dist, 168 IllDec 883, 590 NE2d 520.—Assault 83; Crim Law 641.13(2), 641.13(6), 1042, 1043(3), 1063(1); Rape 40(2).

People v. Skinn, NYAD 1 Dept, 585 NYS2d 206.—Homic 256.

People v. Sleet, MichApp, 484 NW2d 757, 193 MichApp 604.—Const Law 213.1(2), 250.3(1), 270(1); Crim Law 1206.1(1).

People v. Sloan, NY, 583 NYS2d 176, 79 NY2d 386, 592 NE2d 784.—Crim Law 636(1), 636(3), 641.3(2), 641.3(4).

People v. Smalls, NYAD 2 Dept, 587 NYS2d 369.—Crim Law 822(16), 1210(4).

People v. Smallwood, NYAD 1 Dept, 584 NYS2d 16.—Crim Law 814(20).

People v. Smart, NYAD 1 Dept, 585 NYS2d 346.—Crim Law 625.10(1), 625.10(4), 625.35, 1166(12); Ind & Inf 144.1(1).

People v. Smedman, NYAD 2 Dept, 584 NYS2d 627.—Crim Law 303.20, 303.30(1), 339.7(4), 412.2(2); Dist & Pros Attys 8.

People v. Smith, CalApp 4 Dist, 12 CalRptr2d 546, 10 CA4th 178.—Crim Law 1202.14.

People v. Smith, CalApp 4 Dist, 9 CalRptr2d 491.—Crim Law 814(19), 1202.14.

People v. Smith, CalApp 4 Dist, 8 CalRptr2d 846, 13 CA4th 162, review gr and opinion superseded 836 P2d 342, 11 CalRptr2d 890.

People v. Smith, CalApp 5 Dist, 11 CalRptr2d 645, 9 CA4th 196.—Crim Law 789(8), 1208.6(2).

People v. Smith, Colo, 830 P2d 1003.—Atty & C 58, 182(2), 182(3).

People v. Smith, Colo, 828 P2d 249.—Atty & C 44(1), 58.

People v. Smith, ColoApp, 827 P2d 577.—Crim Law 274(3), 980(1), 986.2(2).

People v. Smith, Ill, 178 IllDec 335, 604 NE2d 858, 152 Ill2d 229.—Arrest 68.5(3); Const Law 267, 268(11); Crim Law 338(1), 363, 368(3), 412(5), 412.1(1), 412.1(4), 414, 417(8), 438(1), 438(6), 444, 519(9), 662.8, 730(14), 800(1), 1036.1(5), 1153(1), 1158(4), 1169.1(10); Homic 325; Jury 131(8), 133; Searches 13.1, 172, 198; Witn 40(1).

People v. Smith, Ill, 174 IllDec 804, 599 NE2d 888, 149 Ill2d 558.—Crim Law 23, 1159.5; Homic 31, 34, 144, 255(2), 269.

People v. Smith, Ill, 170 IllDec 644, 593 NE2d 533, 148 Ill2d 454.—Crim Law 44; Rob 12; Weap 4, 17(4).

People v. Smith, IllApp 1 Dist, 177 IllDec 492, 603 NE2d 562, 236 IllApp3d 35.—Crim Law 474.3(3); Infants 20.

People v. Smith, IllApp 1 Dist, 173 IllDec 165, 596 NE2d 789.—Arrest 63.4(2), 63.4(7); Crim Law 339.8(1), 339.10(6), 339.10(9), 339.11(3), 339.11(5), 339.11(6), 996(2), 1023(3), 1081(6), 1158(4).

People v. Smith, IllApp 1 Dist, 173 IllDec 45, 596 NE2d 669.—Crim Law 641.13(1), 641.13(2), 641.13(5), 772(6), 774, 986.2(1), 1036.6, 1063(1), 1147, 1166.11(5), 1170(1), 1208.3(2); Rob 30.

People v. Smith, IllApp 1 Dist, 168 IllDec 495, 589 NE2d 895, 226 IllApp3d 433.—Rec S Goods 1, 2, 8(1), 8(3).

People v. Smith, IllApp 2 Dist, 174 IllDec 708, 599 NE2d 492.—Crim Law 42, 303.30(1), 303.30(4), 303.35(1), 1158(1), 1181.5(1).

People v. Smith, IllApp 3 Dist, 178 IllDec 666, 605 NE2d 105.—Crim Law 317, 330, 374, 661, 721½(2), 814(8), 834(3), 1153(1), 1153(4); Tresp 84; Witn 16, 269(1), 358.

People v. Smith, IllApp 4 Dist, 177 IllDec 51, 602 NE2d 946.—Const Law 221(4); Crim Law 419(1), 419(2), 1158(3); Jury 33(5.1), 120, 121.

People v. Smith, IllApp 5 Dist, 177 IllDec 216, 602 NE2d 1388, 236 IllApp3d 1060.—Crim Law 369.1, 369.2(1), 369.15.

People v. Smith, MichApp, 489 NW2d 135, 195 MichApp 147.—Crim Law 982.9(7), 1216.1(2).

For Later Case History Information, see INSTA-CITE on WESTLAW

Case → **People v. Seawright**

Topics and key number references → [Arrest 68(3); Crim Law 349...]

FIGURE 4–7   Defendant-plaintiff Table of cases with topic and subtopic references (Reprinted by permission of West Publishing Company.)

ENTIRELY   105 F P D 4th—282

ENTIRELY WITHOUT COLOR,
    Sierra Club v. U.S. Army Corps of Engineers, C.A.2 (N.Y.), 776 F.2d 383, 390.

ENTIRE MARKET VALUE RULE,
    Rite-Hite Corp. v. Kelley Co., Inc., E.D.Wis., 774 F.Supp. 1514, 1542.

ENTIRE, SEVERABLE,
    National Iranian Oil Co. v. Ashland Oil, Inc., C.A.5 (Miss.), 817 F.2d 326, 334.

ENTIRETIES PROPERTY,
    Matter of Shader, Bkrtcy.D.Del., 90 B.R. 85, 87.

ENTITIES,
    In re United Const. and Development Co., Bkrtcy.D.Utah, 135 B.R. 904, 907.

ENTITLED TO HAVE PAYMENTS MADE,
    Rybicki v. Hartley, C.A.1 (N.H.), 792 F.2d 260, 261.

ENTITLEMENT,
    Dion v. Secretary of Health and Human Services, C.A.1 (N.H.), 823 F.2d 669, 672.
    Medical Fund-Philadelphia Geriatric Center v. Heckler, C.A.3 (Pa.), 804 F.2d 33, 37.

ENTITY,
    Palestine Information Office v. Shultz, C.A.D.C., 853 F.2d 932, 937.
    Palestine Information Office v. Shultz, D.D.C., 674 F.Supp. 910, 917.
    In re Continental Airlines Corp., D.C.Tex., 50 B.R. 342, 353.
    In re McCown, Bkrtcy.D.Md., 129 B.R. 432, 438.
    In re Canon, Bkrtcy.N.D.Tex., 130 B.R. 748, 752.

Phrases ⟶ ENTITY FOR WHOSE BENEFIT SUCH TRANSFER WAS MADE,
    In re Columbia Data Products, Inc., C.A.4 (Md.), 892 F.2d 26, 29.

ENTITY IN CONTROL,
    In re UVAS Farming Corp., Bkrtcy.D.N.M., 89 B.R. 889, 893.

Word ⟶ ENTRAPMENT,
    U.S. v. Ventura, C.A.11 (Fla.), 936 F.2d 1228, 1230.
    U.S. v. Manzella, C.A.7 (Ill.), 791 F.2d 1263, 1269.
    U.S. v. Carter, C.A.Iowa, 717 F.2d 1216, 1221.
    U.S. v. Ford, C.A.8 (Minn.), 918 F.2d 1343, 1347.
    U.S. v. McLernon, C.A.Ohio, 746 F.2d 1098, 1109.
Defined in
following ⟶   U.S. v. Pfeffer, C.A.8 (S.D.), 901 F.2d 654, 656.
cases   U.S. v. Pruneda-Gonzalez, C.A.5 (Tex.), 953 F.2d 190, 197.
    U.S. v. Arteaga, C.A.5 (Tex.), 807 F.2d 424, 425.
    U.S. v. Punch, C.A.Tex., 722 F.2d 146, 154.
    U.S. v. Beal, C.A.10 (Utah), 961 F.2d 1512, 1515.
    U.S. v. Perez, C.A.10 (Utah), 959 F.2d 164, 169.
    U.S. v. Steinhorn, D.Md., 739 F.Supp. 268, 271.

ENTRAPMENT BY ESTOPPEL,
    U.S. v. Smith, C.A.1 (Mass.), 940 F.2d 710, 714.
    U.S. v. Evans, D.Mont., 712 F.Supp. 1435, 1443.

ENTRAPPED,
    U.S. v. Inigo, C.A.3 (Del.), 925 F.2d 641, 657.

ENTRY,
    Energy Probe v. U.S. Nuclear Regulatory Com'n, C.A.D.C., 872 F.2d 436, 437.
    U.S. v. Aguilar, C.A.9 (Ariz.), 883 F.2d 662, 681.
    U.S. v. Aguilar, C.A.9 (Ariz.), 871 F.2d 1436, 1455.

FIGURE 4–8   Words and Phrases excerpt from digest (Reprinted by permission of West Publishing Company.)

Case Summaries

After locating the topic and key number, the researcher needs to scan the case summaries to find the case or cases that have facts similar to the facts of the researched question. The cases are listed by jurisdiction and by date, with higher level courts listed before lower courts and more recent cases before older cases. Look for cases with similar facts or that use legal principles like the issue you are researching. Look for conflicting cases. Try to discern trends in the law. Determine if different facts in the cases have resulted in different legal conclusions.

These case summaries are the same summaries that were placed in the front of each case in the reporters. In other words, after West Publishing prepares the summaries, or headnotes, for a case, they assign each summary a topic *and* a headnote reference. Then that topic and headnote are printed with the case *and* in the digest under the corresponding topic and headnote reference. (See Figures 4–9 and 4–10.) As new areas of the law develop, West adds new topics to its system. For example, the topic Labor Law has been added, preempting some entries under Master and Servant.

The paralegal must remember that case summaries sometimes are not entirely accurate. As a result, the researcher may miss some cases by using the digest. Also, the researcher should never rely on the information in the headnote, but should always read the case.

Updating Digests

Digests are generally updated by annual pocket parts. In fact, all of the West digests, except the *American Digest System*, uses pocket parts for updating. These pocket parts are supplemented by pamphlets, usually quarterly or biannually. Do not forget to look in the pocket parts as well as the pamphlets to find more recent cases. Cases will have been decided even after these pocket parts and pamphlets have been sent to the subscribers, so to find even more current cases, go directly to the latest volumes of the jurisdiction's reporter system. Each volume of a West reporter and each West advance sheet will have a digest for that volume as well. (See Figure 4–11.) In addition, each West reporter volume contains tables to search for cases within that volume by the name of a party to a case and for cases that have cited a particular constitutional provision, statute, or court rule. For example, if the researcher is looking for a case that deals with a precise statute, a glance at the tables in an advance sheet would alert the researcher to whether any cases in that volume cited that statute.

The *American Digest System* is updated by adding new volumes to a set called the *General Digest Series*. Each month a new volume is published containing the cases most recently decided. A researcher must look in every volume of the *General Digest Series* of this *American*

MAROTTA v. USERY   **615**
Cite as 629 F.2d 615 (1980)

issuing any "certificate." 49 U.S.C. § 307(a). Section 207(a) was enacted in 1935, long before § 206(a)(6) was added in 1962, and we read "certificate" to mean "certificate of public convenience and necessity."

[3] The CPUC addressed the elements of fitness sufficiently in its order, stating:

applicant has the business experience, the facilities, and the ability, including financial ability, to initiate and maintain the proposed service.

WRITTEN DECISION AND ORDER

[4] The APA requires an agency decision to include:

findings and conclusions, and the reasons or basis therefor, on all material issues of fact, law, or discretion presented on the record.[3]

The ICC concluded summarily that CPUC's authorization was "proper and correct in all material respects." We find this an adequate statement of its decision.

After reviewing the CPUC's decision the Commission stated:

[T]he procedures followed [by the CPUC] in reaching such conclusions and findings are in accordance with the requirements of Section 206(a)(6) of the Act, as amended; *Dugan Extension–Certificate of Registration*, 99 M.C.C. 557 [1965].

A short–form expression of finding by the ICC has been held proper. *See Kerner Trucking Service, Inc.*, 108 M.C.C. 888, 889 (1969), *aff'd sub nom. Brake Delivery Service v. United States*, 306 F.Supp. 629 (D.Cal.1969). *Cf. American Farm Lines v. Black Ball Freight Service*, 397 U.S. 532, 90 S.Ct. 1288, 25 L.Ed.2d 547 (1970).

The issuance of the certificate is AFFIRMED.

---

3. Section 557 of the Administrative Procedure Act, 5 U.S.C. § 557, provides in part:

The record shall show the ruling on each finding, conclusion, or exception presented. All decisions, including initial, recommended, and tentative decisions, are a part of the record and shall include a statement of

Eugene F. MAROTTA, Plaintiff–Appellant,

v.

William J. USERY, Secretary of Labor, U. S. Department of Labor, Defendant–Appellee.

No. 78–1341.

United States Court of Appeals, Ninth Circuit.

Argued and Submitted April 16, 1980.

Decided Oct. 6, 1980.

White applicant brought action against the Secretary of Labor alleging employment discrimination in hiring a black applicant for a federal position. The United States District Court for the Northern District of California, William H. Orrick, Jr., J., entered judgment for defendant, and plaintiff appealed. The Court of Appeals, Wyatt, District Judge, sitting by designation, held that, discrimination having been conceded by defendant, defendant met burden of proving, by clear and convincing evidence, that plaintiff would not have been hired even in absence of racial discrimination.

Affirmed.

1. **Federal Civil Procedure** ⟜2069

Jury trials are not a matter of right in employment discrimination actions. Civil Rights Act of 1964, §§ 706(e), 717(c) as amended 42 U.S.C.A. §§ 2000e- 5(f)(1), 2000e–16(c).

2. **Civil Rights** ⟜44(1)

Conceding reverse discrimination in hiring a black for a federal position, federal

(A) findings and conclusions, and the reasons or basis therefor, on all material issues of fact, law, or discretion presented on the record; and
(B) the appropriate rule, order, sanction, relief, or denial thereof.

FIGURE 4–9   Topic and headnote references assigned to a case (Reprinted by permission of West Publishing Company.)

⊶2068 **FEDERAL CIVIL PROCEDURE** 17–9th D Pt 1—892

C.A.Guam 1979. As in cases involving waiver of sovereign immunity, there is no constitutional right to jury trial in action by United States to condemn property under eminent domain. U.S.C.A.Const. Amend. 7.—Franquez v. U. S., 604 F.2d 1239.

Court's discretionary authority to grant jury trial in federal condemnation actions does not result in modification or enlargement of substantive rights in those cases in which statute is silent regarding method of determining just compensation. Fed.Rules Civ.Proc. rule 71A(h), 28 U.S.C.A.—Id.

It was within discretionary authority of district court to grant trial by jury on issue of just compensation in proceeding under statute governing review of claims respecting land acquired by United States on Guam, and such grant was not inconsistent with statute governing such claims or federal rules. 48 U.S.C.A. § 1424c.—Id.

Headnote⟶ ⊶**2069. Employees' actions.**

U.S.N.C. 1978. In face of its extensive knowledge of operation of Fair Labor Standards Act, illustrated by its selective incorporation and amendment of FLSA provisions for the Age Discrimination in Employment Act, Congress could not be assumed to have been unaware that courts had uniformly afforded jury trial under the FLSA nor was Congress, in specifically providing for "legal" relief in the ADEA, oblivious to its long-established meaning or significance and thus, in light of congressional intent, a trial by jury is available in private civil actions for lost wages under the ADEA where sought by one of the parties. Fair Labor Standards Act of 1938, §§ 1 et seq., 16 et seq., 29 U.S.C.A. §§ 201 et seq., 216 et seq.; Age Discrimination in Employment Act of 1967, §§ 2 et seq., 7(b, c), 29 U.S.C.A. §§ 621 et seq., 626(b, c); U.S.C.A. Const. Amend. 7.—Lorillard v. Pons, 98 S.Ct. 866, 434 U.S. 575, 55 L.Ed.2d 40.

C.A.D.C. 1980. Employee who brought Age Discrimination in Employment Act action against federal government could demand jury trial. Age Discrimination in Employment Act of 1967, § 2 et seq. as amended 29 U.S.C.A. § 621 et seq.—Nakshian v. Claytor, 628 F.2d 59, 202 U.S.App.D.C. 59, certiorari granted Hidalgo v. Nakshian, 101 S.Ct. 563, 449 U.S. 1009, 66 L.Ed.2d 467, reversed Lehman v. Nakshian, 101 S.Ct. 2698, 453 U.S. 156, 69 L.Ed.2d 548.

C.A.Ala. 1980. Denial of age discrimination plaintiff's jury demand was prejudicial error where questions for jury existed. Age Discrimination in Employment Act of 1967, § 1 et seq., 29 U.S.C.A. § 621 et seq.; Fed.Rules Civ.Proc. Rules 50(a), 56(b), 28 U.S.C.A.—McCorstin v. U. S. Steel Corp., 621 F.2d 749.

C.A.Ala. 1979. Suit by a discharged employee against employer for breach of collective bargaining contract was common-law claim, and thus one for which jury trial could be invoked. U.S.C.A.Const. Amend. 7.—Cox v. C. H. Masland & Sons, Inc., 607 F.2d 138.

Member of collective bargaining unit had right to trial by jury of his claim that union which represented him violated its duty of fair representation by failing to pursue grievance against employer. U.S.C.A.Const. Amend. 7. —Id.

Where discharged employee chose to seek only remedy of damages in action against employer and union, employee had right to jury trial both on primary claim that employer discharged him in violation of collective bargaining agreement and on corollary contention that union failed fairly to represent him. U.S. C.A.Const. Amend. 7.—Id.

C.A.Ala. 1978. Where defendant contended that the plaintiff's son had signed a receipt for the EEOC right to sue letter and that he was the plaintiff's authorized agent for such purpose, where the plaintiff, in her deposition, denied that her son's signature appeared on the return receipt, and where the receipt was not attached to the deposition, summary judgment in favor of the defendant on the ground that the action had not been brought within 90 days of the receipt of the right to sue letter was improper even though the defendant argued that the failure of the son's signature to appear on the return receipt shown to the plaintiff was explainable by the fact that the receipt shown was only a copy of the record of the postal service. Civil Rights Act of 1964, §§ 701–715, 716(c) as amended 42 U.S.C.A. §§ 2000e to 2000e–15.—Mack v. Anderson Elec. Co., 580 F.2d 191.

C.A.Cal. 1981. Judicial decision did not create right to jury trial in Age Discrimination in Employment Act actions but merely recognized existence of right under existing statutory framework and, in any event, plaintiff should have filed jury demand within ten days of such decision to be timely under his argument, and demand which was made one day after Congress formally incorporated, by amendment, the right to jury trial recognized in judicial decision was not timely. Fed.Rules Civ.Proc. Rule 38(b, d), 28 U.S.C.A.—Sutton v. Atlantic Richfield Co., 646 F.2d 407.

C.A.Cal. 1980. Jury trials are not a matter of right in employment discrimination actions. Civil Rights Act of 1964, §§ 706(e), 717(c) as amended 42 U.S.C.A. §§ 2000e–5(f)(1), 2000e–16(c).—Marotta v. Usery, 629 F.2d 615.

C.A.Ga. 1980. In suit alleging that prison guard was constructively discharged by city for exercising her First Amendment rights, district court should submit to jury those factual issues inherent in balancing test, but ultimate balancing remained province of court and any factual issues decided by jury that might relate to ultimate questions of law were subject to careful review. U.S.C.A.Const. Amend. 1. —Schneider v. City of Atlanta, 628 F.2d 915.

C.A.Ga. 1978. In action brought under Age Discrimination in Employment Act of 1967, trial by jury on claim for lost wages is available when sought by one of the parties. Age Discrimination in Employment Act of 1967, § 2 et seq., 29 U.S.C.A. § 621 et seq.—Murphy v. American Motors Sales Corp., 570 F.2d 1226.

C.A.Ill. 1980. Yardmaster's rights to a jury trial, due process, and equal protection were not violated by fact that under Railway Labor Act dismissal of his NRAB claim for want of exhaustion of administrative remedies precluded a later common-law action on the merits of the claim. Railway Labor Act, § 3, subd. 1(i, p, q) as amended 45 U.S.C.A. § 153, subd. 1(i, p, q); U.S.C.A.Const. Amends. 5, 7, 14.—Essary v. Chicago and N. W. Transp. Co., 618 F.2d 13.

C.A.Ill. 1979. Award of back pay sought by plaintiff on her equal employment claim was an integral part of equitable remedy of reinstatement and, hence, was not something to be characterized as a legal remedy for which plaintiff was entitled to a jury trial. Civil Rights Act of 1964, § 706(g) as amended 42 U.S.C.A. § 2000e–5(g); U.S.C.A.Const. Amend. 7.—Grayson v. Wickes Corp., 607 F.2d 1194.

Jury trial need not be provided to parties in suits under equal employment provision of Civil Rights Act of 1964. Civil Rights Act of 1964, § 706(g) as amended 42 U.S.C.A. § 2000e 5(g); U.S.C.A.Const. Amend. 7.—Id.

C.A.Ind. 1980. Suits for pension benefits brought under Employee Retirement Income Security Act are equitable in nature and, hence, there is no right to jury trial. Employee Retirement Income Security Act of 1974, §§ 502, 502(a), (a)(1)(B), (a)(3), (e)(1), 29 U.S.C.A. §§ 1132, 1132(a), (a)(1)(B), (a)(3), (e)(1); Labor Management Relations Act, 1947, § 301, 29 U.S.C.A. § 185; U.S.C.A. Const. Amend. 7.—Wardle v. Central States, Southeast and Southwest Areas Pension Fund, 627 F.2d 820, certiorari denied 101 S.Ct. 922, 449 U.S. 1112, 66 L.Ed.2d 841.

C.A.La. 1980. Employee Retirement Income Security Act does not entitle plaintiff to jury trial. Employee Retirement Income Security Act of 1974, §§ 401 et seq., 502, 29 U.S.C.A. §§ 1101 et seq., 1132.—Calamia v. Spivey, 632 F.2d 1235.

C.A.Miss. 1980. Inclusion of request for award of attorney fees did not raise right to jury in an otherwise purely equitable employment discrimination action, in view of fact that statutes relied upon by plaintiff for attorney fee provided that it was to be awarded by the court. Emergency School Aid Act, § 718, 20 U.S.C.A. § 1617; Civil Rights Act of 1964, § 706(k), 42 U.S.C.A. § 2000e–5(k): —Whiting v. Jackson State University, 616 F.2d 116, rehearing denied 622 F.2d 1043.

Where employment discrimination complaint requested both compensatory and punitive damages in addition to request for equitable relief, trial court properly placed case on its jury docket. Civil Rights Act of 1964, § 706 as amended 42 U.S.C.A. § 2000e–5; 42 U.S. C.A. §§ 1981, 1983; U.S.C.A.Const. Amends. 5, 14.—Id.

C.A.Mo. 1981. Remedy of back pay in cases brought under section relating to equal rights of all citizens is more appropriately characterized as compensatory, legal damage, and, therefore, there is right to jury trial on legal claims including claim for back pay. U.S. C.A.Const. Amend. 7; 42 U.S.C.A. § 1981.— Setser v. Novack Inv. Co., 638 F.2d 1137, amended and vacated in part 657 F.2d 962, certiorari denied 102 S.Ct. 615.

C.A.Mo. 1980. Employees were properly accorded jury trial in their suit charging union with breach of duty of fair representation. Labor Management Relations Act, 1947, § 301, 29 U.S.C.A. § 185.—Smith v. Hussmann Refrigerator Co., 619 F.2d 1229, certiorari denied Local 13889, United Steelworkers of America v. Smith, 101 S.Ct. 116, 449 U.S. 839, 66 L.Ed.2d 46, on remand 507 F.Supp. 652.

C.A.N.J. 1977. A suit for damages consisting of back wages arising out of the alleged breach of an employment agreement is a routine contract action in which parties are entitled to a jury under the Seventh Amendment. U.S.C.A.Const. Amend. 7.—Rogers v. Exxon Research & Engineering Co., 550 F.2d 834, certiorari denied 98 S.Ct. 749, 434 U.S. 1022, 54 L.Ed.2d 770.

Suits for damages under the Fair Labor Standards Act are within the Seventh Amendment guarantee of a jury trial. Fair Labor Standards Act of 1938, §§ 16, 17, 29 U.S. C.A. §§ 216, 217; U.S.C.A.Const. Amend. 7.—Id.

In view of intrinsic nature of suit for back wages under the Age Discrimination in Employment Act as well as the ADEA's incorporation, in its enforcement provisions, of corresponding sections of the Fair Labor Standards Act, parties were entitled to a jury trial of retired employee's allegations that he had been illegally discriminated against because of his age with respect to, inter alia, promotions

For references to other topics, see Descriptive-Word Index

FIGURE 4–10 The key number and case summaries in the digest (Reprinted by permission of West Publishing Company.)

KEY NUMBER DIGEST

ACTION

I. GROUNDS AND CONDITIONS PRECEDENT.

☞13. **Persons entitled to sue.**

D.C.App. 1995. Zone of interest requirement of standing is "prudential," not constitutionally compelled.—Brentwood Liquors, Inc. v. District of Columbia Alcoholic Beverage Control Bd., 661 A.2d 652.

Under zone of interest requirement of standing, plaintiff must establish that injury he complains of falls within zone of interests sought to be protected by statutory provision whose violation forms legal basis of his complaint.—Id.

In determining whether plaintiff is within zone of interests that legislature has sought to protect for standing purposes, court may look to language of provision and its legislative history.—Id.

Pa.Super. 1995. Before court can proceed to address merits of controversy, it must determine whether standing exists to maintain the action.—In re Barnes Foundation, 661 A.2d 889.

ADMINISTRATIVE LAW AND PROCEDURE

III. SEPARATION OF ADMINISTRATIVE AND OTHER POWERS.

(B) JUDICIAL POWERS.

☞229. —— **Exhaustion of administrative remedies.**

N.J.Super.A.D. 1995. Before presenting to court the issue of whether regulations adopted by Real Estate Commission were inconsistent with the Real Estate Settlement and Procedures Act (RESPA) and whether, if inconsistent, they afforded consumers greater protection, parties had to exhaust administrative remedies with Secretary of Housing and Urban Development (HUD), since issues implicated federal government's strong interest in commerce among states and required exercise of sensitive policy judgments. Real Estate Settlement Procedures Act of 1974, §§ 2–19, as amended, 12 U.S.C.A. §§ 2601–2617.—Mortgage Bankers Ass'n of New Jersey v. New Jersey Real Estate Com'n, 661 A.2d 832, 283 N.J.Super. 233.

ADMINISTRATIVE LAW AND PROCEDURE—Cont'd

V. JUDICIAL REVIEW OF ADMINISTRATIVE DECISIONS.

(C) PROCEEDINGS FOR REVIEW.

☞722.1. —— **In general.**

Pa.Cmwlth. 1995. For purposes of securing filing date for petition for review transmitted by mail, United States Postal Form 3800, receipt of certified mail, is the functional equivalent of United States Postal Form 3817, certificate of mailing. Rules App.Proc., Rule 1514(a), 42 Pa.C.S.A.—Smith v. Pennsylvania Bd. of Probation and Parole, 661 A.2d 902.

Petition for review transmitted by mail is considered filed on the date it is actually received by the prothonotary unless the petition is accompanied by United States Postal Service Form 3817 or 3800, or the form is mailed separately to the prothonotary, the postal form contains the docket number of the matter in the governmental unit, and the postal form is date stamped by the Post Office. Rules App.Proc., Rule 1514(a), 42 Pa.C.S.A.—Id.

Even if private express delivery company delivers petition for review one day past the time for filing, it is unacceptable under rule governing the filing and service of petitions for review because the company's forms are not postal forms and its services are not those of the Postal Service. Rules App.Proc., Rule 1514(a), 42 Pa.C.S.A.—Id.

Under Supreme Court's narrow *Miller* exception to rule that petition for review will be considered filed when received by prothonotary unless there is postal form evidencing mailing, parolee's appeal was not considered timely filed where his petition for review was not received the next business day after the time for filing had elapsed and so it was possible that the petition had been mailed outside the time for appeal. Rules App.Proc., Rule 1514(a), 42 Pa.C.S.A.—Id.

(E) PARTICULAR QUESTIONS, REVIEW OF.

☞783. **Constitutional questions.**

Pa.Cmwlth. 1995. Scope of review of decision of the Pennsylvania Labor Relations Board (PLRB) is limited to determining whether findings of the PLRB are supported by substantial evidence, and whether there has been constitutional violation or an error of law committed.—Association of Pennsylvania State College and University Faculties v. Pennsylvania Labor Relations Bd., 661 A.2d 898.

For Earlier Cases, See Same Topic and Key Number in Any West Key Number Digest

XCII

FIGURE 4–11   Advance sheet with key numbers for *Atlantic Reporter* (Reprinted by permission of West Publishing Company.)

Digest System to find cases decided during the relevant period. This is a laborious and time-consuming process.

Variety of Digests

West publishes specific digests for different jurisdictions. There are digests for every state except Delaware, Nevada, and Utah. West Virginia and Virginia, and North and South Dakota, share digests. A researcher searching for cases from a certain state should always begin by consulting that state's digest. Except for New York state, these state digests also reference federal cases dealing with that state's laws.

West also publishes regional digests that encompass the same geographical breakdown as the regional reporters except for the Northeastern, Southern, and Southwestern digests, which have been discontinued. (See Figure 4–12.) There are also digests for specialized legal matters, such as bankruptcy and social security. (See Figure 4–13.) There are separate digests for federal cases. As discussed below, West publishes a digest specifically for finding Supreme Court cases, as does Lawyers Cooperative Publishing. The *American Digest System* is a national digest covering all cases reported by West Publishing. The paralegal can save considerable research effort by initially selecting the appropriate digest.

FIGURE 4–12
Regional digests generally cover the same geographical territory as the regional reporters

Regional Digest	States Included
Atlantic	Connecticut, Delaware, Maine, Maryland, New Hampshire, New Jersey, Pennsylvania, Rhode Island, Vermont
Northwestern	Iowa, Michigan, Minnesota, Nebraska, North Dakota, South Dakota, Wisconsin
Pacific	Alaska, Arizona, California, Colorado, Hawaii, Idaho, Kansas, Montana, Nevada New Mexico, Oklahoma, Oregon, Utah Washington, Wyoming
Southeastern	Georgia, North Carolina, South Carolina Virginia, West Virginia

Specialty Digests

West's Bankruptcy Digest

West's Military Justice Digest

United States Claims Court Digest

West's Social Security Digest

Figure 4–13 An example of specialty digests

State Digests

A legal professional strives to find any binding precedent. For state precedents, the legal researcher uses a state digest, if available, or a regional digest if there is no state digest (as in Delaware, Nevada, or Utah). As with any digest, the researcher usually will start with the descriptive word index, commonly found in separate volumes at the beginning or end of the digest set. This index provides the topic and key number references. The researcher can then look under the topic and key number in the main volume. If there is more than one series or set of main volumes, the researcher may need to search in several sets. Next, the researcher must check the pocket parts under the same topic and key number, as well as any pamphlets sent out to update the pocket parts.

It is possible that cases have been decided since the last digest pamphlet was published. Each new advance sheet for the reporters contains an abbreviated digest referencing topics and key numbers found in that advance sheet. The researcher must check the most recent advance sheets of the state reporter to complete the research.

Regional Digests

For states that do not have a state digest, the researcher will need to use a regional digest. These regional digests correspond with the regional reporters published by West Publishing.

A regional digest is used in a similar manner to a state digest. First, find a topic and key number reference by using one of the approaches discussed previously. Then find that topic and key number in the main volume. Scan the reference for case summaries fitting the legal problem being researched. Update the search by examining the pocket parts, pamphlets, and advance sheets as discussed above.

Specialty Digests

To assist researchers in finding cases in the specialty reporters discussed in Chapter 3, West Publishing publishes a digest for most of the specialty reporters. The paralegal uses the same process to search for a case in a specialty digest as he of she uses with the other digests. Obviously, the researcher will find only cases on the specialty matter, and the researcher will not be limited by jurisdiction.

Federal Digests

For researching federal case law, West Publishing has published a federal digest, which is in its fifth series. The first series, called the *Federal Digest*, covers cases decided prior to 1939. The second series, called the *Modern Federal Practice Digest*, covers cases decided between 1939 and 1961. The third series is called the *Federal Practice Digest 2d* and covers cases from 1961 to 1975. The fourth series is called the *Federal Practice Digest 3d* and covers cases from 1975 to 1990. The latest series is called the *Federal Practice Digest 4th*. Figure 4–14 is a summary of the federal digests.

Federal digests are used the same way as state digests. Start with the descriptive word index and locate a key number. Because the *Federal Practice Digest* now consists of five series, the paralegal must look under the main volume in each series to find all federal cases dealing with any point of law. Accordingly, the researcher would look under the appropriate topic and key number in all five series. In *Federal Practice Digest 4th*, pocket parts and quarterly pamphlets update this set. To complete the research and obtain all recent federal cases, look in the most recent advance sheets for the *Federal Supplement* (F. Supp.), the *Federal Reporter* (F.2d), and the *Supreme Court Reporter* (S. Ct.).

Figure 4–14
Federal digests published by West Publishing Company

Federal Digest System	
Federal Digest	Prior to 1939
Modern Federal Practice Digest	1939–1961
Federal Practice Digest 2d	1961–1975
Federal Practice Digest 3d	1975–1990
Federal Practice Digest 4th	1990–present

Supreme Court Digest

For researching only United States Supreme Court cases, there is the *United States Supreme Court Digest*, published by West. This digest is used the same way the state and regional digests are used and is updated by pocket parts.

Lawyers Cooperative also publishes a digest for finding Supreme Court cases called the *United States Supreme Court Digest, Lawyer's Edition*. The same methods of use discussed above apply, except the topics and subheadings do not correspond with the topics and subtopics in West's digests and reporters. In other words, this digest has different headings and a different outline. This set is also updated by pocket parts.

Summary of Digest Research Techniques

The process to follow for most digest research is as follows:

Step 1 –   Select a digest for the appropriate jurisdiction. (For example, use a state digest for state cases, a federal digest for federal cases.)

Step 2 –   Use the descriptive word index to find the appropriate topic and key number.

Step 3 –   Look in the main volume of each series, under the topic and key number if using a West digest, and under the topic and section number if using most other digests.

Step 4 –   Examine the pocket parts under the same topic and number.

Step 5 –   Look at the pamphlets, if any, under the topic and number.

Step 6 –   Look in the advance sheets for the reporters covering cases for that jurisdiction.

American Digest System

West has published a series of digests called the *American Digest System* to cover all cases from every jurisdiction (every state as well as the federal court system). It is cumbersome to use, although the technique for using this set is not much different from that used for the other sets. The *American Digest System* begins with the *Century Digest*, covering cases from the beginning of the set until 1896. The *Century Digest* is followed by sets called *Decennials*, covering ten-year periods. For example, the *First Decennial* covers cases from 1896 to 1906. This practice was followed until the *Ninth Decennial*. The *Ninth Decennial* is divided into two parts, each spanning a five-year period. Finally, there is a *General Digest*. Volumes are added to the *General Digest* series on a monthly basis. A researcher must consult each volume of the *General Digest* for more recent cases—not an insignificant task, since it will consist of sixty volumes at the end of a five-year period.

This type of research is clearly time-consuming and burdensome. This set is also expensive because at five-year intervals, West Publishing combines all cases with the same topic or key number in one volume and issues another set. Subscribers then are instructed to discard the *General Digest* series, which may consist of sixty volumes. The main difference between other digests and the *American Digest System* is the updating methodology. The *American Digest System* does not use pocket parts. Instead, it is updated monthly by a new bound volume.

Use this source only if your search is broad-based. You will not use it frequently, but it is effective for locating all cases under a specific point of law. A national encyclopedia or the *American Law Reports* (A.L.R.) sometimes will be more effective than the *American Digest System* for finding cases in other jurisdictions. The process for finding every case under a specific key number in the *American Digest System* is as follows:

Step 1 –   Locate topic and key number reference from descriptive word index. (Remember, key numbers have been added at different times. You may need to look at the descriptive word index for different series.)

Step 2 –   Look under the topic and key number for each volume of the *General Digest*.

Step 3 –   Look under the topic and key number for the *Ninth Decennial* in both Parts I and II.

Step 4 –   Look under the topic and key number in the appropriate volume in each of the remaining eight *Decennials*.

Step 5 –   Convert the topic and key number by using the table in the *First Decennial* to a topic and key number for the *Century Digest*, which has a key numbering system different from the later sets.

Some Research Hints about Digests

Remember that a digest is merely a tool used to find case citations. A headnote summary is the interpretation of a case by a private publishing company and may not be accurate or complete. In any case, the summary should never be quoted or cited. Read the actual case and quote the case instead.

Also remember that the law is always changing. West Publishing and other legal publishing companies may not be on top of changes. Sometimes new topics are not created. As a result, digest summaries may be misclassified, which can frustrate any legal professional. Use some alternative search paths when you do not easily find an answer in a digest. When all else fails, try another approach, such as an A.L.R., treatise, encyclopedia, or periodical. Perseverance is an important research trait.

American Law Reports (A.L.R.)

Lawyers Cooperative Publishing has a philosophy of providing selective access to issues, whereas West Publishing has a philosophy of providing broad access to law, allowing a researcher to draw his or her own conclusions. For example, the digests published by West provide comprehensive coverage of all case principles. The *American Law Reports,* commonly called A.L.R., published by Lawyers Cooperative contain a series of articles on current legal issues. In these articles, the legal professional can find case summaries with citations and explanatory commentary. The A.L.R. is currently in the fifth series. Here is a complete listing of the A.L.R. series:

Series	When Published
A.L.R.1st	1919–1948
A.L.R.2d	1948–1965
A.L.R.3d	1965–1980
A.L.R.4th	1980–1991
A.L.R.5th	1992–present
A.L.R. Fed.	1969–present

What was a current issue of law in 1919 now may be an antiquated concept, or there may have been a shift in the interpretation of the law. As a result, several articles on the same subject or the same issue of law might be found in the A.L.R. The latest article may supersede earlier articles.

The topics covered by the A.L.R. tend to be narrowly focused on issues of importance. The A.L.R. through the A.L.R.3d covered mainly state law topics with occasional articles on federal law. Now there is a separate set covering only federal law called the A.L.R. Fed. Currently, there are more than 14,000 case law articles in the A.L.R. There is an example of an A.L.R.5th article in Appendix B at the end of this book.

Locating Annotations

Lawyers Cooperative publishes a six-volume index covering the A.L.R. Fed. and A.L.R.2d through A.L.R.5th. This index is designed for easy use, and there are pocket parts updating it. Figure 4–15 is a page

ALR INDEX

ALARM SYSTEMS—Cont'd

Limitation of liability
- installation or servicing, liability of person responsible for as to burglar or fire loss, 37 ALR4th 47, §§ 3[b, c], 4[a, b], 5[b, c], 6, 7
- stipulated damages clause in fire or burglar alarm service contract, validity, construction, and effect of limited liability provision, 42 ALR2d 591

Liquidated damages
- contract clause, 42 ALR2d 591
- furnishing, installing, or servicing burglary or fire alarm system, liability of person performing services for burglary or fire loss, 37 ALR4th 47, §§ 4[a, b], 5[b, c], 6[b]

Livestock or animal insurance, risks and losses, 47 ALR4th 772, § 18

Products liability, liability of person furnishing, installing, or servicing burglary or fire alarm system for burglary or fire loss, 37 ALR4th 47

Robbery, liability of storekeeper for death of or injury to customer in course of robbery, 72 ALR3d 1269, § 4[a]

Security services contract, liability of security services company to injured employee as beneficiary of security services contract between company and employer, 75 ALR4th 844

Siren (this index)

Strict or absolute liability of person furnishing, installing, or servicing burglary or fire alarm system for burglary or fire loss, 37 ALR4th 47

Uniform Commercial Code, unconscionability of disclaimer of warranties or limitation or exclusion of damages, under UCC § 2-302 or § 2-719(3), in contract subject to UCC Article 2, 38 ALR4th 25 §§ 3[c], 30, 32

ALASKA NATIVE CLAIMS SETTLEMENT ACT

Class actions, permissibility of action against a class of defendants under Rule 23(b)(2) of Federal Rules of Civil Procedure, 85 ALR Fed 263, § 12

ALCOHOLIC BEVERAGES

Intoxicating Liquors (this index)

ALCOHOLICS AND ALCOHOLISM

For digest treatment, see title **Habitual Drunkards in ALR Digest**

Automobile insurance, cancellation of compulsory or financial responsibility automobile insurance, 44 ALR4th 13, §§ 5[b, c], 20, 23

Bar admission or reinstatement of attorney as affected by alcoholism or alcohol abuse, 39 ALR4th 567

Business compulsion or economic duress, refusal to pay debt as economic duress or business compulsion avoiding compromise or release, 9 ALR4th 942

Confessions, mental subnormality of accused as affecting voluntariness or admissibility of confession, 8 ALR4th 16, § 12[a]

Contempt of court, 46 ALR4th 238

Criminal defense, see group Incompetent and insane persons in this topic

Criminal prosecution of chronic alcoholic for drunkenness offenses, 40 ALR3d 321

Defenses
- criminal defense, when intoxication deemed involuntary, 73 ALR3d 195
- discharge from employment, alcoholism as ground for discharge justifying denial of unemployment compensation, 64 ALR4th 1151

Disability insurance
- chronic alcoholism or its effects as disability entitling claimant to period of disability or disability insurance benefits under §§ 216 and 223 of Social Security Act (42 USCS §§ 416 and 423), 39 ALR Fed 182
- total disability, what constitutes total disability within coverage of disability insurance policy issued to lawyer, 6 ALR4th 422, § 3[b]

Discharge from employment, alcoholism or intoxication as ground for discharge justifying denial of unemployment compensation, 64 ALR4th 1151

Discipline and disciplinary actions
generally, misconduct involving intoxication as ground for disciplinary action against attorney, 17 ALR3d 692

Consult POCKET PART for Later Annotations   **147**

FIGURE 4–15   ALR index

from this index. As a practical matter, the index will be the principal means of locating citations to A.L.R. annotations. The A.L.R.1st has a separate one-volume index that also is easy to use. Below are several alternative methods used to locate A.L.R. annotations.

A.L.R Digest

Lawyers Cooperative, in separate volumes of the A.L.R., publishes digests containing summaries of cases, A.L.R. annotations, and *Lawyer's Edition* cases. There is an *A.L.R. Digest* for the first series, another for the second series, and another that covers the third, fourth, fifth, and the federal series. It is important to remember that the *A.L.R. Digest* uses a different reference system from that used by West Publishing in its digests. Hence, the researcher needs to locate topic references by using the index for this digest or by scanning the alphabetical list of topics in the digest.

Secondary Sources

Other secondary research tools published by Lawyers Cooperative provide citations to A.L.R. annotations. For example, a researcher can find citations for A.L.R. annotations in *American Jurisprudence 2d* (Am. Jur. 2d), the legal encyclopedia published by Lawyers Cooperative.

Computer References

References to A.L.R. annotations can be located on-line through LEXIS or "Auto-Cite," as discussed in Chapter 7.

Tables of Laws, Rules, and Regulations

Sometimes researchers who are researching a particular federal statute, rule, or regulation search for case authority pertaining to that law. The *A.L.R. Index to Annotations* contains several tables of laws, rules, and regulations to assist the researcher in finding annotations that pertain to particular laws. (See Figure 4–16.)

Related Annotations

In each A.L.R. annotation article, there is a section list called "Related Annotations" (previously "Related Matters"). (See Figure 4–17.) Sometimes, if the search by other methods is unsuccessful, the researcher can locate an annotation that is related to the issue, but not really on point. The researcher can look in the related annotations portion of the annotation to see if there are other annotations closer on point.

UNITED STATES CODE SERVICE

Title and section	Vol. and page	Title and section	Vol. and page

1 USCS

1 .. 8 ALR Fed 816 § 4; 24 ALR Fed 631 § 4

3 . 3 ALR Fed 882 § 2-5; 5 ALR Fed 674 § 2, 14; 20 ALR Fed 600 § 2; 91 ALR Fed 547 § 2, 32, 33

4 .... 15 ALR Fed 919 § 4

15 .... 20 ALR Fed 682 § 2

77b(1) .... 3 ALR Fed 592 § 13

109 .... 108 L Ed 2d 1061 § 1 et seq; 63 ALR Fed 328 § 4

112a .... 17 ALR Fed 725 § 2

113 .... 17 ALR Fed 725 § 2

321 .... 58 ALR Fed 312 § 1

322 .... 58 ALR Fed 312 § 1

1531 et seq ...... 107 ALR Fed 827 § 13

2 USCS

72a .... 18 ALR Fed 949 § 1

192 . 3 L Ed 2d 1647 § 1 et seq; 16 L Ed 2d 1231 § 8; 50 L Ed 2d 830 § 20; 53 L Ed 2d 1273 § 30; 84 L Ed 2d 876 § 3

193 .... 88 ALR3d 304 § 5

261 .42 ALR3d 1046 § 2; 3 ALR Fed 770 § 3

261 et seq 2 L Ed 2d 1706 § 19; 16 L Ed 2d 1231 § 8

262 .42 ALR3d 1046 § 2; 3 ALR Fed 770 § 3

263 .42 ALR3d 1046 § 2; 3 ALR Fed 770 § 3

264 .... 16 L Ed 2d 1231 § 8; 42 ALR3d 1046 § 2; 3 ALR Fed 770 § 3

265 .42 ALR3d 1046 § 2; 3 ALR Fed 770 § 3

266 .... 16 L Ed 2d 1231 § 8; 42 ALR3d 1046 § 2; 3 ALR Fed 770 § 3

267 .... 16 L Ed 2d 1231 § 8; 42 ALR3d 1046 § 2; 3 ALR Fed 770 § 3

268 .42 ALR3d 1046 § 2; 3 ALR Fed 770 § 3

269 .42 ALR3d 1046 § 2; 3 ALR Fed 770 § 3

2 USCS—Cont'd

270 .42 ALR3d 1046 § 2; 3 ALR Fed 770 § 3

307 .... 30 ALR3d 9 § 31

431 .. 79 ALR3d 491 § 1; 94 ALR3d 944 § 1; 4 ALR4th 741 § 1; 22 ALR4th 237 § 1; 26 ALR4th 170 § 1; 18 ALR Fed 949 § 1; 66 ALR Fed 750 § 1

431 et seq .... 67 L Ed 2d 859 § 2, 6; 37 ALR Fed 274 § 2

431(a) .... 18 ALR Fed 949 § 1, 5, 6

431(c) .... 18 ALR Fed 949 § 1, 5, 6

431(d) .... 18 ALR Fed 949 § 1, 5, 6

431(e) .... 18 ALR Fed 949 § 1, 5, 6

431(f) .... 18 ALR Fed 949 § 1, 5, 6

432 .. 79 ALR3d 491 § 1; 94 ALR3d 944 § 1; 4 ALR4th 741 § 1; 22 ALR4th 237 § 1; 26 ALR4th 170 § 1; 18 ALR Fed 949 § 1; 66 ALR Fed 750 § 1

433 .. 79 ALR3d 491 § 1; 94 ALR3d 944 § 1; 4 ALR4th 741 § 1; 22 ALR4th 237 § 1; 26 ALR4th 170 § 1; 18 ALR Fed 949 § 1; 66 ALR Fed 750 § 1

434 .. 79 ALR3d 491 § 1; 94 ALR3d 944 § 1; 4 ALR4th 741 § 1; 22 ALR4th 237 § 1; 26 ALR4th 170 § 1; 18 ALR Fed 949 § 1; 66 ALR Fed 750 § 1

434(e) .... 67 L Ed 2d 859 § 6

435 .. 79 ALR3d 491 § 1; 94 ALR3d 944 § 1; 4 ALR4th 741 § 1; 22 ALR4th 237 § 1; 26 ALR4th 170 § 1; 18 ALR Fed 949 § 1; 66 ALR Fed 750 § 1

436 .. 79 ALR3d 491 § 1; 94 ALR3d 944 § 1; 4 ALR4th 741 § 1; 22 ALR4th 237 § 1; 26 ALR4th 170 § 1; 18 ALR Fed 949 § 1; 66 ALR Fed 750 § 1

Consult POCKET PART for Later Entries   **583**

FIGURE 4–16   A page from the table of laws, rules, and regulations in the A.L.R. Index to Annotations

§ 1[a]   ADMISSION OF PRIOR SPOUSAL ABUSE   24 ALR5th
24 ALR5th 465

enactments directly bearing upon this subject. These provisions are discussed herein only to the extent and in the form that they are reflected in the court opinions that fall within the scope of this annotation. The reader is consequently advised to consult the appropriate statutory or regulatory compilations to ascertain the current status of all statutes discussed herein, including those listed in the Jurisdictional Table of Cited Statutes and Cases.

[b] Related annotations

Admissibility of evidence of other offense where record has been expunged or erased. 82 ALR4th 913.

Admissibility of evidence as to other offense as affected by defendant's acquittal of that offense. 25 ALR4th 934.

Admissibility of expert or opinion testimony on battered wife or battered woman syndrome. 18 ALR4th 1153.

Admissibility of evidence of subsequent criminal offenses as affected by proximity as to time and place. 92 ALR3d 545.

Admissibility of evidence of other offenses in rebuttal of defense of entrapment. 61 ALR3d 293.

Admissibility and propriety, in homicide prosecution, of evidence as to deceased's spouse and children. 67 ALR2d 731.

Admissibility of evidence of other crimes, wrongs, or acts under Rule 404(b) of Federal Rules of Evidence, in civil cases. 64 ALR Fed 648.

Admissibility of evidence of habit or routine practice under Rule 406, Federal Rules of Evidence. 53 ALR Fed 703.

Admissibility, under Rule 404(b) of the Federal Rules of Evidence, of evidence of other crimes, wrongs, or acts similar to offense charged to show preparation or plan. 47 ALR Fed 781.

Admissibility, under Rule 404(b) of Federal Rules of Evidence, of evidence of other crimes, wrongs, or acts not similar to offense charged. 41 ALR Fed 497.

§ 2. Summary and comment

[a] Generally

Many defendants who kill their spouse or former spouse have some history of subjecting that individual to some form of abuse, either physical harm or a threat of harm. The prosecution in a marital homicide case often seeks to introduce evidence of the defendant's previous abusive behavior toward the victim during the trial, either through questioning the defendant himself regarding past incidents or by presenting other witnesses to testify as to the defendant's actions. In determining the admissibility of such evidence, the courts are guided by general evidentiary principles.

It is not competent to prove a defendant committed the charged crime or offense by showing he committed other crimes or offenses of a like nature. It is a well-established common-law rule that in a criminal prosecution, evidence which shows or indicates that the defendant committed other crimes or offenses at other times is incompetent and inadmissible for the purpose of showing that he committed the crime or offense for which he is currently being tried, unless the other crimes or offenses are an element of or are legally connected

494

FIGURE 4–17   An example of related annotations in A.L.R.

Contents of A.L.R.

The contents of A.L.R. have changed with the different series. Each series provides detailed case summaries for the cases found within the annotation. The editors of Lawyers Cooperative select a representative case for each article in the first four series and insert that case in front of the annotated article. The fifth series has discontinued the practice of including the representative case. Lawyers Cooperative inserts headnotes summarizing the legal points in the representative case much like West Publishing does for its digest system.

Cases on the same subject may reach different results, or cases may be distinguishable because the facts were different. In other situations, cases may reach the same result but employ different reasoning to reach that result. Lawyers Cooperative groups the case summaries in the A.L.R. annotation under different subheadings to illustrate these variations in the cases. Cases holding for one principle are found under one heading, and cases holding for another principle are found under another heading. Each annotation is given a main title, and after that title is a table of contents for the article. (See Figure 4–18.)

Because these articles may be quite lengthy, there is also a descriptive word index in some of the articles. (See Figure 4–19.)

One feature common to many Lawyers Cooperative articles is the "Total Client-Service Library References." (See Figure 4–20.) This section contains references to other resources published by Lawyers Cooperative that pertain to the annotated subject.

For researchers who are interested only in the law of a particular jurisdiction, there is a "Jurisdictional Table of Cited Statutes and Cases" that shows the reader which subsections of the A.L.R. annotation contain cases from a specific jurisdiction. (See Figure 4–21.) As noted above, there is one section of the A.L.R. annotation called "Related Annotations" that refers the reader to other annotations on related legal matters. There also may be sections near the beginning of the annotation entitled "Summary and Comment" and "Practice Pointers." These sections explain some of the main concerns involved in handling a case in this area of the law.

Using the Different A.L.R. Series

From series to series, Lawyers Cooperative has added or changed the structure of the A.L.R. articles. As mentioned, Lawyers Cooperative has discontinued the practice of placing a representative case before the A.L.R. article beginning with the fifth series. Different A.L.R. series also use different updating methods.

Main topic ←———————————→ "BLOOD SPLATTER" EVIDENCE   9 ALR5th
                                    9 ALR5th 369

Table of Contents

Research References
Index
Jurisdictional Table of Cited Statutes and Cases

ARTICLE OUTLINE

I. PRELIMINARY MATTERS

§ 1. Introduction
    [a] Scope
    [b] Related annotations
§ 2. Summary and comment
    [a] Generally
    [b] Practice pointers

II. ADMISSIBILITY BASED ON TESTIMONY'S EFFECT ON JURY'S ROLE

§ 3. Testimony assisting jury in understanding matters requiring specialized knowledge
§ 4. Testimony concerning matters not beyond common experience

III. ADMISSIBILITY BASED ON WHETHER EVIDENCE IS RELIABLE

A. "GENERAL ACCEPTANCE" TEST FOR DETERMINING RELIABILITY

§ 5. View that evidence may be admitted without proof of general acceptance in scientific community
§ 6. General acceptance in scientific community as circumstance supporting admissibility
    [a] General acceptance established
    [b] General acceptance not established

B. OTHER CONSIDERATIONS IN DETERMINING RELIABILITY

1. EVIDENCE OFFERED BY PROSECUTION

§ 7. Regarding blood at scenes examined during criminal investigation—generally
    [a] Reliability established
    [b] Reliability not established

FIGURE 4–18   An example of a main title and its table of contents from A.L.R.

9 ALR5th   "BLOOD SPLATTER" EVIDENCE ←————————————→ Main topic
                              9 ALR5th 369

RESEARCH SOURCES

The following are the research sources that were found to be helpful in compiling this annotation:

Texts

1 Am Jur Trials 555, Locating and Preserving Evidence in Criminal Cases § 58

3 Am Jur Trials 427, Preparing and Using Experimental Evidence § 23

McDonnell, Flight Characteristics and Stain Patterns of Human Blood (1971)

Torcia, Wharton's Criminal Evidence (14th Ed) §§ 547, 549, 573 (1987)

Encyclopedias

29 Am Jur 2d, Evidence §§ 103, 104, 818, 825, 826, 1104

31A Am Jur 2d, Expert Opinion and Testimony §§ 432-36, 55-59, 214, 300

40 Am Jur 2d, Homicide §§ 413, 421, 422, 444

23 CJS, Criminal Law § 1063, n 50

32 CJS, Evidence §§ 546(70), 546(99)

41 CJS, Homicide § 242

Electronic Search Query

blood w/3 (splatter or splatter or pattern) w/20 (analy! or interpret! or investiga! or evidence)

West Digest Key Numbers

Criminal Law 388(1), (2); 404(2); 448(8); 468, 469; 472; 475; 476(1); 476.6; 477-481; 486(1), (2), (4), (8), (10); 487; 488; 494; 1153(2), (6); 1168(1), (2); 1169.1(3), (7); 1169.2(1), (2), (4), (8); 1169.9; 1170(1)

←——————

INDEX

Accidental injury or death claim, §§ 3, 6[a], 7[a], 12, 14[a], 15[a]
Aggravated battery, §§ 3, 4, 19
Aggravated rape, § 14[a]
Alteration of crime scene, § 15[a]
American Academy of Forensic Science, §§ 12, 15[a]
American Society of Clinical Pathologists, § 12
Angle at which blood struck surface, §§ 6[a], 7[a], 8, 15[a]
Army Criminal Investigation Command, §§ 3, 14[a]
Assault, §§ 3, 5, 14[a]

FIGURE 4–19 An example of a descriptive word index from an annotation article

Main topic ←————————————→ "BLOOD SPLATTER" EVIDENCE   9 ALR5th

9 ALR5th 369

Research References

————→ TOTAL CLIENT-SERVICE LIBRARY® REFERENCES

The following references may be of related or collateral interest to a user of this annotation:

Annotations

See the related annotations listed in § 1[b].

Encyclopedias and Texts

29 Am Jur 2d, Evidence §§ 103, 104, 818, 825, 826; 30 Am Jur 2d, Evidence § 1104; 31A Am Jur 2d, Expert and Opinion Evidence §§ 32-36, 55-67, 300; 40 Am Jur 2d, Homicide §§ 413, 421, 422, 444

12 Federal Procedure, L Ed, Evidence §§ 33:131, 33:145; 33 Federal Procedure, L Ed, Witnesses §§ 80:130-80:140, 80:147-80:149

Practice Aids

7 Federal Procedural Forms, L Ed, Criminal Procedure §§ 20:955, 20:1036

8 Am Jur Pl & Pr Forms (Rev), Criminal Procedure, Form 295; 10 Am Jur Pl & Pr Forms (Rev), Expert and Opinion Evidence, Forms 21-27; 23 Am Jur Pl & Pr Forms (Rev), Trial, Forms 188-190; 25 Am Jur Pl & Pr Forms (Rev), Witnesses, Forms 188-190

2 Am Jur Proof of Facts 585, Blood Tests; 40 Am Jur Proof of Facts 2d 1, Blood Typing

1 Am Jur Trials 555, Locating and Preserving Evidence in Criminal Cases § 58 (Blood Drop Patterns); 2 Am Jur Trials 293, Locating Scientific and Technical Experts; 3 Am Jur Trials 427, Preparing and Using Experimental Evidence § 23 (Blood Drops); 7 Am Jur Trails 477, Homicide

Federal Statutes

USCS, Rules of Criminal Procedure, Rule 16

Digests and Indexes

L Ed Digest, Evidence § 851.5

ALR Digest, Evidence §§ 855.5, 1391, 1392, 1427.5

ALR Index, Blood Tests; Coroners and Medical Examiners; Evidence; Exclusion and Suppression of Evidence; Experiments and Tests; Expert and Opinion Evidence; Homicide; Pictures and Photographs

Auto-Cite®

Cases and annotations referred to herein can be further researched through the Auto-Cite® computer-assisted research service. Use Auto-Cite to check citations for form, parallel references, prior and later history, and annotation references.

Additional resources ←———→

FIGURE 4–20   The Total Client-Service Library References by Lawyers Cooperative Publishing

Jurisdictional Table of Cited Statutes and Cases*

UNITED STATES

Mustafa v United States (1986) 479 US 953, 93 L Ed 2d 392, 107 S Ct 444, 21 Fed Rules Evid Serv 913—§ 2[b]

United States v Mustafa (1986, CMA) 22 MJ 165—§§ 2[b], 3, 5, 14[a]

United States v Russell (Jul 17, 1992, CA4 Va) No. 91-5110, 1992 US App LEXIS 16203—§ 17[b]

ALABAMA

Leonard v State (1989, Ala App) 551 So 2d 1143—§§ 2[b], 12, 14[a], 15[a]

Robinson v State (1990, Ala App) 574 So 2d 910—§§ 2[b], 12, 14[a], 20

ALASKA

Crawford v Rogers (1965, Alaska) 406 P2d 189—§§ 3, 15[a]

Pedersen v State (1966, Alaska) 420 P2d 327—§§ 2[b], 3, 6[a], 15[a]

CALIFORNIA

People v Allen (1969, 5th Dist) 275 Cal App 2d 428, 79 Cal Rptr 793—§ 2[b]

People v Carter (1957) 48 Cal 2d 737, 312 P2d 665—§§ 2[b], 3, 6[a], 11[a]

People v Hogan (1982) 31 Cal 3d 815, 183 Cal Rptr 817, 647 P2d 93—§ 14[b]

FIGURE 4–21 A jurisdictional table of statutes and cases found in the Total Client-Service Library References

A.L.R.1st

The first volume for the first series of A.L.R. was published in 1919. Many of the articles in that series are outdated or have been superseded by other articles in later series. There is a separate index for this set called the "Quick Index for A.L.R." There is also a *Word Book* and *Digest* that can be used to access annotations. This series is kept up-to-date with a set of books called the *Blue Book of Supplemental Decisions*, which consists of seven permanent volumes. This set is updated annually by a pamphlet that replaces the prior year's pamphlet. Figure 4–22 is a page from this *Blue Book of Supplemental Decisions*.

The *Blue Book of Supplemental Decisions* contains citations to cases that relate to each original annotation. The difficulty with using this set is that it includes only the case name and citation, and no summary of any case principles. The researcher must read the cases to see how the principles were used and how the cases were decided.

A.L.R.2d

After Lawyers Cooperative reached volume 175 of the A.L.R., it began renumbering with the next volume as volume 1 of A.L.R.2d. Lawyers Cooperative also changed to a different method of updating with this second series. The A.L.R.2d is updated by the *A.L.R.2d Later Case Service*. (See Figure 4–23.) In hard volumes, each annotation is updated with case summaries of cases that pertain to the original annotation. The *Later Case Service* is updated by pocket parts. A paralegal can locate annotations in the second series rather easily by consulting the *Index to Annotations*, which covers all later series of A.L.R. as well.

A.L.R.3d

Once Lawyers Cooperative reached volume 100 of A.L.R.2d, it began another series. The third series added new features to the annotations. Beginning with the third series, the publisher added the "Total Client-Service Library References" section. Typically, articles in the third series follow this format:

(1) a representative case;
(2) a title and author;
(3) the Total Client-Service Library References section;
(4) a table of contents;
(5) an index (using descriptive terms);
(6) the table of jurisdictions represented;
(7) a scope note;
(8) a related matters section;

102 ALR   SUPPLEMENTAL DECISIONS   388

102 ALR 641-648

U.S.—U. S. v Charles (CA5 Tex) 738 F2d 686

U. S. v Burger (CA2 NY) 739 F2d 805

U. S. v Falcon (CA10 Colo) 766 F2d 1469

Jordan v I. (ED Wis) 567 F Supp 1365

U. S. v Olsen (DC Me) 609 F Supp 1154

U. S. v Shears (DC Md) 614 F Supp 1096

Ala.—Ex parte Shula, 465 So 2d 452

Ex parte Callahan, 471 So 2d 463
Ex parte Weeks, 531 So 2d 643
Shula v S. (App) 465 So 2d 448
Shula v S. (App) 465 So 2d 455

Alaska.—Ridgely v S. (App) 705 P2d 924

Ariz.—S. v Montes, 136 Ariz 491, 667 P2d 191

S. v Reffitt, 145 Ariz 452, 702 P2d 681

S. v Lucas, 146 Ariz 597, 708 P2d 81

S. v Adams (App) 145 Ariz 566, 703 P2d 510

S. v Spence (App) 146 Ariz 142, 704 P2d 272

Cal.—P. v Dingle (4th Dist) 174 Cal App 3d 21, 219 Cal Rptr 707

P. v Underwood (2d Dist) 175 Cal App 3d 745, 221 Cal Rptr 249

Fla.—Roman v S., 475 So 2d 1228, 10 FLW 495

Howard v S. (App D3) 473 So 2d 10, 10 FLW 1740

Ga.—Matthews v S., 167 Ga App 28, 305 SE2d 846

S. v Osborne, 174 Ga App 521, 330 SE2d 447

Ill.—P. v Barber, 116 Ill App 3d 767, 72 Ill Dec 472, 452 NE2d 725

P. v Gore, 116 Ill App 3d 780, 72 Ill Dec 330, 452 NE2d 583

P. v Allen, 116 Ill App 3d 996, 72 Ill Dec 383, 452 NE2d 636

P. v Ellison, 126 Ill App 3d 985,

S. v Hardeman (App 2d Cir) 467 So 2d 1163

S. v Holmes (App 2d Cir) 467 So 2d 1177

S. v Boudreaux (App 5th Cir) 467 So 2d 1335

S. v Allen (App 1st Cir) 470 So 2d 650

S. v Braud (App 4th Cir) 475 So 2d 29

S. v Rogers (App 2d Cir) 476 So 2d 942

S. v Duncan (App 4th Cir) 478 So 2d 992

S. v Phillips (App 1st Cir) 479 So 2d 515

S. v Horton (App 1st Cir) 479 So 2d 528

S. v Roux (App 3d Cir) 487 So 2d 1226

Me.—S. v Franklin, 463 A2d 749
Md.—Brittingham v S., 63 Md App 164, 492 A2d 354
Mich.—P. v Jordan, 149 Mich App 568, 386 NW2d 594
Mo.—S. v Allen (App) 684 SW2d 417

S. v Rogers (App) 686 SW2d 472
S. v Brown (App) 698 SW2d 9
S. v Bailey (App) 714 SW2d 590
S. v Curry (App) 714 SW2d 798
N.M.—Aguilar v S., 106 NM 798, 751 P2d 178
N.Y.—P. v Young (2d Dept) 122 App Div 2d 863, 505 NYS2d 729
S.C.—S. v Adams, 279 SC 228, 306 SE2d 208
Tex.—Perkins v S. (App Tyler) 654 SW2d 534
Vt.—S. v Harvey, 145 Vt 654, 497 A2d 356
W.Va.—S. v Cook, 332 SE2d 147
S. v Fauber, 332 SE2d 625

102 ALR 672

Kan.—S. ex rel. Tomasic v K. C. 237 Kan 572, 701 P2d 1314

102 ALR 716-747

Wash.—Miotke v S., 101 Wash 2d 307, 678 P2d 803

102 ALR 937-938

Supplemented 114 ALR 136♦

102 ALR 943-964

Conn.—Nauss v P., 2 Conn App 400, 480 A2d 568

102 ALR 1019-1031

U.S.—Bashor v R. (CA9 Mont) 730 F2d 1228

Ferrazza v M. (CA6 Mich) 735 F2d 967

Briley v B. (CA4 Va) 742 F2d 155, 16 Fed Rules Evid Serv 1021

Miller v S. (CA9 Cal) 757 F2d 988

Aldrich v W. (CA11 Fla) 777 F2d 630

Harris v S. (CA2 NY) 779 F2d 875

Rogers v C. (CA1 Mass) 833 F2d 379

U. S. v Wagner (CA9 Cal) 834 F2d 1474

Richardson v J. (CA11 Ala) 864 F2d 1536

Godfrey v F. (ND Ga) 613 F Supp 747

Ala.—Ex parte Julius, 455 So 2d 984

Ex parte Baldwin, 456 So 2d 129
Ex parte Wright, 494 So 2d 745
Crowe v S. (App) 435 So 2d 1371
Daly v S. (App) 442 So 2d 143
Lucy v S. (App) 443 So 2d 1335
Wyllie v S. (App) 445 So 2d 958
Bracewell v S. (App) 447 So 2d 815
Wakefield v S. (App) 447 So 2d 1325
Clark v S. (App) 451 So 2d 368
Nelson v S. (App) 452 So 2d 1367
Perry v S. (App) 453 So 2d 762
Perry v S. (App) 455 So 2d 999
Hurst v S. (App) 469 So 2d 720
Eslava v S. (App) 473 So 2d 1143
Horsley v S. (App) 476 So 2d 623
Gray v S. (App) 482 So 2d 1318
Hill v S. (App) 516 So 2d 876
Turner v S. (App) 542 So 2d 1314
Allen v S. (App) 546 So 2d 1009

FIGURE 4–22   An excerpt from the *Blue Book of Supplemental Decisions* for A.L.R. references

LATER CASE SERVICE   **57 ALR2d 242–260**

all net income and earnings in testator's son, and directed that the rest and residue of the estate "then held by said bank . . . be delivered to the child or children of [son] that are living at his death, share and share alike," with the limitation that trustee "will continue to handle and manage said estate until [son's] youngest child reaches the age of twenty-one (21) years," an undivided one-third beneficial interest in the estate vested in each of the minor children of testator's son upon the son's death. Pickering v Miles (1972, **Tex**) 477 SW2d 267.

57 ALR2d 242–260

Liability for injury to property inflicted by wild animal.

§ 1. Scope and related matter, p. 243.

Beekeeping regulation: validity and construction. 55 ALR4th 1223.

Liability of governmental entity for damage to motor vehicle or injury to person riding therein resulting from collision between vehicle and domestic animal at large in street or highway. 52 ALR4th 1200.

Liability for damage to motor vehicle or injury to person riding therein from collision with runaway horse, or horse left unattended or untied in street. 49 ALR4th 653.

Liability for personal injury or death caused by trespassing or intruding livestock. 49 ALR4th 710.

Liability of owner of animal for damage to motor vehicle or injury to person riding therein resulting from collision with domestic animal at large in street or highway. 29 ALR4th 431.

Personal injuries inflicted by animal as within homeowner's or personal liability policy. 96 ALR3d 891.

Governmental liability from operation of zoo. 92 ALR3d 832.

Keeping bees as nuisance. 88 ALR3d 992.

Liability for injury or damage caused by bees. 86 ALR3d 829.

Liability of owner of dog known by him to be vicious for injuries to trespasser. 64 ALR3d 1039.

Zoo as nuisance. 58 ALR3d 1126.

Liability of owner or operator of business premises for injuries to patron caused by insect or small animal. 48 ALR3d 1257.

Dog owner's liability for damages from motor vehicle accident involving attempt to avoid collision with dog on highway. 41 ALR3d 888.

Owner's or keeper's liability for personal injury or death inflicted by wild animal. 21 ALR3d 603.

Liability for injury inflicted by horse, dog, or other domestic animal exhibited at show. 80 ALR2d 886.

Law as to cats. 73 ALR2d 1032.

Liability for damage to motor vehicle or injury to person riding therein by animal at large in street or highway. 59 ALR2d 1328.

Validity, construction, and application of Animal Welfare Act (7 USCS §§ 2131 et seq.). 36 ALR Fed 627.

18 Am Jur Pl & Pr Forms (Rev), Nuisances, Form 141. Complaint, petition or declaration—For equitable relief from nuisance and for damages—Injury to crops from wild geese attracted by artificial pond.

Auto-Cite®: Cases and annotations referred to herein can be further researched through the Auto-Cite® computer-assisted research service. Use Auto-Cite to check citations for form, parallel references, prior and later history, and annotation references.

§ 3. Absolute liability or nonliability, p. 245.

Owner or keeper of zebra held strictly accountable for property damage caused when zebra escaped. Smith v Jalbert (1966) 351 **Mass** 432, 221 NE2d 744.

Pigeons are ferae naturae and in that state their activities create no liability; a private person cannot be held liable for trespasses of animals which are ferae naturae and which have not been reduced to possession. Seaboard A. L. R. Co. v

FIGURE 4–23 An excerpt from the *A.L.R.2d Later Case Service*

(9) practice pointers;

(10) background and summary; and

(11) the article broken down into sections for and
      against the legal principle.

The A.L.R.3d is updated by pocket parts.

A.L.R.4th

The A.L.R.4th series is essentially like the third series. The fourth series is also updated by pocket parts. Since the publication of A.L.R.4th, Lawyers Cooperative has added new features to the fifth series, so as of September 1992, the publisher has added these new features to the A.L.R.4th supplements. These changes include providing references to texts, law reviews, and encyclopedias from other publishers, electronic search queries, and West key number references.

A.L.R.5th

Lawyers Cooperative recently began a fifth series. As already noted, this series heralded some changes. First, this series eliminated the representative case from the front of each annotation. (This case is now placed in the back of the volume.) Second, in addition to the Total Client-Service Library References section that references only materials published by Lawyers Cooperative, this series added a section called "Research References" that references works by other publishers including encyclopedias, law reviews, treatises, and even West digest key numbers. This section also provides words to use in computer searches, called "electronic search queries." These are the same searches Lawyers Cooperative's editors used to compile the articles. Although the syntax of these queries is specific to LEXIS, these queries can be easily modified to search on WESTLAW. Both LEXIS and WESTLAW are on-line computer research methods that are discussed in Chapter 7. This is a helpful aid to legal research. This series is updated by pocket parts.

Lawyers Cooperative has recently added two new updating methods. Subscribers to A.L.R.5th can call the Latest Case Service 800 number to get the latest case citations and references. Also, subscribers receive an *A.L.R.5th Alert* newsletter offering a preview of articles scheduled for the next volume. (See Figure 4–24.)

A.L.R Fed

Most of the early A.L.R. articles dealt with state law problems. In 1969, Lawyers Cooperative began the A.L.R. Fed. to deal with federal

31 ALR 5th Alert

Route To:

☐ _____   ☐ _____
☐ _____   ☐ _____
☐ _____   ☐ _____
☐ _____   ☐ _____
☐ _____   ☐ _____

To Our Subscribers:

This ALR5th Alert is published by Lawyers Cooperative Publishing as a service for ALR users. It reviews annotations in the accompanying volume and previews annotations scheduled for the *next ALR volume.* Advance copies of annotations from the *next* volume can be obtained by calling (716) 546-5530 ext. 3333 between 8:30 a.m. and 4:30 p.m. Eastern Time.

We hope this advance notice saves you the time and expense of research we've already done. This service is one more way we're helping you use your time—and your ALR—more productively.

ANNOTATIONS IN VOLUME 31

▌ MEDICAL MALPRACTICE—Negligent catheterization

Your client, a general surgeon, has been sued by a patient claiming injuries caused by a catheter fragment that became dislodged from an intravenous device inserted by the surgeon. What will the plaintiff be required to prove? Will res ipsa loquitur apply? Is expert testimony necessary to establish negligence on the part of your client? Even if the fragment dislodged for reasons other than negligence, might liability be based on some later act or omission, such as the failure to discover or recover the fragment, or to diagnose and treat a resulting injury or complication? As catheters and catheterization procedures have become indispensible elements of modern medical care, this timely annotation offers an intensive analysis of the legal theories and factual allegations that have been presented on the subject of negligence in connection with all types of catheterization procedures. Listed among several pointed Research References are Am Jur Proof of Facts articles on such topics as the failure to discover breakage of a surgical instrument (10 Am Jur POF2d 605) and negligent injections and infusions (36 Am Jur POF2d 637), as well as Am Jur Trials articles on defending hospitals and physicians in medical malpractice cases (19 Am Jur Trials 431, 16 Am Jur Trials 471). The Practice Pointers include tips on using expert testimony and statutes of limitation. Check the Related Annotations for coverage on issues such as the standard of care owed by a medical specialist (18 ALR4th 603), liability for instrument breakage in the course of treatment (20 ALR4th 1179), and damages for internal injuries (16 ALR4th 238). 31 ALR5th 1

▌ DAMAGES—Measure and elements of damages for injury to bridge

Apart from the London Bridge, most bridges are not bought and sold, and therefore do not have a market value. Accordingly, the market value measure of damages becomes irrelevant when a bridge owner, be it a public entity or a private owner, seeks to recover damages for a bridge that has been damaged or destroyed. Based on the recognition that the market value is not the most appropriate standard for assessing damages for injury to a bridge, courts have used a variety of other measures for evaluating the loss, such as the cost of replacement, repair, or restoration to the original condition. This annotation analyzes the cases discussing the proper measure of damages to be applied when a bridge is injured or destroyed, with consideration also given to the elements of damages recoverable, including consequential damages such as clean-up costs and lost revenue. Evidentiary matters,

FIGURE 4–24   A.L.R. *Alert* newsletter

issues. This series is accessed in the same way as the other A.L.R. series. It also is updated by pocket parts.

Specialty A.L.R.s

Lawyers Cooperative now collects all annotations on certain topics into specialty sets. These annotations can be found in the other A.L.R. series but are collected for the legal professional who deals in a particular area of the law. There are single volumes on such matters as wrongful death, drunk driving, and the Federal Rules of Evidence. There are two multivolume sets on environmental law and federal criminal law. Figure 4–25 is a chart of these specialty A.L.R.s.

FIGURE 4–25
An example of
specialty A.L.R.s

Specialty A.L.R.s

Age Discrimination: Critical Issues and Proof

ALR Critical Issues: Drunk Driving Prosecutions

ALR Critical Issues: Freedom of Information Acts

ALR Critical Issues: Trademarks

ALR Critical Issues: Wrongful Death

Automobile Insurance Practice Guide

Consumer and Borrower Protection: Practice Guide

Consumer Credit: ALR Annotations

Damages: ALR Annotations

Employee Dismissal: Critical Issues and Proofs

Employment Discrimination: Practice Guide

Environmental Law: ALR Annotations

Federal Criminal Law and Procedure: ALR Annotations

Forfeitures: ALR Annotations

Handling Sexual Harassment Cases: Practice Guide

Hedonic Damages: Critical Issues and Proofs Regarding Damages
for Loss of Enjoyment of Life

Pre-Natal Injuries and Wrongful Life: Practice Guide

Some Research Hints about A.L.R.

The A.L.R. provides selective access to case law research. If there is an A.L.R. annotation on an issue of law, that article will provide most, if not all, the research needed on the subject. However, there are many issues that have not been annotated, and the A.L.R. annotation may not include cases from the jurisdiction being researched. In these situations, the researcher will need to look for an alternative research method.

The A.L.R. is simple to use. A paralegal should have little problem using the six-volume index covering A.L.R. Fed. and A.L.R.2d through A.L.R.5th. The annotations are written in understandable language, and updates are found in most sets (except A.L.R.1st and A.L.R.2d) in the pocket parts. When issues are covered by A.L.R. annotations, the paralegal will find the research to be quite beneficial.

Words and Phrases

Courts often decide cases as to the meaning of a word in a statute or transaction document. West Publishing has a set of books called *Words and Phrases* (see Figure 4–26) that collects references to these cases. The books contain summaries of the cases and citations to the cases. The set is updated by pocket parts. When a word has a doubtful meaning in a statute or other authority or in a transaction document, *Words and Phrases* helps you locate cases that may have settled the meaning of the word.

Like the digests and the A.L.R., *Words and Phrases* is basically a case finder. However, *Words and Phrases* is not used nearly as frequently as the digests or the A.L.R. This set is consulted mainly when the researcher needs case authority for word definitions or interpretations.

Minor having temporary automobile driver's permit held "so licensed" within statute imputing negligence to sponsor signing minor's application for "operator's license". Pontius v. McLain, 298 P. 541, 545, 113 Cal. App. 452.

Authorization to do business is not equivalent to "licensed" to do business in the sense used in statute providing that a corporation may be sued in any judicial district in which it is licensed to do business or is doing business. Sawyer v. Soaring Soc. of America, Inc., D.C.N.Y., 180 F.Supp. 209, 213.

A brewing company which has paid into the state treasury the fees required to be paid by manufacturers to obtain the privilege under Act June 21, 1897, P.L. 176, 47 P.S. § 412, and Act July 30, 1897, P.L. 464, 47 P.S. § 341, of selling liquors to dealers, is "licensed" within Act June 12, 1913, P.L. 490, 47 P.S. § 621, prohibiting the offering of premiums by any corporation licensed to sell liquors for the return of caps, stoppers, corks, stamps, or labels, though it has not received a license from the court of quarter sessions. Commonwealth v. Mutual Union Brewing Co., 97 A. 206, 207, 252 Pa. 168.

An incorporated brewing company may be convicted of violating Act June 12, 1913, P.L. 490, 47 P.S. § 621, which prohibits the offering of premiums for the return of caps, stoppers, corks, stamps, or labels, although the company has not received a license from the court of quarter sessions, if it appears that it has availed itself of the provisions of Act June 21, 1897, P.L. 176, 47 P.S. § 412, and has paid into the state treasury the fees required to be paid by manufacturers for the purpose of obtaining the benefits of Act June 21, 1897, P.L. 176, 47 P.S. § 412, and Act July 30, 1897, P.L. 464, 47 P.S. § 341. Such a company is "licensed" within the meaning of Act June 12, 1913, P.L. 490, 47 P.S. § 621. Commonwealth v. Mutual Union Brewing Co., 58 Pa.Super. 647, 649.

LICENSED DOCTOR, PHYSICIAN OR SURGEON

The general term "licensed physicians" comprehends licensed osteopaths. Commonwealth v. Cohen, 15 A.2d 730, 732, 733, 142 Pa.Super. 199.

25 W. & P.—18

Chiropractor held not "licensed physician or surgeon" who, to justify recovery under health policy, must be in regular attendance on insured. Erdman v. Great Northern Life Ins. Co., 235 N.W. 260, 261, 253 Mich. 579.

Although chiropractor may practice medicine, he does not thereby become "licensed doctor, physician, or surgeon". Erdman v. Great Northern Life Ins. Co., 235 N.W. 260, 261, 253 Mich. 579.

In will contest, admission in evidence of confidential statements made by testatrix to Christian Science practitioners held proper, such unlicensed practitioners not being "licensed physicians or surgeons," in statutory sense. In re Mossman's Estate, 6 P.2d 576, 577, 119 Cal.App. 404.

Licensed osteopathic physicians are "licensed physicians," excepted by Anti-Narcotic Act from prohibition of prescription of opium and derivatives thereof. Commonwealth v. Cohen, 15 A.2d 730, 732, 733, 142 Pa.Super. 199.

An osteopathic physician and surgeon licensed by the state medical board to practice osteopathy and surgery in the state is a "licensed physician" within statute defining eligibility for the office of coroner. State ex rel. Kester v. North, 26 N.E.2d 1020, 1021, 136 Ohio St. 523.

The term "licensed physicians" in provision of Anti-Narcotic Act, excepting such physicians from operation thereof, refers to physicians licensed by commonwealth through boards or agencies created by Legislature for such purpose. Commonwealth v. Cohen, 15 A.2d 730, 732, 733, 142 Pa.Super. 199.

Under statute providing that a "licensed physician or surgeon" shall not, without consent of patient, be examined as witness as to any information acquired in attending patient necessary to enable him to prescribe or act for patient the quoted words apply to a person not prohibited by statute regulating practice of medicine, surgery and obstetrics from practicing in the state. State v. Fouquette, 221 P.2d 404, 420, 67 Nev. 505.

The Statutory Construction Act, defining "physician" as individual licensed under laws of commonwealth to engage in practice of medicine and surgery does not affect

FIGURE 4–26 *Words and Phrases,* a West resource, aids in finding legal definitions

Summary

- A digest is a method used to locate citations to relevant court cases.

- The *West digest system*, the most widely used digest system, contains case summaries under subtopics. Each subtopic is assigned a number, which is referred to as a headnote or key number.

- To access the appropriate headnote or key number, the researcher usually refers to the descriptive word index or scans a specific topic.

- Most digests are updated by pocket parts and pamphlets; however, the *American Digest System* is updated by adding new volumes to the set.

- West has published digests for most states. In addition, there are regional digests, federal digests, specialty digests, a digest for locating Supreme Court cases, as well as the *American Digest System* that covers all jurisdictions.

- The *American Law Reports*, commonly called the A.L.R., published by Lawyers Cooperative, contains articles on selected issues of law.

- The main method used to locate articles in the A.L.R. is through the multivolume index that provides citations to all A.L.R. annotations except for the A.L.R.1st series.

- There are different methods for updating A.L.R. annotations. A.L.R.1st is updated by the *Blue Book of Supplemental Decisions* and an annual pamphlet. A.L.R.2d is updated by the *A.L.R.2d Later Case Service* which is, in turn, updated by pocket parts. The other series are updated by annual pamphlets.

- West publishes a set of books called *Words and Phrases* that collects case summaries and citations for cases that have defined or interpreted a word or phrase.

Review Questions

1. Compare the similarities and differences between a digest and an A.L.R.

2. Identify the different sets of digests. How do you decide what digest to begin with in legal research? Explain.

3. Describe the various digests available for researching federal cases.

4. How are the different sets of digests updated?

5. Explain the basic process that is followed in researching with a digest.

6. When does a legal researcher use the *American Digest System?* How is the set different from other digests?

7. What are the similarities and differences of the different series of A.L.R.?

8. What are the methods that can be used to locate A.L.R. articles?

9. Describe the typical contents of an A.L.R. annotation.

10. How are the different A.L.R. series updated?

Research Projects

1. Using the topic and key number Negligence 131, list the citation for the first case that appears under that entry in each of the following digests:

    a. your state or regional digest;

    b. the *Federal Practice Digest 4th*; and

    c. the *Ninth Decennial* digest.

    Update the research of your state's law under Negligence 131 by looking for more recent cases in the pocket parts, any pamphlets, and the advance sheets. List any cases you find by this method.

2. A developer wants to put a zoo on land next to some property owned by John Doe. Locate any A.L.R. annotations that pertain to whether a zoo is a nuisance. In connection with this problem, tell how you updated your search and whether there are any related annotations.

IIII
CHAPTER 5

SECONDARY RESEARCH AIDS

There are times when a legal professional simply does not know how to begin a research project. Maybe the legal professional is researching in an area new to that professional, or maybe the area is quite complicated. When faced with such a situation, the legal professional needs tools that can provide background information on the subject being researched.

There are other times when the legal professional is able to find the applicable law, but has difficulty understanding what he or she has read. Perhaps the case law has conflicting results or draws narrow distinctions. Perhaps the law is convoluted and difficult to sort through. In these situations, the researcher needs tools that can provide the necessary explanation or interpretation of the law.

At even other times, a legal professional may be searching for theoretical support for a novel legal theory. Or the legal professional may need an authoritative statement of a legal expert to support a certain approach. In these cases, the researcher wants resource tools that can provide analysis or opinion on a legal question.

Function of Secondary Sources

Research of the law involves more than looking up law and reading it. The researcher needs a proper perspective of the law. The legal professional, for example, must understand how a law interrelates with other laws, and must appreciate subtle distinctions drawn by the case law. Secondary source materials help legal professionals gain this insight into law.

Earlier chapters have examined primary legal sources and research tools that are used mainly for locating primary law sources; this chapter examines research tools that provide explanations or analysis of law. This grouping is somewhat arbitrary, since some texts already discussed fall into both categories. The A.L.R., for example, not only provides case summaries; it also contains practice pointers, legal explanations, and background information. But even though the A.L.R. contains expository statements about legal principles, it is frequently used for case-finding purposes.

By the same token, legal encyclopedias, treatises, and legal periodicals covered in this chapter do more than just provide explanation and analysis. These sources also can be used, like the digests or the A.L.R., as case-finding sources. In practice, some legal professionals feel more comfortable with an encyclopedia for finding case citations than with a digest, and certainly some researchers use an encyclopedia as a principal method for finding case citations.

Encyclopedias, treatises, legal periodicals, the Restatements, and continuing legal education materials each provide information about the law, although each of these tools uses a different approach. Sometimes, on a major research project, the researcher may consult each of these sources. On other research projects, the researcher may glance at only one of these tools. This chapter is about secondary research tools used by legal professionals to educate themselves about the law.

Encyclopedias

Almost all elementary school students turn to an encyclopedia when writing their first term papers. Faced with panic and little knowledge of the subject, the elementary student usually finds that the encyclopedia is written in a user friendly manner and provides the background information necessary for understanding the topic being researched. The encyclopedia also directs the young researcher to references for follow-up research. Legal encyclopedias serve many of these same purposes for the inexperienced paralegal researcher or any other legal professional who may lack depth of knowledge about the law. The paralegal will find legal encyclopedias to be written in understandable language and loaded with references to cases and statutes.

Function of Legal Encyclopedias

Legal research usually begins with mastering the general principles of law applicable to a particular matter. Then the researcher tries to find even narrower principles that fit more precisely the facts of the problem. An encyclopedia is especially important in the initial phase of this process. Legal encyclopedias provide general background information on most legal topics, whether the researcher is exploring a complex antitrust problem or copyright question, or checking the law on a simple problem such as the grounds for a divorce.

Because paralegals often do not have the in-depth knowledge of attorneys, they may find legal encyclopedias especially useful in starting legal research. The paralegal should be cautioned, however, that a legal encyclopedia often lacks depth of coverage, since encyclopedias are designed primarily to give background or general information.

How to Use a Legal Encyclopedia

Legal encyclopedias are not difficult to use. Topics are arranged alphabetically. Under each main topic are various subtopics that further divide the legal points under that topic. To find any listing in the encyclopedia, you will need both a topic and subtopic reference.

The researcher can locate information in an encyclopedia by several methods: by a general index, by a topic approach, by a volume index, or by a table of authority.

General Index

Most legal encyclopedias have a general descriptive word index at the end of the set. This index is similar to the descriptive word index used with digests. As with most legal research material, this index will work well with the TAPP rule. Using basic vocabulary terms from a research problem, the researcher can identify a specific topic and subtopic. (See Figure 5–1.)

FIGURE 5–1
An example of a general index found in a legal encyclopedia

RIOTS

RINGLEADER
Defined, Vol. 77

RINGWORM
Aliens, exclusion proceedings, dangerous disease, weight of evidence, Aliens § 124
Damages, pleading disease of skin resembling, **Damag** § 135
Workmen's compensation, evidence, Work C § 555(11)

RINKS
Roller Skates and Roller Skating, generally, this index

RINSING DEVICES
Patents, priority of invention, evidence, Pat § 89

RIOTER
Defined, Vol. 77

RIOTOUS
Defined, Vol. 77

RIOTS AND MOBS
Generally, see Title Index to Criminal Law
Obstructing Justice or Governmental Administration
Affray, distinguished, **Affray** § 3

RIOTS AND MOBS—Continued
Constitutional law—Continued
Exemption of municipality for liability as denial of due process, Const Law § 643
Freedom of speech and of press as permitting making of statements inciting, **Const Law** § 213(5)
Liability for acts of, due process of law as violated by statute imposing, Const Law § 637
Municipal liability for damage to property, equal protection of laws, **Const Law** § 553
Violence, criminal trial dominated by as denial of due process, Const Law § 591
Contempt, sheriff making no effort to protect prisoner, Contempt § 21
Corporations, protection from, failure to file acceptance of state constitution as affecting right, **Corp** § 990
Counties, injuries by, liability, **Counties** § 219
Death, actions causing death, parties, **Death** § 64
Defined, **Riot** §§ 1, 2
Disorderly conduct, distinguished, **Disord C** § 1
Extradition, flight because of fear, fugitive from justice, **Extrad** § 10
False imprisonment, deporting from state, **False Imp** §§ 9, 18
Force and Violence, this index
Habeas corpus,

A Topic Approach

Sometimes the legal researcher knows what topic in the encyclopedia to look under, but not the subtopic. For example, you may know that the question you are researching will fall under the Criminal Law topic. In this case, you can turn directly to the volume that deals with that topic and find a summary outline and a detailed outline. These topic outlines can be used to locate a specific subtopic reference. (See Figure 5–2.)

77 C. J. S.

Main topic ━━━━━━━━━━━━━━━━━━━━━━▶ ROBBERY

This Title includes taking, with intent to steal, personal property in possession of another, from his person or in his presence, against his will, by force or by putting him in fear, and attempts and assaults with intent to commit such offenses; nature and elements of the crime of robbery and of degrees thereof; nature and extent of criminal responsibility therefor, and grounds of defense; and prosecution and punishment of such acts as public offenses.

Matters not in this Title, treated elsewhere in this work, see Descriptive-Word Index

Analysis

I. OFFENSES AND RESPONSIBILITY THEREFOR, §§ 1–32

II. PROSECUTION AND PUNISHMENT, §§ 33–59
  A. INDICTMENT OR INFORMATION, §§ 33–44
  B. EVIDENCE, §§ 45–47
  C. TRIAL, §§ 48–50
  D. SENTENCE AND PUNISHMENT, §§ 51–59

III. ATTEMPTS AND ASSAULTS WITH INTENT TO ROB, §§ 60–76
  A. OFFENSES AND RESPONSIBILITY THEREFOR, §§ 60–67
  B. PROSECUTION AND PUNISHMENT, §§ 68–76

IV. BANK ROBBERY, §§ 77–78

V. ROBBERY WITH HOMICIDE, §§ 79-81

VI. ROBBERY WITH RAPE, §§ 82–84

Summary outline *(bracket label)*

Sub-Analysis

I. OFFENSES AND RESPONSIBILITY THEREFOR—p 446

§ 1. Definitions and distinctions—p 446
   2. Nature and elements of offense in general—p 449
   3. Taking or asportation in general—p 450
   4. Nature of property taken—p 451
   5. —— Choses in action and documents evidencing them—p 451
   6. Value of property taken—p 451
   7. Ownership of property taken—p 452
   8. —— Contraband property—p 454
   9. Taking from person, presence, or possession of another—p 454
  10. Force or intimidation—p 455
  11. —— Prior, contemporaneous, and subsequent force or intimidation generally—p 457
  12. —— Previous force without accompanying purpose to rob—p 457
  13. —— Subsequent force to aid escape—p 457
  14. —— Subsequent force to prevent recapture of property—p 458
  15. —— What constitutes force in general—p 458
  16. —— What constitutes intimidation in general—p 459

Subtopic outline *(bracket label)*

FIGURE 5–2 Using the topical approach to legal research with a legal encyclopedia

Volume Index

In the back of the individual volumes of an encyclopedia, there is usually a descriptive word index for matters referenced in that volume. (If a topic is covered in more than one volume, the index for that topic will be in the last volume in which that topic is covered.) Generally, this index is similar to the descriptive word index at the end of the set, although sometimes the index will refer the reader to the index at the end. The volume index is typically used when a researcher has looked under a specific topic and needs to find more specific references in that volume. These volume indexes may not be updated by the pocket parts, so caution must be used when applying this approach.

Tables of Authority

Encyclopedias also provide tables to aid in locating relevant citations. For example, *American Jurisprudence, Second Edition* (Am. Jur. 2d) has a volume entitled "Table of Statutes, Rules and Regulations Cited." (See Figure 5–3.) If you begin your research with a specific citation, this approach can help you quickly find the relevant texts on the topic. However, this is not the most commonly used technique for finding specific references.

Contents of the Encyclopedia

Most encyclopedias begin with the main topic heading. Under this heading may be a **scope note** telling the researcher what is covered and not covered under a particular topic. There also may be a section dealing with matters treated elsewhere. (See Figure 5–4.) The topical index (summary and detailed outlines), discussed above, follows the scope note and provides the various subtopics under the main heading.

Each point of law in the encyclopedia is extensively footnoted. (See Figure 5–5.) Thus, a researcher can find case citations or other law in the footnotes, which is the reason an encyclopedia is used by many legal professionals as a case finder.

LEGAL TERMS

scope note A note following a heading in a reference book that describes what is covered under that particular topic.

TABLE OF STATUTES CITED

This table shows, by reference to title and section, where provisions of the United States Code Service, the Federal Rules of Procedure, and the Uniform Laws are cited in articles in this volume.

UNITED STATES CODE SERVICE

Title and section	Am Jur 2d title and section	Title and section	Am Jur 2d title and section
7 USCS		15 USCS—Cont'd	
§ 1431	WELFARE LAWS § 26	§ 242	WEIGHTS & MEASURES § 40
§ 2011	WELFARE LAWS § 26	§§ 271–278c	WEIGHTS & MEASURES § 37
§ 2012(b)	WELFARE LAWS § 26	§ 272	WEIGHTS & MEASURES § 37
§ 2012(e)	WELFARE LAWS § 26	§ 272(1)	WEIGHTS & MEASURES § 37
§ 2012(f)	WELFARE LAWS § 26		
§ 2012(h)	WELFARE LAWS § 26	§ 272(2)	WEIGHTS & MEASURES § 37
§ 2013	WELFARE LAWS § 27		
§ 2013(a)	WELFARE LAWS § 26	§ 272(3)	WEIGHTS & MEASURES § 37
§ 2013(b)	WELFARE LAWS §§ 26, 27		
§ 2013(c)	WELFARE LAWS § 27	§ 272(4)	WEIGHTS & MEASURES § 37
§ 2014(a)	WELFARE LAWS § 26		
§ 2014(b)	WELFARE LAWS §§ 26–28	§ 272(5)	WEIGHTS & MEASURES § 37
§ 2016(a)	WELFARE LAWS § 26		
§ 2016(b)	WELFARE LAWS § 26	§ 272(a)	WEIGHTS & MEASURES § 37
§ 2017(a)	WELFARE LAWS §§ 26, 28		
§ 2018	WELFARE LAWS § 26	§ 277	WEIGHTS & MEASURES § 37
§ 2019(b)	WELFARE LAWS § 27	§ 903(d)	WEAPONS & FIREARMS § 32
§ 2019(c)	WELFARE LAWS § 27	18 USCS	
§ 2019(h)	WELFARE LAWS § 26	§§ 921–928	WEAPONS & FIREARMS § 33
§ 2019(i)	WELFARE LAWS § 26		
§ 2023	WELFARE LAWS § 105	§ 922(a)(1)	WEAPONS & FIREARMS § 33
§ 2025	WELFARE LAWS § 26		
15 USCS		§ 922(a)(2)	WEAPONS & FIREARMS § 33
§ 201	WEIGHTS & MEASURES § 38		
§ 202	WEIGHTS & MEASURES § 38	§ 922(a)(5)	WEAPONS & FIREARMS § 33
§ 203	WEIGHTS & MEASURES § 38		
§ 204	WEIGHTS & MEASURES § 39	§ 922(a)(6)	WEAPONS & FIREARMS § 33
§ 231	WEIGHTS & MEASURES § 40		
§ 232	WEIGHTS & MEASURES § 40	§ 922(b)(1)	WEAPONS & FIREARMS § 33
§ 233	WEIGHTS & MEASURES § 40		
§ 234	WEIGHTS & MEASURES § 40	§ 922(b)(2)	WEAPONS & FIREARMS § 33
§ 235	WEIGHTS & MEASURES § 40		
§ 236	WEIGHTS & MEASURES § 40	§ 922(b)(4)	WEAPONS & FIREARMS § 33
§§ 237–242	WEIGHTS & MEASURES § 40		
§ 237	WEIGHTS & MEASURES § 40	§ 922(b)(5)	WEAPONS & FIREARMS § 33
§ 238	WEIGHTS & MEASURES § 40		
§ 240	WEIGHTS & MEASURES § 40	§ 922(c)	WEAPONS & FIREARMS § 33
§ 241	WEIGHTS & MEASURES § 40	§ 922(d)	WEAPONS & FIREARMS § 33

xix

FIGURE 5–3 The table of statutes found in Am. Jur., a legal encyclopedia published by Lawyers Cooperative

ᴀMERICAN JURISPRUDENCE

SECOND EDITION

Volume 22

Main topic ────────────────→ **DAMAGES**

by

Jack K. Levin, J.D., Irwin J. Schiffres, J.D.,
Robert R. Crane, J.D. and John B. Spitzer, J.D.

─────→ Scope of topic: This article covers general principles of the law of damages. It includes a discussion of the various kinds of damages—compensatory damages, nominal damages, liquidated damages, and exemplary and punitive damages—as well as of such concepts as general and special damages, prospective damages, and mitigation of damages. The elements and measure of damages in breach of contract, personal injury, and property damage cases are also covered, as are the pleading, proof, and determination of the amount of damages to be awarded in a lawsuit.

Federal aspects: Treatment of the measure and elements of damages awarded under federal statutes is discussed in such articles as 18 Am Jur 2d, Copyright and Literary Property §§ 234 et seq.; 35 Am Jur 2d, Federal Tort Claims Act §§ 103 et seq.; 45B Am Jur 2d, Job Discrimination §§ 2420 et seq.; 54 Am Jur 2d, Monopolies, Restraints of Trade, and Unfair Trade Practices §§ 360 et seq.; 60 Am Jur 2d, Patents §§ 1113 et seq.; and 70 Am Jur 2d, Securities Regulation —Federal §§ 562 et seq. (As to federal taxation relating to the topic, see "Tax References," infra.)

─────→ Treated elsewhere:

Application of general principles governing the award of damages in particular types of tort actions, see, for example, 6 Am Jur 2d, Assault and Battery §§ 178 et seq.; 18 Am Jur 2d, Conversion §§ 105 et seq.; 32 Am Jur 2d, False Imprisonment §§ 134 et seq.; 37 Am Jur 2d, Fraud and Deceit §§ 342 et seq.; 50 Am Jur 2d, Libel and Slander §§ 349 et seq.; 52 Am Jur 2d, Malicious Prosecution §§ 93 et seq.; 75 Am Jur 2d, Trespass §§ 49 et seq.

Measure and elements of damages arising out of breaches of particular types of contracts, see, for example, 13 Am Jur 2d, Building and Construction Contracts §§ 76 et seq.; 43, 44 Am Jur 2d, Insurance §§ 439 et seq., 1771 et seq.; 67A Am Jur 2d, Sales §§ 1109 et seq., 1277 et seq.

Damages in actions arising out of certain relationships, see, for example, 7 Am Jur 2d, Attorneys at Law § 226; 8 Am Jur 2d, Bailments §§ 346 et seq.; 10 Am Jur 2d, Banks §§ 218, 574 et seq., 737 et seq.; 14 Am Jur 2d, Carriers §§ 1197 et seq.; 49 Am Jur 2d, Landlord and Tenant §§ 183 et seq., 1124 et seq.; 61 Am Jur

1

FIGURE 5–4   "Scope of topic" and "Treated elsewhere" narrow and expand, respectively, topical research in a legal encyclopedia

§ 27   BIGAMY   10 Am Jur 2d

ries her to avoid a prosecution for seduction cannot defend against a subsequent bigamy prosecution on the ground that the marriage was coerced.[17]

§ 27. Statute of limitations.

The offense of bigamy is complete when the second marriage is consummated. The statute runs from that time, and unless the indictment is found within the statutory period of limitation from that time, the prosecution is barred.[18] However, where cohabitation following a bigamous marriage is made a crime, the statute does not begin to run until the cohabitation ceases.[19]

IV. PROSECUTION AND PUNISHMENT

A. JURISDICTION AND VENUE

§ 28. Generally; application of bigamy statute to foreign bigamous marriage.

The basic principle that jurisdiction over crimes is local and that no state can punish for a crime committed in another state applies to prosecutions for bigamy; such prosecutions must be brought in the jurisdiction where the crime, which is the second marriage, was committed.[20] The rule that the criminal laws of the state can have no extraterritorial force has been consistently enforced and recognized in jurisdictions making the second marriage the gist of the offense.[1] Thus, although in England a statute allows bigamy to be prosecuted even though the second marriage was solemnized outside the jurisdiction,[2] a statute of like import, enacted in the United States, mak-

---

Footnotes

mous marriage the morning after a peaceful but insistent mob visited him and demanded that he marry his subsequent spouse.

17. Medrano v State, 32 Tex Crim 214, 22 SW 684, involving a promise to the defendant, under arrest on a seduction charge, that the prosecution would be dismissed on his marrying the girl allegedly seduced, no more than what was expressly provided for by statute under such circumstances.

18. Scoggins v State, 32 Ark 205; Gise v Commonwealth, 81 Pa 428 (court rejected contention that offense of bigamy was continuous and limitation did not begin to run as long as the criminal act—"having two wives or two husbands at one and the same time"—continued).

See also Pitts v State, 147 Ga 801, 95 SE 706, where the court rejected the state's contention that by virtue of the statutory definition bigamy was a continuing offense so long as a person who has committed it continued in knowingly having a "plurality of husbands or wives at the same time," so that a prosecution therefor is not barred by limitations if commenced within the period specified after such "having," although not within the statutory period after the second or unlawful marriage ceremony.

19. State v Sloan, 55 Iowa 217, 7 NW 516; Commonwealth v Ross, 248 Mass 15, 142 NE 791.

20. McBride v Graeber, 16 Ga App 240, 85 SE 86; Johnson v Com. 86 Ky 122, 5 SW

365; People v Devine, 185 Mich 50, 151 NW 646; Wilson v State, 16 Okla Crim 471, 184 P 603.

1. Green v State, 232 Ind 596, 115 NE2d 211; State v Stephens, 118 Me 237, 107 A 296; People v Devine, 185 Mich 50, 151 NW 646; People v Mosher (NY) 2 Park Crim 195; State v Ray, 151 NC 710, 66 SE 204.

2. See People v Hess, 286 App Div 617, 146 NYS2d 210, setting out the statute involved, defining the offense as being committed by any person, being married, who "shall marry any other person during the life of the former husband or wife, whether the second marriage shall have taken place in England, or elsewhere," and summarizing Reg. v Topping, Dears CC 647, 169 Eng Reprint 881, in which a British subject who resided in England and contracted a bigamous second marriage in Scotland was held properly tried and convicted on his return to England.

In Rex v Brinkley, 14 Ont L 434, the validity of a statute in effect making punishable the act of a British subject resident in Canada who leaves the jurisdiction with the intent to go through a bigamous marriage and who contracts such a marriage outside the jurisdiction, was sustained on the broad general ground that it is necessary for the welfare of the state to protect it from the effect of lax laws in neighboring states, and on the technical ground that where part of the crime occurs within the jurisdiction, the whole of it may be punished there, and part of the crime is leaving the jurisdiction with intent to contract a bigamous marriage.

988

FIGURE 5–5   Footnotes expand the scope of research and should be considered carefully by the researcher

SIDEBAR   It is important to remember that an encyclopedia reference is not law, but merely a discussion of the law. It is a secondary source of law. It is also important to remember that encyclopedias often oversimplify legal concepts. For these reasons, encyclopedias usually are not cited as authority to a court unless the legal professional is citing them for a background point or for a point that is well-accepted. Some texts even say you should never cite an encyclopedia. If you find a statement in the encyclopedia that supports a position or argument, look at the footnoted cases or other law that supports the statement. Then cite that law, not the encyclopedia, but only after reading it and determining that the cases do indeed support your argument.

Different Types of Encyclopedias

Encyclopedias are classified as national encyclopedias, local encyclopedias, and specialty encyclopedias. National encyclopedias describe generally the law throughout the United States. Because the law may vary, national encyclopedias will be written quite generally. Local encyclopedias describe the law in specific states. Specialty encyclopedias provide coverage of the law on a specific topic.

National Encyclopedias

Both West Publishing and Lawyers Cooperative publish national encyclopedias. The West Publishing set is named *Corpus Juris Secundum* (C.J.S.) and Lawyers Cooperative's set is named *American Jurisprudence, Second Edition* (Am. Jur. 2d). Figure 5–6 is a sample page from C.J.S., and Figure 5–7 is a sample page from Am. Jur. 2d. Basically, these sets summarize general legal principles without emphasis on the law of any particular jurisdiction. Both sets also cover certain areas of federal law.

Corpus Juris Secundum (C.J.S.)

C.J.S. provides a comprehensive overview of case law in the United States with some discussion of federal and state statutory law as well. There are over four hundred topics covered alphabetically in this set, starting with Abandonment and ending with Zoning. Under each topic is a scope note identifying the content of the topic and an analysis section giving a breakdown of the topic. Each subtopic or subtitle contains a thorough discussion that is preceded by statements of **black letter law** that summarize the applicable legal principles.

––––––––––––––––––––– **LEGAL TERMS** –––––––––––––––––––––

black letter law†   Fundamental and well-established rules of law.

§ 1   *GAMING*   38 C.J.S.

I. IN GENERAL

§ 1. Definitions, Descriptions, and Distinctions

    a. In general
    b. Game and terms relating to games
    c. Bet, wager, and terms related thereto
    d. Gambling, gaming, and other terms descriptive of acts
    e. Terms descriptive of persons
    f. Terms descriptive of places
    g. Terms descriptive of things used
    h. Terms relating to speculation
    i. Other and miscellaneous words and phrases

a. In General

The definitions, descriptions, and distinctions of terms germane to this title and contained in the following subdivisions of this section are limited to such terms as used in the criminal law of gaming and its kindred offenses and the civil law governing gambling transactions. Other meanings that such terms may possess are discussed in their proper alphabetical sequence elsewhere throughout this work.

b. Game and Terms Relating to Games

    (1) Game
    (2) Classification of games
    (3) Particular games defined or described

(1) Game

> The term "game" is a very comprehensive one which may embrace any contrivance or institution which has for its object the furnishing of sport, recreation, or amusement.

The term "game" is a very comprehensive one which may embrace any contrivance or institution which has for its object the furnishing of sport, recreation, or amusement,[1] or any sport or amusement, public or private.[2] It may be defined broadly as an amusement or diversion;[3] a contest, physical or mental, conducted according to set rules and undertaken for amusement or recreation or for winning a stake;[4] a contest for success or superiority in a trial of chance, skill, or endurance which may be against other players or against an ideal standard.[5] It includes physical contests, whether of man or beast, when practiced for the purpose of deciding wagers, or for the purpose of diversion, as well as games of hazard or skill by means of instruments or devices,[6] but it is not so comprehensive as to include everything on which a bet or wager may be laid.[7] Questions of what are games within the prohibition of particular penal statutes are considered infra § 86.

The term is also used as meaning a single contest, or a single match at play.[8]

The term "game" or "games" may also be used to designate the instrumentalities used in playing

1. U.S.—Mills Novelty Co. v. U. S., Ct.Cl., 50 F.2d 476, 477.
Cal.—Ex parte Williams, 16 P.2d 172, 173, 127 Cal.App. 424.
Mass.—Commonwealth v. Theatre Advertising Co., 190 N.E. 518, 521, 286 Mass. 405.
27 C.J. p 968 note 5 [a].

Matters held included by term
(1) Betting on horse race.—Sofas v. McKee, 124 A. 380, 382, 100 Conn. 541.
(2) Dog fight.—Grace v. McElroy, 1 Allen, Mass., 563.
(3) Foot race.—Swaggard v. Hancock, 25 Mo.App. 596.
(4) Wrestling game.—Desgain v. Wessner, 67 N.E. 991, 161 Ind. 205.
(5) A machine called "Jig-Saw Blow Ball" with a mechanism producing a current of air which propelled a light ball into holes in the back panel thereof some of which were "live" giving a predetermined score and others "dead" allowing no score, held a game.—C. R. Kirk & Co. v. U. S., Ct.Cl., 37 F.Supp. 934, 936.

Matters held not included by term
(1) Automatic phonographs which dispense what is commonly called "canned music."—Garrison v. Luke, 78 P.2d 1120, 1122, 52 Ariz. 50.
(2) Horseback riding.—White v. Aronson, Mass., 58 S.Ct. 95, 97, 302 U.S. 16, 82 L.Ed. 20, affirming, C.C.A., Aronson v. White, 87 F.2d 272, vacating, D.C., 13 F.Supp. 913, and certiorari granted White v. Aronson, 57 S.Ct. 794, 301 U.S. 675, 81 L.Ed. 1336.
(3) Jig-saw puzzles.—White v. Aronson, supra.
(4) Knitting for diversion.—White v. Aronson, supra.
2. Conn.—Sofas v. McKee, 124 A. 380, 381, 100 Conn. 541, quoting **Corpus Juris.**
27 C.J. p 968 note 3.
Similar definition
A game is any sport.—Lasseter v. O'Neill, 135 S.E. 78, 80, 162 Ga. 826, 49 A.L.R. 1076.
Public game
A game held out or given to the public.—People v. Poole, 89 N.Y.S. 773, 774, 44 Misc. 118.

3. U.S.—White v. Aronson, Mass., 58 S.Ct. 95, 96, 302 U.S. 16, 82 L.Ed. 20, affirming, C.C.A., Aronson v. White, 87 F.2d 272, vacating, D.C., 13 F.Supp. 913, and certiorari granted White v. Aronson, 57 S.Ct. 794, 301 U.S. 675, 81 L.Ed. 1336.
4. U.S.—White v. Aronson, supra.
5. Ariz.—Garrison v. Luke, 78 P.2d 1120, 1122, 52 Ariz. 50.
Similar definitions
(1) "Contest for success or superiority in a trial of chance, skill, or endurance, or any two or all three of these combined."—State v. Prather, 100 P. 57, 79 Kan. 513, 515, 131 Am.S.R. 339, 21 L.R.A.,N.S., 23—27 C. J. p 968 note 3 [a] (1).
(2) Other statements see 27 C.J. p 968 note 3 [a] (2)–(4).
6. Conn.—Sofas v. McKee, 124 A. 380, 381, 100 Conn. 541, quoting **Corpus Juris.**
27 C.J. p 968 note 4.
7. Ind.—Woodcock v. McQueen, 11 Ind. 14.
8. Utah.—People v. Sullivan, 33 P. 701, 9 Utah 195, 198.

FIGURE 5–6 A page from *Corpus Juris Secundum* (C.J.S.) (Reprinted by permission of West Publishing Company.)

I. NATURE AND ELEMENTS; DEFINITIONS

A. IN GENERAL

§ 1. Generally; gaming.

The word "gaming" as a legal term has been variously defined by courts, legal authors, lexicographers, and legislative enactments. Under many statutes having for their object the prohibition of all or various kinds of gaming, the terms "gaming" and "gambling" are defined as the same and treated as synonymous.[1] The definition of gaming as "a contract between two or more persons, by which they agree to play by certain rules at cards, dice, or other contrivances, and that one shall be the loser and the other the winner," is sometimes adopted.[2] A substantially similar statutory definition embodied in some codes provides that to "play at any game for any sum of money or other property of any value" is gambling.[3] A judicial definition is that gaming is "an agreement between two or more persons to risk their money or property in a contest or chance of any kind where one may be gainer and the other loser,"[4] which does not substantially differ from the brief declaration that "to game is to stake money on a chance."[5] It has also been said that the word "gaming" has no technical meaning, but includes every contrivance or institution which has for its object any sport, recreation, or amusement for the public upon which money or any other article of value can be won or lost by the result of such contrivance or institution,[6] and includes bets or wagers made upon any physical contest, whether of man or beast, where practiced for the purpose of deciding such bets or wagers.[7] To condemn a device or program as gambling, there must be involved as a substantial feature in its operation the element of uncontrolled and uncontrollable chance.[8] The element of chance can be supplied by having the happening of some future event determine who gets a prize or how much he gets, at least where that

1. Jackson v State, 30 Ala App 114, 1 So 2d 601, cert den 241 Ala 141, 1 So 2d 602; Maine State Raceways v La Fleur, 147 Me 367, 87 A2d 674; People v Weithoff, 51 Mich 203, 16 NW 442; Opinion of Justices, 73 NH 625, 63 A 505.

A charge of keeping a room for gambling has been held to state no offense under a statute against keeping a room for gaming. State v Bullion, 42 Tex 77.

2. Ansley v State, 36 Ark 67; Shaw v Clark, 49 Mich 384, 13 NW 786.

3. State v Book, 41 Iowa 550.

The Model Anti-Gambling Act, which does not use the word "gaming," in § 2(2) defines "gambling" as "risking any money, credit, deposit or other thing of value for gain contingent in whole or in part upon lot, chance or the operation of a gambling device."

4. Portis v State, 27 Ark 360; Bell v State, 37 Tenn (5 Sneed) 507.

5. Reinmiller v State, 93 Fla 462, 111 So 633; Shaw v Clark, 49 Mich 384, 13 NW 786.

6. James v State (Okla Crim) 113 P 226.

Anything which induces men to risk their money or property without any hope of return other than to get for nothing any given amount from another is gambling. First Nat. Bank v Carroll, 80 Iowa 11, 45 NW 304.

7. § 3, infra.

8. Rouse v Sisson, 190 Miss 276, 199 So 777, 132 ALR 998.

Generally, it may be said that the elements of gambling are payment of a *price* for a *chance* to gain a *prize*. Westerhaus Co. v Cincinnati, 165 Ohio St 327, 59 Ohio Ops 428, 135 NE2d 318.

FIGURE 5–7   A page from *American Jurisprudence* (Am. Jur.)

SIDEBAR

An earlier version of the C.J.S. encyclopedia called *Corpus Juris* (C.J.) will reference very early cases, but it cannot be found in many libraries.

The footnotes to the text in C.J.S. contain citations to case law and references to the West key number system. A researcher can find definitions of words and phrases and legal maxims arranged alphabetically. (See Figure 5–8.)

C.J.S. is updated by annual pocket parts. At times West Publishing also sends replacement volumes for updating purposes.

American Jurisprudence, Second Edition (Am. Jur. 2d)

Am. Jur. 2d provides a comprehensive overview of the case law in the United States. It has greater emphasis on federal statutory law than C.J.S. and discusses uniform state laws (see Chapter 6) as well. Am. Jur. 2d also discusses state statutory law quite broadly. For researching statutes, this set contains a Table of Statutes Cited in each volume (see Figure 5–3). This table covers the *United States Code,* rules of federal procedure, and uniform laws.

The topics in Am. Jur. 2d are arranged alphabetically. There are over four hundred topics in this set. Each topic contains a scope note, a cross-reference section, and an analysis of the section subheadings. The footnotes reference cases, A.L.R. annotations, and other research aids. In fact, Lawyers Cooperative lists Am. Jur. 2d as an important tool for locating citations to A.L.R. articles.

Am. Jur. 2d is updated by cumulative annual pocket parts. In addition, there is a looseleaf book called *New Topic Service* that contains new titles of current interest not covered in the original set. Sometimes the publisher uses a bound volume for the new topic. Am. Jur. 2d is also updated by volume replacement; in fact, Lawyers Cooperative sends new volumes annually to replace the volumes dealing with federal taxation. Am. Jur. 2d replaced an earlier set called *American Jurisprudence,* which superseded a set called *Ruling Case Law.*

Lawyers Cooperative also publishes a *Deskbook* along with Am. Jur. 2d that provides reference information about the court system and the federal government. This set contains professional standards for the legal profession, financial information such as mortality tables and interest tables, and other pertinent information about the legal system. (See Figure 5–9.)

Researchers often find Am. Jur. 2d to be more up-to-date in its coverage because this set was written more recently than C.J.S. More coverage of federal statutory law can be found in Am. Jur. 2d than in C.J.S. While C.J.S. cites more to West Publishing materials, Am. Jur. 2d cites

CRIMEN. The Latin noun "crimen, criminis" means crime; also an accusation or charge of crime.[71]

The Spanish word "crimen" also means, in Spanish law, crime, although a more common term is "delito." A distinction, however, is drawn between the two in this, that "delito" is general and includes all infractions of the penal laws, while "crimen" refers particularly to the most serious ones and those which are punished by afflictive or infamous penalties.[72]

CRIMEN EX POST FACTO NON DILUITUR.[73]

CRIMEN LÆSÆ MAJESTATIS OMNIA ALIA CRIMINA EXCEDIT QUOAD PŒNAM.[74]

CRIMEN OMNIA EX SE NATA VITIAT.[75]

CRIMEN TRAHIT PERSONAM.[76]

CRIMEN VEL PŒNA PATERNA NULLAM MASCULAM FILIO INFLIGERE POTEST.[77]

CRIMINAL.

As a Noun

A person who has committed a crime; one who is guilty of a felony or misdemeanor.[78] The word is of broad significance and includes those who may have committed the most trifling infractions of a penal statute, as well as those guilty of the most heinous offenses.[79]

Phrase: "Apprehending criminals."[80]

As an Adjective

Punishable by law, human or divine;[81] also that which pertains to or is connected with the law of crimes, or the administration of penal justice, or which relates to or has the character of a crime.[82] When used with reference to judicial proceedings, the term "criminal" is opposed to "civil" see Civil 14 C.J.S. p 1154 note 61, and, in its most comprehensive meaning, may be regarded as including all cases for the violation of the penal law.[83]

FIGURE 5–8 Legal definitions found in C.J.S. (Reprinted by permission of West Publishing Company.)

Item No. 340

Accident Reconstruction: Speed and Skidmarks

Speed formula

Total stopping distance = Reaction distance + Braking distance

Reaction distance (in feet) = 1.47 × Speed (in mph)
[This assumes a reaction time of 1 second.]

$$\text{Braking distance (in feet)} = \frac{(\text{Speed in mph})^2}{30.25 \times \text{Coefficient of friction of pavement}}$$

Speed in miles per hour = 0.682 × Speed in feet per second

Speed in feet per second = 1.47 × Speed in miles per hour

Acceleration formula

The following simple acceleration formula enables one to determine the length of time it takes a vehicle to get from a stopped position to some other point:

$$\text{Time required (in seconds) to start and travel a certain distance in feet} = K + \sqrt{\frac{1.365}{a}}$$

S = distance reached in feet

a = acceleration in mph per second

K = perception time plus time to shift gears

From ½ second to one second should be used for K.

Information on the performance characteristics of the particular vehicle involved can be obtained by calling the auto dealer.

The acceleration in miles per hour per second to get from 0 to 10 mph should vary from 1.5 to 6, depending on the type of vehicle and its condition.

This formula should be used in analyzing accidents involving stop signs, red lights, driveway accidents, and the like.

FIGURE 5–9   Sample page from the Am. Jur. *Deskbook* published by Lawyers Cooperative Publishing

more to Lawyers Cooperative materials. The choice of whether to use Am. Jur. 2d or C.J.S. is often a matter of personal preference or a question of which set is more readily available.

Local Encyclopedias

C.J.S. and Am. Jur. 2d are excellent sources for finding general principles of law, but frequently legal researchers are more concerned with the law of a particular state. Local encyclopedias are not published for all states; however, in the states where they are published, these sets cover broadly the case and statutory law for the state. A paralegal who is looking for a particular state law where there is an encyclopedia for that state, will often find it beneficial to start with that encyclopedia. This approach frequently leads to other sources.

State encyclopedias, like Am. Jur. 2d and C.J.S., usually contain scope notes. Many of these state encyclopedias are published by Lawyers Cooperative or West Publishing, so the format is similar to that found in C.J.S. or Am. Jur. 2d. For example, Lawyers Cooperative publishes the following state encyclopedias:

Florida Jurisprudence
New York Jurisprudence
Ohio Jurisprudence 2d
Texas Jurisprudence 2d

These sets use basically the same format as Am. Jur. 2d, except the coverage is restricted to the law of the state. Likewise, West Publishing follows the format of the C.J.S. in publishing the following encyclopedias:

California Jurisprudence 3d
Illinois Law and Practice
Maryland Law and Practice
Michigan Law and Practice

Some states have encyclopedias published by other private publishers.

Topics in these sets are arranged alphabetically, and footnotes reference both cases and statutes as well as other research aids. There is a topical index, a descriptive word index, and usually a volume index. These sets are updated by annual pocket parts and by volume replacement. The publisher also may provide semi-annual pamphlets to update the pocket parts.

Specialty Encyclopedias

In addition to national and local encyclopedias, there are encyclopedias that cover particular areas of the law rather than the entire gamut of law. These encyclopedias are referred to as specialty encyclopedias.

Because these encyclopedias focus on one area of the law, they are more like treatises than encyclopedias. Examples of such encyclopedias are the *Encyclopedia of Crime and Justice* (Sanford H. Kadish, ed., 1983) and the *Encyclopedia of the American Constitution* (Leonard W. Levy *et al.*, eds., 1986). These works cover only a particular topic and are more in-depth than the encyclopedias discussed previously. These encyclopedias are indexed and updated in the same manner as those described above.

Treatises

Treatises are texts written by legal experts on particular legal topics. Many treatises are scholarly works, and some treatises—such as *Williston's Law of Contracts*, *Corbin on Contracts*, and *Wigmore on Evidence*—are legal classics. Treatises can be cited to a court, and some treatises are given great weight by the courts; but even the best treatise is only persuasive authority. A court can accept or reject the reasoning of even the most authoritative treatise.

SIDEBAR   Treatises vary in quality. Some treatise writers are highly respected by legal professionals; other treatises are given little attention. Because some authors are more respected than others, the paralegal should not assume that any particular treatise will be given credence by courts or other legal professionals. In selecting a treatise, ask law librarians, attorneys, or other legal professionals whether the author is a respected authority. You might also determine whether the publisher of the treatise is one of the established law book publishers (West Publishing, Lawyers Cooperative, etc.), whether the treatise is current (that is, whether it has a current publication date or whether the pocket parts are recent), and whether the coverage is complete (for example, whether the topics correspond with any research you have already done). Remember that law is ever-changing and what was an accepted position twenty years ago may not be accepted now.

Function of Treatises

Treatises focus on certain areas of the law, such as personal injury, contracts, or evidence. A treatise usually is written to explain or interpret the law in that particular area. Some treatises are written to critique or analyze the law. A treatise might argue how the law ought to be. A treatise might even present a philosophical overview of the law.

Usually treatises provide more in-depth coverage of topics than encyclopedias. Unlike encyclopedias, which are not usually cited as authority to a court, treatises can prove quite persuasive to buttress a party's position, especially if the author of the treatise is well-respected. When a treatise is available, a paralegal invariably finds it useful in explaining the intricacies of the law on the topic covered by the treatise. Before asking an attorney for assistance on a research problem, read a treatise and try to answer your questions yourself.

Many treatises have multiple volumes—as many as twenty to thirty. Some treatises are only one volume. West Publishing publishes single volume treatises called **hornbooks.** A hornbook is used by many law students to educate themselves about the law, and certainly paralegals find them just as useful.

Content of Treatises

The format of a treatise will vary from publisher to publisher. Typically, however, there will be a descriptive word index or table of contents. There may be a summary table of contents for larger sets. Treatises usually are broken into chapters with detailed section headings and contain a table of authorities (cases and statutes) with exact page references to the text. The text of the treatise is extensively footnoted, like the text of the encyclopedia, so a treatise can be used to locate case or statutory authority. (See Figure 5–10.)

How to Use a Treatise

A treatise is used basically like an encyclopedia. The researcher consults either the descriptive word index or the detailed table of contents to locate the appropriate heading reference. These methods usually lead to a volume and page reference or a chapter and subtopic reference. The researcher also can check the table of authorities if a case or other citation is available. After reading the text, the researcher can identify citations from the footnotes that are pertinent to the research.

To find treatises in large law libraries, consult a card or computer catalog as you would to find a book in any other library. In card catalogs, you can access treatises by subject, author, or title. With computerized card catalogs, you also can use word search methods.

SIDEBAR

Under the Library of Congress system, look under the call letters "KF." In the Dewey Decimal system, look under numbers 340 to 349. Treatises also can be found on-line on a computer, and on CD-ROM.

───────────────── LEGAL TERMS ─────────────────

hornbook† A book that explains the fundamental aspects of an area or field of the law in basic terms. A hornbook is usually concise.

CIRCUMSTANCES CREATING EMOTION §390

alleged criminals have raised questions which ought to have been silently ignored by the courts — a treatment which would tend much to the discouragement of crime and the lightening of the profession's burden of precedents.

The *criminality* of the circumstances involved in proof of the motive has no doubt often been the ground of objection, the character rule (§194 *supra*) being invoked in exclusion. But it has already been seen (§216 *supra*) that the fact that the circumstance offered involves a crime by the defendant other than that charged is in itself no objection, if the circumstance is relevant for the present purpose.

A natural arrangement of the precedents would be according either to the various circumstances offerable or to the various emotions to be proved. Practically, however, it is not possible to attempt a consistent grouping on either principle; the precedents are therefore arranged in part on each principle.

§390. **Motives for murder.** The circumstances which might excite a desire to kill are innumerable. It must be understood that the rulings of the courts cover only those circumstances which counsel have cared to question, and that nowadays the fact that counsel care and dare to question a circumstance is not necessarily an indication that there is the slightest rationality in the question. The annals of trials illustrate many other circumstances judicially recognized as capable of becoming motives; and the absence of a ruling by an appellate court upon a particular circumstance casts no doubt upon its propriety. Among the instances most commonly offered for adjudication, the following may be noted:

Circumstances involving the *sexual passion,* in one aspect or another, and usually operating through the emotion of jealousy, may lead to a desire to kill.[1]

Footnotes

§390. 1 *Alabama:* Johnson v. State, 17 Ala. 618 (1850) (wife murder; the fact admitted that in the preceding year he had attempted to carry on a liaison with an unmarried woman nearby); Gafford v. State, 122 Ala. 54, 25 So. 10 (1889) (deceased's adulterous relations with the defendant's sister admitted to show the deceased's probable aggression; Tyson and Haralson, JJ., dissenting; Caddell v. State, 136 Ala. 9, 34 So. 191 (1903) (wife murder; defendant's relations with a paramour admitted); Rollings v. State, 160 Ala. 82, 49 So. 329 (1909) (murder; bad character of defendant's wife, without other evidence, excluded); Spicer v. State, 188 Ala. 9, 65 So. 972 (1914) (wife murder; defendant's relations with other women admitted); Powell v. State, 219 Ala. 557, 123 So. 34 (1929) (illicit relations with the deceased's sister); Woodard v. State, 253 Ala. 259, 264, 44 So. 2d 241, 245 (1950) ("The defendant admitted that during the first week after Dean's death he began to have sexual intercourse with the woman known as Dean's wife and who was living with Dean as his wife at the time of his death. It was not reversible error, therefore, for the State to show that prior to the death of Dean the defendant sought to have dates with this woman and asked her to go on long trips with him. Such testimony was admissibile as tending to show motive"); Williams v. State, 255 Ala. 229, 51 So. 2d 250 (1951) (infatuation with wife of deceased); Ray v. State, 257 Ala. 418, 59 So. 2d 582 (1952) (wife murder; defendant's relations with various girls).

Arkansas: Edmonds v. State, 34 Ark. 720 (1879) (murder of a paramour; violence of the defendant, a few days before, to their child in the deceased's presence, admitted to show his feelings towards the deceased); Ware v. State, 91 Ark. 555, 121 S.W. 927 (1909) (murder; defendant's seduction of deceased's daughter, unknown to deceased, excluded).

California: People v. Gress, 107 Cal. 461, 40 Pac. 752 (1895) (the defendant's efforts to induce the deceased's wife to leave the deceased excluded, because the killing was admitted and self-defense was the issue; this seems erroneous, because on the question whether the defendant was the aggressor, his prior motive to kill the deceased would be useful); People v. Brown, 130 Cal. 591, 62 Pac. 1072 (1900) (defendant's relations with the deceased's wife admitted); People v. Wright; 144 Cal. 161, 77 Pac. 877 (1904)

419

FIGURE 5–10 An example of an extensive footnote in a treatise on evidence (*Wigmore on Evidence,* Chadbourn, © 1979. Published by Little, Brown and Company.)

Treatises are not always available in small law libraries. Those that are available may not be particularly authoritative or widely accepted. When a good treatise is available, however, it almost always provides some insight and direction to the research. Before citing a treatise in a legal writing, the paralegal should see if the law does support the position taken by the treatise by reading the applicable primary authority, which often can be found in the footnotes.

Some treatises are not updated at all; others are updated only by printing new editions of the treatise. The most common method of updating treatises is probably pocket parts or supplemental pamphlets. Some treatises are in looseleaf binders and are updated by page replacements or looseleaf supplements that are inserted into the front or back of the binder. Looseleaf supplements often are tabbed, or the new pages may have different colors than the rest of the text, so the researcher can spot supplemental materials quickly.

Legal Periodicals

Legal periodicals are journals of articles written by judges, professors, law students, and legal experts on various legal topics. Legal periodicals are published by law schools, professional organizations, and law associations. The paralegal will almost certainly find new theories and ideas in legal periodicals.

Many law schools have a group of top law students who publish a law review for their school. The law review, as these students are called, decides what articles to publish. A law review may publish articles written by professors or by the students themselves. Some law schools also publish specialized scholarly journals that may be edited by professors or other scholars rather than law students. Some bar associations publish journals of articles. For example, the *American Bar Association Journal* contains articles on many practical issues of current interest. Other legal periodicals are published by special interest groups that deal only with certain topics, for example, the *Environmental Law Journal* and the *Products Liability Journal*.

Legal periodical articles usually are scholarly and provide considerable depth about issues of current interest. In a large university law library, the researcher will find aisle after aisle of these journals. However, paralegals working in smaller metropolitan areas may not have access to collections of legal periodicals except through interlibrary loan or computerized legal databases such as LEXIS or WESTLAW.

Legal periodicals may be published weekly, monthly, quarterly, or annually. Often legal periodicals are published in paperback format, and these pamphlets may be bound together. Journal articles span the body of law, dealing with multiple facets of law.

Because some articles are written by students and others by leading legal experts, and because some are published by the best law schools and others by schools of lesser quality, the depth and coverage of periodicals varies greatly. This is not to say that a particular article by a student from a smaller school might not be a classic, but only that the reader must be alert to the fact that not all statements made in these articles can be accepted without question. The paralegal should read every article critically.

Function of Legal Periodicals

Legal periodicals serve a variety of functions. It is not unusual for a legal periodical to identify an evolving area of law. A legal periodical can help sort through apparently confusing cases or complicated statutory developments and provide a rationale for the law. Typically, legal periodicals give researchers additional insight into the law. And because periodical literature is published so often, it is a rich source for the current thoughts on most topics of legal interest.

Some legal periodicals provide basic background information about the law. A legal periodical may survey the law. Other legal periodicals provide opinions or analysis of law. A legal periodical may be critical of a law or a trend in the law. Although legal periodicals are not used routinely in the initial phase of a research project, the articles in them do provide back-up citations for research. They can prove particularly productive, even in the initial phase of research, for the researcher looking into a unique or new area of the law.

In short, legal periodicals cover the gamut of legal issues: the routine and the unique, the simple and the complex. Figure 5–11 is an example of a page from the *Notre Dame Law Review*.

How to Find Legal Periodicals

The researcher sometimes stumbles upon a citation to a relevant article in a legal periodical when using a digest, encyclopedia, or other source. Citations are to particular journals (for example, the *Harvard Law Journal*) and provide volume and page references. The researcher simply looks for the correct volume of the journal and turns to the indicated page to locate the article.

To search for specific legal periodical articles, use one of the indexes that are available. The two most commonly used indexes are the *Index to Legal Periodicals* and the *Current Law Index*.

Corporate Sponsorships of Charity Events and the Unrelated Business Income Tax: Will Congress or the Courts Block the IRS Rush to Sack the College Football Bowl Games?

I. INTRODUCTION

On August 16, 1991 the Internal Revenue Service (IRS) issued a technical advice memorandum (TAM) which imposed an unrelated business income tax (UBIT) on corporate title sponsorship payments to two tax-exempt college football bowl games (bowl games).[1] Because exempt organizations received an estimated $1.1 billion from corporate sponsors in 1991,[2] the ruling created a wave of concern among all exempt organizations.[3]

The IRS must overcome several hurdles to impose UBIT on corporate sponsorships. First, exempt organizations can raise several legal challenges against the IRS position.[4] Second, the IRS must distinguish between the corporate sponsorships that are subject to UBIT and those that are exempt.[5] Finally, three bills are pending

---

1 Tech. Adv. Mem. 91-47-007 (Aug. 16, 1991). The IRS released the TAM to the public in late November 1991. The TAM has been referred to as the Cotton Bowl ruling, because the ruling applied specifically to the Mobil Cotton Bowl. The other bowl game initially affected was the John Hancock Bowl. *See, e.g.,* Thomas S. Mulligan, *IRS Ruling May Force Business Out of Athletics; Sponsors: A Decision to Make Nonprofits Pay Taxes on Corporate Contributions Could Affect Events All the Way to the Olympics,* L.A. TIMES, Dec. 24, 1991, at D2.

Title sponsors refer to corporate sponsors whose names are included in the name of the exempt organization's event, such as Mobil and John Hancock above. Twelve of the eighteen 1991/92 bowl games had title sponsors. *Id.*

2 *See* Dennis Zimmerman, *Corporate Title Sponsorship Payments to Nonprofit College Football Bowl Games: Should They Be Taxed?,* 1992 Rep. Cong. (CSR) No. 157E at 2-3 (Feb. 11, 1992), *available in* LEXIS, FedTax Library, TNT File (92 TAX NOTES TODAY 41-18 (1992)) (In 1991 total corporate sponsorship payments to tax-exempt organizations was "$1.1 billion, of which about $64 million was paid to the college football bowl organizations. Of this $64 million, an estimated $19.6 million was received for corporate title sponsorships rather than as corporate royalty payments.").

3 *See, e.g.,* Nancy Churnin, *IRS Move Threatens to Sack Key Stage Funding Source,* L.A. TIMES, Jan. 30, 1992, at F2; Mulligan, *supra* note 1; Dick Rosenthal & John D. Crow, *BACKTALK; Bowl-Game Taxes Hurt Charity, Schools and Business,* N.Y. TIMES, Feb. 9, 1992, § 8, at 11; Paul Streckfus, *Cotton Bowl Ruling Draws Fire at ASAE Roundtable Discussion,* 92 TAX NOTES TODAY 12-6 (1992), *available in* LEXIS, FedTax Library, TNT File.

4 *See infra* Parts III and V.

5 The IRS issued proposed examination guidelines to address this administrative

---

FIGURE 5–11 An excerpt from a law review article (Volume 67, Issue 4, *The Notre Dame Law Review* (1992) 1079–1120. Reprinted with permission. © by *Notre Dame Law Review,* University of Notre Dame.)

Index to Legal Periodicals

The paralegal who has researched magazine articles through the *Readers Guide to Periodical Literature* will feel comfortable with the *Index to Legal Periodicals* (H. W. Wilson Company). This index is the most commonly used index for finding legal periodicals. It is broken down into three categories: a subject and author index, table-of-cases and table-of-statutes indexes, and a book review index. Figure 5–12 is a page from the subject and author index. There is a cumulative index for the period 1926 to 1976, with supplemental volumes covering the period after 1976, including monthly pamphlets for the most recent year. These monthly pamphlets are cumulated quarterly in soft cover pamphlets and in a bound volume at the end of the year. Look at each monthly or quarterly pamphlet, at each supplemental volume, and under the appropriate subject in the cumulative volume to complete the search for articles.

The *Index to Legal Periodicals* provides access to over five hundred legal periodicals. It covers legal periodicals published since 1900 and can be searched on-line through both LEXIS and WESTLAW. There is a CD-ROM version of this index called WILSONDISC, also published by H. W. Wilson, but the CD-ROM version only covers journal articles since 1981.

SIDEBAR

The *Index to Legal Periodicals* publishes a thesaurus to help you penetrate the index. This thesaurus provides words that are narrower or broader than words you may have already tried. The thesaurus also tells the user what words are commonly used in the index.

Current Law Index

The *Current Law Index* (Information Access Corporation) covers legal periodicals published since 1980 and provides access to over seven hundred journals. The index is issued in pamphlets that are cumulated annually. The index is organized into a subject index, a table of cases, a table of statutes, and an author/title index. This index is also available in a CD-ROM format called *LegalTrac,* and it is available on-line to subscribers.

The advantage of using a CD-ROM version like *LegalTrac* or WILSONDISC is that the researcher does not have to look through volume after volume (a year-by-year search) for articles. The researcher can look under a particular heading and find all relevant references. *LegalTrac* covers approximately one hundred more journals than the *Current Law Index.*

INDEX TO LEGAL PERIODICALS

Handicap discrimination—*cont.*

Societal prejudice reflected in our courts: the unfavorable treatment of the mentally retarded. L. A. Lorenzo, student author. 2 *Seton Hall Const. L.J.* 771-803 Spr '92

Statutory sources of protection for the handicapped traveler. V. Jensen, student author. 57 *J. Air L. & Com.* 907-36 Summ '92

Tennis everyone?: The impact of the Americans with Disabilities Act on state recreational facilities. J. Muller, student author. 10 *Thomas M. Cooley L. Rev.* 169-85 '93

Wynne v. Tufts University School of Medicine [932 F.2d 19 (1991)]. K. Rottinghaus, student author, W. Wilds, student author. 19 *J.C. & U.L.* 185-98 Fall '92

New Mexico

Discrimination of people with disabilities and their federal rights—still waiting after all these years. P. Cubra. 22 *N.M. L. Rev.* 277-94 '92

Virginia

AIDS and the law of Virginia. K. E. Labowitz. 3 *Geo. Mason U. Civ. Rts. L.J.* 67-112 Fall '92

Handicapped persons

See also
  Handicap discrimination
  Mental health

Access to medical care for HIV-infected individuals under the Americans with Disabilities Act: a duty to treat. J. Cohen. 18 *Am. J.L. & Med.* 233-50 '92

Amateur athletes with handicaps or physical abnormalities: who makes the participation decision? M. J. Mitten. 71 *Neb. L. Rev.* 987-1032 '92

Architectural barriers legislation and the range of human ability: of civil rights, missed opportunities, and building codes. R. W. Andersen. 28 *Willamette L. Rev.* 525-45 Summ '93

Communicating with your deaf client. J. V. McCoy. 65 *Wis. Law.* 16-19+ N '92

Community mental health treatment for the mentally ill—when does less restrictive treatment become a right? S. E. Seicshnaydre, student author. 66 *Tul. L. Rev.* 1971-2001 Je '92

The conflict between "disabling" and "enabling" paradigms in law: sterilization, the developmentally disabled, and the Americans with Disabilities Act of 1990. J. C. Dugan, student author. 78 *Cornell L. Rev.* 507-42 Mr '93

Disability issues in legal education: a symposium. Introduction. L. F. Rothstein; Identifying and accommodating learning disabled law school students. M. K. Runyan, J. F. Smith, Jr.; Law schools and disabled faculty: toward a meaningful opportunity to teach. S. L. Mikochik; Accommodating hearing-impaired law students and faculty members. B. P. Tucker. 41 *J. Legal Educ.* 301-61 S/D '91

Disabling ambiguities: confronting barriers to the education of students with emotional disabilities. T. Glennon. 60 *Tenn. L. Rev.* 295-364 Wint '93

Employing and accommodating workers with disabilities: mandates and guidelines for labor relations. J. A. Mello. 44 *Lab. L.J.* 162-70 Mr '93

Federal policy on forgoing treatment or care: contradictions or consistency? B. J. Uddo. 8 *Issues L. & Med.* 293-308 Wint '92

The killing words? How the new quality-of-life ethic affects people with severe disabilities. T. HarveyParedes, student author. 46 *SMU L. Rev.* 805-40 Wint '92

The logic of identity and the politics of justice: establishing a right to community-based treatment for the institutionalized mentally disabled. B. A. Arrigo. 18 *New Eng. J. on Crim. & Civ. Confinement* 1-31 Wint/Summ '92

Medical treatment rights of older persons and persons with disabilities: 1991-92 developments. D. Avila. 8 *Issues L. & Med.* 429-66 Spr '93

Medical treatment rights of older persons and persons with disabilities: 1992 developments. D. Avila. 26 *Clearinghouse Rev.* 1267-76 Ja '93; 1303-16 F '93

No place to go: refusal of life-sustaining treatment by competent persons with physical disabilities. S. S. Herr, B. A. Bostrom, R. S. Barton. 8 *Issues L. & Med.* 3-36 Summ '92

Part H and EPSDT: helping at-risk infants and toddlers. T. E. Shanahan, student author, L. E. Cunningham. 27 *Clearinghouse Rev.* 2-10 My '93

Preserving the sixth amendment rights of the deaf criminal defendant. M.-L. Berko, student author. 97 *Dick. L. Rev.* 101-30 Fall '92

'Program accessibility': how courts can accommodate people with disabilities. J. A. Dooley, E. F. Wood. 76 *Judicature* 250-3 F/Mr '93

Publicly financed interpreter services for parochial school students with IDEA-B disabilities. D. S. Huefner, S. F. Huefner. 21 *J.L. & Educ.* 223-39 Spr '92

Voluntary active euthanasia: the next frontier? M. Johnson. 8 *Issues L. & Med.* 343-59 Wint '92

Withdrawing life-sustaining treatment from people with severe disabilities who request it: equal protection considerations. D. Coleman. 8 *Issues L. & Med.* 55-79 Summ '92

Arizona

Establishment clause prohibits provision of state-paid sign language interpreter to student attending pervasively religious high school: Zobrest v. Catalina Foothills School District, 963 F.2d 1190 (1992). I. M. Humphrey, student author. 25 *Ariz. St. L.J.* 449-59 Summ '93

Australia

Sexuality and the disabled: legal issues. <u>J. Blackwood.</u> ◄—— Author
11 *U. Tas. L. Rev.* 182-90 '92

Canada

La protection juridique des personnes âgées ou handicapées et la Charte canadienne des droits et libertés. D. Poirier. 23 *Ottawa L. Rev.* 553-79 '91

Illinois

Let's get off the floor: the call for Illinois to adopt a higher substantive standard for special education. M. F. Tomasek, student author. 24 *Loy. U. Chi. L.J.* 375-411 Wint '93

Michigan

"Handicapper services": they are for seniors, too. C. Braun, H. Turnham. 72 *Mich. B.J.* 56-8 Ja '93

Netherlands

Life-prolonging and life-terminating treatment of severely handicapped newborn babies: a discussion of the report of the Royal Dutch Society of Medicine on "life-terminating actions with incompetent patients: Pt. 1 severely handicapped newborns". H. Jochemsen. 8 *Issues L. & Med.* 167-81 Fall '92

New Hampshire

Special education and the juvenile justice system. G. M. Zelin. <u>34 *N.H. B.J.* 21-9 Mr '93</u> ◄—— Source

Pennsylvania

Estate planning for disabled beneficiaries: Pennsylvania Supreme Court confirms effectiveness of properly drafted discretionary trusts. F. S. Goldman, Jr., C. K. Rarig. 63 *Pa. B.A.Q.* 154-8 Jl '92

Vermont

Act 230: cost containment, deregulation, and the reform of special education in Vermont. G. M. Eaton, student author. 17 *Vt. L. Rev.* 195-234 Fall '92

Handler, Adam M.
<u>Proposed Regs. coordinate deferred exchange and install-</u> ◄—— Title
<u>ment sale rules.</u> 79 *J. Tax'n* 44-9 Jl '93

Handler, Milton, 1903-
The dilemma of the antitrust practitioner. 22 *Sw. U. L. Rev.* 393-8 '93

Haney, Marian C.
Litigation of a sexual harassment case after the Civil Rights Act of 1991. 68 *Notre Dame L. Rev.* 1037-56 '93

Haney, Thomas D.
The child victim/witness: balancing of defendant/victim rights in the emotional caldron of a criminal trial. 62 *J. Kan. B.A.* 38-43 Ja '93 ◄—— Date

Hankey, David Lawrence
A corporate counsel's primer on restrictive covenants. 39 *Prac. Law.* 31-47+ Ja '93

Hanks, Peter
Adjusting Medicare benefits: acquisition of property? 14 *Sydney L. Rev.* 495-503 D '92

Can the state's rewrite Mabo (No 2) [Mabo v. Queensland, [1992] 107 A.L.R. 1]? Aboriginal land rights and the Racial Discrimination Act. 15 *Sydney L. Rev.* 247-53 Je '93

FIGURE 5–12 An excerpt from the *Index to Legal Periodicals* (*Index to Legal Periodicals,* 1993, Vol. 86, no. 11, page 10. Copyright ©1993 by the H.W. Wilson Company. Material reproduced with permission of the publisher.)

Contents of Legal Periodicals

Typically, the articles found in legal periodicals can be classified into several categories:

Articles written by law professors, practicing lawyers, or other experts.

Comments, or *notes*, which are articles submitted by law students.

Case notes, usually written by law students, summarizing or discussing particular cases.

Commentaries, which are short discussions, usually following a feature article.

Book reviews, typically written by professors.

Some legal periodicals devote particular issues to recent developments in the law or to symposium topics. For example, a law review might devote an issue to recent cases from a federal circuit or from a particular state. Another law review might devote an entire issue to a survey of the law on a particular topic. A law review might publish articles from, or devote an entire issue to, a symposium, which is a meeting of legal experts who are invited to give speeches or present articles on a given subject.

The text of articles in legal periodicals is extensively footnoted to other legal authority, so a researcher can locate law through a law journal article as well as through a treatise. You can even find citations to other law review articles on the same topic. Like magazine articles, journal articles are not updated.

Restatements of the Law

The American Law Institute publishes the Restatements of the Law. The Restatements are written by a reporter who assembles the views of a committee of experts—lawyers, judges, and professors. The Restatements cover different legal topics. The first edition of the Restatements developed black letter principles (fundamental statements of the law) from the majority case law trend on an issue. In other words, the committee of experts collected all the cases on a particular principle of law and wrote a legal principle based upon the trend on that issue. If a majority of the states had decided a law a certain way, these experts "restated" the principle to mirror this majority approach.

More recently, in the second series, the committee developed legal principles on how its members think the law *ought to be decided,* not on how the majority of the cases may have decided that principle. There is now even a third series on several topics.

The paralegal should not confuse the Restatement principles with law. The Restatements are not law, but merely demonstrate what experts feel the law should be. However, courts give considerable weight to Restatement principles because they represent the analyses of leading legal experts on the particular subject.

Contents of the Restatements

The Restatements cover such subjects as agency, conflicts of law, contracts, foreign relations, judgments, property, restitution, security, torts, and trusts. In each Restatement, the subjects are arranged in chapters, which are further divided into sections. The black letter principle is printed in bold face. (See Figure 5–13.) Each principle is explained by comments and illustrations. The comments explain the rationale for the rule, and the illustrations are examples of how the principle works. Notice in Figure 5–14 how actual examples are used to demonstrate the operation of the rule.

The Restatements also contain citations to cases that have cited the Restatement principles, citations to A.L.R. annotations, and West topic and key number references that relate to the Restatement principles. There are also tables of statutes and cases to cross-reference research. Figure 5–15 is a table showing the different restatements.

How to Use the Restatements

To research using the Restatements, first decide what Restatement subject applies to your research. Then locate a specific chapter and section reference by looking in the table of contents in the front of the volumes or by using the descriptive word index found in the last volume of each set.

Read the Restatement principle carefully. Every word of that principle was written with deliberate care. In fact, each Restatement principle is a product of several drafts. Each draft is sent to the members for discussion and review. There may be considerable debate about each word of the principle. After reading the principle, check your understanding of that principle by reading the comments and illustrations. The comments tell how the principle operates and the illustrations give concrete examples of how the rule applies to particular fact situations. The Restatements are updated in several ways—pocket parts, supplemental volumes, and appendix volumes.

§ **150.** Factors Involved in Determining Reasonableness of Punishment

In determining whether force or confinement is reasonable for the control, training, or education of a child, the following factors are to be considered:

(a) whether the actor is a parent;

(b) the age, sex, and physical and mental condition of the child;

(c) the nature of his offense and his apparent motive;

(d) the influence of his example upon other children of the same family or group;

(e) whether the force or confinement is reasonably necessary and appropriate to compel obedience to a proper command;

(f) whether it is disproportionate to the offense, unnecessarily degrading, or likely to cause serious or permanent harm.

Black letter principle

See Reporter's Notes.

Comment:

a. The factors listed in this Section are not intended to be exclusive.

b. As to the more extensive privilege of discipline of a parent, see § 147, Comment *c.*

FIGURE 5–13   An example of a black letter principle (Copyright 1965 by the American Law Institute. Reprinted with the permission of the American Law Institute.)

§ **19.** What Constitutes Offensive Contact

A bodily contact is offensive if it offends a reasonable sense of personal dignity.

See Reporter's Notes.

Caveat:

The Institute expresses no opinion as to whether the actor is liable if he inflicts upon another a contact which he knows will be offensive to another's known but abnormally acute sense of personal dignity.

Explanation of the rationale ——→ **Comment:**

a. In order that a contact be offensive to a reasonable sense of personal dignity, it must be one which would offend the ordinary person and as such one not unduly sensitive as to his personal dignity. It must, therefore, be a contact which is unwarranted by the social usages prevalent at the time and place at which it is inflicted.

Examples of how the principle works ——→ **Illustrations:**

1. A flicks a glove in B's face. This is an offensive touching of B.

2. A, while walking in a densely crowded street, deliberately but not discourteously pushes against B in order to pass him. This is not an offensive touching of B.

3. A, who is suffering from a contagious skin disease, touches B's hands, thus putting B in reasonable apprehension of contagion. This is an offensive touching of B.

4. A, a child, becomes sick while riding in B's taxicab. B takes hold of A in order to help her. This is not an offensive touching.

FIGURE 5–14 An example of how the "Comment" and "Illustrations" sections are used in the Restatements (Copyright 1965 by the American Law Institute. Reprinted with the permission of the American Law Institute.)

FIGURE 5–15
The Restatements
available for
legal research

Subject of Restatement	Series	Date of Adoption
Agency	1st	1933
	2d	1957
Conflict of Laws	1st	1934
	2d	1969, 1988
Contracts	1st	1932
	2d	1979
Foreign Relations	2d	1962
	3d	1986
Judgments	1st	1942
	2d	1980
Property	1st	1936, 1940, 1944
	2d	1976 (Landlord and Tenant)
		1981, 1984, 1986 (Donative Transfers)
Restitution	1st	1936
Surety	1st	1941
Torts	1st	1934, 1938, 1939
	2d	1963, 1964, 1976 1977
Trusts	1st	1935
	2d	1957
	3d	1990 (Prudent Investor Rule)
Unfair Competition	3d	1994

Sometimes you may want to consult both the first and second editions of the Restatements to note how the law has evolved or is evolving. The appendix volumes collect cases that have cited the Restatement principles so you can see how widely the principle has been accepted and whether there are exceptions to the principle.

The Restatements are seldom used in the initial phase of legal research, but often a Restatement provides polish for ending a research project or provides you with a new theory to pursue in your research. Remember that the Restatement of the Law is a highly respected source.

Continuing Legal Education (C.L.E.) Materials

States are now requiring lawyers to attend annual continuing education seminars. As lawyers are required to attend these seminars in order to maintain their licenses to practice law, professional groups are sponsoring such seminars. Paralegals can and often do attend these continuing education seminars. Sponsors may include local bar associations, national associations, or organizations such as the American Law Institute/ American Bar Association (ALI-ABA), the National Institute of Trial Advocacy (NITA), the Defense Research Institute (DRI), or the Practicing Law Institute (PLI). Panelists at these seminars prepare materials that are published in books or pamphlets. These materials are called **C.L.E. materials** and are a burgeoning source of legal information.

The C.L.E. materials tend to be practice-oriented, and many are specific to a particular jurisdiction. Although not always as scholarly as treatises, legal periodicals, or restatements, these materials can provide invaluable guidance on the law.

C.L.E. materials often cover topics not yet covered by other sources. For example, if a state is adopting child support guidelines for the first time, a C.L.E. seminar may be held to show attorneys how to apply them. New laws are hot topics for seminars. Lawyers who must attend a seminar frequently choose a seminar in an area of the law that has changed because of recent legislation or a recent court decision. Sponsors of these seminars compete with each other to provide topics that will interest the widest audience. Thus, the C.L.E. materials may contain the most up-to-date theories on a new area of the law. Because the lawyers who are asked to speak at these seminars usually have been involved in this breaking area, their materials contain some practical information about the area as well.

Sometimes the bar association for a particular state publishes lists or catalogs of the C.L.E. materials available for that state. For example, PLI publishes an *Index to Course Handbooks,* and the ALI-ABA publishes the *C.L.E. Journal and Register.* Otherwise, the best way to locate a publication on a specific topic is by browsing in the library for these materials or by consulting a card catalog. Some C.L.E. materials can be found on-line with a computer.

C.L.E. materials are footnoted, but perhaps not as extensively as the other sources discussed in this chapter. These materials often are not

---

LEGAL TERMS

C.L.E. materials Books and pamphlets containing materials prepared by panelists for continuing legal education seminars.

well indexed, except for a listing of the titles in the book, and are rarely updated in any manner.

Often cassette tapes are made of the lectures and workshops given as part of the continuing legal education programs. Purchasing these tapes can be an effective way to keep up with the law in a certain area.

C.L.E. materials, like other secondary source materials, enable paralegals to answer their own questions about law. If you work as a paralegal for a law firm with a specialty practice, read C.L.E. materials in that specialty area to further your legal education. Many young legal professionals spend too much time asking questions and not enough time looking for answers. Consult secondary source materials to answer your own questions before asking for advice from others.

Summary

- Legal professionals rely upon secondary research materials to help them understand and apply legal principles.

- The two main national encyclopedias are *Corpus Juris Secundum* (C.J.S.) published by West Publishing and *American Jurisprudence, Second Edition* (Am. Jur. 2d), published by Lawyers Cooperative.

- A treatise is a text written by a legal expert on a particular legal topic.

- A legal periodical contains journal articles published by law schools, professional organizations, and law associations. To search for a journal article, use the *Index to Legal Periodicals* or the *Current Law Index*. Researchers also can search the indexes by using a CD-ROM version of the indexes or by using an on-line computer service.

- The American Law Institute publishes a set of books called the Restatements of the Law. The Restatements reflect the opinions of a committee of legal experts on different aspects of the law.

- In most states, attorneys are required to attend so many hours of seminars each year as part of a continuing legal education requirement. The materials handed out at these seminars are often good secondary research tools.

Review Questions

1. What is the role of a secondary research tool in legal research?

2. What are the different methods used to locate information in an encyclopedia?

3. What are the two main national encyclopedias?

4. How are encyclopedias updated?

5. What is the difference between a treatise, a legal encyclopedia, legal periodicals, and a restatement? Discuss what factors would influence you to select one of these tools over another.

6. What is the main difference between the first series of the Restatements and the later series of the Restatements?

7. What are different media that can be used to index law review articles?

8. What are C.L.E. materials?

Research Projects

1. If an establishment serves liquor to a patron who is intoxicated and that patron injures a third party, the third party can sue the establishment in most states. After finding the relevant law relating to this issue in your state, use the secondary source materials discussed in this chapter to answer these questions:

   a. What is the trend of the law on this issue in your state?

   b. Are there any peculiarities in the law of your state on this issue?

   c. Are there any law review articles on this issue from law schools in your state?

   d. Can you locate any C.L.E. materials on this topic?

||||

CHAPTER 6

ADDITIONAL METHODS FOR RESEARCHING STATUTORY LAW

CHAPTER OUTLINE

Statutory research is often completed by using an annotated code. Annotated codes provide the researcher with the actual text of the statute, so the legal professional only needs to read the statute to answer most questions. In addition, annotated codes provide background information about the statute, with case citations, secondary source citations, and cross-references to other laws. A paralegal who knows how to use an annotated code can master most statutory research situations. There are other methods, however, that can be used for researching statutory law.

Some paralegals work in legal departments of large firms that concentrate their practice in complex areas such as tax law, employment law, or securities law. These firms often rely upon looseleaf services in researching such specialized areas. A paralegal must know how to use a typical looseleaf service. A paralegal may find it necessary to research the legislative history of a statute in more detail, look for model or uniform laws, or search for the opinion of an Attorney General on a particular topic. This chapter explores methods for expanding the research of statutory law.

Looseleaf Services

With the growth of administrative agencies, there has been a proliferation of looseleaf services. In fact, there are thousands of different looseleaf services. Many law books are published in looseleaf format; however, when lawyers use the term **looseleaf services**, they usually mean law books published in binder format that comprehensively cover the different aspects of a particular area of law. These looseleaf services typically cover areas of law related to administrative agencies. Unlike annotated codes, which provide the text of statutes with case summaries and some citations to regulations, looseleaf services may provide the text of statutes with the full text of relevant cases and regulations. Looseleaf services also provide commentary about the areas of the law they cover. The researcher, therefore, can find all pertinent primary sources in one set of reference materials. A lawyer who practices discrimination law, for example, can find applicable statutes, regulations, cases, administrative opinions, and explanations of the law similar to those found in treatises in one looseleaf service.

Treatises traditionally deal with common law concerns. If a treatise deals with other sources of law, it usually only cites to the law, rather than including the law verbatim. There are three distinguishing features of a looseleaf service: (1) looseleaf services include the full text of all primary sources that pertain to a specific area of the law; (2) they are supplemented frequently, often weekly; and (3) they provide information from all sources on the topic covered, whether the source law is federal or state, or an agency or a court. The difference between looseleaf services and treatises often is blurred. It is not so important that the paralegal knows the difference between a looseleaf service and a treatise as it is for the paralegal to know how to use a looseleaf service when it is encountered.

Because there are thousands of looseleaf services, it is difficult to generalize about them. However, the typical looseleaf service provides the following:

- the actual text of any statutes or regulations (federal or state) relevant to the subject covered by the service;

- the text of relevant cases and administrative decisions;

- explanatory text that helps the subscriber understand the law in the area covered;

- extensive indexes, usually tabbed;

- extensive updating materials; and

- a system of identifying outdated pages to be replaced with new pages.

Other features provided by many looseleaf services include:

- newsletters that alert subscribers to new developments;

- collections of administrative or judicial decisions relevant to the subject covered by the service;

- summary indexes or new development indexes to aid readers in finding references in the service; and

- the text or summary of proposed laws or regulations.

How to Use a Looseleaf Service

Perhaps the most important fact to remember when using a looseleaf service is that most services use paragraph (¶) references rather than page references. (See Figure 6–1.) Many legal researchers become frustrated when using looseleaf services until they remember this simple fact.

2016QF   Fair Employment Practices   372   10-29-93

Duty to Accommodate Religious Needs.—Both employers and labor unions may be excused from the ban on religious discrimination with respect to those practices that are needed to conduct their operations so long as efforts to accommodate employees and job applicants in observing their religious commitments have been made. Moreover, the United States Supreme Court has indicated that an employer is not required to accept an employee's proposal for accommodating his or her religious needs—any reasonable method of accommodation is sufficient.[11]

The U.S. Supreme Court has held that a public employer may violate the guarantee of free exercise of religion contained in the first amendment to the U.S. Constitution if it fires an employee for sacramental use of illegal drugs. Whether or not the employer's actions violate the Constitution depends on whether religious use of a particular drug is exempted from the controlled substances law of the state where the employees works. For example, if religious drug use in the state is legal, the employer's discharge of the employee would violate the Constitution. However, in a state where such use is illegal, the discharge would be proper.[12]

An employee seeking protection under the NLRA from forced unionism may be required to contribute an amount equal to the union initiation fees or dues to a nonreligious, nonlabor organization. Similar requirements have been placed on employees demanding that their religious needs be accommodated under Title VII.[13]

The U.S. Supreme Court has held that an employer need bear only a minimum of costs, otherwise it would be discriminating against other employees for whom no similar expenses are borne to allow them time off. Also, a labor union need not agree to shift changes that would violate the seniority system established under its bargaining contract.[14]

Imposition of this duty on employers does not run counter to the constitutional bar to laws "respecting an establishment of religion," it has been held by a majority of the courts. Granting state employees time off with pay to attend religious services, however, may be considered violative of the attitude that is required of state governments by the constitutional prohibition against the establishment of a religion.[15]

¶ 112.4   *Sex Discrimination*

The disparate treatment of male and female workers is often based on stereotyped characterizations of the sexes. For example, the assumption that females are less capable than males of performing strenuous physical work has been viewed as wrongfully foreclosing many job opportunities to women.

References are to paragraphs of CCH Employment Practices Guide.

[11] See ¶ 238, 1018   [13] See ¶ 237, 238   [15] See ¶ 238
[12] See ¶ 238   [14] See ¶ 238

©1993, Commerce Clearing House, Inc.

FIGURE 6–1   The Labor Law Reporter, a looseleaf service from Commerce Clearing House, Inc. (Reproduced with permission from CCH's *Labor Law Reports Quick Finder,* published and copyrighted by CCH Incorporated, 2700 Lake Cook Road, Riverwoods, Illinois 60016.)

The second most important fact to remember when using a looseleaf service is that there may be multiple indexes for any set with names like rapid finder index, new development index, topical index, and descriptive word index. These indexes are usually tabbed for easy reference. The best advice is to read any instructions before you begin.

Summary Indexes

Looseleaf services are usually multi-volume sets. The index itself may be quite extensive. Some sets provide a summary index that is shorter than the main index. This index might be called a "Rapid Finder Index." The purpose of the index is to provide researchers with a quick orientation to the set.

Cumulative Indexes

Sometimes there is an index for new developments. In such instances, the researcher will first use the main index, and then use this updated index for more recent references.

Main Indexes

Like most other legal research tools, looseleaf services typically have both topical and subject matter indexes, so you can find information by scanning the table of contents or by using a descriptive-word approach, or both.

SIDEBAR

A researcher using an index to a looseleaf service might find a reference to a paragraph such as ¶ 30,130, then look through the looseleaf set and find that it ends with ¶ 10,000. Some sets have accompanying volumes that collect court cases or administrative decisions, and usually such a high paragraph number refers to one of these volumes rather than to the looseleaf volumes.

Finding Tables

Often looseleaf services furnish lists or tables of relevant primary sources including cases, rules, orders, and regulations. (See Figure 6–2.)

Digests

When a looseleaf service collects administrative or judicial decisions, it may have its own miniature digest. (See Figure 6–3.)

When you use any looseleaf service, first read the instructions for that set. The instructions will explain the various indexes. Typically

Barbour v. Merrill (CA DC, 93-7219 etc., 5/16/95; den'g rehear'g of 67:369) 126
Bassett-Walker Inc.; Derthick v. (DC WDVa, 94-0026-D etc., 5/18/95) 139
Baufield v. Safelite Glass Corp. (DC Minn, 3-91-214, 5/10/93, 831 FSupp 713) 107
Beadle v. Tampa, City of (US SupCt, 94-1705, 6/19/95; den'g cert 66:1540) .. 64
Beckett v. Prudential Insurance Co. of America (DC SNY, 94-CV-8305 (SAS), 5/15/95) 74
Bentsen; Robbins v. (CA 7, 94-1743 etc., 12/8/94, 41 F3d 1195) 295
Board of Education, see name of locality
Board of School Comrs., see name of locality
Board of, see name of locality
Board of Trustees, see name of locality
Bob Chinn's Crab House, see Chinn Enterprises Inc.
Boeing Co.; Steinle v. (DC Kan, 90-1337-SAC, 3/30/95; see also 62:272, 62:279, 64:1310) 69
Bonner v. Guccione (DC SNY, 94 Civ. 7735 (DLC), 3/24/95) 47
Boone v. Federal Express Corp. (CA 8, 94-3451, 7/3/95) 353
Booth v. Intertrans Corp. (DC ELa, 94-2359, 5/26/95) 433
Borough of, see name of borough
Bowles; Woolf v. (CA 4, 94-2337, 6/16/95) 161
Boyd v. Harding Academy of Memphis Inc. (DC WTenn, 93-2867-M1/Bro, 5/31/95) 238
Bradley v. Pizzaco of Nebraska Inc. (CA 8, 89-2271NE etc., 7/25/91, 939 F2d 610; aff'g, rvs'g & rem'g in part 51:811; supersed'g 55:347) 242
—(US SupCt, 91-640, 1/21/92, 502 US 1057; den'g cert 68:242) 245
Bradley v. Pizzaco of Nebraska (CA 8, 92-3781, 10/21/93, 7 F3d 795; see also 51:811, 55:347, 68:242, 68:245) 245
Bramesco v. Drug Computer Consultants (DC SNY, 93 Civ. 0923 (VLB), 10/23/93, 834 FSupp 120) 387
Brannon; Catchpole v. (Calif CtApp, A062338, 6/27/95) 270
Brothers v. NCR Corp. (DC NOhio, 1:94CV0461, 5/10/95) 6
Bryn Mawr Hospital; Robertson v. (DC EPa, 94-2489, 6/20/95) 393
Burggraf Construction Co.; Gross v. (CA 10, 94-8054 etc., 4/25/95) 88

C

Caddo Parish, Bd. of Education; U.S. v. (DC WLa, 94-0155, 4/21/95) 4
Camillo v. Coca-Cola Bottling Co. of New York Inc. (CA 2, 91-9110, 2/25/92, 962 F2d 2; aff'g 66:365) 256
Carlson v. American Meter Co. (DC Neb, 8:CV93-356, 4/24/95) 193
Carpenters, Local 971; Herman v. (CA 9, 93-16819, 6/21/95) 181
Case Corp.; Gehring v. (US SupCt, 94-1780, 6/26/95; den'g cert 66:1373) ... 64
Catchpole v. Brannon (Calif CtApp, A062338, 6/27/95) 270

Chinn Enterprises Inc.; Curcio v. (DC NIll, 95 C 0821, 6/5/95) 290
Chojar v. Levitt (DC SNY, 90 Civ. 3402 (RWS), 9/25/91, 773 FSupp 645) 259
Cigna Financial Advisors Inc.; Williams v. (CA 5, 94-11030, 6/19/95) 65
Citizens Savings Bank/Citizens Trust Co.; Reid v. (DC RI, 94-0622ML, 4/21/95) . 361
City of, see name of city
CJA, see Carpenters
Clarke v. Kentucky Fried Chicken of California Inc. (CA 1, 94-1950, 6/14/95) ... 34
—(CA 1, 94-1950, 6/14/95; amend'g 68:34) 352
Coca-Cola Bottling Co. of New York Inc.; Camillo v. (CA 2, 91-9110, 2/25/92, 962 F2d 2; aff'g 66:365) 256
Commissioner of Internal Revenue; Downey v. (US SupCt, 94-999, 6/19/95; den'g cert 65:1192) 64
Commissioner of Internal Revenue v. Schmitz (US SupCt, 94-944, 6/19/95; grant'g cert, vac'g judgm't & rem'g 65:1195) 63
Commonwealth of, see name of commonwealth
Correctional Medical Systems; Walker v. (DC WPa, 94-203, 5/16/95) 42
County Commissioners, Bd. of, Kearny County, Kansas; Gallardo v. (DC Kan, 94-4064-SAC, 6/13/94, 857 FSupp 783) 365
County of, see name of county
Cox v. National Football League (DC SNY, 94 Civ. 5440 (HB), 6/21/95) 350
Craven Community College, Bd. of Trustees; Strag v. (CA 4, 94-2170 etc., 6/1/95) 163
Crighton v. Schuylkill County (DC EPa, 94-5658, 3/6/95) 122
Cumberland Carpet Mills, see Queen Carpet Corp.; Anderson v.
Curcio v. Chinn Enterprises Inc. (DC NIll, 95 C 0821, 6/5/95) 290

D

Dailey v. Societe Generale (DC SNY, 94 Civ. 1649 (JGK), 6/20/95) 345
Daly v. Unicare Corp.—Township Manor Nursing Center (DC EPa, 94-6838, 4/26/95) 208
Daughters of Jacob Nursing Home Inc.; Piasecki v. (DC SNY, 91 Civ. 7748 (DNE), 12/22/92, 808 FSupp 1136) 203
Davis v. Fleming Companies Inc. (CA 8, 94-3431, 6/8/95) 17
De Los Santos v. J.R. Simplot Co. (Idaho SupCt, 20760, 5/23/95) 150
Dean Witter Reynolds Inc.; Hansen v. (DC SNY, 92 Civ. 7946 (HB), 6/5/95) 370
Department of, see name of agency
Derthick v. Bassett-Walker Inc. (DC WDVa, 94-0026-D etc., 5/18/95) 139
Diehl v. Tele-Solutions Inc. (CA 6, 93-3911, 6/14/95) 86
Domino's Pizza, see Pizzaco of Nebraska
Doral Mortgage Corp.; Rodriguez v. (CA 1, 94-2227, 6/23/95) 331

FIGURE 6–2   An excerpt from a looseleaf service illustrating a list of primary sources. (Lab. Rel. Rep.) (Reprinted with permission from *Labor Relations Reporter*. Copyright by the Bureau of National Affairs, Inc. (800-372-1033))

FILE in Master Index Binder II or Binder 7 under Cumulative Digest & Index — FEP tab. DISCARD previous Supp. and Master CDI (67 FEP Cases) beginning with pages D-II A601 and D-II A701.

LABOR
RELATIONS
REPORTER®

July 10, 1995

Final
CUMULATIVE DIGEST
and INDEX (CDI)
Fair Employment Practice Cases
(67 FEP Cases)

March 6 — June 26, 1995

(See also bound FEP-CDI volumes.)

Classification numbers identified by the symbol "▶" in this CDI represent specific points of fair employment practice law. They are located by topic in the General Index (Tab A in Master Index Binder) or in the FEP Topic Finder. The Outline of Classifications FEP (Tab D-1) provides the description of each number.

Each descriptive entry below provides the particulars in a given case relating to the classification number.

Included are descriptive entries from Americans with Disabilities Cases (AD Cases) that construe points of law that overlap in FEP Cases and AD Cases (e.g., employment remedies and procedures).

▶ 106.01   Shareholders who obtained order requiring employer to include in corporate proxy materials reports about its EEO and affirmative action programs are entitled to attorneys' fees under common-benefit theory, even though proposal was overwhelmingly defeated, where all shareholders benefited substantially from promotion of corporate suffrage regarding significant policy issue, and action also facilitated communications among shareholders and between shareholders and management. —Clothing & Textile Workers v. Wal-Mart Stores Inc. (CA 2) 67 FEP Cases 882

▶ 106.0410   Lower court erroneously concluded that homosexuals had been deprived of their right to petition municipal legislative forum for enactments designed to protect and advance their collective agenda by amendment to city charter that precludes creation of special class status or laws based on sexual orientation, since amendment does not deprive homosexuals of right to, or reduce relative weight of, any homosexual's vote. —Equality Foundation of Greater Cincinnati Inc. v. Cincinnati, City of (CA 6) 67 FEP Cases 1290

Section 1b

FIGURE 6–3   An example of a looseleaf service digest (Lab. Rel. Rep.) (Reprinted with permission from *Labor Relations Reporter*. Copyright by the Bureau of National Affairs, Inc. (800-372-1033))

you will begin with a summary index. You may consult the main index and then any updated indexes to ensure that you did not miss any new developments. Then you will read the text and check for any supplemental material.

Updating Looseleaf Services

A distinguishing feature of looseleaf services is that they are supplemented regularly and frequently. Most looseleaf services are updated by one of two methods: (1) insert pages, or (2) cumulative updates. Some services that are now available on computer are updated through multi-media means as well.

Insert Pages

The unique feature of a looseleaf binder is that pages can be removed and replaced with new pages. Publishers of looseleaf services provide almost continual updates with new pages to replace pages with outdated material. Be sure all previous releases have been inserted before you begin filing any new release.

Cumulative Updates

Another updating method used by publishers of looseleaf services is to provide new pages to be inserted (like a pocket part) in the front or back of the looseleaf service. These pages may be a different color from the white pages in the main text.

Multi-Media Updates

Many on-line computer services have posed a threat to looseleaf services. Some looseleaf publishers have responded to the competition by providing more frequent updates, but others have put their looseleaf services on-line or on CD-ROM. For example, the *CCH Standard Federal Tax Reporter* is found in looseleaf format, on CD-ROM, and on-line. Subscribers who purchase the on-line service receive daily updates.

When to Use a Looseleaf Service

A looseleaf service has both advantages and disadvantages. The sets usually are expensive, and sometimes become outdated if the subscription lapses. It takes time to master the indexes of some looseleaf services, and it may take the researcher time to find an exact reference to a question. Sometimes looseleaf services are rather technical. Despite these disadvantages, the researcher who has some experience with looseleaf services will find not only the law, but also detailed explanations of that law. These explanations provide insight easily missed by simply reading the law. For subscribers who follow the newsletters and updates, the looseleaf service offers tips and solutions for dealing with current legal problems. For example, a federal income tax looseleaf service may advise readers of a possible new deduction created by changes in the tax law, or an employment law looseleaf may advise readers of a new ruling on what constitutes discrimination in the workplace.

Simply put, the more experience a researcher has with looseleaf services, the more often the researcher will select a looseleaf service as a resource for finding answers to legal questions. A researcher who is not comfortable with looseleaf services should make an effort to use these sets whenever possible to gain experience with them. Most nagging questions that cannot be answered by other methods can be answered by a looseleaf service.

Model and Uniform Codes

The *Restatements* discussed in Chapter 5 summarize how common law principles ought to be decided. Model and uniform codes have a similar function in that they provide prototype versions of how statutory law ought to be written.

Uniform Codes

A **uniform code** provides proposed statutory language, the purpose of which is to standardize an area of the law throughout the United States. By publishing a uniform code, the authors, who are legal experts in the area, provide a version a state legislature can simply enact word-for-word. Sometimes the state legislature enacts the uniform code word-for-word, sometimes the legislature makes changes before enacting the statute, and at other times the legislature completely ignores the uniform version. Both uniform codes and model codes are secondary source materials.

Perhaps the best example of a uniform code is the Uniform Commercial Code (U.C.C.), which now has been adopted in some version by all fifty states. The U.C.C. is a comprehensive code that was

---

LEGAL TERMS

uniform code† Model legislation, the purpose of which is to promote uniformity throughout the country with respect to statutes governing significant areas of the law.

written to promote commercial uniformity throughout the United States. The U.C.C. was a joint project of the National Conference of Commissioners on Uniform State Laws (NCCUSL) and the American Law Institute (ALI). The ALI publishes the *Restatements*, and the NCCUSL is an organization consisting of commissioners appointed by the governors of all fifty states for the purpose of establishing uniform laws in areas of national concern. Faced with different commercial laws in each of the fifty states, the ALI and the NCCUSL wrote the U.C.C. with the help of leading legal experts. Commercial laws dealing with sale of goods, with money and checks, and with secured transactions are fairly standardized throughout the United States now that the fifty states have adopted the U.C.C.

Today, NCCUSL is a leading source for developing uniform statutes, although there are other public and private organizations that publish similar proposals from time to time. All the uniform laws published by the NCCUSL have been compiled by West in a multi-volume set called the *Uniform Laws Annotated* (U.L.A.). This set contains every uniform law that has been adopted by at least one state. The U.L.A. contains comments of the commissioners of the NCCUSL on each statute and short summaries of court decisions that have interpreted that uniform provision. (See Figure 6–4.) The U.L.A. has tables indicating which states have enacted the uniform code and whether they changed any of the language of that code.

The U.L.A. is updated by annual pocket parts. The NCCUSL also supplements this set with its annual *Handbook of the National Conference of Commissioners on Uniform State Laws*.

Model Codes

A **model code** is similar to a uniform law except it is written more from the perspective of how the law should be ideally written. There may be less compromising in the drafting of the language of a model code because the model code is not seeking as widespread support as the uniform code. Model codes seek to provide modern methods in revamping laws on certain subjects. For example, most states have laws relating to the probate of the estate of a deceased person. These laws have developed helter-skelter over the years and can cause estate administration to become quite expensive. The ALI has studied the probate laws in the fifty states and has written a model probate code incorporating simpler and more efficient probate practices.

──────────────── LEGAL TERMS ────────────────

model code   Model legislation that is written from the perspective of how the law should be ideally written.

§ 1–208.   Option to Accelerate at Will.

A term providing that one party or his successor in interest may accelerate payment or performance or require collateral or additional collateral "at will" or "when he deems himself insecure" or in words of similar import shall be construed to mean that he shall have power to do so only if he in good faith believes that the prospect of payment or performance is impaired. The burden of establishing lack of good faith is on the party against whom the power has been exercised.

[Official Comment]

Prior Uniform Statutory Provision: None.

Purposes:

The increased use of acceleration clauses either in the case of sales on credit or in time paper or in security transactions has led to some confusion in the cases as to the effect to be given to a clause which seemingly grants the power of an acceleration at the whim and caprice of one party. This Section is intended to make clear that despite language which can be so construed and which further might be held to make the agreement void as against public policy or to make the contract illusory or too indefinite for enforcement, the clause means that the op-

tion is to be exercised only in the good faith belief that the prospect of payment or performance is impaired.

Obviously this section has no application to demand instruments or obligations whose very nature permits call at any time with or without reason. This section applies only to an agreement or to paper which in the first instance is payable at a future date.

Definitional Cross References:

"Burden of establishing". Section 1–201.

"Good faith". Section 1–201.

"Party". Section 1–201.

"Term". Section 1–201.

[Notes of Decisions]

Generally 1
Additional collateral, demand for 7
Burden of proof 17
Damages 21
Default, acceleration upon 9
Demand instruments 12
Due-on-sale clause 13
Duress 6
Good faith 2
Instructions 20
Mistake 10
Notice to debtor 11
Objective or subjective standard 3
Pleadings 16
Punitive damages 21
Questions of fact 18
"Reasonably" 5
Remedies 15
Repossession 8
Secured transactions 14
Subjective or objective standard 3
Unconscionability 4
Weight and sufficiency of evidence 19

1. Generally

Acceleration clauses are designed to protect creditor from actions by debtor which jeopardize or impair creditor's security; they are not to be used offensively, e.g., for commercial advantage of creditor. Brown v. Avemco Inv. Corp., C.A.Mont.1979, 603 F.2d 1367.

2. Good faith

Under Iowa statute providing that a provision whereby one party is authorized to accelerate payment is to be construed to mean that he shall have the power to do so only if he in good faith believes that prospect of payment is impaired; good faith is presumed when a creditor accelerates a debt. Jensen v. State Bank of Allison, C.A.Iowa, 1975, 518 F.2d 1.

Although security agreement contained so-called insecurity clause in broadest possible terms, under this section mortgagee could accelerate only if it in good faith believed that prospect of payment or performance was impaired. Sheppard Federal Credit Union v. Palmer, C.A.Tex.1969, 408 F.2d 1369.

Test was one of good faith under Colorado law in determining whether brokerage firm breached contract or its fiduciary duty to customer either when customer's account was liquidated or when it demanded that he sign promissory note for net debit balance. Clayton Brokerage Co. of St. Louis, Inc. v. Stansfield, D.C.Colo.1984, 582 F.Supp. 837.

By incorporating Uniform Commercial Code's remedies into note secured by real estate, parties also incorporated the Code's limitations on the exercise of those remedies, including good faith limitation on acceleration under insecurity clause. Bartlett Bank & Trust Co. v. McJunkins, 1986, 100 Ill.Dec. 420, 497 N.E.2d 398, 147 Ill.App.3d 52.

FIGURE 6–4   An excerpt from Uniform Laws Annotated illustrating comments and decision summaries. (Copyright 1989 by the American Law Institute and the National Conference of Commissioners for Uniform State Laws. Reprinted with permission of the Permanent Editorial Board for the Uniform Commercial Code.)

Model codes published by the NCCUSL are included in the U.L.A. The ALI occasionally drafts and publishes model codes that can be located in a law library or on-line through a computer.

Attorney General Opinions

Attorneys are frequently called upon to give their opinions on legal issues. These opinions are sent by letter to the clients. The United States Attorney General represents the federal government and is often asked to render opinions on federal legislation. These opinions are published in a set of books called the *Opinions of the Attorney General*. These opinions are merely persuasive authority. A court may accept or reject the reasoning of an opinion, depending upon the court's interpretation of the legislation.

State governments also are represented by state attorneys general. Like their federal counterpart, state attorneys general also issue opinions, and in most states, these opinions are published in a format similar to those of the United States Attorney General. Figure 6–5 is an example of an Indiana attorney general opinion.

Legislative History

Occasionally a legal professional may need to research the legislative history of a statute—maybe for the purpose of gaining some background knowledge or insight about the law. Perhaps the legal researcher is examining the legislative process to identify the effect of impending legislation on existing law. Or a researcher might reference legislative history to discern the meaning of a statute without asking for help from others. Courts use legislative history to resolve ambiguities in statutes.

The paralegal who is researching legislative history may not find all the necessary sources in a law library and may need to resort to other libraries. United States government documents usually are printed by the Government Printing Office (G.P.O.) and are sent to federal depository libraries.

A **federal depository library** is a library that has agreed to keep federal documents for use by the public. Regional depository libraries contain even larger collections of federal documents. Some federal publications can be purchased in retail stores. Because federal depository libraries are not always convenient, the researcher may need

FIGURE 6–5
An example of an
Indiana attorney
general opinion
(87 Op. Att'y
Gen. 21 (Nov. 2,
1987))

OPINION NO. 87-21

OFFICIAL OPINION NO. 87-21

November 2, 1987

The Honorable Baron P. Hill
　Indiana State Representative
　　4A-8 State House
　　　Indianapolis, Indiana 46204

Dear Representative Hill:

This is written in response to your request for an opinion regarding the legality of Bingo games in the State. Your question necessarily encompasses four areas of inquiry:

　　1. What constitutes a lottery under Article 15, § 8 of the Constitution of Indiana?

　　2. Is Bingo a lottery?

　　3. What have other jurisdictions, all having similar lottery prohibitions, ruled regarding the status of Bingo as a lottery?

　　4. Does Indiana statutory law prohibit Bingo?

ANALYSIS

I. What constitutes a lottery under Article 15, § 8 of the Constitution of Indiana?

The Constitution of Indiana, Article 15, § 8 provides:

　　No lottery shall be authorized; nor shall the sale of lottery tickets be allowed.

The term "lottery" has no precise technical meaning, but traditionally has been defined as a scheme whereby, for consideration, a participant has an opportunity, which is to be determined by chance through the selection of lots, for gaining a prize greater than his consideration. *Lesher v. Baltimore Football Club* (1986), Ind. App., 496 N.E.2d 785, 789. In *State v. Nixon* (1979), 270 Ind. 192, 201, 384 N.E.2d 152, 161, the Indiana Supreme Court ruled that a pari-mutuel system constituted a constitutionally proscribed lottery:

　　... that the concern of those who drafted and adopted our Constitution, including Article XV, section 8, was to minimize the harmful effects of gambling by sheltering the people from gaming enterprises promoted and operated for monetary

FIGURE 6–5
(continued)

OPINION NO. 87-21

gain by those who, because of the methods employed, are, in essence, purveyors rather than players.

The focus of the *Nixon* case was on the element of "chance" and the court ruled that, notwithstanding the fact:

that a degree of skill is involved in selecting the horses most likely to perform well, the unpredictability of the odds to be paid and the limited predictability of the performance of the animals combine to provide the degree of "chance" required to meet the traditional textbook definitions of the term "lottery." However, whether or not it is a lottery, in the classical sense, is immaterial. Its effects are precisely those sought to be prevented by Article XV, section 8; and, it is, therefore, a "lottery" within the meaning of that term as therein employed.

Id. at 161.

II. Is Bingo a lottery?

The game of Bingo is played by participants paying an individual a sum of money for the use of one or more cards upon which are printed twenty-five squares, each containing a number except for the central square which is blank. No participant can obtain a card without paying money for it. Payment of money for the card constitutes consideration.

When the game commences, numbers are drawn by chance from a receptacle, one by one, and announced. The receptacle continues rotating and the numbers are continually withdrawn at random until a participant announces that he has matched up, on his pre-numbered purchased card, enough randomly drawn numbers to complete the desired winning pattern of numbers. At this time, the participant calls out "bingo" and is declared the winner of a prize. In view of the definition of the term "lottery," the game of Bingo clearly constitutes a lottery.

III. What have other jurisdictions, all having similar constitutional lottery prohibitions, ruled regarding the status of Bingo as a lottery?

The game of Bingo has uniformly been recognized as a lottery and prohibited as such. *State v. Mabrey* (1953), 245 Iowa 428, 60 N.W.2d 889; *A.B. Long Music Co. v. Commonwealth* (1968), Ky.,

FIGURE 6–5
(continued)

1987-1988 O.A.G.

429 S.W.2d 391; *Loder v. City of Canton* (1951), 65 Ohio Law Abst. 517, 111 N.E.2d 793; *People v. Kiefer* (1940), 173 Misc. 300, 16 N.Y.S.2d 858; *Italian Community Home Federation v. Kelly* (1958), 12 Misc. 33, 178 N.Y.S.2d 694; *State v. Nelson* (1972), 210 Kan. 439, 502 P.2d 841.

Secondary authorities of both a legal and a general nature agree that Bingo is a lottery. 54 CJS Lotteries § 10 (1948) ("although there is some authority to the contrary, it is generally held that a game variously designated as bingo, beano, lotto, or the like is a lottery"); 3 Wharton, Criminal Law and Procedure § 942 (Anderson ed. 1957) ("Bingo and Keno are lotteries"). In addition, in "The Bingo Bungle," 105 Sol. J. 597, 598 (1961), the author states:

> Quite clearly, bingo is a lottery. The distinction between lotteries and gambling is by no means a hard and fast one, but participation in the game of bingo is not confined to a payment for a ticket, and the act of marking off on a card the numbers drawn from the bag, and the making of a claim for a prize when the requisite numbers have been drawn, is sufficient to constitute bingo a game of chance. But it is also a distribution of prizes by lot, without the use of skill, and as such it is also a lottery.

IV. Does Indiana statutory law prohibit Bingo?

Indiana Code Section 35-45-5-1 (Burns Repl. 1985) defines gambling and gambling devices:

> "Gambling" means risking money or other property for gain, contingent in whole or in part upon lot, chance, or the operation of a gambling device; but it does not include participating in:
>
> (1) Bona fide contests of skill, speed, strength, or endurance in which awards are made only to entrants or the owners of entries; or
>
> (2) Bona fide business transactions that are valid under the law of contracts.
>
> "Gambling device" means:
>
> (1) a mechanism by the operation of which a right to money or other property may be credited, in return for con-

FIGURE 6–5
(continued)

OPINION NO. 87-21

sideration, as the result of the operation of an element of chance;

(2) a mechanism that, when operated for a consideration, does not return the same value or property for the same consideration upon each operation;

(3) a mechanism, furniture, fixture, construction, or installation designed primarily for use in connection with professional gambling;

(4) a policy ticket or wheel; or

(5) a subassembly or essential part designed or intended for use in connection with such a device, mechanism, furniture, fixture, construction, or installation.

In the application of this definition, an immediate and unrecorded right to replay mechanically conferred on players of pinball machines and similar amusement devices is presumed to be without value.

In addition, Indiana Code Section 35-45-5-2 (Burns Repl. 1985) proscribes gambling:

A person who knowingly or intentionally engages in gambling commits unlawful gambling, a Class B misdemeanor.

The element of skill is not present in the game of Bingo. Indeed, a person has no control over the card he receives. The selection of numbers which are announced is determined solely by chance. One cannot win, regardless of how many years one has played the game, until the announced numbers form a winning pattern on a pre-numbered purchased card. Since Bingo is a game of chance, it constitutes gambling within the meaning of Indiana Code Sections 35-45-5-1 and 35-45-5-2.

CONCLUSION

It is, therefore, my Official Opinion that Bingo is a lottery and consequently is prohibited by Article 15, § 8 of the Constitution of Indiana. While Bingo is often played for benevolent purposes, i.e., fundraising for charities or community projects, Bingo is still prohibited by the Indiana Constitution and by Indiana Code Sections 35-45-5-1 and 35-45-5-2.

FIGURE 6–5
(continued)

1987-1988 O.A.G.

Bingo cannot be legalized in Indiana without an amendment to the Indiana Constitution. *In State v. Nixon* (1979), 270 Ind. 192, 202, 384 N.E.2d 152, 162, the Supreme Court ruled:

The determination that the need for such protection no longer continues can be made only by those who have the authority, the people of Indiana acting by referendum upon a proposed constitutional amendment.

---

to use interlibrary loans, contact a United States representative or senator for assistance, or write to the G.P.O. or another commercial publisher such as the Congressional Information Service, Inc. (CIS) for information.

The G.P.O., which prints a massive amount of materials annually, publishes catalogs and indexes for accessing information. The most useful catalog of government publications is the *Monthly Catalog of United States Government Publications*, which is abbreviated MoCat. MoCat is a catalog of all legislative, executive, and administrative documents available from the G.P.O. There is an index to this catalog that allows a researcher to find a document by author, title, subject, stock number, title keyword, and other methods. MoCat is available in many public libraries and can be used to locate and order legislative documents. Figure 6–6 is a page from MoCat.

SIDEBAR

The federal government prints information not only about government, but also on topics of everyday interest such as child abuse, home repairs, hobbies, and many other such matters. Also, the National Technical Information Service (N.T.I.S.) publishes over 80,000 titles per year of unclassified federal reports of government-sponsored research. Many of these documents can be obtained free or at little cost from the agency that has published the report.

How Laws Are Made

All federal legislation is passed by Congress. The United States Congress is bicameral, meaning that it has two coequal branches: the

--- LEGAL TERMS ---

federal depository library   A library that has agreed to keep federal documents for use by the public.

MONTHLY CATALOG

NOVEMBER 1994

AGRICULTURE DEPARTMENT
Washington, DC 20250

94-22935

A 1.34:871

Ranking of states and commodities by cash receipts [[microform]] / United States Department of Agriculture, Economic Research Service. Washington, DC : The Service ; Herndon, VA : ERS-NASS [distributor], Paper version available from: ERS-NASS, 341 Victory Dr., Herndon, VA 22070

v. ; 28 cm. (Statistical bulletin ; no. 871)

Annual Shipping list no.: 94-0352-M. 1992. Description based on: 1990; title from cover. Microfiche. 1990- [Washington, D.C.] : Supt. of Docs., U.S. G.P.O. microfiches : negative. ●Item 0015 (MF)

1. Farm produce — Economic aspects — United States — States — Periodicals. 2. Livestock — Economic aspects — United States — States — Periodicals. 3. Poultry — Economic aspects — United States — States — Periodicals. I. United States. Dept. of Agriculture. Economic Research Service. II. Series: Statistical bulletin (United States. Dept. of Agriculture) ; no. 871. sn-93027869 OCLC 28160494

94-22936

A 1.34:873

Ali, Mir B.

Soybeans [[microform]] : state-level production costs, characteristics and input use, 1990 / Mir B. Ali, William D. McBride. — Washington, D.C. : U.S. Dept. of Agriculture, Economic Research Service ; [Herndon, VA : ERS-NASS, distributor, 1994]

iii, 39 p. ; 28 cm. — (Statistical bulletin ; no. 873) Cover title. Distributed to depository libraries in microfiche. Shipping list no.: 94-0328-M. "February 1994"—P. i. Chiefly tables. Includes bibliographical references (p. 5). Microfiche. [Washington, D.C.?] : Supt. of Docs., U.S. G.P.O., [1994] 1 microfiche : negative. ●Item 0015 (MF)

1. Soybean — United States — Statistics. 2. Soybean industry — United States — Statistics. I. McBride, William D. II. United States. Dept. of Agriculture. Economic Research Service. III. Title. IV. Series: Statistical bulletin (United States. Dept. of Agriculture) ; no. 873. OCLC 30834616

94-22937

A 1.34:874

Livestock and meat statistics (1989)

Livestock and meat statistics [[microform].] Washington, DC : U.S. Dept. of Agriculture, Economic Research Service ; Herndon, VA : ERS-NASS [distributor, Paper version available from: ERS-NASS, 341 Victory Dr., Herndon, VA 22070

v. ; 26-28 cm. (Statistical bulletin ; no. 874)

Irregular Shipping list no.: 94-0352-M. 1970-92. Description based on: 1984-88; title from cover. Report coverage varies. Microfiche. ⟨1984-88-⟩ [Washington, D.C.] : Supt. of Docs., U.S. G.P.O. microfiches : negative. ●Item 0015 (MF) Continues: Livestock and meat statistics. Supplement

1. Animal industry — United States — Statistics — Periodicals. 2. Meat industry and trade — United States — Statistics — Peri-

odicals. 3. Livestock — United States — Statistics — Periodicals. I. United States. Dept. of Agriculture. Economic Research Service. II. Series: Statistical bulletin (United States. Dept. of Agriculture) ; no. 874. sn-93027857 OCLC 26983317

94-22938

A 1.47:993

Agricultural statistics (Washington, D.C.)

Agricultural statistics / United States Department of Agriculture. Washington, D.C. : The Department : For sale by the Supt. of Docs., U.S. G.P.O., Supt. of Docs., U.S. Govt. Print. Off., Washington, D.C. 20402

v. ; 24 cm.

Annual

$19.00

Began with 1936. Shipping list no.: 94-9056-P. 1993. Description based on: 1980. Prior to 1936 the information contained in the present volume was published in the statistical section of the Yearbook of agriculture (Washington, D.C. : 1926). Cf. 1936, p. 1. ●Item 0001 S/N 001-000-04609-8 @ GPO ISSN 0082-9714

1. Agriculture — United States — Statistics — Periodicals. I. United States. Dept. of Agriculture. II. United States. National Agricultural Statistics Service. HD1751.A43 sn-87042980 338.10973 OCLC 01773189

94-22939

A 1.75:644-10

Brown, Dennis M.

Value-added agriculture as a growth strategy [[microform]] / Dennis M. Brown, Mindy F. Petrulis. — [Washington, D.C.?] : U.S. Dept. of Agriculture, Economic Research Service, [1993]

[2] p. ; 28 cm. — (Agriculture information bulletin ; no. 644-10) Caption title. At head of title: Issues for the 1990's : rural economy. Distributed to depository libraries in microfiche. Shipping list no.: 93-0302-P. "April 1993." Includes bibliographical references (p. [2]). Microfiche. [Washington, D.C.?] : Supt. of Docs., U.S. G.P.O., [1994] 1 microfiche : negative. ●Item 0004 (MF)

1. Food industry and trade — Southern States. 2. Agricultural processing plants — Southern States. 3. Rural development — Southern States. I. Petrulis, Mindy F. II. United States. Dept. of Agriculture. Economic Research Service. III. Title. IV. Title: Value added agriculture as a growth strategy. V. Title: Issue for the 1990's, rural economy. VI. Series. OCLC 30855956

94-22940

A 1.75:664-4

Madell, Mary Lisa.

EC agricultural policy reform [[microform]] / Mary Lisa Madall. — [Washington, D.C.?] : U.S. Dept. of Agriculture, Economic Research Service, [1993]

[2] p. ; 28 cm. — (Agriculture information bulletin ; no. 664-4) Caption title. At head of title: Issues for the 1990's: trade. Distributed to depository libraries in microfiche. Shipping list

Page 1

FIGURE 6–6   The *Monthly Catalog of United States Government Publications* is an excellent resource for finding federal documents (Mo Cat, Nov. 1994, p.1)

Senate with 100 members, and the House of Representatives with 435 members. Before legislation can become law, it must pass both chambers and then be presented to the president for signature.

The legislative process can be quite complicated and even convoluted. The process for passing legislation varies from situation to situation. Figure 6–7 is a capsule version of the manner in which a statute becomes law. Remember, steps of this process may be repeated or abbreviated in particular situations.

Introducing Legislation

Most legislation can be introduced in either the Senate or the House (except for revenue measures, which must be introduced in the House). Legislation may begin as a bill, a joint resolution, a concurrent resolution or a simple resolution. **Bills** are the typical vehicle by which legislation is introduced. The language of a bill may change during the legislative process. Several bills may be introduced on the same subject, and there may be a Senate version of a bill and a House version of a bill. A member or members of Congress (called a sponsor or cosponsors) introduce legislation. After a bill is introduced into Congress, it is assigned a number. A Senate bill will be assigned a number that begins with the letter "S," and a House bill will be assigned a number that begins with the letters "H.R." Figure 6–8 is a sample bill. Bills die if they are not enacted by the end of a congressional term. If a bill is reintroduced, it may be given a new number.

Often a legal researcher can gain considerable insight into the legislative process by comparing the words of the original bill with the words of the actual statute that has been enacted into law. By studying the changes, a researcher may see that the law is broader or narrower in scope than the original bill, that certain exceptions were essential to the passage of the law, that Congress left certain issues to be handled by an administrative agency or a court, or that there were compromises on key words in the law. Any amendments to the bill will tip the researcher to clues about the legislative intent of Congress because changes to a bill usually are made deliberately, perhaps after considerable debate.

In addition to bills, Congress adopts resolutions. A resolution refers to the adoption of a motion by a legislative body. A **simple resolution** (abbreviated "H.Res." or "S.Res.") is passed only by one body of

---

LEGAL TERMS

bills† Proposed laws that are presented to the legislature for enactment.

simple resolution A motion passed by only one body of Congress that is used mainly for procedural housekeeping purposes.

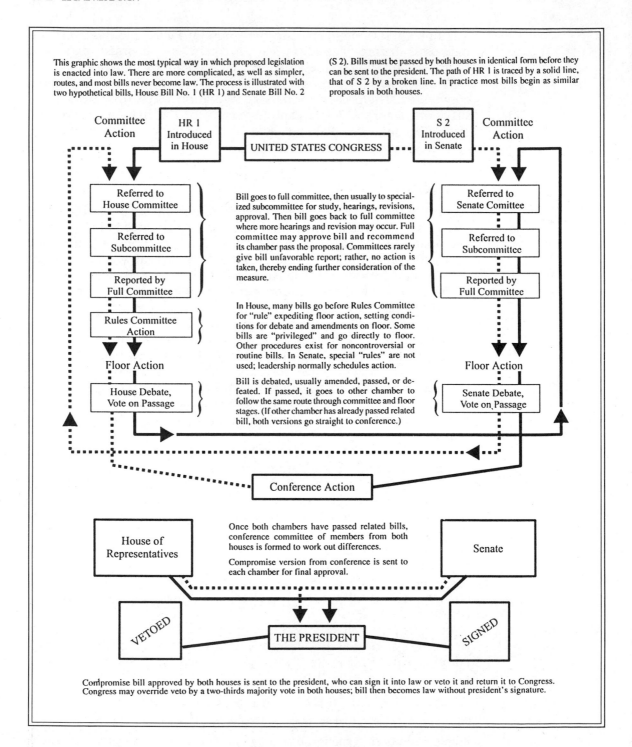

This graphic shows the most typical way in which proposed legislation is enacted into law. There are more complicated, as well as simpler, routes, and most bills never become law. The process is illustrated with two hypothetical bills, House Bill No. 1 (HR 1) and Senate Bill No. 2

(S 2). Bills must be passed by both houses in identical form before they can be sent to the president. The path of HR 1 is traced by a solid line, that of S 2 by a broken line. In practice most bills begin as similar proposals in both houses.

Committee Action

HR 1 Introduced in House

UNITED STATES CONGRESS

S 2 Introduced in Senate

Committee Action

Referred to House Committee

Referred to Subcommittee

Reported by Full Committee

Rules Committee Action

Floor Action

House Debate, Vote on Passage

Bill goes to full committee, then usually to specialized subcommittee for study, hearings, revisions, approval. Then bill goes back to full committee where more hearings and revision may occur. Full committee may approve bill and recommend its chamber pass the proposal. Committees rarely give bill unfavorable report; rather, no action is taken, thereby ending further consideration of the measure.

In House, many bills go before Rules Committee for "rule" expediting floor action, setting conditions for debate and amendments on floor. Some bills are "privileged" and go directly to floor. Other procedures exist for noncontroversial or routine bills. In Senate, special "rules" are not used; leadership normally schedules action.

Bill is debated, usually amended, passed, or defeated. If passed, it goes to other chamber to follow the same route through committee and floor stages. (If other chamber has already passed related bill, both versions go straight to conference.)

Referred to Senate Comittee

Referred to Subcommittee

Reported by Full Committee

Floor Action

Senate Debate, Vote on Passage

Conference Action

House of Representatives

Senate

Once both chambers have passed related bills, conference committee of members from both houses is formed to work out differences.

Compromise version from conference is sent to each chamber for final approval.

VETOED

THE PRESIDENT

SIGNED

Compromise bill approved by both houses is sent to the president, who can sign it into law or veto it and return it to Congress. Congress may override veto by a two-thirds majority vote in both houses; bill then becomes law without president's signature.

FIGURE 6–7 The standard procedure by which a federal bill becomes public law.

VERSION   As Introduced in the House
              102d CONGRESS
                 1st Session
BILL   H.R. 25
TITLE   To protect the reproductive rights of women.

IN THE HOUSE OF REPRESENTATIVES
JANUARY 3, 1991

Mr. Edwards of California (for himself, Mrs. Schroeder, Mr. Anderson, Mr. Atkins Mr. AuCoin, Mr. Beilenson, Mr. Berman, Mr. Boehlert, Mrs. Boxer, Mr. Bryant, Mr. Bustamante, Mr. Campbell of Colorado, Mr. Campbell of California, Mr. Cardin, Mr. Clay, Mrs. Collins of Illinois, Mr. Conyers, Mr. DeFazio, Mr. Dellums, Mr. Dicks, Mr. Dixon, Mr. Downey, Mr. Engel, Mr. Evans, Mr. Fascell, Mr. Fazio, Mr. Feighan, Mr. Ford of Tennessee, Mr. Frank of Massachusetts, Mr. Frost, Mr. Gallo, Mr. Gejdenson, Mr. Gray, Mr. Green, Mr. Hayes of Illinois, Mr. Hoyer, Mrs. Johnson of Connecticut, Mr. Jontz, Mr. Kennedy, Mr. Kopetski, Mr. Kostmayer, Mr. Lehman of Florida, Mr. Lehman of California, Mr. Levin of Michigan, Mr. Levine of California, Mr. Lewis of Georgia, Mrs. Lowey of New York, Mr. Machtley, Mr. Markey, Mr. Matsui, Mr. McDermott, Mr. Miller of California, Mr. Miller of Washington, Mr. Mineta, Mrs. Mink, Mr. Moody, Mrs. Morella, Mr. Mrazek, Mr. Owens of New York, Mr. Pallone, Mr. Payne of New Jersey, Ms. Pelosi, Mr. Porter, Mr. Price, Mr. Richardson, Mrs. Roukema, Mr. Roybal, Mr. Sabo, Mr. Scheuer, Mr. Schumer, Mr. Shays, Mr. Skaggs, Ms. Slaughter of New York, Mr. Smith of Florida, Ms. Snowe, Mr. Solarz, Mr. Stark, Mr. Stokes, Mr. Studds, Mr. Swift, Mr. Torres, Mr. Towns, Mr. Udall, Mrs. Unsoeld, Ms. Waters, Mr. Waxman, Mr. Weiss, Mr. Wheat, Mr. Wolpe, Mr. Wyden, and Mr. Yates), introduced the following bill; which was referred to the Committee on the Judiciary.

TEXT   A BILL
To protect the reproductive rights of women.
       Be it enacted by the Senate and House of Representatives of the United States of America in Congress assembled,
SECTION 1. SHORT TITLE.
       This Act may be cited as the 'Freedom of Choice Act of 1991'.
SEC. 2. RIGHT TO CHOOSE.
       (a) In General. - Except as provided in subsection (b), a State may not restrict the right of a woman to choose to terminate a pregnancy -
              (1) before fetal viability; or
              (2) at any time, if such termination is necessary to protect the life or health of the woman.
       (b) Medically Necessary Requirements. - A State may impose requirements medically necessary to protect the life or health of women referred to in subsection (a).
SEC. 3. DEFINITION OF 'STATE'.
       As used in this Act, the term 'State' includes the District of Columbia, the Commonwealth of Puerto Rico, and each other territory or possession of the United States.

FIGURE 6–8   An excerpt from a bill introduced in the House of Representatives

Congress and is used mainly for procedural or housekeeping purposes. A **joint resolution** (abbreviated "H.J.Res." or "S.J.Res.") is a resolution adopted by both houses of Congress. If a joint resolution has been approved by the president, it has the effect of law. A joint resolution can be used to introduce a bill, but more typically is used to amend a pending bill. A joint resolution may be used in connection with a constitutional amendment or may pertain to money matters. A **concurrent resolution** (abbreviated "H.Con.Res." or "S.Con.Res.") is a resolution passed by one house and sent to the other house for its concurrence. A concurrent resolution may be used to send a message to a foreign country or to fix the time to adjourn Congress.

Locating Bills and Resolutions

The original text of a bill or resolution can be located at United States depository libraries. A researcher also can obtain copies of legislation from a congressional representative by writing the Clerk of the House or Senate, or by ordering a copy from the Government Printing Office. Private publishers provide bills and resolutions to their subscribers. Commerce Clearing House (CCH), for example, provides this information to subscribers of the Electronic Legislative Search Service (ELSS) and to subscribers of the *Legislative Reporting Services*. Congressional Information Service provides this information on microfilm to subscribers. In fact, "CIS/Congressional Bills, Resolutions and Laws on Microfiche" has a most complete collection of bills and resolutions. West Publishing provides the full text of slip laws in the *U.S. Code Congressional and Administrative News* (U.S.C.C.A.N.). The *United States Code Service* offers advance sheets with this information.

SIDEBAR

Billcast is a database available on-line on LEXIS and WESTLAW. This service contains a summary of public bills introduced in Congress with odds of whether the legislation will pass. This service is updated weekly.

Assigning Legislation to Committee

Preliminary action on legislation takes place in committee. A committee may hold hearings, commission a study called a committee

────────────── LEGAL TERMS ──────────────

joint resolution A resolution adopted by both houses of Congress. If it has been approved by the president, it has the effect of law.

concurrent resolution A resolution that originates and is passed by one house of Congress and is sent to the other house for its concurrence.

print, and issue a report on the legislation. These actions may be performed by a subcommittee rather than the whole committee.

Committee Hearings

Before a bill becomes law, it usually is assigned to a committee for study. This committee may hold **hearings** on the bill. Government officials, experts, scholars, and concerned citizens may testify at these hearings about the merits of the proposed legislation. Hearings are held for various reasons such as to gather facts, to survey political opinion, or even to stall legislation. Transcripts are kept of these proceedings.

Hearing transcripts are not always available to the public. Those that are available can be purchased from the Government Printing Office. The *CIS/Index* published by Congressional Information Service indexes each hearing and provides a brief abstract about the hearing. Microfiche copies of the hearing transcripts are also available from CIS.

Committee Prints

A committee sometimes commissions a study about proposed legislation called a **committee print.** These studies are conducted by the committee staff or by outside consultants. As with transcripts of committee hearings, the researcher can identify whether committee prints are available by searching the *CIS/Index.* Committee prints can be purchased from the G.P.O. or found at federal depository libraries.

Committee Reports

Considerable legislation simply dies in committee. Only a small percentage is reported from the committee to the floor of Congress. Occasionally the report of the committee recommends against passage of the legislation, but most often if a bill is reported from committee, the committee is recommending passage. A written **committee report** is prepared that analyzes and discusses the opinions of the committee.

Committee reports are an important source of legislative history because these reports detail the intent and rationale of the committee members. Committee members who disagree with the bill may even

---
LEGAL TERMS

hearing† A proceeding in which evidence is introduced and witnesses are examined so that findings of fact can be made and a determination rendered.

committee print A study of proposed legislation commissioned by a committee and conducted by the committee staff or by outside consultants.

committee report A written report of a committee analyzing and discussing proposed legislation, and recommending whether or not it should be passed.

prepare a minority report. Committee reports provide objective evidence of the legislature's intent and can assist in understanding the meaning of a statute.

Committee reports are published in individual pamphlets and collected in a set of volumes referred to as the *Serial Set*. This set also collects other important congressional documents. The West Publishing set called the *United States Code Congressional and Administrative News* (U.S.C.C.A.N.) collects committee reports for more important legislation. Each U.S.C.C.A.N. edition covers a session of Congress and contains a section reprinting the text of the statutes and another section containing the legislative history of these statutes. There is a subject index at the end of the final volume of each edition to direct the researcher to precise page references. The U.S.C.A. provides cross-references to U.S.C.C.A.N., and committee reports also can be identified by the *CIS/Index*.

Floor Action

After the bill is reported favorably from a committee, it is placed on a calendar and called upon for action through the parliamentary process. The members then debate the bill. Amendments may be proposed and voted upon on the floor of Congress. After the bill has been fully debated, a vote is taken. If approved, the bill or resolution becomes an act, and the act is referred to the other chamber of Congress for a similar process. In the second chamber, the act may be accepted, rejected, or amended. The second chamber may even ignore the act or pass its own version. The process in the second chamber is similar to the process in the first chamber with an assignment of the bill to a committee, hearings, preparation of committee prints, and reports from the committee for floor action. The Congressional Record, an official government publication, as well as its predecessors (the *Annals of Congress, Register of Debates,* and the *Congressional Globe*) are the main sources for following what happens on the floor of Congress. The *Congressional Record* is also a source for finding the vote tallies on a piece of legislation.

SIDEBAR The paralegal should know that in the past, the *Congressional Record* was not necessarily a verbatim transcript of the floor debate and speeches. After a transcript has been prepared of the floor proceedings, a member is permitted under the rules to revise and extend his or her remarks. This allows members to insert remarks never given and even to change the entire content of the actual remarks. The official record of congressional proceedings can be found in the *House Journal* and the *Senate Journal*. These journals contain minutes of the daily sessions and details of any amendments, motions, and notes. Both journals have a "History of Bills and Resolutions" section that traces the action taken on a particular bill or resolution.

The *Congressional Record* is published daily when Congress is in session. It is found on-line on both LEXIS and WESTLAW, both of which are discussed in the next chapter. Each issue of the *Congressional Record* contains four sections: the proceedings of the House; the proceedings of the Senate; a "Daily Digest"; and the "Extensions of Remarks." A separate biweekly index also is published.

Proceedings of the House and Senate

The *Congressional Record* is like a daily newspaper of Congress. The daily edition contains the floor debates and proceedings, speeches, amendments, and sometimes even the full text of bills or resolutions. The daily edition also contains messages from the president and notices of upcoming actions.

Daily Digest

Each issue of the *Congressional Record* contains a "Daily Digest" that highlights the day's activities, including what bills and resolutions were passed or rejected as well as the actions taken by the committees. Figure 6–9 is an example from the "Daily Digest." This digest is cumulated annually. This annual cumulation contains a "History of Bills Enacted into Public Law" section and is arranged by public law number.

Extensions of Remarks

Members of Congress are permitted to include supplemental remarks and extraneous materials such as poems, letters, and even recipes. This section of the *Congressional Record* is not cumulated in the annual bound volumes. It is sometimes referred to as the Appendix to the *Congressional Record*. Figure 6–10 is from the "Extension of Remarks" section of the *Congressional Record*.

Biweekly Index

Every two weeks the *Congressional Record* prints an index in a separate pamphlet. This biweekly *Congressional Record Index* contains a subject and member's name index as well as a "History of Bills and Resolutions" section that is organized by bill number. (See Figure 6–11.) The "History of Bills and Resolutions" section contains bill status information including information about cosponsors, amendments, the date legislation is passed, and conference reports.

CW03, U.S. Marine Corps; Herbert J. Smith and Pam Smith, both of Ijamsville, Maryland; John P. Riggs, St. Marys, West Virginia; Christopher Dauer, Leominster, Massachusetts; and Brian Martin, Niles, Michigan.

YAVAPAI PRESCOTT WATER RIGHTS SETTLEMENT

Committee on Indian Affairs: Committee concluded hearings on S. 1146, to provide for the settlement of the water rights claims of the Yavapai-Prescott Indian Tribe in Yavapai County, Arizona, after receiving testimony from John Duffy, Counselor to the Secretary and Chairman of the Working Group on Indian Water Settlements, and William Swan, Office of Field Solicitor (Phoenix, Arizona), both of the Department of the Interior; Robert Ogo, David Bodney, and Jack Utter, all on behalf of the Yavapai-Prescott Tribal Council, and John R. Moffitt and Brad Huza, both of the City of Prescott, all of Prescott, Arizona; and Richard H. Silverman and John Weldon, both on behalf of the Salt River Project, Phoenix, Arizona.

PHARMACEUTICAL MARKETPLACE REFORM

Special Committee on Aging: Committee concluded hearings to examine the Administration's national health care reform proposal's impact on the effectiveness of marketplace competition for prescription drugs, after receiving testimony from Philip R. Lee, Assistant Secretary for Health, and Helen M. Smits, Deputy Administrator, Health Care Financing Administration, both of the Department of Health and Human Services; Judith L. Wagner, Senior Associate, Health Program, Office of Technology Assessment; Mark Whitener, Deputy Director, Bureau of Competition, Federal Trade Commission; Abbey S. Meyers, National Organization for Rare Disorders, New Fairfield, Connecticut; Benji K. Wyatt, Pace Alliance, Lawrence, Kansas; Morton H. Katz, Clay-Park Labs Inc., Bronx, New York, on behalf of the National Association of Pharmaceutical Manufacturers; and Gerald J. Mossinghoff, Pharmaceutical Manufacturers Association, Washington, D.C.

House of Representatives

Chamber Action

Bills Introduced: 11 public bills, H.R. 3511–3521; and 1 resolution, H. Con. Res. 181 were introduced.
Page H9853

Reports Filed: Reports were filed as follows:

H.R. 1425, to improve the management, productivity, and use of Indian agricultural lands and resources, amended (H. Rept. 103–367);

H.R. 3511, rescinding certain budget authority (H. Rept. 103–368); and

H. Res. 311, providing for consideration of H.R. 3450, to implement the North American Free Trade Agreement.
Page H9853

Journal: By a yea-and-nay vote of 250 yeas to 157 nays, Roll No. 567, the House approved the Journal of Monday, November 15.
Pages H9707–08

Meeting Hour: Agreed that the House will meet at 9 a.m. on Wednesday, November 17.
Page H9719

Memorial Cairn in Arlington National Cemetery: House passed S.J. Res. 129, to authorize the placement of a memorial cairn in Arlington National Cemetery, Arlington, Virginia, to honor the 270 victims of the terrorist bombing of Pan Am Flight 103—clearing the measure for the President.
Pages H9719–21

Veterans Health Administration Officials: House passed S. 1534, amend title 38, United States Code, to repeal a requirement that the Under Secretary for Health in the Department of Veterans Affairs be a doctor of medicine.
Pages H9721–23

Agreed to the Montgomery amendment in the nature of a substitute.
Pages H9722–23

Agreed to amend the title.
Page H9723

Suspensions: House voted to suspend the rules and pass the following measures:

Veterans health care services: H.R. 3313, amended, to amend title 38, United States Code, to improve health care services of the Department of Veterans Affairs relating to women veterans, to extend and expand authority for the Secretary of Veterans Affairs to provide priority health care to veterans who were exposed to ionizing radiation or to Agent Orange, and to expand the scope of services that may be provided to veterans through Vet Centers;
Pages H9723–31

FIGURE 6–9   An excerpt from the *Daily Digest* (*Congressional Record,* Nov. 16, 1993, Vol. 139, No. 159)

November 18, 1993   CONGRESSIONAL RECORD — *Extensions of Remarks*   E 2933

ameliorate the problem: they are part of the problem.

Career paths in the U.S. Foreign Service do not generally include more than one tour within the U.N. system. Such assignments are not in any case perceived as especially career-enhancing, and so they are not sought after by the best and brightest FSOs. The experience gained in such a tour is only rarely exploited later on. If, however, the United States wants to have a major influence in these increasingly important multilateral settings, this self-defeating situation needs change. It could be accomplished by the creation of a multilateral "career cone" for FSOs, or simply by making it clear that multilateral experience will be rewarded in future assignments—up to and including career ambassadorships. Either way, this is a matter that deserves attention at the highest levels of the U.S. government.

U.S. leadership in the world begins at home. The U.S. role in the United Nations can be effective only as it reflects clear and coherent U.S. foreign policies generally. It also has to be based on an informed assessment of what the U.N. can, and cannot, be expected to contribute to U.S. interests. The reverse also is true: an "effective" U.N. has to receive clear and coherent signals from the United States, among all of the world's major powers. A U.N. with strong U.S. leadership, and with a reasonable degree of managerial efficiency and a persistent focus on its collective security responsibilities, can make measured progress toward the goals of the Charter—which is important for the United Nations, and for the United States.

TRIBUTE TO EDWARD FREEMAN

HON. EDOLPHUS TOWNS
OF NEW YORK

IN THE HOUSE OF REPRESENTATIVES

Thursday, November 18, 1993

Mr. TOWNS. Mr. Speaker, it is with great pleasure that I rise today to recognize a dear friend, great athlete, and outstanding educator, Mr. Edward Freeman. I pay tribute to this honorable man because he has unselfishly dedicated his time and expertise to so many of New York's youth.

Edward received his academic training at New York University, Texas State University, and Boston University. He concentrated his studies in the areas of sports medicine, biology, health, and physical education. Mr. Freeman played professional football with the Boston Patriots and New York Titans. He pursued his graduate studies and won an annual fellowship in safety education.

An exceptionally talented man, Mr. Freeman is ranked in the top 20 among USPTA Tennis Professionals—Pro.1. He has used his expertise in tennis to coach many youth groups, namely the Pee Wee program at Wimbledon, a group he created for children 3–6 years of age. He has also coached the boys and girls tennis teams at Hempstead Public High School, and the children of Roslyn Racquet Club.

When Edward is not coaching tennis, he is diligently committing himself to working with youth in community centers and participating in tennis tournaments. He annually participates in the Stop the World Hunger tennis tournaments. As a concerned and dedicated athlete and educator, Edward dedicates his summers to directing tennis camps and spe-

cial youth programs. During the school year he teaches physical education.

I applaud Edward Freeman for his generosity and dedication to our children. He is rich in character and very deserving of each and every honor that is bestowed upon him. Please join me in commending Mr. Freeman on his outstanding achievements.

SALUTE TO THE VENTURA COUNTY PROFESSIONAL FIREFIGHTERS' ASSOCIATION

HON. ELTON GALLEGLY
OF CALIFORNIA

IN THE HOUSE OF REPRESENTATIVES

Thursday, November 18, 1993

Mr. GALLEGLY. Mr. Speaker, I rise today to pay special honor to the members of the Ventura County Professional Firefighters' Association, who on Saturday will hold their second annual charity ball.

This year, some 350 people will attend the event, which will raise funds for a very special organization, the Alisa Ann Ruch California Burn Foundation. The foundation is a living memorial to an 8-year-old girl who was fatally burned in a common backyard barbecue accident—and to our heroic firefighters who are concerned about the prevention and proper treatment of burn injuries.

Since its inception in 1971, the foundation has grown to become the only agency providing burn assistance and burn prevention education throughout California. I'm sure my colleagues are aware that the foundation developed the nationally recognized Stop, Drop, Roll program that informs children what to do if their clothes catch fire.

I also want to take this opportunity to once again thank Ventura County's firefighters for their dedication and professionalism. Once again, during our recent series of devastating brushfires in southern California, the men and women of the Ventura County Fire Department made the heroic look ordinary as they battled the searing flames and gale-force winds that blackened so many thousands of acres. It is truly a monument to their skill and bravery that so few lives were lost and that so many homes were saved.

Mr. Speaker, I ask my colleagues to join me in honoring the members of the Ventura County Professional Firefighters' Association.

MICHAEL BROWN AND RAYMOND FIELDS, EAGLE SCOUTS

HON. JACK REED
OF RHODE ISLAND

IN THE HOUSE OF REPRESENTATIVES

Thursday, November 18, 1993

Mr. REED. Mr. Speaker, I rise today to salute two distinguished young men from Rhode Island who have attained the rank of Eagle Scout in the Boy Scouts of America. They are Michael Brown and Raymond Fields of Troop 2 Arctic in West Warwick and they are honored this week for their noteworthy achievement.

Not every young American who joins the Boy Scouts earns the prestigious Eagle Scout Award. In fact, only 2.5 percent of all Boy Scouts do. To earn the award, a Boy Scout

must fulfill requirements in the areas of leadership, service, and outdoor skills. He must earn 21 merit badges, 11 of which are required from areas such as citizenship in the community, citizenship in the Nation, citizenship in the world, safety, environmental science, and first aid.

As he progresses through the Boy Scout ranks, a Scout must demonstrate participation in increasingly more responsible service projects. He must also demonstrate leadership skills by holding one or more specific youth leadership positions in this patrol and/or troop. These young men have distinguished themselves in accordance with these criteria.

For their Eagle Scout projects, Michael painted the lines on the much-used basketball court of St. John the Baptist Church, while Raymond spent his summer helping to clean up Phenix Square Park for residents to use.

Mr. Speaker, I ask you and my colleagues to join me in saluting Eagle Scouts Michael Brown and Raymond Fields. In turn, we must duly recognize the Boy Scouts of America for establishing the Eagle Scout Award and the strenuous criteria its aspirants must meet. This program has through its 80 years honed and enhanced the leadership skills and commitment to public service of many outstanding Americans, two dozen of whom now serve in the House.

It is my sincere belief that Michael Brown and Raymond Fields will continue their public service and in so doing will further distinguish themselves and consequently better their community. I join friends, colleagues, and family who this week salute them.

WORLD AIDS DAY

HON. JAMES H. BILBRAY
OF NEVADA

IN THE HOUSE OF REPRESENTATIVES

Thursday, November 18, 1993

Mr. BILBRAY. Mr. Speaker, December 1, 1993 is World AIDS Day. Las Vegas, NV, my home town, has been exemplary in their struggle dealing with HIV/AIDS. Our community has shown compassion and diligence, providing one of the most comprehensive coordinated HIV/AIDS care programs in the Nation.

On this day, the Clark County Coalition of HIV/AIDS Service Providers will be sponsoring a gathering of local, State, and Federal agencies, community based organizations, as well as businesses that deal specifically with HIV/AIDS patients. The participants will be distributing literature and information to the public. The goal is to educate and enlighten the public to the facts about HIV and AIDS. I am delighted that my constituents will have the opportunity to live in the light of the truth.

World AIDS Day provides an opportunity to focus on HIV infection and AIDS; caring for people with HIV infection and AIDS, and learning about the disease. I urge all citizens to take part in activities and observances designed to increase awareness and understanding. Only through understanding will we be able to meet the challenge of HIV/AIDS.

FIGURE 6–10   An excerpt illustrating the extensions of House of Representative members. (*Congressional Record,* Nov. 18, 1993, Vol. 139, No. 161)

Joint Conference Action

If an act passes one chamber and substantial amendments are made to that act in the other chamber, then the matter is referred to a conference committee. A conference committee consists of members from both the House and the Senate. This committee studies the differences in the legislation and reports on whether the committee can agree on a final version. Another committee may need to be called if the first committee is unsuccessful in reporting on a final version. Both the Senate and the House vote on whether to adopt the revised legislation or recommit the changes to the conference committee. Like the committee reports of the House and the Senate, these conference committee reports are important sources of legislative history. Like the

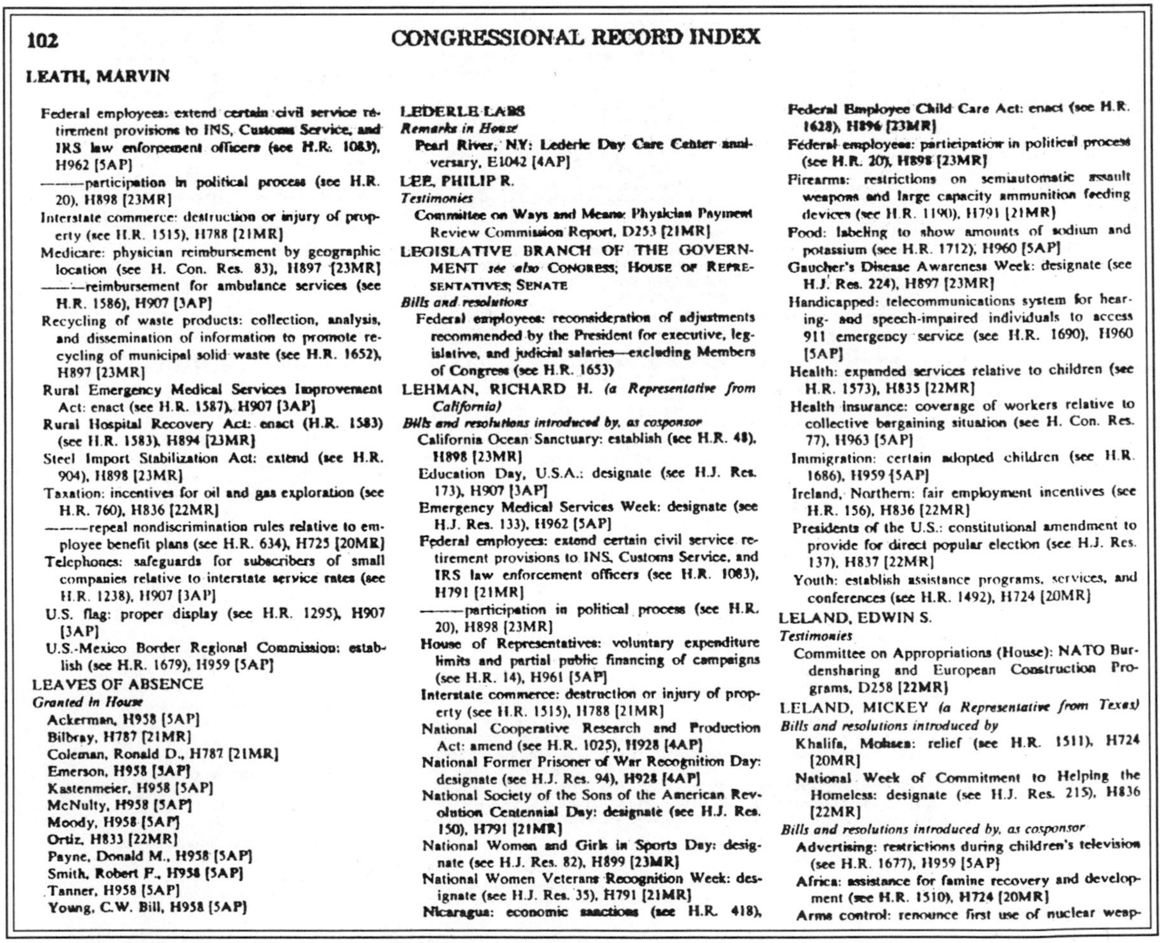

102 CONGRESSIONAL RECORD INDEX

LEATH, MARVIN

Federal employees: extend certain civil service retirement provisions to INS, Customs Service, and IRS law enforcement officers (see H.R. 1083), H962 [5AP]
———participation in political process (see H.R. 20), H898 [23MR]
Interstate commerce: destruction or injury of property (see H.R. 1515), H788 [21MR]
Medicare: physician reimbursement by geographic location (see H. Con. Res. 83), H897 [23MR]
———reimbursement for ambulance services (see H.R. 1586), H907 [3AP]
Recycling of waste products: collection, analysis, and dissemination of information to promote recycling of municipal solid waste (see H.R. 1652), H897 [23MR]
Rural Emergency Medical Services Improvement Act: enact (see H.R. 1587), H907 [3AP]
Rural Hospital Recovery Act: enact (H.R. 1583) (see H.R. 1583), H894 [23MR]
Steel Import Stabilization Act: extend (see H.R. 904), H898 [23MR]
Taxation: incentives for oil and gas exploration (see H.R. 760), H836 [22MR]
———repeal nondiscrimination rules relative to employee benefit plans (see H.R. 634), H725 [20MR]
Telephones: safeguards for subscribers of small companies relative to interstate service rates (see H.R. 1238), H907 [3AP]
U.S. flag: proper display (see H.R. 1295), H907 [3AP]
U.S.-Mexico Border Regional Commission: establish (see H.R. 1679), H959 [5AP]

LEAVES OF ABSENCE
Granted in House
Ackerman, H958 [5AP]
Bilbray, H787 [21MR]
Coleman, Ronald D., H787 [21MR]
Emerson, H958 [5AP]
Kastenmeier, H958 [5AP]
McNulty, H958 [5AP]
Moody, H958 [5AP]
Ortiz, H833 [22MR]
Payne, Donald M., H958 [5AP]
Smith, Robert F., H958 [5AP]
Tanner, H958 [5AP]
Young, C.W. Bill, H958 [5AP]

LEDERLE LABS
Remarks in House
Pearl River, NY: Lederle Day Care Center anniversary, E1042 [4AP]

LEE, PHILIP R.
Testimonies
Committee on Ways and Means: Physician Payment Review Commission Report, D253 [21MR]

LEGISLATIVE BRANCH OF THE GOVERNMENT *see also* CONGRESS; HOUSE OF REPRESENTATIVES; SENATE
Bills and resolutions
Federal employees: reconsideration of adjustments recommended by the President for executive, legislative, and judicial salaries—excluding Members of Congress (see H.R. 1653)

LEHMAN, RICHARD H. *(a Representative from California)*
Bills and resolutions introduced by, as cosponsor
California Ocean Sanctuary: establish (see H.R. 48), H898 [23MR]
Education Day, U.S.A.: designate (see H.J. Res. 173), H907 [3AP]
Emergency Medical Services Week: designate (see H.J. Res. 133), H962 [5AP]
Federal employees: extend certain civil service retirement provisions to INS, Customs Service, and IRS law enforcement officers (see H.R. 1083), H791 [21MR]
———participation in political process (see H.R. 20), H898 [23MR]
House of Representatives: voluntary expenditure limits and partial public financing of campaigns (see H.R. 14), H961 [5AP]
Interstate commerce: destruction or injury of property (see H.R. 1515), H788 [21MR]
National Cooperative Research and Production Act: amend (see H.R. 1025), H928 [4AP]
National Former Prisoner of War Recognition Day: designate (see H.J. Res. 94), H928 [4AP]
National Society of the Sons of the American Revolution Centennial Day: designate (see H.J. Res. 150), H791 [21MR]
National Women and Girls in Sports Day: designate (see H.J. Res. 82), H899 [23MR]
National Women Veterans Recognition Week: designate (see H.J. Res. 35), H791 [21MR]
Nicaragua: economic sanctions (see H.R. 418),
Federal Employee Child Care Act: enact (see H.R. 1628), H896 [23MR]
Federal employees: participation in political process (see H.R. 20), H898 [23MR]
Firearms: restrictions on semiautomatic assault weapons and large capacity ammunition feeding devices (see H.R. 1190), H791 [21MR]
Food: labeling to show amounts of sodium and potassium (see H.R. 1712), H960 [5AP]
Gaucher's Disease Awareness Week: designate (see H.J. Res. 224), H897 [23MR]
Handicapped: telecommunications system for hearing- and speech-impaired individuals to access 911 emergency service (see H.R. 1690), H960 [5AP]
Health: expanded services relative to children (see H.R. 1573), H835 [22MR]
Health insurance: coverage of workers relative to collective bargaining situation (see H. Con. Res. 77), H963 [5AP]
Immigration: certain adopted children (see H.R. 1686), H959 [5AP]
Ireland, Northern: fair employment incentives (see H.R. 156), H836 [22MR]
Presidents of the U.S.: constitutional amendment to provide for direct popular election (see H.J. Res. 137), H837 [22MR]
Youth: establish assistance programs, services, and conferences (see H.R. 1492), H724 [20MR]

LELAND, EDWIN S.
Testimonies
Committee on Appropriations (House): NATO Burdensharing and European Construction Programs, D258 [22MR]

LELAND, MICKEY *(a Representative from Texas)*
Bills and resolutions introduced by
Khalifa, Mohsen: relief (see H.R. 1511), H724 [20MR]
National Week of Commitment to Helping the Homeless: designate (see H.J. Res. 215), H836 [22MR]
Bills and resolutions introduced by, as cosponsor
Advertising: restrictions during children's television (see H.R. 1677), H959 [5AP]
Africa: assistance for famine recovery and development (see H.R. 1510), H724 [20MR]
Arms control: renounce first use of nuclear weap-

FIGURE 6–11 The *Congressional Record* Index provides biweekly information about legislative activity (*Congressional Record Index,* Vol. 135, Nos. 32–40, Mar. 20 to Apr. 7, 1989)

committee reports of either the House or the Senate, conference reports are cataloged in MoCat and the *CIS/Index*. These reports also can be obtained from the G.P.O. The most important of these reports can be found in the U.S.C.C.A.N. and in the *Congressional Record*. These reports are collected in an official compilation called the *Serial Set* and in full text on microfiche available from the Congressional Information Service. The CIS is an important source of information about committee actions.

When an act is passed by Congress, it is presented to the president (as required by the Constitution), and the president can sign it or veto it. Congress may override a veto by a two-thirds majority vote in both houses. A law may be either a public or private law. A public law is a law that affects the public generally. A private statute is a law for a particular individual or situation. For instance, a private statute might award damages or a pension to a citizen. Both public and private law numbers are in sequence and reference the session of Congress. For example, Public Law 103-1 (cited as P.L. 103-1) references the first public law passed by the 103d Congress.

Compiling a Legislative History

As already seen, a bill or resolution can go through a circuitous process before becoming a statute. In some instances, the government or a private group will retrace the legislative history for a particular statute in a compiled legislative history. More often researchers need to compile the history themselves. Fortunately, a researcher can track legislation now by using on-line computer services. For example, the House of Representatives operates LEGIS, which contains bill status information. All information is updated, and the public can use LEGIS. Other computer on-line services for tracing legislative history include Legi-Slate, CCH's Electronic Legislation Search System (ELSS), Congressional Quarterly's Washington Alert Service, and WESTLAW or LEXIS.

The following are some noncomputerized methods that can be used to compile the legislative history of a particular bill or resolution.

CIS/Index

The *CIS/Index to Publications of the U.S. Congress*, published by the Congressional Information Service, Inc., indexes and abstracts most of the major documents of Congress including committee prints and reports, hearings, and other House and Senate documents. It has a status table for legislation that is quite complete. This index can be researched manually or on-line on computer through several different services. The *CIS/Index* is organized by subject, title, member's name, and number. In-depth indexes with numerous titles are published by CIS, including the *CIS U.S. Congressional Committee Hearings Index*, the *CIS U.S. Congressional Committee Prints Index*, and the *CIS Index to Unpublished U.S. Senate Committee Hearing*. Overnight delivery of microfiche copies is available from CIS.

Congressional Record

A researcher can reconstruct a legislative history by using the "Daily Digest" and the "History of Bills and Resolutions" sections found in the *Congressional Record*. The "History of Bills and Resolutions" is a table that gives a summary of each bill or resolution, the committee that considered the matter, and the action taken on the bill or resolution. This table is published biweekly in the index to the *Congressional Record* and is cumulated for each session in the bound volumes.

Each daily issue of the *Congressional Record* also summarizes legislative actions in the "Daily Digest" section. The "Daily Digest" contains a subject index that tells the status of pending legislation. The "Daily Digest" is cumulated at the end of each session in a separate volume of the *Congressional Record*. This cumulation is entitled the "History of Bills Enacted into Public Law." Notice that this section identifies legislation by public law number rather than bill number.

CCH Congressional Index

Commerce Clearing House provides an index of legislative action in its *Congressional Index*. This looseleaf service contains a "Status of House Bills" section and a "Status of Senate Bills" section that show the current status of bills and resolutions. These features are cumulated. Enacted legislation can be found in the "Enactments-Vetoes" section. This section contains listings by public law number and original bill number and is indexed by subject and sponsor.

Congressional Calendars

Both bodies of Congress publish calendars that are sent to federal depository libraries. The most useful is the *House Calendars,* which details Senate actions as well as House actions. One section of the *House Calendars* entitled "Numerical Order of Bills and Resolutions Which Have Passed Either or Both Houses, and Bills Now Pending on the Calendars" provides the status of all bills and resolutions. There is also a section that is organized by public and private law number. Another section is organized by bill number, and this section provides committee report number, dates of passage, conference report information, and public law numbers.

State Legislative History

State legislatures pass laws in much the same way as does Congress. However, in many states, legislative history is difficult to locate or is not kept in any official manner. In a few states, private companies provide legislative materials to subscribers, and some states have computer access to information about legislative history. State libraries located in state capitols are sometimes a source for this information.

It is not uncommon for commissions or agencies to make proposals for new legislation. These commissions or agencies may publish studies or comments about the legislation that can be helpful in explaining the legislative intent. Some of these materials have been summarized in the *Legislative Research Checklist* published by the Council of State Governments. Another method of research is to contact a local state representative for assistance.

Summary

- A looseleaf service is a comprehensive collection of statutes, regulations, cases, and other source materials pertaining to an area of the law. A looseleaf service also provides commentary about the law.

- Uniform codes provide model language for state legislatures to follow in enacting laws. The goal of a uniform code is to promote uniformity in law throughout the United States. A model code, on the other hand, is written more from the perspective of how the law should be ideally written.

- Legal opinions of the United States Attorney General and of state attorneys general are published frequently and can be used as persuasive authority.

- The Government Printing Office publishes a massive amount of materials annually. The *Monthly Catalog of United States Government Publications* (MoCat) provides a means to access these materials.

- A committee may hold hearings, commission studies, and issue reports. The *CIS/Index* published by the Congressional Information Service provides a brief abstract about committee hearings, identifies committee prints, and provides references to committee reports.

- The *United States Code Congressional and Administrative Names* (U.S.C.C.A.N.), a West publication, is a good source for obtaining committee reports for important legislation.

- The *Congressional Record*, a government publication, is an excellent source for following what is happening on the floor of Congress.

Review Questions

1. Explain how to access and update looseleaf services.

2. Discuss the difference between a uniform code and a model code.

3. What is an attorney general opinion?

4. What is the difference between a joint resolution, a concurrent resolution, and a simple resolution?

5. How would you research committee reports?

6. What are different methods that can be used to keep abreast of what is happening on the floor of the House or the Senate?

7. What is important in the *Congressional Record?*

8. Discuss the on-line computerized and the noncomputerized methods for tracing legislative history.

9. What is a committee print?

Research Projects

1. The Civil Rights Act of 1964 is landmark legislation. Identify the looseleaf services available to you that deal with this law.

2. Trace the legislative history of the Civil Rights Act of 1964. What did Strom Thurman say about this law? What did Hubert Humphrey say about this law?

IIII
CHAPTER 7

COMPUTER-ASSISTED
LEGAL RESEARCH

For centuries, law was read from books, and the legal professional needed to learn how to master these books. In the past several decades, however, legal research has joined the information revolution. Legal professionals have begun to use computers, computer networks, and CD-ROM to assist in the legal research process. **Computer-assisted legal research (CALR)** provides new ways for legal professionals to find and read law. Paralegals entering the job market in the next decade will need to be familiar with computer research technology. This chapter explores the use of computer technology in legal research.

Development of CALR

In the early 1970s, Mead Data Central, Inc., introduced a method for researching law by computer that is now called LEXIS®, and soon thereafter West Publishing Company developed a comparable system called WESTLAW®. LEXIS was developed from the research efforts of a not-for-profit organization of lawyers named the Ohio Bar Automated Research (OBAR) that had been commissioned to develop a computer method for researching law. Today, most legal professionals use either LEXIS or WESTLAW.

Prior to the development of either LEXIS or WESTLAW, many computer users were using the **Internet.** The Internet is over 30,000 computer networks linked together. There are tens of millions of users on the Internet. The Internet, which was created in 1969 as a means to connect the United States Defense Department with university researchers who were working on government projects, is rapidly opening new opportunities for legal and nonlegal research. The Internet originally was designed to be a decentralized system of computers that would be protected from a nuclear strike, but it has become a worldwide system that links domestic and foreign governments as well as universities, libraries, private businesses, and individual computer users.

Whether researching with LEXIS and WESTLAW or on the Internet, the legal researcher is researching **on-line.** On-line means that the

---

LEGAL TERMS

computer-assisted legal research (CALR) Research by legal professionals that is conducted with the use of computers, computer networks, and CD-ROM.

Internet A computer network linking over 30,000 computer networks together that is opening new opportunities for legal and nonlegal research.

on-line Used to describe a researcher who is using a computer, usually a personal computer (PC), to connect by a modem with the memory of another computer stored at a remote location.

researcher is using a computer, usually a personal computer (PC), to connect by a modem with the memory of another computer stored at a remote location. With LEXIS and WESTLAW, for instance, the legal researcher's computer dials one of these services, and information is transmitted by telephone line to the researcher's terminal.

In addition to on-line legal research, legal professionals are using CD-ROM technology on their computers. **CD-ROM** stands for Compact Disc with Read-Only Memory. A CD-ROM stores the information on a plastic disc and a laser beam reads the information from that disc.

Advantages of CALR

In traditional legal research, publishers provide indexes, tables, and digests for locating points of law. Sometimes these methods have pinpoint accuracy; other times these methods prove quite frustrating. Before computers, a researcher was not able to efficiently locate a case or statute without finding aids because no legal professional could possibly read every case and every statute to find a point of law, given the huge numbers of cases and statutes that exist. However, a computer *can* read every case and every statute to look for a certain word or phrase.

Computers perform other functions not possible by traditional methods. A researcher with a computer can not only search the full text of documents, but also browse documents, retrieve documents, and update legal research on-line.

Searching on a Computer

A computer permits a researcher to bypass traditional research methods. With computer technology, a legal researcher can search millions of pages of documents for a particular word or phrase. In effect, the computer reads in seconds or minutes its **database** to find that word or phrase. A database is a compilation of searchable information found in a computer's memory.

Suppose a researcher wants to know the name of every case in the United States that mentions the word *abortion*. In computer parlance, a

---

LEGAL TERMS

CD-ROM (Compact Disc with Read-Only Memory) A technology by which information is stored on a plastic disc and a laser beam reads the information from that disc.

database A compilation of searchable information found in a computer's memory.

search for a particular word or phrase is called a **query** or **search request**. Given several commands, the computer can scan a database for that word in minutes. This is a main feature of on-line legal database systems such as WESTLAW and LEXIS. By connecting to an on-line database, an individual researcher can devise his or her own search query. Searching with traditional indexes, tables, and digests can be frustrating and time-consuming, but of course, a computer can search only for documents that have been previously entered into its database.

A computer search can be quite sophisticated. A query can command the computer to identify only documents where two different words appear. So the researcher might search for documents where the words *abortion* and *picketing* both appear, or the researcher might ask the computer to identify documents where a phrase such as *due process of law* appears. The researcher might be even more specific and ask the computer to identify Florida court cases where the word *abortion* and the word *picket* appear in the same sentence.

Both WESTLAW and LEXIS have included many types of legal documents in their databases:

- Primary sources - cases, statutes, regulations, and other administrative materials.

- Secondary sources - law reviews, A.L.R. annotations, and looseleaf services.

- Other legal resources - newspapers, patent and trademark information, medical information, magazines, and financial information.

So the researcher can search, for example, Kansas statutes or Mississippi cases and find relevant secondary sources as well as primary ones. As a result, an individual researcher can scan a wide variety of documents quickly and thoroughly for a particular word or phrase. A computer permits a researcher to devise his or her own search strategy without relying upon traditional methods.

SIDEBAR

Rarely should a researcher rely totally upon computers. Most legal professionals begin research projects with books such as digests, encyclopedias, A.L.R., and treatises, all of which have been discussed in previous chapters. These sources permit the researcher to refine the search before turning on the computer terminal. Computer time is relatively expensive, and a researcher will often devise a wrong query for a problem without background information on the law.

——————————— LEGAL TERMS ———————————

query or search request A command that tells a computer to search for a particular word or phrase.

A researcher should always remember that a computer can only search for data that has been put into memory. Neither LEXIS nor WESTLAW has included all the law in their databases. In fact, older cases and authority cannot be searched on either WESTLAW or LEXIS. For example, a researcher who selects the North Dakota Library on LEXIS will find the search for cases limited to North Dakota Supreme Court cases since January 1965 and to Court of Appeals cases since November 1987. North Dakota attorney general opinions written before January 1977 cannot be searched on LEXIS.

Retrieving Documents by Computer

Computers provide not only a unique way to search for documents, but also a means to retrieve documents that might not be readily available otherwise to legal professionals. Many researchers, for example, do not have access to government documents found in federal depository libraries. Although legal professionals almost always have access to statutes from their own state, seldom do they have ready access to statutes from other states. Likewise, many researchers do not have access to legal periodicals unless they live near a large university library. On-line legal databases as well as the Internet provide the researcher with a means to retrieve documents without leaving the computer terminal. Computers provide access to a wealth of documents, including official and unofficial sources as well as primary and secondary material. Legal professionals can research federal and state constitutions, statutes and regulations, legislative history, and attorney general opinions on-line. There are law reviews, A.L.R., digests, and looseleaf services on computer.

In addition, both LEXIS and WESTLAW have court cases on-line that will not be found in any other media. A citation will be assigned to a case on both LEXIS and WESTLAW. An example of a LEXIS citation is:

1993 U.S. LEXIS 250,6.

The 1993 at the beginning is the year the case was decided, the U.S. refers to the court, LEXIS is the computer service, the 250 is the assigned case number, and the 6 is the page reference. A researcher can retrieve documents by entering either the computer citation or the book citation into the computer. For example, on WESTLAW, the researcher can key find (fi) and a citation, and the computer will retrieve the document. On LEXIS, the researcher can locate cases and many other documents by pressing the LEXSEE® key or keying LEXSEE with the citation, and can locate a statute by pressing the LEXSTAT® key or keying LEXSTAT with the citation. A researcher also can retrieve documents by entering the names of the parties to the case.

Once a document has been located, the researcher can simply print the document from the screen. Or the researcher can print a list of all documents that have answered the particular query and look at the documents in books. Remember that reading a printout or a book is less expensive than reading the document on-line.

Browsing Documents on a Computer

After a search, the computer can display a list of citations of relevant documents or display the full text of the documents on the screen. Depending on the on-line service, the computer may display the documents it has located in a reverse chronological order, by jurisdiction, or by relevancy.

A unique feature of computer research is the way in which a user can browse applicable documents once the search has found them. Suppose the search retrieves a list of twenty documents. On both LEXIS and WESTLAW, the researcher can strike a key on the computer to display only the part of each of these documents that contains a search word. On LEXIS, the user can hit the function key KWIK on a LEXIS keyboard and the screen will display the search term surrounded by twenty-five words on either side of that term. For instance, if the researcher was searching for the word *abortion*, KWIK would turn to the exact page of the document on which this word appears so the researcher would not need to wade through the entire document to see whether it is relevant. Using this approach, a researcher can scan many documents quickly to see if any of them are relevant.

Updating Research

Computers can provide researchers with new information more quickly than other means. Consider, for example, a case decided by the Supreme Court only hours ago. A publisher will need to print the decision and mail it to subscribers—a process that may take a week or more. That case will be entered into WESTLAW and LEXIS, however, within an hour of the decision. Any users on-line can read the case immediately on their computer screen.

A computer also can be used to update changes in the law—to tell whether a case has been overruled by another case or whether a statute has been amended or repealed. The manner in which computers are used for updating purposes is discussed in the next chapter.

Legal Research on LEXIS and WESTLAW

Most legal professionals use either WESTLAW or LEXIS for their computer research needs. In many respects, WESTLAW and LEXIS are similar. Both are on-line services that provide quick and easy access to a wide range of legal authority. The researcher can locate and read cases, statutes, regulations, and most other legal authority from a computer screen. Because WESTLAW and LEXIS are competing services, however, there are differences as well as similarities. For instance, some legal authority might be found on WESTLAW but not on LEXIS, and vice versa. WESTLAW, developed by West Publishing, is structured to rely upon West features such as the American Digest System. WESTLAW queries can incorporate the West topic and key number system, so a researcher who already knows a relevant topic and key number can save considerable effort by combining this information with a word search. On the other hand, through a licensing venture with Veralex, Inc., LEXIS provides Lawyers Cooperative material such as the full text of the A.L.R., L. Ed. 2d, and *United States Code Service*. As a result, a subscriber to LEXIS has on-line access to many of the Lawyers Cooperative publications that are not available on WESTLAW.

Another difference between WESTLAW and LEXIS is the scope and breadth of coverage. Many early cases have not been included in either LEXIS or WESTLAW, so the researcher cannot be assured that a computer search has covered all relevant authority. Some law reviews and government publications can be found on one service, but not on the other.

Both LEXIS and WESTLAW offer quasi-legal and nonlegal information to subscribers. The NEXIS service, for example, is provided to LEXIS subscribers, while DIALOG, MEDLINE®, and PHINET® are provided to WESTLAW subscribers. These services provide up-to-the-minute news on a wide range of topics. There are databases on medical developments and financial matters, governmental activities, and scientific developments. A researcher can access scientific or medical journals on-line just like the researcher accesses cases or statutes. The researcher also can access information about settlements and verdicts of cases throughout the country, obtain information about expert witnesses, or research trademarks and patents on-line. Although only a few states are covered at present, a researcher can even learn about whether a particular individual has a mortgage or other financing by checking public documents.

For the paralegal, the main difference between researching on WESTLAW and LEXIS is simply that the paralegal must learn different function keys on each system to perform the same tasks. These systems rely upon either a search word or term method, or a natural language or relevance method.

Search Word or Term

When on-line searching was first introduced, a user relied upon a **search word or term** method. Basically, this is the method described at the beginning of this chapter that allows a user to command a computer to search all the documents in a database for a certain word or term. The computer's memory is divided into units. Each unit is called a database. When a researcher selects a database, the researcher is telling the computer what part of the computer's memory should be searched.

With the search word or term method, a researcher might ask a computer to search for all district court cases with the word *abortion*. In a search word or term method, the computer will not search for any other word, nor will it automatically search for the words *abort* or *aborting*, unless the search request is formulated to do so. The computer does not search for a synonym or an antonym, nor will the computer search for a narrower term or a broader term. In other words, if a researcher searches for cases with the word *dog* and a case uses the word *hound*, the computer will not identify the case as relevant to the search. If the researcher misspells the query words, the computer will look only for the misspelled word. Consequently, the search is only as accurate as the query.

Often a search of statutes or cases for a particular word will result in an unmanageable list of documents. For example, if the researcher searched the case law for all cases with the word *abortion,* the list would include hundreds or thousands of documents. That is why the search might be reformulated to include only cases with both the words *abortion* and *picketing.* Then the list of relevant cases would be shortened. The process that enables a computer to search for a combination of terms is based upon a Boolean logic technique (named after a nineteenth century mathematician).

A search word or term approach requires the user to identify any words that are critical to the legal issue. The word or term can be a common noun or even a legal phrase. For instance, the computer can search for any document where the phrase *equal protection of the law* appears with the word *student*. A search can be for cases with multiple phrases. For instance, the computer can search for any document in which the phrase *doing business* and the term *minimum contacts* appear.

LEGAL TERMS

search word or term   A method by which a user can command a computer to search all the documents in a database for a certain word or phrase.

When searching on either LEXIS or WESTLAW, the phrase needs to be placed within quotation marks. The computer looks for that phrase exactly as quoted.

Natural Language or Relevance Searches

In 1992, West Publishing announced an enhancement to WESTLAW called WIN ("WESTLAW Is Natural"). WIN is a **natural language or relevance method** for researching law. The following year LEXIS announced that it had developed a natural language program for its system called FREESTYLE. Instead of formulating a word search, the researcher using a natural language approach composes a sentence that is descriptive of the legal issue. For example, instead of asking the computer to search for the terms *abortion* and *picketing,* the researcher might type one of these sentences: "What are the rights of picketers at an abortion clinic?" or "What restrictions apply to picketers at an abortion clinic?" The computer will search the content words and synonyms of those words, as well as root stems of the words. The computer also identifies and ranks the authority that the computer determines most closely deals with that issue.

With a natural language or relevance search, instead of simply locating words or terms, the computer matches the search words or terms with the number of times the search words or terms appear in the documents. This approach assumes that the more frequently a word appears, the more likely it is that the document is relevant. The computer ranks the cases for relevance based upon this principle. The computer determines which document is most likely to answer the query and ranks that document first. This feature is called **concept ranking.**

WIN is now available to search on most of West's databases, including the following:

- Cases

- State statutes

- *United States Code Annotated*

- *Federal Register*

--LEGAL TERMS--

natural language or relevance A method by which a user can command a computer to search all the documents in a database using a sentence that is descriptive of the legal issue in question.

concept ranking A feature of computer software programs by which documents are ranked according to how likely they are to be relevant to the legal issue in question.

- *Code of Federal Regulations*
- Legislative history (state and federal)
- Legal periodicals
- Restatements
- C.L.E. articles
- Attorney general opinions (state and federal)

The more precisely the sentence is written for the natural language query, the more successful is the computer's response. The difficulty with both the natural language approach and the search word approach is that the English language has many words with the same meaning, and a researcher can easily frame an approach that misses the most appropriate word or term. As a result, either search approach can lead to inaccurate results.

Basics of Computer Research

Each computer software program is written differently, whether it is a computer game, a data processing system, or a legal research method. Each comes with a separate instruction booklet. It would require another text to describe in detail how to format a computer search. The format is different for LEXIS than it is for WESTLAW. Also, natural language searches are different from a search word and term approach for each program. In addition, LEXIS or WESTLAW are being upgraded constantly. There are training courses for LEXIS and WESTLAW, and both services offer training modules on-line and software to walk students through the computer research process. West Publishing, for example, publishes a manual for WESTLAW called *Discovering WESTLAW: The Student's Essential Guide* (1991). For LEXIS users, Carrick, *LEXIS: Legal Research Manual* (1989) is quite informative.

Whether using LEXIS or WESTLAW, the basic steps involved in CALR are quite similar. The next section presents a capsule view of that process.

Formulating the Search

Before going on-line, the researcher should have a working knowledge of the legal issue or issues being researched. Remember that on-line computer research can be expensive, especially when the researcher is not prepared. Consequently, the researcher initially should try to become familiar with the law relating to the issue by using traditional research methods and the same thought processes used in researching with an index in a book.

Try to state the issue in one or two sentences. Putting the issue on paper will help to check the thought process, and later to identify search terms. Consider concrete search words (*car, dog, store*) as well as legal terms (*res ipsa loquitur, due process of law, equal protection*). Think in terms of narrow concepts as well as broader concepts. The TAPP rule, discussed in Chapter 1, works well with computers. Remember, computers look for words, not ideas. Any legal professional with good vocabulary skills can formulate a workable query.

Getting On-line

To begin, the researcher must have access to a computer terminal with a modem and must be a subscriber to either WESTLAW or LEXIS. After the computer system has contacted WESTLAW or LEXIS, the researcher will be asked to provide a password. Upon entering the password, the researcher will be asked to identify client information for billing purposes. A logo screen then appears welcoming the researcher to WESTLAW or LEXIS, then a directory screen appears describing the available services or databases.

Entering a Database

In traditional legal research, there are different sets of books. There are state, regional, and federal case reporters, federal and state codes, and numerous secondary source materials. A researcher must decide which set to use.

A legal researcher using a computer has a similar choice. Instead of selecting a set of books, however, the subscriber must select a database on WESTLAW, or what is termed a **library** on LEXIS. Each LEXIS library is subdivided into **files** that are narrower collections of documents. A database or library typically contains a collection of documents. Perhaps the database is Missouri, and it contains the statutes, cases, regulations, and other laws from that state. Or the database might be ALLSTATES and contain all the cases from all the states. LEXIS has a library called General Federal (GENFED) that contains a broad collection of federal statutes, cases, and secondary sources. A file in that library includes the federal district court decisions known as DIST.

──────────────────── **LEGAL TERMS** ────────────────────

library The name given to describe a database, or a compilation of searchable information, in the LEXIS computer program.

files The term used to describe subdivisions of a library (database) in the LEXIS computer program; narrower collections of documents.

Both WESTLAW and LEXIS provide detailed descriptions of their databases or libraries on-line and through printed guides. For instance, the researcher can use the SCOPE command on WESTLAW to see a detailed description of WESTLAW databases.

When searching statutes, the researcher can choose between annotated and unannotated codes. In a search of an unannotated code, only the text of the actual statutes is searched by the computer. In searching an annotated code, the computer searches both the statute text and the explanatory text for the query word or term.

Some databases or libraries are divided into topical areas such as criminal justice, family law, and workers' compensation. Others are grouped by jurisdiction. LEXIS, for example, groups the statutes, cases, and regulations of each state in a separate library. There are separate libraries for federal statutes, cases, and regulations. A database or library may contain law reviews, treatises, and legal periodicals. Other databases provide updating information. There are even databases furnished by other services. For example, Commerce Clearing House (CCH) provides databases to WESTLAW subscribers. A researcher may be able to locate all relevant authority in several different databases or libraries. The researcher can look, for instance, in the Michigan library to find a Michigan case, or search cases in a library for all fifty states. The same query in either database will locate the same Michigan cases. The only difference is that the search in the wide database may locate many cases from other jurisdictions that are not really needed for the project, and it will be more expensive.

SIDEBAR On-line computer research can be expensive, and the cost is usually billed to the client. A paralegal must learn the practices and restrictions of the firm regarding this type of research *before* incurring substantial costs!

The best developed query is useless if the researcher selects the wrong database or library; therefore, it is imperative to select the proper database.

Formulating the Query

To search efficiently, the researcher must format the query properly. A query must be written in a way the computer will accept it. There are certain conventions to use in formatting a query that will ensure a more reliable search. Three basic concerns are involved in writing a query for a search word or term request: (1) selecting the most appropriate search word or words; (2) adding any necessary expanders; and (3) using the correct connectors.

Selecting the Search Word or Words

A word in a computer database is one or more characters without any spaces. *CD-ROM* is one word, but *XYZ Company* is two words. A space between letters is interpreted by a computer as an "or." Thus, if the researcher keys *dog bite*, then the computer automatically looks for documents with either the word *dog* or the word *bite*. The computer database program searches for whatever is keyed. If the researcher keys a nonsensical word, the computer looks for the word as it is spelled, and for no other. Hyphenated words are treated differently by LEXIS and WESTLAW. LEXIS treats a hyphen as a space. Because a space between words not in quotation marks means "or" to a computer database program, LEXIS looks for either the word before the hyphen or the word after the hyphen. WESTLAW, on the other hand, retrieves the hyphenated word, the hyphenated word where it is written as a compound word without the hyphen, and the two separate words without a hyphen. Some words, called **noise** or **stop words** (such as *the, one, he, she, or, it, and, be, is,*) cannot be searched on either LEXIS or WESTLAW.

Both LEXIS and WESTLAW automatically search for singular, plural, and possessive forms of words. However, LEXIS does not automatically search for irregular plurals of words, such as *mice* or *geese*. On LEXIS, the query would need to specify *mouse* and *mice* or *goose* and *geese*.

In selecting a search word, the researcher must be able to identify a word or term that a court would have used. In selecting search words, the researcher should use the TAPP rule used in traditional research to flush out possible approaches. A court may use different vocabulary words, so the researcher should consult a thesaurus or dictionary for alternative words. There are dictionaries and thesauri on-line as well as other aids to facilitate a word search. WESTLAW has a menu-driven search aid called EZ ACCESS that walks the user through the search word or term approach. It is also helpful to write out the issue before going on-line. Try to incorporate as many significant facts into the statement of the issue as possible. If the search results in too many or too few documents, try to reformulate the issue with alternative terms.

There are different search strategies. The researcher can start with broad terms and then narrow the terms in subsequent queries, or start with a narrower term to try to zero in on a few key documents. The pricing structure of LEXIS encourages researchers to search in levels; each modification of the original query is a different level. On WESTLAW, each modification is considered a new search in its pricing structure.

————————————————————— **LEGAL TERMS** —————————————————————

noise or stop words Words (such as the, one, he, she, or, it) that cannot be searched on either the LEXIS or the WESTLAW computer programs.

Expanders

The computer does not search for variations of a word, so if a researcher types *insurance,* the computer will not search for *insure, insured,* or *insuring.* However, the insertion of an exclamation point after the root stem of a word will tell the computer to search for any derivative words. For instance, the entry *abort!* will tell the computer to look for *aborted, aborting,* and *abortion.* Likewise, entering *insur!* will mean the computer will search for *insure, insuring, insured,* and *insurance.*

Another **expander** is the asterisk (*). An asterisk tells the computer to substitute any character that might form a word. So if the researcher enters *f**t,* the computer will search for documents containing the words *foot, feet, fret, font,* and so on; but it will not search for *fat, fit,* or *footing.*

Connectors

In many situations, the researcher needs to search for a combination of words or terms. One word or term would be insufficient or would result in locating too many documents. When the researcher is searching for more than one word, the researcher must use **connectors.** A connector tells the computer how to search for multiple terms. For instance, if the researcher keys *dog* and *bite,* the computer will look only for cases where both of these words appear. But if *dog* or *bite* is entered, the computer will look for cases where either of these words appear.

In many situations, the researcher wants documents where words appear in close proximity to each other. In such cases, the researcher can use a **grammatical connector** to tell the computer to look for documents where *dog* and *bite* appear in the same sentence or where these words appear in the same paragraph; or the researcher can use a **numerical connector** to tell the computer to look for terms that appear within a certain number of words. The *w/n* connector retrieves words on LEXIS that are found within a specified number of words of each other. (Simply replace the *n* with a number.) For instance, by

---

LEGAL TERMS

expander   A character or symbol that tells a computer to search for documents containing variations or derivatives of words.

connector   A word that tells a computer to search for documents containing multiple words or terms or a combination of words or terms.

grammatical connector   A word that tells a computer to search for documents in which multiple words or terms appear in the same sentence or paragraph.

numerical connector   A command that tells a computer to search for documents in which words or terms appear within a specified number of words of each other.

keying *abortion w/5 picketing* the computer will search for documents where *abortion* and *picketing* are within five words of each other. The researcher also can use a combination of connectors.

The query can even tell the computer what not to search for. Keying *not* in the query will tell the computer to ignore certain words. Assume the researcher wants to find cases dealing with RICO. The query might exclude cases where the word *Puerto* appears. On WESTLAW, the *not* command is written *but not* or *%*. So the command is written *RICO but not Puerto*, or *RICO % Puerto*. On LEXIS, the command is written *and not*.

SIDEBAR   In math, the formula 2 + 4 x 6 will produce different results, depending on whether the addition or multiplication operation is performed first. When a computer is told to process several operations, it will do them in a certain order. The researcher needs to consult a WESTLAW or LEXIS guide to learn this order to ensure that the computer will process the query in the proper manner.

Writing the Natural Language Search

Generally, a natural language search is easier to formulate. The natural language approach allows the computer to search without connectors or expanders. For example, instead of using the query *abort! and const! and picket!,* the user might ask the computer: "What are the constitutional rights of someone who pickets an abortion clinic?" WESTLAW, in its search system, automatically removes the noncontent words (that is, words without legal significance) and any stop words. The computer also uses a thesaurus to recognize relevant synonyms or terms.

When using the natural language approach, the researcher cannot be sure how broadly the computer has searched or even the precise method the computer has used to rank the relevant documents. With either the natural language or the search word or term methods, however, the researcher must be sure to include all the critical words in the query.

Modifying the Search

The computer tells the user how many documents satisfy the search query. Sometimes no document answers the query; at other times, too many documents satisfy the query. In either case, the search must be reformulated. The researcher may consider first changing from a search word or term approach to a natural language search, or vice versa. If there are no documents that satisfy a search word or term query, however, merely putting the words into a natural language query may not produce any better result.

If too few documents are identified, the researcher must either rewrite the query, use a broader connector if a search word method was tried (*or* rather than *and,* for example), or change to a different database or library. If the search finds too many documents, the researcher can edit the query by deleting broader terms, adding different words, or using different expanders or connectors. The researcher also may decide to restrict the search to a particular part of a document, which is called a field or segment search.

There is no "correct" way to write or edit queries. Sometimes it is better to start with a narrow word or term to find a manageable list of documents, and then expand to more general words or terms. In other situations, a researcher will start with a broader word or term and add on other words that narrow the search if the original word or term results in too many documents. This latter strategy is currently more economical on LEXIS than on WESTLAW because of the pricing practices, but price strategies are always changing.

Searching Fields or Segments

WESTLAW divides documents into **fields,** and LEXIS divides documents into **segments.** Depending upon the database, the author of a document may be in one field or segment, and the title of a document may be in another. WESTLAW divides each case in its database into a number of fields:

ATTORNEY (AT)
CITATION (CI)
COURT (CO)
DIGEST (DI)
HEADNOTE (HE)
JUDGE (JU)
OPINION (OP)
SYNOPSIS (SY)
TITLE (TI)
TOPIC (TO)

LEGAL TERMS
---

fields The term used to describe the subdivisions of documents in the WESTLAW computer program.

segments The term used to describe the subdivisions of documents in the LEXIS computer program.

Sometimes a search of a field or segment may be more advantageous than a search of the full text of a document. The following are some reasons to search fields or segments.

Locating a Case by Name

Sometimes a researcher knows the name of a case but does not have a citation for it. To search for a case by name, the researcher can type *TI* to access the title field on WESTLAW. On LEXIS, the researcher would type *name*. If the researcher needs to find the citation for *Roe v. Wade,* for example, the following information will be entered, depending on the service:

WESTLAW: TI (Roe and Wade)

LEXIS: Name (Roe and Wade)

Roe v. Wade is a case that has been cited thousands of times in other cases. If the researcher were to search the full text for this information rather than by field or segment, the researcher would waste considerable time and would have to sift through much extraneous information.

Searching by Topic or Headnote

West Publishing adds topics, key numbers, headnotes, and synopses to the full text of each case. (See Chapter 4.) These editorial enhancements aid researchers in using the West digest system. When WESTLAW was first introduced, it did not include the full text of cases in its databases. Instead, WESTLAW contained only editorial enhancements such as topics, key numbers, and headnotes. As a result, the researcher using WESTLAW could search either by topic and key number or by search word or term, but the search was not of the actual text of the case, only of the summaries West prepared of the case. West soon adopted the approach of LEXIS and began entering the full text of the cases to WESTLAW while retaining the editorial enhancements. So, users can still search by topic, key number, and headnote on WESTLAW, and each of these elements is a separate field.

The researcher also can combine a topic and key number search. WESTLAW assigns a number to each of its topics. Typing the topic number with the letter "K," which stands for the West key symbol, and the key number will prompt WESTLAW to search for relevant cases. For example, in the entry *116 K 110,* the 116 is the topic reference, the *K* is the symbol for the West key, and the 110 is the West key number.

A researcher can search using the digest method on LEXIS as well. For instance, to search cases from all jurisdictions using a digest on LEXIS, enter the *General Digest* library.

Searching by Judge

Suppose the supervising attorney is working on a case that will be handled by a particular judge. The researcher can locate quickly other cases that this judge has handled. If the judge is named Mary Hughes, the researcher can search on LEXIS with an entry that reads *Writtenby (Mary W/3 Hughes)*.

Searching by Citation

A researcher can find most documents by citation on either LEXIS and WESTLAW. By entering *fi* for find on WESTLAW or LEXSEE on LEXIS, the computer can locate the document on screen in seconds.

Searching by Date

Sometimes a researcher wants to search by date—a researcher, for instance, may want cases decided before or after a certain date. This type of search is easily accomplished on either LEXIS or WESTLAW. The researcher can ask the on-line service to retrieve cases decided before a certain day or month or to retrieve cases decided between certain dates. On WESTLAW, for example, by typing *da(aft 5-17-75) and abortion,* the researcher can find all cases decided after May 17, 1975, that contain the word *abortion.*

Searching for Attorney Information

Suppose the researcher needs to know what attorney has handled a certain type of case. The researcher who wants to know if Steve Barber has handled any class action lawsuits can enter *(Steve + 3 Barber) and "class action"* on WESTLAW to locate this information.

Signing Off the Service

After the research is completed, the researcher signs off the on-line subscription service. On LEXIS, for example, the researcher presses the SIGN OFF key. The screen asks if the search should be saved. The computer will save the latest request for the rest of the day.

Legal Research on the Internet

The Internet is providing up new research opportunities for legal and nonlegal research and prompting new computer applications in law firms and businesses. Because the Internet is a worldwide network of computers, a researcher is not constrained by a limited database like LEXIS or WESTLAW. Instead, the researcher can search around the world for legal and nonlegal information. A researcher using the Internet can connect with computers at the Library of Congress, the House of Representatives, or the White House. Or the Internet user can send a communication to Microsoft, General Motors, or even the publisher of this book. A researcher can locate a United States Supreme Court decision, the Code of Federal Regulations, or patent information on the Internet. Reference questions can be posed to law librarians around the world, or the user can connect directly into a computer card catalog.

Accessing the Internet

There are different ways to gain access to the Internet. You need a computer and the appropriate software, along with a high-speed modem or special telephone connections—although you can, in fact, connect with the Internet by radio, antenna, or cable. Larger law firms and companies wire into the Internet through a dedicated high-speed telephone line or by special telephone connectors known as SLIP or PPP. Unless your business or law firm has a special connection, you probably will need to open an account with an on-line commercial service (Prodigy, Delphi, CompuServe) or with an Internet access provider. In selecting an access provider, remember that some services are text-based and require that you type commands, while other services have developed more user-friendly graphical interfaces. There are even specialized on-line services that provide legal research access. For instance, Law Journal EXTRA!^{sm} (developed by the publisher of the *New York Law Journal* and the *National Law Journal*) provides customized Internet services for legal professionals. Delphi provides full Internet access, and many other on-line services will soon follow in that direction.

Using the Internet

The Internet is used for a wide variety of functions. Legal professionals use the Internet primarily to send e-mail, to participate in bulletin board discussions, to retrieve files, and to log-in to remote locations.

E-mail

The most popular use of the Internet is to send e-mail. E-mail is simply electronic mail sent almost instantaneously from one user to another. Some estimates suggest that there are over fifty million users of e-mail, and certainly that number is increasing at an amazing rate. Most major on-line services have established gateways for exchanging electronic mail on the Internet. Many law firms are already connected to the Internet and communicate with other firms or clients with e-mail.

SIDEBAR

There is much concern about the possible interception of e-mail. Because legal professionals are sensitive to confidentiality concerns, the paralegal should be cautious about the types of messages sent by e-mail. There are methods that can be used to encrypt messages.

Bulletin Boards

A bulletin board is so named because it is a computer message center. Information posted on an electronic bulletin board will be distributed to a large group of people. Most on-line services offer some form of the bulletin board as part of the service.

On the Internet, Usenet is the way that information is disseminated through the bulletin board format. At present, there are thousands of Usenet newsgroups on a wide array of topics. You can subscribe to a Usenet newsgroup through your Internet service provider. As a member of a newsgroup, you may receive hundreds of messages every day.

Paralegals can access information from a bulletin board. For instance, a legal professional might post a notice on a bulletin board and may receive responses from legal professionals around the world. The paralegal can download this information from the bulletin board onto the hard drive and share it with members of the firm. Bulletin boards have become very specialized, and legal bulletin boards are becoming popular. The American Bar Association, through ABA/net, has a service paralegals can join for on-line access to legal bulletin boards. The largest law bulletin board at present is the Legal Forum, or LAWSIG, a CompuServe feature.

SIDEBAR

An electronic bulletin board service can be very specialized. For instance, the LERN™ Service, a product of Legal Research Network, assists legal professionals who handle product liability, personal injury, or medical malpractice litigation. You can obtain information about attorneys, expert witnesses, and documents relating to these specialized areas.

Retrieving Files

From a research standpoint, one of the most significant resources on the Internet is Ftp, or file transfer protocol. Ftp is a method that allows you to access and download files from other Internet computers. In other words, you can transfer information from a Ftp site onto your personal computer. Many universities, libraries, and businesses make files publicly available through a procedure called **anonymous Ftp.** Ftp also allows you to search the directories of a remote computer for information.

Remote Log-in

Telnet, or remote log-in, allows you to tap into a remote computer to gain access to that computer's publicly available files as though you were directly connected to that computer. This tool is useful for perusing a card catalog at a remote library or a database at a remote location. In effect, your computer becomes a guest visiting another computer. For instance, if you were going to connect to the Cornell Law School Legal Information Institute from a dialing account, you would type: telnet fatty.law.cornell.edu at the system prompt. You would then be able to access information about various legal topics from the files of that computer.

Researching on the Internet

Legal professionals are increasingly relying upon the Internet for locating and downloading legal and nonlegal information. The Internet provides a link to many repositories of information. Via the Internet, you can access the Columbia Law Library, the Indiana University Law Library, or the Legal Information Institute. You can access many universities, libraries, businesses (including law firms), and government agencies (foreign and domestic) on the Internet. Remember, with the appropriate tools, you can communicate with any computer on the Internet, so you can do a worldwide search for information.

Because the Internet is so vast, however, there is no "phone book" for locating Internet connections. As a result, you need to be familiar with some basic search tools available to Internet users. Most of these tools have interesting names.

LEGAL TERMS

anonymous Ftp (file transfer protocol)   A procedure by which files at universities, libraries, and businesses that are publicly available can be accessed and downloaded onto a personal computer through the Internet.

Archie

With WESTLAW and LEXIS, you can search for a word in legal documents. The Internet takes this process a step further with Archie. Using Archie, host computers share lists of file names, and users can search these lists or databases for a particular word. Archie maintains a database from about fifteen hundred hosts. Archie servers continually share information to update new files. To make an Archie search, you Telnet to an Archie computer. Once you are connected to that computer, you can search the files by file type or by keyword. You then generate the files matching that request, and you can use Ftp to retrieve the files.

Gopher

Gopher is a software that follows a simple protocol for tunneling through the Internet. There are about sixteen hundred Gopher sites on the Internet. This software provides a menu-based search and retrieval function. With simple keyboard functions, you can pass through menu after menu. These menus are like tables of contents. You can make a selection from the menu, which will lead to a more detailed menu, to another host computer for more Gopher menus, or to the text of a document. Gopher actually takes you to the computer that has the information for which you are looking. After you have found your answer, you can download the information.

Veronica

Veronica was Archie's girlfriend in the comic strips and is an acronym for Very Easy Rodent-Oriented Netwide Index to Computerized Archives. Archie and Veronica are interrelated on the Internet. When you use Gopher, you connect to a particular Gopher. The file you are looking for might not be listed at that Gopher site. Because there are sixteen hundred Gopher sites, a complete search requires a search of each of these sites. Veronica continually contacts the various Gopher sites and updates its database. Veronica maintains a list of all the menu selections at all of the Gopher sites. When you use Veronica to search for a word or words, Veronica compiles a menu of the different files that contain the words for which you are searching. Veronica searches the directories at the various Gopher sites and, when it has located a document, retrieves it for you.

WAIS

Unlike Archie, Gopher, and Vernoica, all of which search for words in titles, WAIS actually searches inside files for search words. At a WAIS site, files are indexed much like this book is indexed. Similar indexed files are grouped together into databases. At a WAIS site, there are lists of available databases that can be searched for information. Like WIN, which is used on WESTLAW, WAIS prioritizes its search results. The more the search word appears in the document, the higher the document appears on the list.

World Wide Web

The World Wide Web, sometimes called the Web or WWW, is one of the hottest items on the Internet. The Web provides an easy-to-use graphics screen based upon a hypertext language. Hypertext sets up links between key concepts in the text. If you are reading a document and are interested in searching further about a word or concept in that document, you simply click the word, phrase, or an icon to lead you to other related information. Because the Web is multi-media, the clicking might lead to an audio, video, or graphical link, or even to another document. In short, the Web allows you to jump from file to file at different WWW sites with a click of a word, phrase, or icon. Many commercial services provide Web access.

Internet Browsers

A browser translates computer language into an interesting graphical display on your screen. Instead of looking at meaningless figures, you see the graphics you are used to seeing on a commercial service. The Mosaic, for instance, is a software program designed to help users browse the Web and retrieve information from it. This is a free application that can be downloaded from a number of sites. There are also commercial browsers available such as WinGopher and Internet-in-a-Box. Perhaps the most exciting browser is the Netscape Navigator which allows the user to view the World Wide Web through a graphical format.

SIDEBAR

A paralegal will learn about the Internet only by getting lost on it. Paralegals who are computer literate are a scarce resource. The more expertise you have with computer networks, the more valuable you will become as an employee because most lawyers have little training on the Internet.

CD-ROM Libraries

As stated earlier, CD-ROM stands for Compact Disc with Read Only Memory. A CD-ROM can store around 250,000 to 300,000 typed pages of information. A CD-ROM disc takes up only negligible office space. Thus, a publisher can put a considerable amount of information on a single disc. West Publishing, for instance, has started four CD-ROM libraries: Bankruptcy, Federal Civil Procedure, Federal Taxation, and Government Contracts. West is also offering CD-ROM libraries that contain state cases, annotated codes, and encyclopedias. Lawyers Cooperative offers the A.L.R.s on CD-ROM. Other publishers are competing in the CD-ROM market.

On one or two discs, the researcher can find:

- Primary authority dealing with the topic, such as statutes, regulations, and case law.

- Digests.

- Treatises and other secondary sources dealing with the topic.

With a CD-ROM, a user can "turn" from page to page or jump from document to document on a screen. If a researcher discovers a citation on the screen, the researcher can use the cursor to have the computer find that document. Instead of reading materials in books, the researcher is accessing material electronically. If the researcher finds some relevant text or a relevant quote, the information can be downloaded into an electronic notebook that can be retrieved through a word processing system.

The main feature of a CD-ROM disc is that it allows a legal professional to find anything relevant to a topic on a disc instead of searching through various sets of books or even through various libraries for these materials. (See Figure 7–1.) In other words, by purchasing a CD-ROM disc, the legal professional can have electronic access to a library of materials. For instance, if you purchase Social Security Plus™ from Clark, Boardman, Callaghan, you will get:

- The full text of over nine thousand cases.

- The applicable statutes of the Social Security Act.

- The complete Code of Federal Regulations relating to Social Security.

- The full text of over six hundred Social Security rulings.

- The complete text of a treatise on Social Security.

And there is more to be found on that disc. If this information could be purchased only by purchasing whole sets of other books, or even

CD-ROMS

Topic	Publisher
Personal Injury Verdicts and Settlements	LRP Publications
Disability Law	LRP
Special Education Law	LRP
Environmental Law	Matthew Bender (MB)
Immigration Law	MB
Federal Practice	MB
Collier Bankruptcy	MB
Business Law	MB
Intellectual Property	MB
Personal Injury	MB
Employment Law	MB
Workers' Compensation	MB
Tax	MB
Real Estate	MB
Banking Law	MB
Insurance Law	MB
Code of Federal Regulations	Counterpoint Publ (CP)
Federal Register	CP
State Environmental Regulations	CP
Gould's USCU	Gould Publications Inc.
Americans with Disabilities LawDesk	Lawyers Cooperative Publishing (LCP)
CFR LawDesk	LCP
The LawDesk Regulatory Library	LCP
US Supreme Court Reporters Lawyers Edition 2D, LawDesk	LCP
Compensation and Benefits Guide	BNA
Medicare and Medicaid Guide	Commerce Clearing House (CCH)
SmartTax	CCH
OSHA	U.S. Government Printing Office (GPO)
Supreme Court Reporter	West Publishing (West)
American Law Institute Restatements of the Law	West
Legal Directory Attorney Library	West
US Tax Reporter	RIA
USSC+ CD-ROM	Infosynthesis

FIGURE 7–1   CD-ROM technology provides researchers with a vast amount of information, but there are limitations.

just the related materials, the cost likely would exceed the cost of the disc.

Because CD-ROM can be searched through indexes or by word or phrase searching, it has many of the advantages of on-line services. For example, cases on West's CD-ROMs can be searched by the following methods:

- By West topic and key number.

- By words or phrases with sentence and paragraph connections.

- By moving to another cited case by highlighting a cite.

Thus the researcher can search for a particular word or phrase from a disc—an approach that cannot be used with a book. The methods are similar to those used on LEXIS or WESTLAW.

In addition, new and updated discs are sent to subscribers when there are new developments. Updated discs are sent to subscribers on a periodic basis (monthly, quarterly, and so on). Before new discs are sent, subscribers can find out about new information by accessing an on-line database.

The researcher should keep in mind that there are limitations to this new technology. They generally involve computer hardware capabilities, cost, accuracy, and timeliness.

Summary

- WESTLAW and LEXIS are on-line services that provide legal professionals with a means to search law on computer.

- The Internet is a worldwide network of computer networks that can be used to search for legal and nonlegal information, to send e-mail, and to participate in discussion groups.

- A computer can search documents for a keyword or phrase, which in computer language is called a query or search request.

- A researcher typically will search a database on WESTLAW or a library on LEXIS.

- A search request must be written precisely, with the most appropriate search word or words, and with any necessary expanders or connectors.

- CD-ROM discs are being used instead of law books in many law offices. The information on the disc can be searched with methods similar to those used on WESTLAW and LEXIS.

- Information can be retrieved from remote computers on the Internet by Ftp, or file transfer protocol.

- There are various search tools like Archie, Gopher, Veronica, WAIS, and the World Wide Web that can be used to look for information on the Internet.

Review Questions

1. What is on-line legal research?

2. What is CD-ROM? Describe the advantages of this media for legal research.

3. Describe a query or search request on WESTLAW or LEXIS.

4. What is the NEXIS service? How would a paralegal use it in a law practice?

5. Compare the natural language search method with a search word or term method.

6. How do you formulate a query or WESTLAWor LEXIS?

7. Why would you search a field or segment on WESTLAW or LEXIS?

8. What is the Internet? How do you search for documents on the Internet?

9. What is the difference between Ftp and Telnet?

Research Project

1. Using either LEXIS or WESTLAW, run a word search for any cases in your state that involve dog bites. After completing this search, isolate the cases that involve pit bulls. Print lists for each search.

2. Using a commercial service or by directly accessing the Internet, do the following:

   a. send an e-mail message;
   b. participate in a discussion group; and
   c. contact a remote library and peruse its card catalog.

IIII
CHAPTER 8

UPDATING AND VERIFYING LEGAL RESEARCH

A legal professional must know how to update his or her research. A tax attorney, for example, cannot give competent legal advice using last year's tax code. A litigation attorney must keep abreast of any new court cases that might have an impact on the client's case. A lawyer who represents a medical care provider must be in tune with any new regulations that are passed concerning health care. This text has already explored some methods used by legal professionals to keep up-to-date, that is, pocket parts for books, advance sheets, pamphlets, looseleaf services, and updated discs for CD-ROM. In addition to these tools, legal professionals need methods to find changes made in the last week or month.

In legal research, there are unique tools designed primarily for updating purposes, or just for checking the accuracy of citations. These updating and verification tasks can be accomplished by using printed sources or computers.

Shepard's

Virtually every workday, cases are decided, statutes are passed, and regulations are enacted. A case may overrule an existing precedent; a statute may repeal another statute; and a newly enacted regulation may amend another regulation. Legal professionals must spot and react quickly to changes in the law. Imagine, for instance, the embarrassment to a lawyer who argues to a court that a certain case is a controlling precedent, only to learn from an opposing lawyer that this case has been reversed by a higher court.

Over a hundred years ago, Frank Shepard recognized that legal professionals needed a means to update legal research. As a result, he developed Shepard's citators. Today, these citators are published by Shepard's/McGraw Hill, Inc. What is unique about a Shepard's citator is that it provides up-to-date information in a column format. This method of updating law by using citators, developed by Frank Shepard, is now referred to as **shepardizing**. Whenever a source authority is important to the result, it should be shepardized. Shepard's citators update primary sources—including constitutions, cases, statutes, regulations, and administrative decisions—and even some secondary sources such as law reviews.

Shepardizing Cases

A **citator** consists of lists of citations for documents that refer to another document. The document that is shepardized is called the **cited source,** and the document that makes reference to the cited source is called the **citing source.** A citator enables a legal professional to locate any later case, statute, or other authority that references an earlier source. A case citator contains lists of citations of every instance in which a reported case has been cited by subsequent cases. A statutory citator contains lists of citations of citing sources for statutes. Shepard's publishes case citators covering state and federal cases. Legal professionals use case citators for various purposes.

Why Use a Case Citator?

Suppose a legal professional has located a case that seems to pertain to a client's situation. By reading the case, a researcher will not know if the case has been appealed to a higher court or remanded from a higher court to a lower court. This is highly relevant information. If it was appealed to a higher court, the higher court may have reversed the case or affirmed the case on logic different from that used by the lower court. This would be part of the **history of a case,** or **direct history of a case.** A history of a case, or direct history, traces the same case through the court system. For example, a federal case might begin in a district court, go to a circuit court of appeals, be remanded back to the district court, be appealed again to the circuit court, and ultimately be decided by the supreme court. It is important that the legal professional know how to trace the course of a case through the court system.

After a case has been finally decided, its value as a precedent can be strengthened or weakened by later cases. A later case may criticize or distinguish the cited case without overruling it, or a later case may even overrule the case that the researcher is relying upon. How different

---
LEGAL TERMS
---

citator† A system of books, the use of which allows a person doing legal research to locate every court opinion in which a particular case is cited, and to determine the context in which it is cited as well as whether it has been affirmed, distinguished, followed, overruled, or simply mentioned.

cited source† A document that is shepardized; the document to which a Shepard's entry (a citing course) refers.

citing source† A document that is entered in Shepard's because it makes reference to another document (the cited source).

history (direct history) of a case† The path a particular case takes through the court system.

courts have treated a case is called the **treatment of a case**, or the **indirect history of a case.**

Although it is not a principal use of Shepard's, a researcher can use a citator as a tool for finding citations to other relevant authority, including both primary and secondary sources. By combing through the list of citations in a Shepard's, a researcher may uncover a case overlooked by other methods. Shepard's citators reference some law review articles, and some citators reference the Restatements of the Law. In some cases, a citator may be the most convenient means by which to locate these sources.

SIDEBAR

Sometimes an enacted statute overrides the effect of a case. In that event, the editorial letter "q" will be placed on the case that has been overruled or superseded by the statute.

How to Use a Case Citator

Whenever a researcher has located a relevant case, the researcher should shepardize it before citing it in any legal writing. Although there are different case citators for shepardizing state and federal cases, the process for using a case citator is basically the same. Here is that process.

Step 1—Select the appropriate citator. The first step in shepardizing a case is to identify the appropriate set of Shepard's. Shepard's publishes a different case citator for each state as well as the District of Columbia and Puerto Rico. In addition, Shepard's publishes regional citators that correspond with West's regional reporters. There are also federal citators that cover federal cases. The federal case citators include the *Shepard's United States Citations, Case Edition,* covering United States Supreme Court cases, and separate units of a set called the *Federal Citations.* One unit of the *Federal Citations* covers federal district court cases, and another unit covers federal circuit court of appeals decisions.

Step 2—Check all relevant volumes of the set. The second step in using a citator is to ensure that all volumes are available. Typically a set consists of permanent volumes, perhaps an interim or annual pamphlet, a monthly pamphlet, and possibly a small advance sheet. The latest issue contains a part entitled "What Your Library Should Contain." This section explains the components of the set. Read it. The

---

LEGAL TERMS

treatment (indirect history) of a case The manner in which different courts have treated a case, which will affect the value of the case as a precedent.

information in each volume is not cumulative, so if a volume is missing, the researcher may be missing critical information.

Each Shepard's volume may have several sections or divisions—one part of a volume may cover the official citation, and another part the unofficial citation. In *Shepard's United States Citations, Case Edition*, for example, there are three subsets, each devoted to a particular Supreme Court reporter. For instance, volumes 1.1 to 1.8 are utilized for shepardizing a *United States Reports* citation, volumes 2.1 to 2.8 feature citations to the *United States Supreme Court Reports*, and volumes 3.1 to 3.7 cover the *Supreme Court Reporter*. Each state citator also has a means for checking not only citations to official material, but also unofficial citations, such as to West regional reporters.

It is noteworthy that the researcher will not find exactly the same information in all citators even if the researcher is looking under entries for parallel citations. A state citator, for instance, cites to cases from the same jurisdiction, to state attorney general opinions, and to some local law review articles—whereas a regional citator cites to cases from *every* state in its region, but not to the local law review articles. Both regional and state citators provide parallel citations and trace the direct history of a case.

Step 3—Look up the citation. The next step is to look up the citation in the applicable Shepard's citator. Suppose the citation of a case is *Board of Education of Rockford School District No. 205 v. Rockford Education Association*, 150 Ill. App. 3d 198, 103 Ill. Dec. 317, 501 N.E.2d 338 (1986). A researcher can check in *Shepard's Illinois Citations* for the Illinois citations or in *Shepard's Northeastern Citations* for the regional citations.

SIDEBAR

Because the state version has different information from the regional version, the researcher may want to consult both editions.

After locating the appropriate citator, turn to the page that has the applicable volume number at the top of the page. Figure 8–1 is an exerpt from *Shepard's Northeastern Citations*. Notice that "Vol. 501" appears at the top of the page, which matches the volume number for the *Northeastern Reporter* reference in the *Board of Education* citation example above. The page references are in bold and centered within the columns. Find the page reference of the citation (page 338 in the example) in the column of the citator. Under each page reference is a number of case citations. There may be a citation in parentheses. For example, see the citations in parentheses under page 338 in column 2 (see Figure 8–1). These citations are parallel citations and will be found

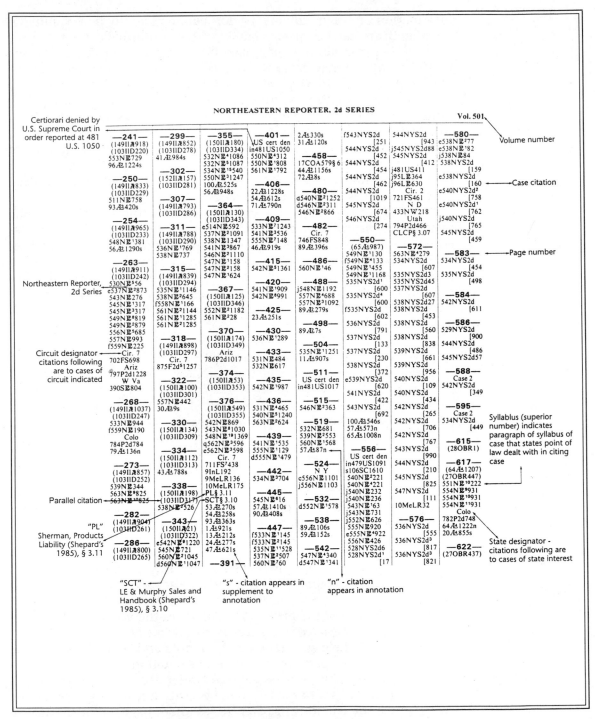

FIGURE 8–1 An example of the range of functions performed by Shepard's (Reproduced by permission of Shephard's/McGraw-Hill, Inc. Further reproduction of any kind is strictly prohibited.)

only in the first volume covering a citing case. Sometimes even the first entry for a citation will have no parentheses because not all citations have parallel references. The other citations under the page number are to cases and other authorities that have mentioned the cited source. The most recent Shepard's citators have changed in format. They now feature references to names and years and have only six (as opposed to eight) columns per page.

Step 4—Check for letter and small superior numbers. In front of some of the citations are letter abbreviations describing the history or treatment of a case, and in back of some of the citations are small superior numbers. For example, in the citation *o 526 N.E.2d 151^2*, the *o* is the letter abbreviation, and it means that this case overruled the cited case, so the cited case is no longer valid authority for the point of law. Figure 8–2 explains some of the various abbreviations used by Shepard's in its case citators. Shepard's customizes its abbreviation tables for each citator; therefore, the table of abbreviations in the federal case citators is different from those in each of the state case citators.

The letter abbreviations often contain valuable information about a case. In some situations, there are hundreds or even thousands of citing sources for a cited source. The notations added by Shepard's helps the legal professional spot which of the sources may be particularly relevant to the research.

Almost every case deals with more than one point of law. A researcher usually is concerned with only one particular point of law in any one case, even though numerous points may be covered in the case. To enable a researcher to look for only a particular point of law, Shepard's adds small superior numbers to the right of the citing case that correspond with the headnote numbers in West's reporters. The headnotes are consecutively numbered (see Figure 4–8 in Chapter 4), and each headnote deals with a different point of law. The first headnote of a case, for example, may deal with a procedural question, while the second headnote deals with a substantive issue. The researcher who is concerned with the substantive issue and not the procedural question can tell from Shepard's whether a case is relevant by noting whether the superscript number is 1 or 2. Some citations are not assigned a superscript number if the citing source does not refer to a particular principle of law or does not relate directly to the point expressed by the headnotes in the reporter.

SIDEBAR

Remember that case reporters may have several editions or series. Make sure you check the citation for the correct edition or series. For example, if a citation is to 501 N.E.2d 338, make sure the citator you use corresponds to the second series of the *Northeastern Reporter*, not to the first edition.

ABBREVIATIONS—ANALYSIS

History of Case

a	(affirmed)	Same case affirmed on appeal.
cc	(connected case)	Different case from case cited but arising out of same subject matter or intimately connected therewith.
D	(dismissed)	Appeal from same case dismissed.
m	(modified)	Same case modified on appeal.
r	(reversed)	Same case reversed on appeal.
s	(same case)	Same case as case cited.
S	(superseded)	Substitution for former opinion.
v	(vacated)	Same case vacated.
	Cert den	Certiorari or appeal denied or dismissed by Illinois Supreme Court.
US	cert den	Certiorari denied by U. S. Supreme Court.
US	cert dis	Certiorari dismissed by U. S. Supreme Court.
US	reh den	Rehearing denied by U. S. Supreme Court.
US	reh dis	Rehearing dismissed by U. S. Supreme Court.

Treatment of Case

c	(criticised)	Soundness of decision or reasoning in cited case criticised for reasons given.
d	(distinguished)	Case at bar different either in law or fact from case cited for reasons given.
e	(explained)	Statement of import of decision in cited case. Not merely a restatement of the facts.
f	(followed)	Cited as controlling.
h	(harmonized)	Apparent inconsistency explained and shown not to exist.
j	(dissenting opinion)	Citation in dissenting opinion.
L	(limited)	Refusal to extend decision of cited case beyond precise issues involved.
o	(overruled)	Ruling in cited case expressly overruled.
p	(parallel)	Citing case substantially alike or on all fours with cited case in its law or facts.
q	(questioned)	Soundness of decision or reasoning in cited case questioned.

FIGURE 8–2   One needs to recognize the Shepard's abbreviations before undertaking the research (Reproduced by permission of Shepard's/McGraw-Hill, Inc. Further reproduction of any kind is strictly prohibited.)

Step 5—Repeat the process in each volume. The final step in using a Shepard's is to repeat the process in each relevant volume of Shepard's, since the volumes do not cumulate. Each volume is formatted in the same fashion, so the same process applies to each volume.

SIDEBAR

Shepard's publishes a pamphlet entitled *How to Shepardize* that is used in many law schools to explain the shepardizing process. Paralegal students may want to purchase the pamphlet, as it is quite comprehensive and easy to follow.

Shepardizing Statutes

Annotated codes usually update statutes on a periodic basis. As a result, legal professionals may rely upon any pocket parts or pamphlets accompanying the annotated code for bringing their research up-to-date. Nonetheless, there are situations where a Shepard's citator is an integral part of this research process.

Why Use a Statute Citator?

New statutes may amend or repeal statutes. A case might construe a statute or even hold that a statute is unconstitutional. Although annotated codes provide updating information, a statute citator may be used to double-check for changes or to check for all citing sources for a statute. As with a case citator, a researcher might locate a citation not found by other sources. A Shepard's statute citator references any statutes that have an impact on the cited source statute. It also references any case or other source—such as A.L.R. annotations, legal periodicals, attorney general opinions, and other secondary sources—that has cited the source statute.

Some statutory citators also include tables of statutes with citations that have been referred to by a popular name or by a short title.

How to Use a Statute Citator

The process for using a statute citator is similar to that for using a case citator. The researcher begins with a statutory citation, such as 28 U.S.C. § 1331.

Step 1—Locate the appropriate Shepard's volumes. *Shepard's United States Citations, Statutes and Court Rules* covers federal statutes. This citator references the *United States Code* citations unless a particular statute is not codified, in which case it references the *Statutes at Large* citation. Shepard's also publishes a state statute citator for each state. These state citators typically reference a code citation. If there is no code citation, the state citator references the session law.

In addition to providing information about statutes, a statute citator also may cover constitutions, municipal charters, ordinances, court rules, and jury instructions. Thus, a researcher can shepardize a provision of the United States Constitution by using *Shepard's United States Citations* and a provision of the Alabama Constitution by using the *Alabama Citations*. Figure 8–3 is an example of how a Shepard's statute citator references the freedom of religion clause of the United States Constitution.

Step 2—Locate all relevant volumes to the set. Case citators and statute citators come in sets consisting of burgundy permanent volumes, perhaps a gold interim pamphlet, a red monthly or quarterly pamphlet, and sometimes a white advance sheet. The statute citators, like the case citators, do not cumulate information. Make sure that every volume of the set is there! If a volume predates the cited source statute, it does not need to be consulted.

Step 3—Look up the citation. The form of statute citations varies from state to state. The researcher must match the year, title, article, chapter, or section number of the statute citation with the information located at the upper outside corner of the citator page. Then the researcher can search the columns for a more precise match of the information. Suppose, for example, the researcher wants to shepardize 42 U.S.C. § 2000(e). This particular entry in *Shepard's United States Citations* covers more that fifteen pages. Figure 8–4 is an excerpt from one of these pages. Title 42 is at the top right of the page, and § 2000(e) would be found in the column of a preceding page.

Step 4—Check any letter abbreviations. Statute citators provide letter abbreviations to the left of the citing source. These letter abbreviations indicate how the citing source treats the cited statute. If the citing source is a statute that amends the statute, Shepard's places an "A" before the citing source. If the citing source is a case that holds the statute unconstitutional, Shepard's places a "U" before the citing source. Figure 8–5 explains some of the abbreviations used by Shepard's in statute citator volumes.

Step 5—Repeat the process in all the volumes. The final step is to repeat the process in any cumulative supplement or advance sheet, making certain all relevant volumes have been searched before considering the research complete.

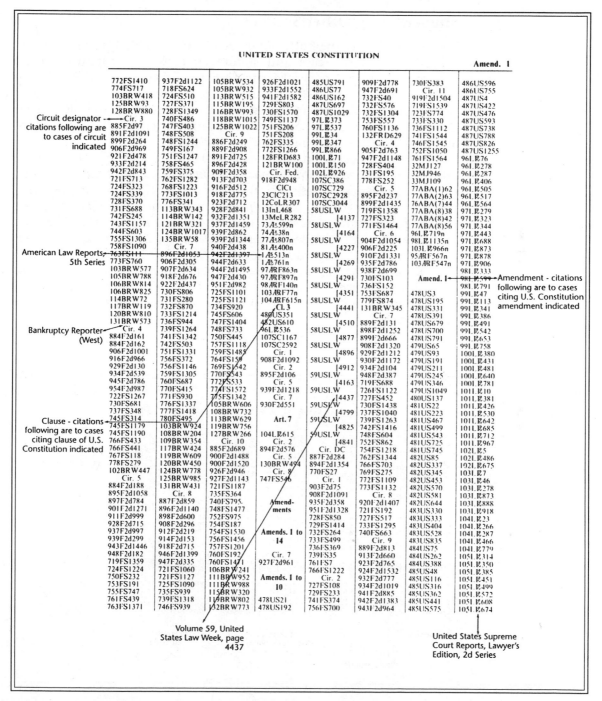

FIGURE 8–3 Shepard's can provide information on cases involving the United States Constitution (Reproduced by permission of Shepard's/McGraw-Hill, Inc. Further reproduction of any kind is strictly prohibited.)

Shepardizing Other Sources

There are a variety of other Shepard's, each of which is as simple and easy to use as the case and statute citators. For instance, federal regulations can be shepardized in *Shepard's Code of Federal Regulations Citations*. Citations to C.F.R. are checked using basically the same process as that used for checking federal statutes. Shepard's also covers decisions rendered by some administrative agencies in a set called *Shepard's United States Administrative Citations*.

There are specialized Shepard's citators—including one covering ethical matters called *Professional and Judicial Conduct Citations*, one covering the federal rules called the *Federal Rules Citations*, one covering commercial law called the *Uniform Commercial Code Citations*, one covering bankruptcy law called the *Shepard's Bankruptcy Citations*, and one covering tax law called *Shepard's Federal Tax Law Citations*. There is even a citator for shepardizing legal periodical articles named *Shepard's Law Review Citations*, a citator for shepardizing A.L.R. annotations named the *Shepard's Citations for Annotations*, and a citator for shepardizing the Restatements of the Law named the *Restatement of the Law Citations*.

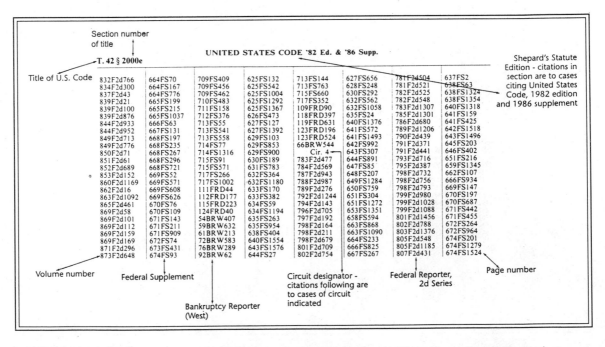

FIGURE 8–4 Shepard's can provide updating information about any title in the *United States Code* (Reproduced by permission of Shepard's/McGraw-Hill, Inc. Further reproduction of any kind is strictly prohibited.)

ABBREVIATIONS—ANALYSIS

Form of Statute

Amend.	Amendment	Proc.	Proclamation
App.	Appendix	Pt.	Part
Art.	Article	Res.	Resolution
Ch.	Chapter	§	Section
Cl.	Clause	St.	Statutes at Large
Ex. Ord.	Executive Order	Subch.	Subchapter
H.C.R.	House Concurrent	Subcl.	Subclause
	Resolution	Subd.	Subdivision
No.	Number	Sub ¶	Subparagraph
¶	Paragraph	Subsec.	Subsection
P.L.	Public Law	Vet. Reg.	Veterans' Regulations
Pr.L.	Private Law		

Operation of Statute

Legislative

A	(amended)	Statute amended.
Ad	(added)	New section added.
E	(extended)	Provisions of an existing statute extended in their application to a later statute, or allowance of additional time for performance of duties required by a statute within a limited time.
L	(limited)	Provisions of an existing statute declared not to be extended in their application to a later statute.
R	(repealed)	Abrogation of an existing statute.
Re-en	(re-enacted)	Statute re-enacted.
Rn	(renumbered)	Renumbering of existing sections.
Rp	(repealed in part)	Abrogation of part of an existing statute.
Rs	(repealed and superseded)	Abrogation of an existing statute and substitution of new legislation therefor.
Rv	(revised)	Statute revised.
S	(superseded)	Substitution of new legislation for an existing statute not expressly abrogated.
Sd	(suspended)	Statute suspended.
Sdp	(suspended in part)	Statute suspended in part.
Sg	(supplementing)	New matter added to an existing statute.
Sp	(superseded in part)	Substitution of new legislation for part of an existing statute not expressly abrogated.
Va	(validated)	

FIGURE 8–5   Shepard's statute abbreviations (Reproduced by permission of Shepard's/McGraw-Hill, Inc. Further reproduction of any kind is strictly prohibited.)

National Reporter Blue Book

Frequently, the researcher has a citation to a case but lacks a parallel citation. Perhaps the researcher has the official citation and not the unofficial one, or vice versa. There are a number of approaches to use to find parallel citations.

- Some parallel citations are found in reporters at the beginning of the case.

- Parallel citations can be found in digests by looking at the alphabetical table of cases.

- Shepard's case citators put the parallel citations in parentheses or as the first entry under the cited source.

- Parallel citations can be found on LEXIS and WESTLAW.

If the only information needed is the parallel citation, the *National Reporter Blue Book* provides a quick method for finding it. This set provides official citations to the researcher who has unofficial citations and unofficial citations to the researcher who has official citations. Figure 8–6 is a sample from this set. Notice that this set is merely a cross-reference table. Locate the volume and page numbers of the citation, then read the chart to locate the parallel citation.

Using Computers to Update

A researcher can use a computer to shepardize and verify citations. In fact, on-line computer services provide more up-to-date information than that available in printed matarials.

WESTLAW Updating Methods

WESTLAW provides a number of sources to its subscribers for updating legal authority: Shepard's, Shepard's PreView, Quickcite, Insta-Cite, and West*Check*. Each of these programs serves a different function.

Shepard's on WESTLAW

Shepardizing on WESTLAW is achieved by keying "sh" with a citation or by keying "sh" for any case that is on screen. The computer finds the applicable Shepard's cases volumes for the researcher, and

Illinois Court of Appeals Reports, 3d Edition

Northeastern Reporter, 2d Series → Volume number / Page number

150 ILLINOIS APPELLATE REPORTS, THIRD SERIES

Ill.App.3d Pg.	N.E.2d Vol.	N.E.2d Pg.	Ill.Dec. Vol.	Ill.Dec. Pg.	Ill.App.3d Pg.	N.E.2d Vol.	N.E.2d Pg.	Ill.Dec. Vol.	Ill.Dec. Pg.	Ill.App.3d Pg.	N.E.2d Vol.	N.E.2d Pg.	Ill.Dec. Vol.	Ill.Dec. Pg.
1	501	802	103	485	328	501	904	103	587	733	501	1380	103	842
6	501	133	103	112	331	500	1083	103	12	750	502	85	103	938
21	501	343	103	322	343	501	887	103	570	755	502	730	104	233
30	501	794	103	477	350	501	901	103	584	765	501	983	103	666
34	501	1323	103	785	355	501	828	103	511	782	502	450	104	187
38	501	840	103	523	357	501	723	103	406	787	501	948	103	631
41	501	821	103	504	402	501	907	103	590	797	502	332	104	69
48	501	825	103	508	406	501	891	103	574	806	502	53	103	906
53	501	374	103	353	421	501	805	103	488	812	502	756	104	259
56	501	882	103	565	431	501	781	103	464	818	502	422	104	159
62	501	764	103	447	445	501	830	103	513	827	502	357	104	94
67	501	702	103	385	459	501	923	103	606	832	502	414	104	151
75	501	979	103	662	472	501	812	103	495	840	502	428	104	165
81	501	391	103	370	479	501	817	103	500	845	502	341	104	78
90	501	349	103	328	486	501	1354	103	816	850	502	396	104	133
100	501	322	103	301	500	501	998	103	681	854	502	355	104	92
112	501	334	103	313	506	501	774	103	457	857	502	393	104	130
118	501	848	103	531	516	501	1003	103	686	862	503	1055	105	49
125	501	367	103	346	518	502	57	103	910	870	502	436	104	173
130	501	364	103	343	524	501	1010	103	693	874	502	464	104	201
134	501	330	103	309	531	502	80	103	933	879	502	439	104	176
139	502	23	103	876	535	501	1347	103	809	885	502	447	104	184
146	501	875	103	558	545	502	83	103	936	890	502	459	104	196
158	501	767	103	450	549	501	376	103	355	897	502	78	103	931
168	501	695	103	378	572	502	48	103	901	900	501	1363	103	825
174	501	370	103	349	578	502	31	103	884	911	502	431	104	168
180	501	355	103	334	584	502	42	103	895	915	501	937	103	620
192	501	954	103	637	589	502	61	103	914	932	502	378	104	115
198	501	338	103	317	594	502	40	103	893	944	501	910	103	593
206	501	934	103	617	597	502	45	103	898	959	502	433	104	170
211	501	856	103	539	601	501	958	103	641	962	502	373	104	110
216	501	752	103	435	608	501	1015	103	698	971	502	474	104	211
224	501	842	103	525	617	501	790	103	473	979	502	467	104	204
232	502	29	103	882	623	501	971	103	654	988	502	385	104	122
234	502	17	103	870	634	501	1332	103	794	999	501	1021	103	704
242	501	1027	103	710	645	501	1339	103	801	1009	502	345	104	82
248	501	1312	103	774	657	502	35	103	888	1025	502	454	104	191
264	501	932	103	615	664	502	74	103	927	1033	502	337	104	74
267	501	699	103	382	669	502	69	103	922	1039	501	1370	103	832
272	501	175	103	154	673	502	72	103	925	1052	502	315	104	52
278	501	852	103	535	677	502	370	104	107	1075	502	304	104	41
283	501	963	103	646	681	501	1290	103	752	1092	502	862	104	365
288	501	995	103	678	692	502	273	104	10	1098	502	866	104	369
293	502	27	103	880	696	502	268	104	5	1160	514	1241	113	230
296	501	966	103	649	703	502	298	104	35	1160	514	1242	113	231
304	501	920	103	603	712	502	366	104	103	1161	514	1242	113	231
310	501	1325	103	787	717	502	276	104	13	1162	514	1242	113	231
319	501	1004	103	687	729	502	419	104	156	1162	514	1243	113	232

FIGURE 8–6   The *National Reporter Blue Book* provides both official and unofficial citations (Reprinted by permission of West Publishing Company.)

then the relevant pages appear on screen. If there is both an official and unofficial edition, the computer provides both versions.

Shepard's on WESTLAW integrates information from multiple volumes for the user. For example, with the printed version, the researcher may need to look in a permanent volume, separate interim volumes, and a supplementary monthly pamphlet. The researcher must be careful not to miss any of these materials. The computer, however, brings all this relevant information together on screen for the researcher. The screen version of Shepard's information is in a slightly different format than the printed version (see Figure 8–7), but otherwise both the printed version and the WESTLAW version contain the same information.

The computer version of Shepard's is no more up-to-date than the printed version. The advantage of using the computer version is that the researcher can browse the listed citations with a stroke of a key. And when the researcher locates an applicable case, he or she can retrieve that case on the screen. Another advantage is that the researcher can customize searches in Shepard's on WESTLAW. The researcher can tell the computer to scan for authority that meets certain specifications—for example, only cases that have overruled or reversed an authority.

Shepard's PreView

Although the publisher strives to keep Shepard's current, very recent authority is not included. Shepard's obtains copies of federal court decisions electronically within hours of the filing of those decisions, but there is a delay before the next Shepard's is printed and mailed to subscribers. As soon as an advance sheet is prepared, Shepard's and West work together to update its Shepard's database on WESTLAW with the new information from that advance sheet. This information can be accessed through Shepard's PreView by typing "sp" with a citation or just "sp" to search authority if the authority being researched is already displayed on the screen.

Shepard's PreView does not provide either the abbreviations for the treatment of the case or the small superior numbers that reference West headnotes.

Quickcite

Even using both Shepard's and Shepard's PreView, the researcher will have a gap that is not covered for the most recent activity in the courts and legislatures. To bring research more up-to-date, the researcher can use Quickcite. In a manner similar to that used for searching for a word or term, the researcher using Quickcite formulates a query that tells the computer to search for a citation, and then to search the appropriate

```
                                SHEPARD'S    (Rank 1 of 2)   Page 1 of 4

CITATIONS TO: 520 N.E.2d 617
CITATOR: NORTHEASTERN REPORTER CITATIONS
DIVISION: Northeastern Reporter 2nd
COVERAGE: First Shepard's volume through Nov. 1993 Supplement
Retrieval                                          Headnote
   No.       —Analysis—-    —-Citation—-           No.
   1 > Shep  Same Text    ( 121 Ill.2d 36)
   2 > Shep  Same Text    ( 117 Ill.Dec. 266)
   3     SC  Same Case      380 N.E.2d 903
   4     SC  Same Case      477 N.E.2d 82
   5     SC  Same Case      499 N.E.2d 174
   6     SC  Same Case      507 N.E.2d 554

                                Ind
   7     SC  Same Case      504 N.E.2d 552
   8     E   Explained      520 N.E.2d 792, 794
   9     F   Followed       521 N.E.2d at 936
  10     F   Followed       521 N.E.2d at 937

   > Display only NEGATIVE history and treatment code references (LOC NEG)
   > Insta-Cite > Shepard's PreView > QuickCite > Commands > SCOPE
Copyright (C) 1994 McGraw-Hill, Inc.; Copyright (C) 1994 West Publishing Co.



                                SHEPARD'S    (Rank 1 of 2)   Page 2 of 4

CITATIONS TO: 520 N.E.2d 617
CITATOR: NORTHEASTERN REPORTER CITATIONS
DIVISION: Northeastern Reporter 2nd
Retrieval                                          Headnote
   No.       —Analysis—-    —-Citation—-           No.
   1     F   Followed     521 N.E.2d at 938
   2               521 N.E.2d at 939
   3     F   Followed     521 N.E.2d at 939
   4     F   Followed     521 N.E.2d at 940
   5     F   Followed     521 N.E.2d at 941
   6     F   Followed     521 N.E.2d at 1171
   7               525 N.E.2d 30, 36
   8     F   Followed     525 N.E.2d 30, 38        21
   9     F   Followed     530 N.E.2d 1104, 1108     2
  10               541 N.E.2d 182, 198             2
  11               542 N.E.2d 881, 890             4
  12     E   Explained    558 N.E.2d 479, 482      1
  13     E   Explained    558 N.E.2d 479, 482      2
  14               561 N.E.2d 1188, 1195           2

   > Insta-Cite > Shepard's PreView > QuickCite > Commands > SCOPE
Copyright (C) 1994 McGraw-Hill, Inc.; Copyright (C) 1994 West Publishing Co.
```

FIGURE 8–7   Computer printout of a Shepard's report (Reprinted by permission of West Publishing Company and Shepard's/McGraw-Hill, Inc. Further reproduction of any kind is strictly prohibited.)

database for that citation. Quickcite limits the search by date, so it does not repeat sources found by Shepard's or Shepard's PreView. Any recent authority that refers to the cited source will be identified. The researcher only needs to type "qb" with a citation to access this service.

Insta-Cite

Sometimes a researcher wants to verify a citation or a case history. Suppose the researcher has prepared a written memoranda explaining his or her research results. Now the researcher wants to see if all the citations and dates are accurate. The researcher may want to include a parallel citation as well. Insta-Cite provides the following information with the command "ic" and a citation:

- a means to verify the accuracy of a citation;

- any parallel citations;

- current direct case history; and

- any negative indirect history.

The information on Insta-Cite is put on-line within days after the information is received by West. As a consequence, if there are any recent negative developments, they are identified by Insta-Cite. The information retrieved by Insta-Cite is not nearly as complete as the information retrieved by a Shepard's search. Because Insta-Cite picks up any negative events, however, it is helpful. The fact that the information is current also makes Insta-Cite a useful tool to use in the last check of citations before submitting them to a court or for publication.

West*Check*

By installing West*Check* (a new software produced by West Publishing) with a data processing system, a researcher can automatically check any citation. West*Check* automatically extracts citations from a typed document, accesses WESTLAW, and checks the citations on Shepard's, Shepard's PreView, and Insta-Cite. Then the program prints a report of its findings. West*Check* provides details of any mistakes or critical developments concerning the citations.

LEXIS Updating Methods

Basically, the techniques used by WESTLAW are also available on LEXIS with a few exceptions.

Shepardizing on LEXIS

It is relatively easy to shepardize a case on LEXIS. Type "shep" with a citation. There is one difference, however, between shepardizing on WESTLAW and shepardizing on LEXIS. The researcher can enter either an official or an unofficial citation on WESTLAW and retrieve all applicable Shepard's entries. If the researcher uses an official citation on LEXIS, the computer will retrieve only the Shepard's entries for that citation, and not those for any parallel citations. The researcher must enter the parallel citations to obtain this information.

LEXIS does not have a service comparable to Shepard's PreView. Instead the researcher will need to use LEXIS as a citator for the next step. Remember that Shepard's PreView provides citation information for cases in its National Reporter System days or weeks before the information is available anywhere else. If you are using LEXIS and need to find, for example, any cases decided within the past several weeks that cite a particular case, you need to key in that citation and search for any cases that reference that particular citation. This method takes a little more effort, but should lead to the same results.

LEXCITE™

LEXCITE is a system comparable to Quickcite on WESTLAW. It uses a search word or term approach, but instead of searching for a word, it searches for a particular citation. It also looks for parallel citations. The researcher can browse the documents found by LEXCITE by using the KWIC display key, which displays the citation along with a window of text material, so the researcher can ascertain quickly whether the cited material was treated favorably or unfavorably.

Auto-Cite

Auto-Cite is an on-line citator service of LEXIS. It verifies that a citation is accurate (spelling of parties' names, volume and page reference, year of decision) and that the citation is still good law, and it provides some research information. Auto-Cite performs the following tasks:

- verifies the case name, year of decision, and jurisdiction for a citation;
- provides the history of the case;
- references parallel citations;
- lists any citations affecting the validity of the case; and
- provides citations to A.L.R. annotations.

Insta-Cite and Auto-Cite are more up-to-date than Shepard's. These services usually are updated within a week after the materials are received by West Publishing (Insta-Cite) or Mead Data Central (Auto-Cite). Although Shepard's is more comprehensive in citing to other sources, both Insta-Cite and Auto-Cite report any adverse authority, which is the primary reason a researcher uses these services. Certainly either Insta-Cite or Auto-Cite should be used as part of the last check before research is submitted to a court or for publication.

CheckCite™

Mead Data Central also markets a software program that verifies citations much like Westlaw's West*Check*. This program automatically contacts LEXIS and uses Auto-Cite and Shepard's. CheckCite produces a report that tells whether the legal citations in a brief or memorandum are accurate. It checks the date, parties' names, and volume and page numbers of the citation. The report shows any adverse treatment of the cited material by other sources. CheckCite, however, does not provide nonadverse authority or many of the other citations provided by Shepard's. It is a citation verification tool.

Summary

- A citator is a book or pamphlet that contains a list of citations for sources that reference a cited source.

- The primary noncomputer citation method used to update law is the Shepard's citators.

- A case citator provides both the history of a case and the treatment of a case.

- A researcher can locate parallel citations by using a Shepard's or the *National Reporter Blue Book*.

- A researcher can shepardize primary sources such as constitutions, cases, statutes, regulations, and administrative decisions. A researcher also can shepardize secondary sources such as ethical canons and legal periodicals.

- A researcher can shepardize on-line with either WESTLAW or LEXIS.

- To obtain recent authority not yet included in Shepard's, a researcher can use Shepard's Preview and Quickcite on WESTLAW.

- A researcher can verify a citation or case history on WESTLAW with Insta-Cite and on LEXIS with Auto-Cite.

Review Questions

1. Describe what is meant by the term *sheparding*.

2. What is a citator? What is the difference between a cited source and a citing source?

3. What is the difference between the history (direct history) of a case and the treatment (indirect history) of a case?

4. Describe how to use a typical case citator.

5. What does the letter in front of a citator entry represent? What does the superior number after a citator entry represent?

6. How can you check whether a specific point of law has been affected by a later case?

7. Compare the process of sheparding a case and that of sheparding a statute.

8. What are the different primary and secondary sources that can be shepardized?

9. Describe how to use WESTLAW and LEXIS to shepardize sources.

10. What are Insta-Cite and Auto-Cite?

Research Projects

1. Shepardize *Irvin v. Dowd*, 366 U.S. 717 (1961). List all cases that constitute the direct history of that case. What is the full parallel citation for that case? How many books or pamphlets would you check to find the indirect history of that case?

2. Using either LEXIS or WESTLAW, again shepardize *Irvin v. Dowd*. Print the pages that show the direct and indirect history of that case.

IIII
CHAPTER 9

PRACTICE AIDS

CHAPTER OUTLINE   Form Books

Practice Guides

Trial Practice Books

Reference Works

Directories

Magazines, Newspapers, and Newsletters

Although a legal professional may be preparing a document or a case for the first time, other legal professionals already may have spent countless hours preparing similar documents or similar cases. One way this experience is passed on is by various "how to" books. There are books that provide forms for writing a simple will, a complex trust, or a complaint at the beginning of a lawsuit. There are books that provide sample questions for a lawyer to ask a witness. Legal professionals even have magazines and newspapers specific to their profession.

This chapter explores various practice-oriented materials used by legal professionals in their day-to-day practice. Many of these books walk the legal professional through a transaction or describe in detail how to handle a particular type of case. Many of them are especially relevant to a practicing paralegal.

Form Books

Paralegals should be able to prepare most legal documents with a minimal amount of attorney supervision. A paralegal who works in a litigation practice, for instance, should be able to prepare pleadings and motions that can be filed with a court. A paralegal who works in the general practice of law is expected to know how to prepare basic documents such as wills, trusts, and real estate contracts. A business practice paralegal may prepare commercial leases, corporate documents, or promissory notes. No paralegal, however, is expected to prepare any of these documents without a form or model to follow. Private publishers provide a variety of form books to guide legal professionals in the preparation of legal documents.

Categories of Form Books

Some form books show legal professionals how to prepare **transaction documents.** A transaction document describes and memorializes events. A contract memorializes a business transaction; a will memorializes the intent of the person upon death; and a lease memorializes the rights and responsibilities of the parties with respect to property. Transaction documents are prepared to prevent or solve later disputes about the transaction. Because many transactions involve significant financial investments, these documents must be carefully

LEGAL TERMS

transaction documents Documents that describe and memorialize business transactions that are prepared to prevent or solve later disputes about the transactions.

written. Transaction form books contain sample contracts, leases, promissory notes, wills, and trusts. Litigation form books, on the other hand, show legal professionals how to prepare documents that are filed with a court such as complaints, motions, and pleadings.

Some form books provide only sample forms for a specialty area. For instance, there are form books dealing only with wills and estates. Such a set may include practice forms for opening an estate, filing a claim in the estate, and preparing simple wills and trusts. Many form books include features other than just forms. It is common for a form book to include tax advice along with the forms. Some books combine treatise materials and forms together in the same set. Such a set may include some explanatory text or provide extensive references to other legal sources. For instance, *Midwest Transaction Guide* is a looseleaf set that discusses the laws of Indiana, Illinois, and Michigan on various business topics. This set intersperses forms from these three states with the text. This approach allows the researcher to review the underlying law before preparing a transaction document. Let us consider some examples of the categories of form books.

Transaction Form Books

A legal professional may use the same forms over and over. There are a myriad of forms needed for transactions—for example, a contract for the sale of real estate, a promissory note, a deed, a simple will, an incorporation form, the bylaws of a corporation, and a mortgage. In each of these situations, there are forms that have been drafted already by legal experts to fit the transaction. Private publishers collect these forms and sell them as form books. There are very few transactions that must be drafted completely from scratch. Even for transactions that are new or rare, many boilerplate provisions can be copied from other forms.

West Publishing, Lawyers Cooperative Publishing, and many other private companies publish comprehensive sets of form books covering a wide range of legal transactions. The West set is titled *West Legal Forms*, 2d ed. (West, 1981–1986 with pocket parts), and the Lawyers Cooperative set is titled *American Jurisprudence Legal Forms 2d* (Lawyers Cooperative, 1971 with pocket parts).

Am. Jur. Legal Forms 2d combines many of the features of a typical transaction form book. This multi-volume set provides procedural guidance, including tax implications in preparing business and legal documents. The forms in this set are classified under more than 260 broad chapter topics such as aviation, atomic energy, patents, public utilities, and trusts. This set also has a separate General Index at the end of the set for locating specific forms and a detailed table of contents at the beginning of each chapter.

Each chapter in *Am. Jur. Legal Forms 2d* has a section called General Considerations that provides introductory comments with references to *Am. Jur. 2d* and applicable *A.L.R.* annotations. (See Figure 9–1.) Other introductory sections present a concise discussion of the law applicable to the transaction. Another section, entitled Form Drafting Guide, gives detailed guidance for drafting a document. Each chapter also provides cautions and recommendations (including checklists) to help legal professionals customize forms to fit a particular transaction. (See Figure 9–2.) Each chapter contains a complete form for the particular transaction, and sometimes several different forms for a transaction. (See Figure 9–3.) For instance, there may be a sample form for leasing an apartment and another for leasing a commercial establishment. After the sample forms, there may be some optional provisions. Not all forms fit all transactions, so the optional provisions help the document drafter find substitute language to meet different situations. When appropriate, the researcher can substitute an optional provision in place of the corresponding provision from the sample form. Whenever any transaction has any tax consequences, there are some tax notes. *Am. Jur. Legal Forms 2d* is updated by annual pocket parts and sometimes by replacing volumes in the set.

Other popular sets that provide forms for a wide variety of legal transactions are J. Rabkin and M.H. Johnson's *Current Legal Forms with Tax Analysis* (Matthew Bender, 1968 to date, with looseleaf supplementation) and *Nicholas Encyclopedia of Legal Forms Annotated* (Callaghan, 1936 to date with pocket parts).

SIDEBAR

It is good practice to consult several form books before drafting a legal document. The legal professional who consults multiple sources will gain more depth of knowledge than the one who consults only a single source.

Litigation Form Books

Many novice litigation practitioners rely upon form books for drafting pleadings and motions for use in court proceedings. Some form books are tailor-made for a particular jurisdiction. The major publishers such as West, Lawyers Cooperative, Matthew Bender, and Clark, Boardman & Callaghan publish practice forms for different states. Sometimes the researcher will find a set covering civil litigation matters and another set covering criminal litigation matters. Because some states have unique rules respecting pleading and practice, it is a good idea to review form books from the particular jurisdiction in which the documents are to be filed.

For practicing in the federal courts, there are several form books that can be consulted: *Bender's Federal Practice Forms,* West's Federal Forms,

I. GENERAL CONSIDERATIONS

§ 28:1 Introductory comments

The nonmilitary use of atomic energy is subject to extensive governmental regulation. The primary regulatory agency is the United States Nuclear Regulatory Commission, [1] charged with administering the provisions of the Atomic Energy Act of 1954.[2] This comprehensive statute was enacted to encourage broader participation by private industry in the development of peacetime uses of atomic energy, subject to the prime necessity of providing for national defense and security.[3]

1. *Text references:* Authority of Nuclear Regulatory Commission. 6 AM JUR 2d, Atomic Energy §§ 5 et seq.

2. *Statutory references:* See 42 USCS §§ 2011 et seq.

(For Tax Notes and Notes on Use of form, see end of form)

3. *Text references:* Background and purposes of Atomic Energy Act of 1954. 6 AM JUR 2d, Atomic Energy § 3.

§ 28:2 Annotation references

ALR and ALR Fed annotations treating generally the subject of atomic energy are set forth below. Additional annotation references discussing specific matters are set forth in pertinent divisions of this topic and in the Notes on Use that follow particular forms.

ALR annotations:

Tort liability incident to nuclear accident or explosion, 21 ALR3d 1356.

Construction and application of zoning regulation in connection with bomb or fallout shelters, 7 ALR3d 1443.

State regulation of nuclear power plants, 82 ALR3d 751.

ALR Federal annotations:

Applicability of federal antitrust laws to licenses and permits issued under Atomic Energy Act of 1954 (42 USCS §§ 2131 et seq.), 15 ALR FED 599.

FIGURE 9–1   An example of the "Introductory Comments" section in *Am. Jur. Legal Forms 2d*

§ 34:12 Form drafting guide

As with any similar contract, a contract for the sale of an aircraft must

(For Tax Notes and Notes on Use of form, see end of form)

be supported by a valuable consideration and must meet the other requirements of a valid contract.[5] Such contract should be in writing to preclude future misunderstandings between the parties and, where applicable, to comply with the statute of frauds. The draftsman should ensure that the contract contains the entire agreement between the parties, with special emphasis on such matters as warranties and representations by the seller, accessories to be transferred with the aircraft, and the effect of either party's inability to perform the contract.

→ ☑ **Reminder:** In drafting a contract for the sale of an aircraft, consequences of the federal Truth-in-Lending Act[6] and applicable regulations,[7] and of similar state laws and regulations, must be considered if (1) credit is offered by the seller to the buyer, and (2) the seller regularly extends or arranges for the extension of consumer credit in the ordinary course of business.[8]

☑ **Comment:** In certain contracts of conditional sales involving large civil aircraft registered by the United States, a "truth in leasing" clause, as prescribed by federal regulation, must be appended to the contract in large print immediately preceding the space for the parties' signatures.[9]

5. *Text references:* Formation of contracts generally. 17 AM JUR 2d, Contracts §§ 10 et seq.

6. *Statutory reference:* Provisions of Federal Truth in Lending Act. 15 USCS §§ 1601 et seq.

7. *Regulations references:* Provisions of Regulation Z. 12 CFR §§ 226.1 et seq.

8. *Cross references:* For checklist of matters to be considered in connection with drafting instruments affected by the Federal Truth in Lending Act, see CONSUMER CREDIT PROTECTION ACTS (Ch 66).

9. *Regulations references:* Truth in leasing clause, requirement in leases and conditional sales contracts. Fed Aviation Reg Part 91 § 91.54.

§ 34:13 Form drafting guide—Checklist—Matters to be considered in drafting contract for sale of aircraft

→ ☑ **Checklist** of matters that should be considered in drafting a contract for the sale of an aircraft:

- Seller.
  —Name.
  —Address.
- Buyer.
  —Name.
  —Address.

(For Tax Notes and Notes on Use of form, see end of form)

FIGURE 9–2 The Form Drafting Guide sections found in *Am. Jur. Legal Forms 2d* provide guidance and an opportunity for customization to meet particular needs

any, of such change on design, performance, weight, balance, and time of delivery. The term "Federal Aviation Administration", as used in this agreement, shall include the Federal Aviation Administration or any other agency or authority of the federal government having jurisdiction.

☑ **Tax Notes:**

(See also Tax Notes following § 34:16)

General reference: For tax aspects of sales agreements generally, see FEDERAL TAX GUIDE TO LEGAL FORMS, Sales Agreements ¶¶ 170-C-11 et seq.

For tax implications of agreements to sell or purchase, see FEDERAL TAX GUIDE TO LEGAL FORMS, Sales Agreements ¶¶ 170-F-61, 62.

☑ **Notes on Use:**

(See also Notes on Use following § 34:16)

Text references: Federal regulation and control of aircraft generally. 8 AM JUR 2d (Rev), Aviation §§ 11 et seq.

§ 34:26 Bill of sale—Aircraft

Bill of sale executed __1_____ *[date]*, by __2_____, of __3_____ *[address]*, City of __4_____, County of __5_____, State of __6_____, referred to as seller, to __7_____, of __8_____ *[address]*, City of __9_____, County of __10_____, State of __11_____, referred to as buyer.

In consideration of __12_____ Dollars ($____), receipt of which is acknowledged, seller, the owner of the full legal and official title of an aircraft described as follows: __13_____ *[make, year, and model]*, Serial No. __14_____, Registration No. __15_____, on __16_____ *[date]*, sells and transfers to buyer, and buyer's legal representatives, successors, and assigns, all of seller's right, title, and interest in the aircraft described above, and certifies that such aircraft is not subject to any security interest or any other encumbrance __17_____ *[if applicable, add:* except __18_____ *(type of encumbrance)* in the amount of __19_____ Dollars ($____), in favor of __20_____, dated __21_____.

In witness whereof, the parties have executed this bill of sale at __22_____ *[place of execution]* the day and year first above written.

[Signatures]

[Acknowledgments]

☑ **Tax Notes:**

(See also Tax Notes following § 34:16)

General reference: For tax aspects of sales agreements generally, see FEDERAL TAX GUIDE TO LEGAL FORMS, Sales Agreements ¶¶ 170-C-11 et seq.

For tax implications of agreements to sell or purchase, see FEDERAL TAX GUIDE TO LEGAL FORMS, Sales Agreements ¶¶ 170-F-61, 62.

(For Tax Notes and Notes on Use of form, see end of form)

Form that can be used *(label pointing to the bracketed form section)*

3 Am Jur Legal Forms 2d (Rev)

FIGURE 9–3   An example of a document template provided in *Am. Jur. Legal Forms 2d*

and *Federal Procedural Forms—Lawyer's Edition*. Because federal courts deal with some matters not handled by state courts, these form books may be the best source for many federal forms.

A comprehensive set of litigation forms published by Lawyers Cooperative can be found in *American Jurisprudence Pleading and Practice Forms Annotated*, revised edition. *Am. Jur. Pleading and Practice Forms* is organized similar to *Am. Jur. Legal Forms*. There are hundreds of chapter topics covering a wide range of litigation matters such as abandoned property disputes, fence disputes, fraud claims, and zoning matters. Under each chapter topic, there are tables of contents, references to other research sources, textual material summarizing the substantive law relating to that topic, a checklist to follow, and a variety of forms. There may be sample complaints, answers to the complaint, motions, jury instructions, notices, court orders, affidavits, and many other forms used in connection with litigation. In addition to the table of contents at the beginning of each chapter, there is a two-volume descriptive word index at the end of the set. *Am. Jur. Pleading and Practice Forms* is updated by pocket parts and volume replacement.

Am. Jur. Pleading and Practice Forms deals with most phases of litigation. There are some form books, however, that deal with only a particular phase of a case. For example, there are form books dealing with only the discovery process and other form books that deal with only jury instructions.

Discovery Forms

During the course of a case, a party may conduct discovery to learn about the opposing party's case. As part of this discovery process, a party may submit written questions, called **interrogatories,** to the other party; direct questions to a witness before a court reporter at a **deposition;** or request the other party to produce documents or things for inspection or copying. There are form books that specifically help with this discovery process such as *Bender's Forms of Discovery* (twenty volumes, 1963 to present) and a series of books published by Lawyers Cooperative, written by Douglas Danner, with titles like *Pattern Discovery: Automobiles, Pattern Discovery: Products Liability, Pattern Discovery: Premises Liability,* and *Pattern Discovery: Employment Discrimination.*

————————————————————————LEGAL TERMS————————————————————————

interrogatories† Written questions put by one party to another, or, in limited situations, to a witness in advance of trial; a form of discovery.

deposition† The transcript of a witness's testimony given under oath outside of the courtroom, usually in advance of the trial or hearing, upon oral examination or in response to written interrogatories.

These works provide actual questions or requests to send to opposing parties.

Jury Instruction Forms

At the end of a jury trial and before the jury begins to deliberate, a judge reads instructions to the jury. The parties to a case may prepare proposed instructions for the judge's consideration. There are form books that deal specifically with **jury instructions.** These form books often are written for a specific jurisdiction.

It is not unusual for a party who loses at a trial to argue to a higher court that the judge gave erroneous instructions. To prevent some of these arguments between litigants, legal professionals in most states use **pattern** or **model jury instructions.** Similar to a model code, pattern or model jury instructions are secondary sources. These instructions may have been prepared by a bar or judge's association, or in some cases by a state supreme court. Pattern jury instructions may contain some commentary about the instructions such as a description of what cases have considered the language used in the proposed instruction. Figure 9–4 is an example of an Illinois pattern jury instruction.

For legal professionals who are working on a federal matter, there are some model or pattern sets for use within particular circuits such as the *Fifth Circuit Pattern Jury Instructions* (civil cases) and the *Ninth Circuit Model Criminal Jury Instructions*. In addition, there are two works that provide sample instructions: G. J. Dewitt, C. B. Blackburn, and M. A. Wolff, *Federal Jury Practice and Instructions* (West, 1977 to date), and L.B. Lord *et al.*, *Modern Federal Jury Instructions* (Matthew Bender, 1985 to date). Both sets cover civil and criminal instructions.

Specialty Form Books

Certain form books that contain forms for a specialty area may include both litigation and transaction forms in the same set. The specialty area may be property law, family law, wills and estates, pension law, or corporate law. Some of these sets limit coverage not only to a specialty area, but also to a particular jurisdiction. A set might cover, for instance, Kentucky wills and estates or North Dakota corporate practice.

LEGAL TERMS
---

jury instructions† Directions given to the jury by the judge just before he or she sends the jurors out to deliberate and return a verdict, explaining the law that applies in the case and spelling out what must be proven and by whom.

pattern or model jury instructions† In many jurisdictions, sample jury instructions that trial judges are required to follow when charging a jury.

DRAM SHOP ACT   **150.01**

150.01 Dram Shop Act—Injury to Person or Property
by an Intoxicated Person—Statutory Provisions

There was in force in the State of Illinois at the
time of the occurrence in question a statute called the
Dram Shop Act providing that every person who shall
be injured in person or property by any intoxicated person as a result of his intoxication shall have a right of
action [in (his) (her) own name] against any person
who shall, by selling or giving alcoholic liquor, have caused the intoxication of such intoxicated person.

→ Pattern instructions

Notes on Use

→ Commentary

This instruction is to be used when the seller alone is sued
for injury to person or property by an intoxicated person. This
instruction should be followed by IPI 150.02 (elements), Instruction 150.15 (defining intoxicated), IPI 150.16 (defining alcoholic
liquor). These dramshop instructions should be used with as
much of IPI 30.01–30.16 on damages as is applicable under the
pleadings and proof. IPI 30.01 should be changed from "have
resulted from the negligence [wrongful conduct] of the defendant" to "caused by the intoxicated person."

Comment

Injury to the person means actual personal violence. *Al-
brecht v. Walker*, 73 Ill. 69 (1874). Injury to "property" applies
only to tangible real or personal property. *Howlett v. Doglio*,
402 Ill. 311, 83 N.E.2d 708, 6 A.L.R.2d 790 (1949).

FIGURE 9–4   An example of jury instructions found in *Illinois Pattern Jury Instructions—Civil,* 2d ed.

Legal professionals should become familiar with the available form books in any area in which they practice. The paralegal who refers to these form sets will save considerable time and effort, end with a more complete legal document, and spot any potential legal problems with the proposed transaction.

SIDEBAR

A form book provides a good starting point for drafting a legal document. In a few situations, a form can be copied word-for-word. In most situations, however, a form needs to be altered to fit the transaction. Paralegals should never hesitate to change a form to fit the situation. Remember that the form is only a guide or starting point for drafting a legal document.

How to Select Forms

Form books are a tool of the legal professional that saves hours of time. By selecting good forms and gaining some experience, a paralegal will be able to draft a document as well as any other legal professional. In researching and selecting forms, the paralegal should remember that legal documents vary from state to state, so it is sometimes critical to start with forms specific to the jurisdiction in which the paralegal is employed. Some jurisdictions require that specific words be incorporated into documents. For instance, a statute may require that a warranty deed contain the words "convey and warrant" or that an option be "irrevocable."

The paralegal also should be forewarned that not all forms found in books necessarily are well written. Many forms found in form books, in fact, are poorly written. Do not copy a form word-for-word. Search for documents that are thorough and easily understood. In fact, a good rule is not to use any form that cannot be easily understood.

Many publishers are now marketing CD-ROM and software versions of forms. This recent trend has several advantages over more traditional form books. Especially advantageous is that the form does not need to be typed but can be simply read and printed by word processing equipment. For large documents, this can save a substantial amout of time.

Finally, a paralegal should know that sometimes the best forms are those that have been honed by the legal professional. Many legal professionals save forms. Do not be bashful about asking other legal professionals whether they have forms to start a project. By the same token, a legal professional who finds or drafts a good form should save it for future use. A paralegal should develop his or her own form books.

Practice Guides

Chapter 5 discusses treatises and C.L.E. materials, both of which provide practical as well as scholarly advice to legal practitioners. A **practice manual or guide** is a book or set of books that provides practical step-by-step information and how-to advice in a specific area of the law. Some of these materials reference the law of a particular state on a specific subject, and others reference the law generally on a specific subject.

A practice guide typically consists of one or more volumes published in hard cover or looseleaf format. These guides cover almost every area of law in which attorneys practice. Many of them deal with rules and procedures of particular states or federal courts. For example, Lawyers Cooperative's *Federal Procedure* and West's *Federal Procedure Manual*, 2d ed. are useful guides for dealing with basic questions concerning the federal rules of civil procedure.

Some legal publishers like Clark, Boardman & Callaghan and John Wiley & Sons publish a wide variety of practice manuals dealing with both general and specific subjects. One example of a general practice manual is *Actions and Remedies* (1985, two volumes), which provides practical information about what it takes to prove various causes of action such as a nuisance action, a business tort, a defamation action, a fair debt collection practice claim, or a truth-in-lending violation.

An example of a specific practice manual is *Social Security Disability Practice* (1983, two volumes updated as a looseleaf service). This practice manual, published by Clark, Boardman & Callaghan, covers various matters that may arise in pursuing a claim for benefits from the Social Security Administration. Another example of a specific practice manual is *Making Trial Objections*, published by John Wiley & Sons, which illustrates how to make trial objections in all sorts of situations. A legal professional can educate himself or herself quite thoroughly in a new area by reading some of these manuals.

SIDEBAR

Although some practice manuals are accurate, others are of uneven quality. Many of these works are low budget publications. Always approach these guides with some caution. They are good starting points, but information from them should be cross-checked through other resources as well.

-------------------- LEGAL TERMS --------------------

practice manual or guide A book or set of books that provides practical step-by-step information and how-to advice in a specific area of the law.

Trial Practice Books

A paralegal may be asked to interview a witness or a client and have little idea of what to ask. There are books that provide sample questions. Although many of these books are meant for lawyers who do trial work, a paralegal will find them useful in preparing to interview a client or witness.

Proof of Facts

Legal professionals ask a lot of questions—to clients, to witnesses, and to opposing parties. A paralegal may be asked to take a statement from a witness, interview a client, or gather information from an expert. A paralegal must learn to converse with experts from any vocation. The legal professional may question a financial expert, an engineer, and a physician in the same case.

Lawyers Cooperative Publishing publishes a set of books called *Proof of Facts* that provides sample questions in a variety of situations—for instance, child neglect, employment discrimination, automobile accident, and products liability. Now in the third series, this set contains a number of features, including articles that offer practical and technical background and suggestions to educate the legal professional about the particular area covered by the article. (See Figure 9–5.) This set also contains extensive citations to other sources that relate to the subject of the article, including citations to law review articles, A.L.R.s, *American Jurisprudence 2d*, and other texts. The main feature of this set, however, is the sample questions and answers that illustrate the interchange between a lawyer and witness. (See Figure 9–6.) Some questions and answers were created from reported decisions and actual trial transcripts. *Proof of Facts* is practically written and can be helpful to any legal professional who must interview or question a client or witness.

Am. Jur. Trials

A set of books that is similar to *Proof of Facts* is *Am. Jur. Trials,* which consists of forty-eight volumes, plus two index volumes. The first six volumes of this set provide a general guide for preparing and trying cases: how to interview a client, control trial publicity, locate and preserve evidence, handle cross-examinations, and present a final argument. The remaining forty-two volumes, which are continually expanding, are titled *Model Trials*. These volumes describe how to prepare and try specific cases. For instance, there are articles on how to

3-265
§ 13
CHILD NEGLECT

is sought, a court may refuse to order surgery or blood transfusions, where there is no certainty that such treatment would in fact be helpful, and where the parent's objections are based in part on the danger inherent in the treatment.[95]

§ 14. Educational neglect

In the absence of statutory exemptions, most states require persons having control of a child between certain ages, usually the ages of six to sixteen, to send the child to a full-time public or private school. States may enforce compulsory attendance laws through provisions proscribing truancy, through penal sanctions making failure to comply with the compulsory education laws a crime, or by making such failure to comply a ground for a neglect finding. It has been noted that, although the standards to be applied in educational neglect cases thus are quite specific, cases involving educational neglect are frequently difficult to resolve.[96]

One reason for this difficulty is that when a child does not attend school, it may constitute either delinquency or neglect, depending on the circumstances. If the child is out of school without the parent's knowledge, such absence constitutes truancy and generally is not a basis for a neglect finding, unless the truancy can be traced to the attitudes or actions of the parents. Nonattendance, in which the child is absent from school with the parent's knowledge, is a more common basis for a neglect finding.[97]

---

95. See Brown, Parental Right to Refuse Medical Treatment for Child, 12 Crime & Delin 377, for such a case. In that case a neglect petition was brought on behalf of a six-year-old black child with sickle cell anemia. The recommended treatment included, in part, a splenectomy, which would require a blood transfusion, and blood transfusions if his hemoglobin level fell below four grams. Such treatment was not customary for sickle cell anemia and was relatively experimental, and there was no assurance that the child would benefit. The court, after overruling the mother's objections on religious grounds, sustained her objections on medical grounds and held the child was not neglected.

96. See Gill, 6 Nat Probation & Parole AJ 12, 13.

97. See generally, Gill, 6 Nat Probation & Parole A J 12.
    As used herein, nonattendance denotes a child's absence from school with parental knowledge or approval.
    It has been noted that when parents allow their children to remain away from school, without any apparent reason or justification, the entire family situation should be examined, as such parental indifference frequently accompanies other family problems and may indicate other types of neglect. See id., p. 13.

FIGURE 9–5   *Proof of Facts,* published by Lawyers Cooperative Publishing, provides sample questions, practical and technical insight, and citations for various topics (3 *Am. Jur. Proof of Facts 2d* 294)

EMPLOYMENT DISCRIMINATION—HIRING   **3-221**
§ 19

A.   We put notices on the bulletin boards.

Q.   Are these bulletin boards accessible to persons other than company employees?

A.   No.

☐ **Case Illustration: Failure to publish job opportunities.** It is unlawful for an employer to limit notice of future opportunities in job classifications to word-of-mouth recruitment, where the company had traditionally white job classifications and relied solely on word-of-mouth recruitment for its job classifications; where there was no "help-wanted" announcement posted to notify incumbent employees in other job classifications who might be interested in transferring; and where the company never advertised job vacancies or used community sources such as the State Employment Service to obtain applicants for those jobs. United States v Central Motor Lines, Inc. (DC NC) 338 F Supp 532, supp op (DC NC) 352 F Supp 1253.

§ 18. Word-of-mouth recruiting

Q.   How is the posting of job vacancies on bulletin boards effective in filling such openings?

A.   We encourage our present employees to make job openings known to their friends.

Q.   Wasn't it obvious to you that if new employees were selected from friends of present employees your work force would generally exclude minorities?

A.   No. That didn't occur to me.

☐ **Case Illustration: Word-of-mouth recruiting.** The district court's refusal to supplement or change an employer's word-of-mouth recruiting practice was clearly an abuse of discretion where 92.8 percent of all personnel likely to see the job vacancy notices posted were white, and where no business necessity compelled the company to rely so heavily on that recruiting practice. United States v Georgia Power Co. (CA5 Ga) 474 F2d 906.

§ 19. Recruitment of walk-in applicants

Q.   Does the _____ Company advertise job openings in order to secure applicants for employment?

A.   No, except for the posting of notices on bulletin boards and with the State Employment Service, we do not advertise employment openings.

3 POF 2d   **243**

FIGURE 9–6   *Proof of Facts* is also an ideal reference for researchers who need to interview others

prepare and try a motorboat accident case, a kerosene heater accident case, a tractor rollover case, and a pit bull injury case. These volumes provide sample questions like those in *Proof of Facts*, but they provide more legal, practical, and technical information than questions. This set also provides legal theories as well as expert witness information.

Legal professionals involved in a litigation can gain considerable insight by reading *Am. Jur. Trials*. For instance, suppose a client is injured in a pit bull attack. There is an article on such a case in *Am. Jur. Trials*. This article describes how the pit bulldog was bred and how the propensity of that breed for violence evolved. It describes the standard of care owed by the owner of the pit bulldog to the public, as well as different legal theories that may apply to such a case.

Am. Jur. Trials contains practical hints about how to evaluate whether to accept a case, set a fee, and undertake settlement negotiations. It gives hints about how to locate and interview witnesses. It tells how to prepare a complaint to file in the case and how to prepare interrogatories. Finally, there are many pages covering trial tactics, including tips for opening and closing arguments and sample cross-examination questions.

Reference Works

There are certain materials that are kept readily available by legal professionals for reference purposes such as legal dictionaries and thesauri, desk rule books, desk references, and checklists.

Dictionaries and Thesauri

There are several dictionaries published solely for legal professionals. The two most popular legal dictionaries are *Black's Law Dictionary*, 6th ed. (West, 1979) and *Ballantine's Law Dictionary*, 3rd ed. (Lawyers Cooperative, 1969). These dictionaries are arranged alphabetically, just like nonlegal dictionaries. Remember that *Black's Law Dictionary* can be searched on WESTLAW as well. Figure 9–7 is a sample page from *Black's Law Dictionary*. An especially well-written work is Bryan A. Garner, *A Dictionary of Modern Legal Usage* (Oxford University Press, 1987), which provides definitions for legal words and phrases in an understandable fashion. Another easy-to-understand dictionary is J. Lynton, *Ballentine's Legal Dictionary and Thesaurus* (Delmar/LCP, 1995).

Every paralegal should have access to a quality legal dictionary. Legal terms have precise meanings. When in doubt about a word or phrase, look it up. Often paralegals find it difficult to penetrate a descriptive

DELEGATION   384

Term → **Delegation of powers.** Transfer of authority by one branch of government in which such authority is vested to some other branch or administrative agency.

creditor. *Imperfect delegation* exists when the creditor retains his rights against the original debtor.

U.S. Constitution delegates different powers to the executive, legislative and judicial branches of government. Exercise by the executive branch of the powers delegated to the legislative branch offends this separation and delegation of powers and hence is unconstitutional. Schechter Poultry Corp. v. U. S., 295 U.S. 495, 55 S.Ct. 837, 79 L.Ed. 1570. Certain powers may not be delegated from one branch of government to another such as the judicial powers or such congressional powers as power to declare war, impeach, or admit new states.

For distinction between delegated powers and various other types of constitutional powers, see **Power** *(Constitutional powers).*

De legatis et fidei commissis /díy ləgéydəs èt fáydiyay kəmísəs/. Of legacies and trusts. The name of a title of the Pandects.

Pronunciation →

Delegatus non potest delegare /dèlagéydəs nòn pówdəst dèləgériyə/. A delegate cannot delegate; an agent cannot delegate his functions to a subagent without the knowledge or consent of the principal; the person to whom an office or duty is delegated cannot lawfully devolve the duty on another, unless he be expressly authorized so to do.

Delete /dəlíyt/. To erase; to remove; to strike out.

Deleterious /dèlətíriyəs/. Hurtful, morally or physically; injurious, as influence; poisonous; unwholesome.

De libera falda /díy líbərə fóldə/. Writ of free fold. A species of *quod permittat.*

De libera piscaria /díy líbərə pəskériyə/. Writ of free fishery. A species of *quod permittat.*

Deliberate, *v.* To weigh, ponder, discuss, regard upon, consider. To examine and consult in order to form an opinion. To weigh in the mind; to consider the reasons for and against; to consider maturely; reflect upon, as to deliberate a question; to weigh the arguments for and against a proposed course of action. People v. Thomas, 25 Cal.2d 880, 156 P.2d 7, 17, 18. See also **Deliberation.**

Legal Source →

Deliberate, *adj.* Well advised; carefully considered; not sudden or rash; circumspect; slow in determining. Willful rather than merely intentional. Formed, arrived at, or determined upon as a result of careful thought and weighing of considerations, as a deliberate judgment or plan. Carried on coolly and steadily, especially according to a preconceived design; given to weighing facts and arguments with a view to a choice or decision; careful in considering the consequences of a step; slow in action; unhurried; characterized by reflection; dispassionate; not rash. People v. Thomas, 25 Cal.2d 880, 156 P.2d 7, 17, 18.

By the use of this word, in describing a crime, the idea is conveyed that the perpetrator weighs the motives for the act and its consequences, the nature of the crime, or other things connected with his intentions, with a view to a decision thereon; that he carefully considers all these, and that the act is not suddenly committed. It implies that the perpetrator must be capable of the exercise of such mental powers as are called into use by deliberation and the consideration and weighing of motives and consequences. See also **Deliberation; Premeditation.**

← Additional terms to research

Deliberately. Willfully; with premeditation; intentionally; purposely; in cold blood. Averheart v. State, 158 Ark. 639, 238 S.W. 620, 621.

Deliberate speed. Phrase used in mandate to desegregate public schools and means such speed as is consistent with the welfare of all people of the state, with the maintenance of law and order and with the preservation, if possible, of the common school system. Calhoun v. Members of Bd. of Ed., City of Atlanta, D.C.Ga., 188 F.Supp. 401, 404; Brown v. Board of Education, 347 U.S. 483, 74 S.Ct. 686, 98 L.Ed. 873.

Deliberation. The act or process of deliberating. The act of weighing and examining the reasons for and against a contemplated act or course of conduct or a choice of acts or means. As used in context of an essential element of first-degree murder, is a weighing in the mind of consequences of course of conduct, as distinguished from acting upon a sudden impulse without exercise of reasoning powers. Davis v. State, 251 Ark. 771, 475 S.W.2d 155, 156. See also **Deliberate; Premeditation.**

De libero passagio /díy líbərow pəséyjiow/. Writ of free passage. A species of *quod permittat.*

De libertate probanda /díy libərtéydiy prəbǽndə/. Writ for proving liberty. A writ which lay for such as, being demanded for villeins or niefs, offered to prove themselves free.

De libertatibus allocandis /díy libərtéydəbəs ǽləkǽndəs/. A writ of various forms, to enable a citizen to recover the liberties to which he was entitled.

De licentia transfretandi /díy ləsénsh(iy)ə trænsfrətǽnday/. Writ of permission to cross the sea. An old writ directed to the wardens of the port of Dover, or other seaport in England, commanding them to permit the persons named in the writ to cross the sea from such port, on certain conditions.

Delict. Criminal offense; tort; a wrong.

In Roman law this word, taken in its most general sense, is wider in both directions than our English term "tort." On the one hand, it includes those wrongful acts which, while directly affecting some individual or his property, yet extend in their injurious consequences to the peace or security of the community at large, and hence rise to the grade of crimes or misdemeanors. These acts were termed in the Roman law "public delicts;" while those for which the only penalty exacted was compensation to the person primarily injured were denominated "private delicts." On the other hand, the term appears to have included injurious actions which transpired without any malicious intention on the part of the doer. A quasi delict in Roman law was an act whereby a person, without malice, but by fault, negligence, or imprudence not legally excusable, caused injury to another. They were four in number, viz.: (1) *Qui*

FIGURE 9–7 Legal dictionaries are an essential resource when beginning legal research (Reprinted by permission of West Publishing Company.)

word index in a digest or code. In such cases, it is helpful to consult a legal thesaurus, such as J. Lynton's *Ballentine's Legal Thesaurus for Legal Research and Writing* (Delmar/LCP, 1994), to find synonyms and antonyms.

Deskbooks

A booklet commonly found on most legal professionals' desks is a **deskbook** that contains the rules of trial and appellate procedure, the rules of evidence, ethical canons, and other pertinent rules for a particular jurisdiction. Many of these deskbooks, such as the *Maine Rules of Court,* are published by West. Figure 9–8 is an outline of the matters covered by the *Federal Civil Judicial Procedure and Rules,* which is a deskbook that covers the rules of the federal courts. These deskbooks are revised annually, so the prior year's deskbook is usually discarded. Most litigation legal professionals keep a deskbook readily available. Deskbooks are prepared by publishers as a convenience to legal professionals. The information in a deskbook almost always can be found in another source such as an annotated code, but deskbooks are easier to carry to court or around the office.

Desk References

An excellent source for law-related information is the **desk reference.** Desk references contain information about the court system, federal and state agencies, statistical information, medical diagrams, financial tables, and other reference materials. *American Jurisprudence 2d Deskbook* (Lawyers Cooperative, 1979) is one of the more available of these references because it is published as part of the *Am. Jur. 2d* encyclopedia set. This desk reference book directs the user to other references such as *Am. Jur. 2d* that may be relevant. This set is updated by pocket parts. A similar work is *Shepard's Lawyer's Reference Manual* (1983, with annual pocket parts).

LEGAL TERMS

deskbook A booklet that contains the rules of trial and appellate procedure, the rules of evidence, ethical canons, and other pertinent rules for a particular jurisdiction.

desk reference A reference book that contains information about the court system, federal and state agencies, statistical information, medical diagrams, financial tables, and other reference materials.

FIGURE 9–8
A topical
index to the
rules of
federal court

SUMMARY OF FEATURES:

A more specific desk reference book is the popular three-volume work by Philo & Philo, *Lawyers Desk Reference*, published by Lawyers Cooperative Publishing Co. & Bancroft-Whitney Co. This work contains a wealth of information about the preparation of a personal injury or product liability lawsuit. It contains names of expert witnesses, titles for technical articles, and numerous helpful hints on trying the personal injury lawsuit. This set also is updated by pocket parts.

Checklists

Checklists provide legal professionals with a means to spot-check whether all items of importance have been covered. Checklists serve a number of functions. Some checklists help the legal professional to prepare to interview clients. Such a checklist outlines areas to cover at the interview so that all items of importance will be covered. Other checklists help legal professionals make sure all items have been covered in drafting litigation or transaction documents. Some checklists are included in form books. Some books consist only of sample checklists for different situations. Lawyers Cooperative Publishing publishes a book, for example, called Danner, *Pattern Deposition Checklists* (1973, with a supplementary pamphlet) that outlines the basic elements for taking a deposition in various types of cases. (See Figure 9–9.)

Directories

A client may need to hire an attorney in another state, or a lawyer may need to contact a lawyer in another state for some advice. There are legal directories that help legal professionals learn about lawyers in other states.

Martindale-Hubbell Law Directory

The most popular law directory is *Martindale-Hubbell Law Directory* (twenty-seven volumes in 1994, replaced annually). *Martindale-Hubbell* can be searched on-line on LEXIS/NEXIS and is available on CD-ROM. WESTLAW has a similar service available on-line called the *West's Legal Directory* that provides basic information (name, address, education, and so on) about attorneys nationwide.

Martindale-Hubbell compiles information about attorneys in the United States and in over 130 foreign countries. The set includes volumes that summarize the statutory law in the United States, the District of Columbia, Puerto Rico and the Virgin Islands, Canada and its provinces, and over 60 other countries. Although a *Martindale-Hubbell* is mainly a directory of attorneys, it also contains an extensive digest of domestic and foreign laws.

Attorney Directory Information

A paralegal, like any other legal professional, may be asked to find the name, address, or other information about an attorney in another

Chapter 1   **§ 1:81**

Specific Deponents

§ 1:81   Specific Deponent—Witness to Occurrence

RESEARCH REFERENCES

Am Jur:
    58 Am Jur (1st ed), Witnesses.

---

1. Identification—See 1:01 or 1:41
2. Relationship to Legal Action—See 1:43
3. Presence at Place of Occurrence
   (a) location of deponent in relation to other persons
       (1) preceding occurrence
       (2) at moment of occurrence
       (3) after occurrence
   (b) reason for presence in vicinity
       (1) purpose in being there
       (2) activities
       (3) time of arrival
       (4) intended length of time in vicinity
       (5) time of departure
   (c) view of events preceding and including occurrence
       (1) distance from events
       (2) obstructions to view
           (aa) identification
           (bb) description
           (cc) location relative to persons involved
       (3) ability to observe events

131

FIGURE 9–9   An example of a useful outline from a book of checklists

city or state. The most common use of *Martindale-Hubbell* is to look up an attorney in another city or state. Attorneys are listed in a number of ways by this set:

- Several volumes list all attorneys alphabetically. These volumes identify only the attorney's place of practice.

- Several volumes list all attorneys by their area of practice.

- Multiple volumes list United States attorneys (sixteen volumes in 1994) and attorneys in over 130 countries (three volumes in 1994) with practice profiles and biographical information.

- One volume contains listings for corporate law departments and law schools.

The volumes that provide the practice profiles and biographical information are arranged alphabetically by state. Within a volume, the entries are arranged alphabetically by city or town. For each city or town in the United States, there is an alphabetical roster of the attorneys who practice there. In the blue pages of the volume, there is a practice profile for each attorney consisting of the name, year of birth, first year of admission to the bar, college attended, degree received (undergraduate and law school), and where the attorney practices.

Martindale-Hubbell also rates attorneys. This rating is obtained by interviews and questions submitted to lawyers and judges familiar with the attorney who is being rated. If a rating is assigned, it is included in the profile.

In the white pages, there is a more complete professional biography. Because a fee is required from attorneys included in this section, not all attorneys are listed here. This section may contain considerably more information about the attorney, including any practice areas, awards, cases handled, publications, and representative clients.

Law Digests

A *Martindale-Hubbell* set contains volumes entitled *Digest of Laws* that provide summaries of the statutory laws for the fifty states as well as for sixty other countries. For each state or territory, these legal summaries are listed under subject headings with numerous subheadings as well. There are separate summaries for copyright, patent, and trademark laws; the complete text of selected uniform and model acts; and ethical standards for the profession.

The laws that are digested in this set may not be readily available to some legal professionals by any other means, so *Martindale-Hubbell* can provide a quick answer to a problem. For instance, if a legal professional needs to know the statute of limitations for bringing a negligence action in Arizona, the answer can be found in a *Martindale-Hubbell*.

SIDEBAR

The biographical listings also may list nonlawyer support personnel such as paralegals and CPAs. *Martindale-Hubbell* is finalizing details for listing law school students, which is intended to be used for recruiting purposes.

Blue Book Directories

There are directories available that list attorneys in a certain state and others that list attorneys in a certain region. Many of the state directories have a blue cover and are marketed as a "blue book" directory. These directories typically have a separate biographical section like that is found in *Martindale-Hubbell*.

Specialized Directories

In addition to *Martindale-Hubbell* and state directories, there are directories that contain lists of lawyers who practice in specialized areas. For example, *Markham's Negligence Counsel*, published by Markham Publishing Corporation, is a directory of lawyers who practice in the personal injury area, and *Directory of Bankruptcy Attorneys* (Prentice Hall Law and Business, annual) is a directory of lawyers who practice in the bankruptcy area. It is also available on-line on WESTLAW.

SIDEBAR

When a paralegal is job hunting, a law directory can provide insight and information about a firm or attorney, especially in the biographical section of the set. Before interviewing with a firm, review biographical sketches about members of the firm.

Magazines, Newspapers, and Newsletters

The legal professional is even kept informed by magazines, newspapers, and newsletters.

Magazines

Some bar associations or law interest groups publish magazines for their members. These magazines typically provide articles featuring practical advice about developments in the law. Articles may deal with law office management concerns, upcoming events, membership information, and new cases. These magazines are often a good means to stay current on developing areas of the law. Paralegals should make it a habit to read several magazines to stay current with trends and new ideas.

Newspapers

Although legal newspapers have long covered large cities like Chicago and New York, recently several legal newspapers, national in scope, have become quite popular. For example, the *National Law Journal* is a newspaper that provides national coverage of law and law-related news. It covers breaking news about important cases across the country and new legal theories. It contains articles about legal personalities, law firms, and government.

Another national newspaper, the *American Lawyer*, focuses on news about lawyers and law firms. This newspaper is a little more gossipy than the *National Law Journal*. It covers law firm breakups, profiles controversial legal figures, and follows the course of interesting cases.

In addition to the national newspapers, several publishers have started legal newspapers covering a state (for example, the *Indiana Lawyer*) or region. Such newspapers keep the subscribers up-to-date on changes in state laws and court rules, and even provide information about court calendars, including what cases have been docketed or argued and what cases are pending for decision. There may be feature articles about firms or trends as well.

Newsletters

Another way for legal professionals to keep up-to-date are newsletters. As legal practice becomes more technical and specialized, more and more publishers have put out "niche" newsletters. Many of these newsletters cover narrow areas of the law. Some provide abstracts or summaries of court cases from a certain court or jurisdiction. There may be a newsletter for public defenders in a state and another for prosecutors in the same state. There may be a newsletter that provides abstracts of new cases in a particular area. For example, a group called National Organization of Social Security Claimant's Representatives (NOSSCR) publishes a newsletter dealing with new developments in Social Security law. This newsletter provides a synopsis of laws and recent court decisions. It also provides practice tips, includes sample forms, and even alerts readers to proposed changes so the members can lobby for or against the change. Newsletters are a good way to stay abreast of the law in a particular area of practice.

Summary

- Many legal documents such as transaction documents and litigation documents can be prepared by referencing a form book. For instance, *American Jurisprudence Pleading and Practice Forms Annotated* contains a comprehensive set of litigation forms, and *Am. Jur. Legal Forms 2d* is a comprehensive set of transaction documents.

- A practice manual or guide provides basic how-to information about a specific area of the law.

- Some trial practice books like *Proof of Facts* and *Am. Jur. Trials* actually provide sample questions for a variety of situations.

- To master the jargon of the law, every paralegal should have a legal dictionary readily available.

- *Martindale-Hubbell* is a legal directory of attorneys.

- There are a number of magazines and newspapers that provide news coverage of legal issues. For example, the *National Law Journal* is a national newspaper providing coverage of legal developments, lawyers, and government.

Review Questions

1. Identify examples of a transaction form book, a specialty form book, and a litigation form book.

2. What is a practice guide? List several examples.

3. Why would a paralegal use *Proof of Facts* or *Am. Jur. Trials*?

4. Explain how to look up an attorney in *Martindale-Hubbell*.

5. Give some examples of reference books used by legal professionals.

6. Identify different ways a paralegal might keep abreast of news in the law.

7. If you were asked to prepare jury instructions, what would you do?

Research Projects

1. A client has been injured in an automobile accident and has sustained a postconcussion injury. Using the practice aids identified in this chapter, copy the following:

   a. a complaint to file in court from a form book;

   b. questions that might be used to question the treating physician from *Proof of Facts*; and

   c. applicable jury instructions that your court might give in this case.

2. Look up a famous lawyer in the United States in *Martindale-Hubbell*. What is his or her address and rating?

‖‖

CHAPTER 10

THE LEGAL
RESEARCH PROCESS

A paralegal can gain expertise at legal research only by actual in-the-library practice, not by textbooks and lectures. In fact, it is questionable whether any researcher can become good at legal research without years and years of practice. As researchers gain experience, they learn that there is no "right" way to approach legal research. If a group of legal experts were asked to research a legal question of some complexity, each would probably approach the problem with a different method—and each might even reach different conclusions about the law and the answer. To verify this statement, simply read a decision of the United States Supreme Court on a controversial issue. There may be a majority opinion with, perhaps, several concurring opinions, and even several dissenting opinions. Not only do Supreme Court justices reach different results, but each of them may even rely upon different authority.

Because legal research is an art and not a science, there are no hard-and-fast rules that can be taught about the process that fit every circumstance. At best, the legal student can be taught only the basic steps of the legal research process. Although some of these steps do not apply in all research situations, most need to be done at some point in the process. As legal professionals gain expertise, many of these steps are done routinely and without much thought.

With these caveats in mind, Chapter 10 discusses the basic steps of the legal research process.

GATHERING THE FACTS

Before opening any law book, the legal professional first must ascertain all the relevant facts. The facts are the events that happened prior to the client seeking legal advice. Learning the facts may involve learning the details of a transaction or the details of an accident. A client may have slipped and fallen in a grocery store, stolen some clothes from a retail outlet, or failed to file a necessary form with a regulatory agency.

A paralegal may gather facts by interviewing a client or witness, or a supervisor may relate the facts to the paralegal in a narrative form. Sometimes a paralegal learns the facts from reading the file. Learning the necessary facts usually involves nothing more than asking enough questions. During the course of a research project, it is not unusual for a paralegal to go back to a supervisor or client to learn more details. The more thorough the paralegal is at the beginning of the project, however, the more likely it will be that the paralegal can minimize these follow-up sessions.

The importance of learning all the facts cannot be underscored enough. One set of facts may occasion the application of a certain principle; but the addition of several additional details to those facts may occasion the application of an entirely different principle. Inexperienced lawyers and paralegals often are so enamored with legal principles that they overlook pertinent factual distinctions.

Suppose, for example, that a supervisor asks a paralegal to see if a husband can prevent his wife from testifying against him in a criminal proceeding. In most states, if not all, there is a spousal privilege. The researcher may give the wrong answer, however, if the case involves a child molesting charge because there is an exception to the spousal privilege in those cases in some jurisdictions.

FRAMING THE ISSUES

After gathering all the essential facts, the next step is to try to formulate the issue or issues that must be researched. In law, an issue is the question that is posed by the facts. Often the legal professional cannot state readily the issue in any coherent manner before beginning the research, and sometimes the issue cannot be framed until the researcher is almost finished with the legal research process. Trying to write the issue before researching, however, serves a number of functions. First, different issues are approached by different means. One of the issues may be a statutory question, and another may be a common law question. A researcher would research these issues with different books and methods. Second, by framing the issue, the researcher begins to focus on key words and ideas that can help in penetrating an index. Third, as the research progresses, a researcher can more easily organize his or her findings by issue on separate pages or in separate files. Finally, writing usually helps the thinking process.

As the research progresses, the researcher often finds subissues or new issues. What was formulated as a broad question or issue can be restated as a more narrow question or issue in later stages of the research. In fact, legal research often progresses from broad principles to a narrowly focused issue. It is not unusual to begin researching a particular issue only to learn that there are better issues that can be posed. In short, writing issues is an important step in legal research.

Identifying the Source Authority and Jurisdiction

There are two threshold questions every researcher should answer before proceeding with any legal research. First, what is the source authority? Is it a constitutional provision, a statute, a regulation, a court rule, a case, or some other authority? Second, what jurisdiction's law will determine the outcome of the case? Answering these questions frames the research project and saves many hours of research time. For example, it would not make sense to look first for Kansas cases when researching an Ohio law problem, nor would it make sense to look through regulatory authority when the answer to the query is in the case law.

Identifying the Source Authority

As the chapters in this text demonstrate, a researcher selects different books, depending on whether the source law is a statute, a case, a constitutional provision, or an ordinance. In some situations, the researcher is not able to pinpoint the source law before starting the research. For instance, the researcher may not know whether the issue is a common law concern or a statutory problem. In the beginning, the researcher may not spot a constitutional problem. Nonetheless, to the extent that the researcher can identify what source authority controls, the more likely that the researcher will find an answer. The researcher who cannot identify the type of source authority needs to ask for some direction at the beginning, or at least consult some background materials for help.

What Is the Applicable Jurisdiction?

Another essential inquiry is which jurisdiction's law will answer the question. In many cases, identifying jurisdiction is as simple as noting that Florida law or Oregon law applies. Basically the researcher decides whether a particular state's law applies or whether the problem involves a federal matter. In most situations, the researcher can easily recognize what state's law applies and whether it is a state or federal matter. Sometimes, however, these decisions are more difficult, as in a **diversity case** (a federal lawsuit involving parties who live in different states), or in cases where the facts or transaction happened in multiple

---

LEGAL TERMS

diversity case   A federal lawsuit involving parties who live in different states.

jurisdictions. These are not the sorts of problems a paralegal usually researches without considerable experience or significant direction from a supervising attorney.

Sometimes a researcher starts a project and discovers there is no case law that answers the question in the relevant jurisdiction, or the researcher wants to search for case law from other jurisdictions that have interpreted a similar statute or constitutional provision. A decision to search for persuasive authority from other jurisdictions is a fairly routine practice. A paralegal who is accustomed to making broad searches should never lose sight of the ultimate goal: to find source authority from the relevant jurisdiction that answers the issue.

When there is no source authority for the relevant jurisdiction, the researcher needs to search for persuasive authority, which might be a case from another jurisdiction or a commentary like a treatise or law review article.

Learning the Vocabulary

The greatest handicap for a novice researcher is usually a limited vocabulary. Legal professionals use their own jargon. Terms like res ipsa loquitur, writ of certiorari, burden of persuasion, collateral estoppel, res judicata, and adverse possession may have little meaning to a layperson but must be part of most lawyers' common vocabulary. Although many legal indexes can be penetrated quite simply without a legal vocabulary by using the TAPP rule discussed in Chapter 1, some legal principles cannot be located through an index unless the researcher knows the appropriate legal terms. For example, in many annotated codes, the researcher will not find a statutory citation under drunk driving, but will find that citation under "driving while intoxicated." Although publishers tout the TAPP rule, sometimes it does not work.

Perhaps the most frustrating feeling of a legal professional is having no clue where or how to begin. The researcher has tried the TAPP approach but is still unable to pinpoint any law relevant to the problem. Often, in such situations, the problem is that the researcher lacks the relevant vocabulary. There are resources and methods to assist the researcher who needs help at this stage of the research process.

Use a Legal Dictionary or Thesaurus

Legal vocabulary is not the same as a layperson's vocabulary, which may mean the researcher must develop a more abstract vocabulary. The TAPP rule allows researchers to access legal principles through concrete words, yet sometimes indexes can be accessed only with more abstract terms. The easiest way to overcome a deficient vocabulary is to use a legal dictionary or thesaurus like those discussed in Chapter 9. By looking for synonyms, the researcher may find a more apt word or phrase to use in the search.

SIDEBAR

Every paralegal student should own a good legal dictionary. Paralegals should develop a habit of looking up any new word or term when it is encountered. Vocabulary skills are critical to the legal profession.

Use Alternative Approaches

In a new area of the law, usually the best approach is to try first a descriptive-word index. If vocabulary problems hinder this approach, try scanning the topics or chapter headings or looking at a table of contents to see if any topic seems to relate to the situation. When a researcher's vocabulary is deficient, sometimes the best approach is to try to categorize the area of law (for example, negligence, trademark, contract) that will answer the question. When indexes or chapter headings do not help, try another set of books. If a digest does not help, try an A.L.R. When an annotated code does not produce an answer, try a looseleaf service. Some indexes are better than others, and even the best indexes sometimes are not very good for a particular matter.

Read Related Materials

When other alternative methods fail, the next, and probably last, approach is to consult a secondary source to educate oneself about the law. Background reading introduces new vocabulary terms that, in turn, permits the researcher to retrace his or her previous attempts with better results.

Consulting Secondary Sources

A paralegal should not finish reading this text with the impression that legal research is simply a matter of finding a law and reading that law to find an answer. A more accurate picture would show a paralegal who is frustrated because he or she cannot find the law, partly because the indexes and the paralegal are using different terms, and partly because the paralegal has no familiarity in the area of the law. After spending too much time looking, the paralegal finally finds a statute that is steeped in legal terms that the paralegal does not really understand, along with several cases that seem to contradict themselves. The cases seem similar to the problem, but are not similar enough to it to be on point. Even after reading and rereading the statute and cases, the paralegal still does not understand the rationale of the legal principles applicable to the problem.

The paralegal may be surprised to learn that this scenario is a fairly typical daily occurrence for lawyers as well as paralegals. Lawyers, like paralegals, often are stymied by the research process. Legal professionals often research in areas in which they have no background knowledge. Before starting the research, they may not be able to identify the source authority or frame the issue intelligently.

As a result, many researchers need to read background sources (such as treatises, legal periodicals, and encyclopedias) before starting to look for the law. That is why there are so many secondary sources to explain the law. Sometimes the researcher, while reading background materials, finds the answer to the initial problem.

Thus, a legal researcher must decide at the outset whether to first consult a secondary source to learn about an area of the law or whether to look initially for a primary source authority. As a practical matter, this choice often is made by trial and error. If a researcher begins looking for the law and is frustrated in that search, the researcher needs to restart the process by looking at secondary sources. At other times, the researcher may consult a secondary source and find nothing, but go directly to an annotated code and find a statute that answers the question.

A legal professional consults secondary sources to gain knowledge about law. Sometimes the professional needs a secondary source such as an encyclopedia to even get started with the research project. As researchers read secondary sources, they learn more legal terms and can more effectively "crack" an index. A treatise or law review may explain how different cases fit a pattern or rule, or how a statute is to be applied. Even a researcher who has found the law, such as a particular statute, and read it may need to go back to secondary sources to help explain that law. A secondary source may explain the policy behind a rule or even provide an argument why a certain law should be changed. Some works explain how different rules fit together. If the secondary source is written by a respected legal writer, it may be cited later as a persuasive authority to a court or administrative agency.

Secondary sources are used throughout the research process—to get started, to explain what has been found, and to suggest what ought to be. It is not unusual for a researcher to go from secondary source to primary source and back to secondary source repeatedly throughout a project. Nor is it unusual for a legal professional to begin with an encyclopedia for basic knowledge, then read a treatise to find how to interpret or apply the law, then read a law review for the latest scholarly thought in the area, and then conclude by looking at a restatement to cite to a court. Secondary sources are consulted at every step of the process. A paralegal learns about the law in the same way a lawyer learns about the law: by consulting secondary sources.

Finding the Law

A main objective of any researcher is to locate primary authority (law) that pertains to an issue. Sometimes researchers tend to forget this objective during the course of a research project. Nonetheless, a researcher cannot answer a question without reading the law. More precisely, the researcher is always looking first for any binding primary authority and second, if there is no binding primary authority, for any persuasive authority. A persuasive authority may be a case from another jurisdiction or from a lower court in the same jurisdiction. If there is neither binding primary authority nor any persuasive law, then the researcher's last resort is to look for any secondary source that might pertain to the situation.

The process of looking for law depends upon the source authority. If the source authority is a case, the researcher must find that case; if the source authority is a statute, the researcher must find that statute. There are different approaches, depending upon the primary source.

Finding Cases

As discussed in Chapters 4 and 5, there are a wide variety of search tools available for finding cases: digests, encyclopedias, A.L.R.s, treatises, C.L.E. materials, law reviews, and computer services (WESTLAW and LEXIS). Unless a paralegal is especially skillful on a computer, a good rule to follow is to start with a digest, encyclopedia, or A.L.R. to find cases. It would not be inappropriate to start with some of the other tools mentioned above, and some professionals routinely do so. Some researchers, for example, start with treatises if they are available. But for routine research, digests, encyclopedias, and A.L.R.s are the tools most relied upon by researchers.

None of these search tools works best in all circumstances, and the decision to start with one of them over another is often based on personal preference or intuition. In some situations, the researcher consults all these sources in looking for a particular case.

Finding Constitutional Provisions

When the source authority is a constitutional provision, the initial concern is to identify the precise provision of the constitution that applies. For example, the issue might involve due process of law, freedom of speech, or the right to bear arms. Most constitutional provisions are written in general language, so identification of the provision will not necessarily answer the question. As a consequence, the second step is to look at the cases that have interpreted the provision. Both steps, identifying the precise constitutional provision and locating any applicable cases, can be accomplished by using an annotated code. At the federal level, for example, the researcher can use either the U.S.C.A. or the U.S.C.S. for this purpose. An annotated code provides case summaries with citations. By reading the case summaries, a researcher can identify any relevant cases. In fact, the process for researching a constitutional question is the same as the process for researching a statute.

In addition, a researcher can locate cases dealing with constitutional issues in the same way the researcher locates any case—by using digests, encyclopedias, A.L.R.s, and so on. Both law reviews and treatises are especially helpful to explain how constitutional provisions should be applied to particular fact patterns. Constitutional questions certainly can be researched effectively on either WESTLAW or LEXIS.

Finding Statutes

A good rule for all researchers to remember is: when the source authority is a constitution, statute, or court rule, start with an annotated code. A paralegal who remembers only this rule will be able to research in a wide variety of situations. The only choice the paralegal must make in selecting the annotated code is whether to use a federal or state version. Although it is usually good practice to start with an annotated code to find a statute, it also is appropriate to start with a looseleaf service if the researcher is comfortable with the set, or even to start with WESTLAW or LEXIS.

After locating a statute, the next step is to read that statute. In many instances, the researcher can answer a question simply by reading the statute. After reading the statute, the researcher should check the case summaries to find any cases that have dealt with the statute. Remember that cases explain and interpret statutes, so case law is quite pertinent to this form of research.

Each case summarized under a statute must be checked for validity! Contrary to what some researchers think, cases that are overruled by later cases are *not* automatically "dropped" from the annotated codes. Also, remember that amendments to a statute may invalidate prior case law—hence the importance of checking pocket part supplements and citators to update your research.

Because cases are relevant to statutory research, any of the case finding techniques discussed above can be used. Researchers also can use secondary sources such as law reviews, treatises, encyclopedias, and C.L.E. materials to gain an overview of or insight into the source authority.

Finding Rules of Court and Rules of Evidence

Court rules detail the procedure to be followed in litigation matters. There are rules for criminal matters and rules for civil matters, rules for appellate procedure, and even rules specifically for practice before the United States Supreme Court. In addition, the federal courts as well as many state courts have adopted rules of evidence.

Most litigation specialists keep a deskbook that contains these rules on their desk for ready reference, and frequently a researcher can answer a question pertaining to the rules simply by reading the rule. In some cases, even after reading the rule, parties still disagree about the proper interpretation of the rule. In these circumstances, a researcher probably will need to use an annotated code and research the rule just like a statute. An annotated code has cases that have interpreted the rule. In addition, the annotated code may contain commentary from the committee that recommended the adoption of the rule, which gives some insight into the background and policy underlying the rule.

Whenever the researcher is looking for cases that have interpreted the rule or explanations about the rule, the researcher can use other tools such as digests, encyclopedias, A.L.R.s, or treatises.

In addition to rules of evidence and rules of procedure, there are ethical standards for lawyers and judges that can be researched by the same techniques as those used to research other rules. Some states even have adopted ethical codes that apply to legal assistants. See Appendix C for rules recently adopted by the Indiana Supreme Court governing the activity of legal assistants in that state. Although only a few states have adopted ethical standards for legal assistants at the time of the publication of this text, it is anticipated that most states will follow with similar standards. Paralegals should thoroughly acquaint themselves with any rules that pertain to their work. Failure to do so can lead to serious consequences. If these rules have been adopted in your state, they usually can be accessed with an annotated code.

Finding Regulations

To locate a regulation, the researcher almost always will start with the *Code of Federal Regulations* for locating federal regulations, or the applicable administrative code if available for finding regulations applicable to a certain state. Because the indexing is generally poor, both WESTLAW and LEXIS are recommended alternatives. Just as cases interpret statutes and constitutional provisions, cases also interpret regulations. A researcher can look for relevant cases pertaining to a regulation by using case finding methods.

Finding Ordinances

To locate a charter or ordinance, usually the researcher must start with the official volumes of the ordinances, which usually are available from the public entity that issued them. Occasionally a researcher can locate case law pertaining to a local charter or ordinance by using case finding methods.

Updating the Research

A case decided today or a statute passed yesterday can upset all the research that has been done. A statute can supplant cases dealing with a common law issue; a case can hold an ordinance to be unconstitutional; a new regulation may change another regulation; a statute may be amended or repealed; a rule of evidence can change the existing law; and so on. Anytime a researcher has located relevant authority, the researcher must update the search. As a matter of habit, every legal professional should always check every pocket part or supplemental pamphlet. All cases and statutes important to the research project should be shepardized. In fact, if a case is of critical importance to a client, the researcher also should thumb through the latest advance sheet to check for later cases. Federal regulations should be updated through the *Federal Register* or through Shepard's. Many researchers continually update any important leads through Shepard's even in the early stages of a research project. This is a good practice that is often rewarded with new leads. Paralegals should know how to shepardize all authority on-line with a computer, with books, and on CD-ROM.

Verifying Citations for Form and Accuracy

The last step of the research process is to verify citations, which means that the researcher must check the final version of each citation with the actual source—in other words, check the citation against the original. Look to see that the parties to a case are correctly named and the names are correctly spelled, that all volume and page references are accurate, and that all dates are provided. Check the form of the citation with the so-called *Bluebook* (*A Uniform System of Citation* discussed in Chapter 1). Find any parallel citations by looking in Shepard's or the *National Reporter Blue Book* (not to be confused with *A Uniform System of Citation,* which also is called *The Bluebook*.) Remember that WESTLAW has Insta-Cite and LEXIS has Auto-Cite for all these purposes. Citation verification is often a delegated task in the legal profession.

Building Research Skills

Because there is no "right" way or method for conducting legal research, ingenuity and perseverance often are more successful than following any process. There is considerable satisfaction in finding a case or statute that the other side has missed. Here are some tips to aid researchers during the research process:

1. *Use multiple approaches.* Seldom should a researcher rely on only one approach. Alternative approaches sometimes lead to new ideas or citations. One publisher may have covered a topic that was ignored by another. A rule of law may be classified in an obscure way in one set of books but in a more logical way in another set of books. Remember that law books have different functions. Some are written to provide an overview, and others are written to provide depth or insight. Some are

meant to categorize, and others are meant to expand. Different sets of books provide different slants on the research problem.

2. *Build on what is known.* Too frequently, researchers ignore good clues. Suppose the researcher knows that a particular case from another state seems to relate to the researched situation. With this knowledge, the researcher can latch onto a key number or shepardize the case to locate other pertinent authority. Or a researcher can check the table of cases in a treatise to see if the case is discussed; and if it is, the researcher can read the text to locate other references. A researcher who is frustrated with the research process should reassess what he or she has found already to see if this information can be traced by other methods.

3. *Use tables of cases, statutes, rules, and regulations.* Most law books contain tables of authority. These tables provide references to a page number, paragraph number, or topic reference in that set for a particular citation. A good example is found in the A.L.R.s. If the researcher has a citation to the *United States Code* or *Code of Federal Regulations,* the researcher can check a table to see if there are any relevant annotations pertinent to that citation. (See Figure 10–1.)

4. *Take careful notes.* Legal researchers frequently are under time pressure. As a result, they tend to scurry from set to set of books looking for authority. In their hurry, they may fail to take note of materials they later decide are relevant. The best practice is to write down key citations and copy any source that may be used later.

Some researchers keep index cards, but most legal researchers simply use legal pads. Whatever approach is used, it is a good idea to keep citations separate by issue—for example, the researcher may start a new page of citations for each issue.

5. *Retrace steps.* In the earlier stages of the research process, the researcher may be fairly uneducated about the law on a particular topic. As a consequence, the researcher may have missed some pertinent commentary or even some law. As a researcher becomes more educated, it is not a bad idea to retrace earlier steps to see if anything of substance was missed.

6. *Browse the shelves or scan books.* A researcher who is stymied may want to simply browse the shelves or scan the available books for guidance. Often a researcher will stumble onto a new approach or idea, so do not give up too soon.

7. *Be thorough.* Legal research sometimes can be tedious. If the case justifies a substantial library effort, the researcher may spend weeks going through pages of the different digests under various key numbers, combing the card catalog to find relevant books on the subject, and formulating and reformulating computer queries. The researcher who reads page after page of digest headnotes may scan too quickly and skip over the only entry relevant to the search.

TABLES

Title and section	Vol. and page	Title and section	Vol. and page
ARKANSAS—Cont'd		**ARKANSAS—Cont'd**	
Ark Stat Ann—Cont'd		**Ark Stats—Cont'd**	
41-203(2)......... 7 ALR5th 758 § 13[a]		56-128(H) .. 1 ALR5th 469 § 14[d], 20[a]	
41-301 et seq (Repl 1977). 7 ALR5th 758 § 16		71-1307 .... 7 ALR5th 474 § 5	
41-503 (Repl. 1977) . 7 ALR5th 758 § 16		71-1307(g) ...... 7 ALR5th 474 § 155[a]	
41-507.1 (Supp 1983) .... 7 ALR5th 758 § 13[a]		71-1307(h) ...... 7 ALR5th 474 § 155[a]	
41-701(b) (Repl 1977) .... 7 ALR5th 758 § 9[a], 13[a]		71-1307(j) .... 7 ALR5th 474 § 155[a]	
41-1001 (Repl 1977) ..... 7 ALR5th 263 § 7[c]		82-2629 (Supp 1977) . 1 ALR5th 346 § 9, 10	
41-1001(2) (Repl 1977) ... 7 ALR5th 263 § 5[a]		**CALIFORNIA**	
41-1501 (Repl 1977) . 7 ALR5th 758 § 5, 9[a], 13[a]		**Constitution**	
41-1501(1)(a) (1977) . 7 ALR5th 758 § 4		Art 9 § 2 .... 7 ALR5th 455 § 3[a]	
41-1501(1)(a) (Repl 1977). 7 ALR5th 758 § 4, 9[a], 14, 15, 16, 18[a]		Art I § 1.......... 1 ALR5th 622 § 16[a]	
		Art I § 13 .... 1 ALR5th 622 § 16[a]	
41-1502(1)(a) (1977) . 7 ALR5th 758 § 4		Art I § 13; implemented by Pen. Code § 1023 .... 4 ALR5th 273 § 23	
41-1502(1)(a) (Repl 1977). 7 ALR5th 758 § 9[a], 13[a], 18[a]		Art I § 14 .... 1 ALR5th 622 § 16[a]	
41-1503(1) (Repl 1977) ... 7 ALR5th 758 § 13[a], 16		**1982 Cal Stat**	
		ch 1339 27 .... 7 ALR5th 263 § 7[c]	
41-1503(1)(b) (Repl 1977) 7 ALR5th 758 § 13[a, b], 16		**Admin Code**	
41-1503(a)(b) ..... 7 ALR5th 758 § 13[a]		2795 .... 7 ALR5th 474 § 92	
41-1601(1)(a) ..... 5 ALR5th 243 § 50[a]		2831 ....7 ALR5th 474 § 160[a]	
41-1601(1)(c) ..... 5 ALR5th 243 § 59[a]		2831.1 .... 7 ALR5th 474 § 160[a]	
41-1602(1)(a) ..... 5 ALR5th 243 § 59[a]		**Admin Code tit 10**	
41-1602(1)(d) (Criminal Code 1976) ...5 ALR5th 243 § 60[a]		2831.1 .... 7 ALR5th 474 § 160[a]	
		2950(b) .... 7 ALR5th 474 § 160[a]	
		Bus and Prof Code	
		6101 .... 1 ALR5th 874 § 9[f]	
		6106 .... 1 ALR5th 874 § 9[f]	
		7025-7031 .... 4 ALR5th 772 § 78	
		10026 ....7 ALR5th 474 § 159[a]	
		10146 ....7 ALR5th 474 § 159[a]	

FIGURE 10–1 Cross-referencing tables are a useful tool for conducting legal research

8. *Anticipate the opponent's research.* Lawyers are advocates and, as advocates, tend to see problems from only one side. As much as possible, try to see the problem from the perspective of the opposing side. Certainly it is critical that a researcher not ignore any contrary authority. By the same token, a researcher should not quit because he or she has found some adverse authority. That researcher always should try to ferret out other law that supports the client's position, if possible. The competent researcher finds the law, good or bad. The competent researcher notices trends in the law. Try to look at the law objectively. Someone who can see both sides of an argument will be a better advocate.

9. *Use traditional library techniques.* All paralegals have used a card catalog to locate materials in a library. A law library may have a card catalog for finding law books. Do not hesitate to use it. Similarly, many paralegals get started researching by reading a magazine or newspaper article about a legal problem. Most, if not all, paralegal students have used the *Readers Guide to Periodical Literature* to find a magazine article. Finding a magazine article about the area of the law may help the researcher. The researcher should use any library skills he or she already has acquired.

10. *Know when to ask for help.* By law, a paralegal's work must be supervised by an attorney. Paralegals do not have law school training. Some paralegals can research better than some lawyers, but most cannot. A good researcher needs to know when the project is too complicated and, when it is, ask for help. The most successful paralegals can work with minimal supervision, so before asking for help, a paralegal should try to solve the problem by using the tools discussed in this book. If a reasonable effort produces no results, however, the paralegal should ask for assistance rather than waste more time.

Deciding When to Quit

Perhaps the hardest decision to make in the legal research process, even for experienced researchers, is when to stop. If the researcher has found a case or statute that clearly deals with the problem situation, and the researcher understands the case or statute, the decision may be simple to make. A more common situation, though, is when the researcher has located some cases or statutes that seem to pertain to the problem, but the researcher is not sure of the answer. In this situation, the researcher must make a decision whether to stop or continue.

If the court is taking a five-minute recess, the researcher is asked by his or her superior to find an answer within that time, and the five minutes is up, the decision to stop is easy to make. It is also easy to stop when the client or the superior has budgeted only so much time for you to devote to research and that time is up. There are many instances, however, in which the decision of whether to stop or continue is quite difficult.

In many situations, the researcher finds conflicting cases or vague statutes and, as a result, is unable to answer definitely the original query. Assuming he or she has exhausted the available sources, the researcher must accept that there is no definite answer. Remember that legal experts do not always agree about the law.

In other situations, the researcher discovers that there is *no* law. Although the best practice is always to assume that there is some relevant authority, there are exceptions. Imagine that a diligent student is assigned a legal research problem in the *Resource Manual* that has no answer. That student might spend many frustrating hours looking for the law. The more diligent the student, the longer the student would look. Diligence will not find law where there is none, so a researcher needs to recognize when there is no law to be found.

If the researcher has not found any binding authority in the applicable jurisdiction, the researcher usually should look for persuasive precedent in other jurisdictions or for general principles from the existing body of law within the same jurisdiction to answer the inquiry. In these situations, the researcher may look for analogous law or for patterns in the existing law.

Before expanding the search for persuasive precedents in other jurisdictions, however, double-check the law by using alternative finding tools. If you use a digest first, use an encyclopedia to see if the answer is the same. Look at the A.L.R. or a treatise. Sometimes this will expose errors in the method used. Assuming no error was made, the search should be expanded to look for persuasive precedents or analogous law in the same or other jurisdictions.

In practice, the research process can be both challenging and frustrating, but it never stops. The researcher is constantly reading law. When researching one project, the researcher may uncover a law review article that pertains more to another project or find a treatise that was not available earlier. Researchers who are stymied on Monday may have a fresh idea on Tuesday. A good researcher quits only when he or she runs out of time.

Summary

- The first step in answering any legal question is to ascertain all the relevant facts.

- After gathering the relevant facts, the researcher should try to formulate the issues to be researched. As the research progresses, the researcher may need to narrow or broaden an issue or even reformulate it.

- The researcher should remember the two threshold legal research questions: What is the source authority? What jurisdiction's law will determine the outcome of the case?

- In many situations, the researcher needs to develop a vocabulary before making progress with the research. This can be done by consulting a legal dictionary or thesaurus, using the TAPP rule, categorizing the area of law, or reading background materials.

- When researching in an area in which you have no background knowledge, start with a secondary source to gain knowledge about the law.

- If you are looking for case law, use finding tools designed for that purpose such as digests, encyclopedias, A.L.R.s, treatises, C.L.E. materials, law reviews, and computer services.

- An annotated code can be used for researching constitutions, statutes, and court rules.

- To research regulations, use the *Code of Federal Regulations* for federal regulations and an administrative code for state regulations.

Review Questions

1. If you are stymied with a legal research problem, what techniques can you use to try to break through the problem?

2. Describe the similarities and differences between researching statutory law and case law.

3. How do you research a constitutional provision?

4. How do you research rules of court or rules of evidence?

5. How do you research regulations?

6. Discuss in detail the different methods used in law to update legal research.

7. Why is it important to verify citations?

8. How do you decide when to quit your legal research?

Research Projects

1. Discuss how you would proceed in each of these research situations:

   a. to find out about COBRA;

   b. to find out how points are calculated against residents of your state for speeding violations; and

   c. to find out what law deals with the work product principle in federal courts.

2. Make a chart of the various types of research tools discussed in this text. For each tool, identify the index methods and updating methods used with that set.

APPENDIX A

UNITED STATES VS. SPROED

Co. v. Deliso Construction Co., 315 Mass. 313, 52 N.E.2d 553, 556–57 (1943) (pumping cement into ground harming plaintiff's underground equipment constitutes trespass); *Ball v. Nye*, 99 Mass. 582 (knowing contamination of groundwater by manure causing injury to plaintiff's well and cellar is actionable tort). Nor do plaintiffs' physical injuries support an injunction. Plaintiffs' exposure to the contaminated water ceased in May of 1979, when Wells G and H were closed. The requested relief would not mitigate plaintiffs' special injuries; it would only remedy the public nuisance of groundwater contamination.

[26] This same logic requires that plaintiffs' claim for expenses for abating the nuisance be denied. *See Bousquet v. Commonwealth*, 374 Mass. 824, 372 N.E.2d 257, 258 (1978) (rescript); *Parker v. American Woolen Co.*, 215 Mass. 176, 102 N.E. 360, 361 (1913). In both *Bousquet* and *Parker*, the damages awarded were to compensate for costs incurred in "preventing, reducing or abating" the damage done to plaintiffs' property. Plaintiffs in the instant action have alleged no damage to their land other than the contamination of groundwater with which they claim no contact.

[27] Defendants argue that plaintiffs' claims for damages on a theory of nuisance are merely duplicative of their negligence claims. This may well be true in regard to the personal injury claims. However, plaintiffs are entitled to present alternative theories of liability to the jury, so long as appropriate instructions are given to prevent double recovery for any element of damage. Accordingly, defendants' motion for summary judgment on plaintiffs' nuisance claims will be ALLOWED with respect to the claims for injunctive relief and expenses for abating the nuisance and is otherwise DENIED.

To summarize, defendants' joint motion for partial summary judgment is ALLOWED in regard to (1) the claims of Carl Robbins, III; (2) plaintiffs' claims of emo-

tional distress for witnessing a family member die of leukemia; and (3) plaintiffs' claims for injunctive relief on a theory of nuisance and the damage claims for the expenses of abating the alleged nuisance. The motion is otherwise DENIED.

UNITED STATES of America, Plaintiff,

v.

David Leroy SPROED, Defendant.

CVB No. P127482.

United States District Court,
D. Oregon.

Jan. 6, 1986.

Defendant sought to have dismissed prosecution charging him with catching butterflies in national park. The District Court, James M. Burns, J., held that prosecution would be dismissed.

Ordered accordingly.

Criminal Law ⟜303

Prosecution charging defendant with catching butterflies in national park would be dismissed.

OPINION AND ORDER

JAMES M. BURNS, District Judge.

Judges seldom get a chance to wax lyrical. Rarer still does a judge have an opportunity to see a case centered around a butterfly.[1] Those who read this opinion will, therefore, recognize that this case presented me with a temptation which I obviously could not resist.

---

1. Butterflies are normally grist for the poet's mill, not that of the judge. Occasionally, even the august Court of Appeals finds itself cerebrat-

ing over butterfly related causes, *Friends of the Endangered Species v. Jantzen*, 760 F.2d 976 (9th Cir.1985).

628 FEDERAL SUPPLEMENT

supervisory power as a District Judge to review the ruling of the Magistrate, 28 U.S.C. § 636.[4]

In his letter to the Court, Sproed says that he and his son "have always loved and enjoyed the out-of-doors and never knowingly disregard laws.... [W]e were out catching butterflies. We have a collection and wherever we go we try to add to it. It never entered my mind that it was unlawful to catch a butterfly in the park."

Sproed said he and his son "saw no signs and there was nothing even hinting [that butterfly-catching was a crime] in the paper given to us when we entered the park." Thus, he felt "that a friendly explanation and a warning was all that was necessary—it would have made this a learning experience instead of a bitter remembrance." He said that "It will take some time for me to restore my boy's previous respect for park rangers. I trust that your decision will make that job easier for me."

The Sproed's experience exemplifies the axiom "Nature Imitates Art," as one can see from Appendix B. It is a copy of a recent strip from the widely syndicated comic "BLOOM COUNTY." Permission to reproduce this copyrighted strip has been graciously granted by the Washington Post Writers Group, which syndicates this comic strip.

Judge Hogan, AUSA Kent, the sharp-eyed young lady in the Clerk's office and I have now done our bit. Restoring the younger Sproed's respect—if this will help somewhat in achieving that worthy aim—seems, somehow, a fitting way to close the year 1985. It is a small victory, perhaps, but well worth the effort.

Mr. Sproed's young son, as a part of the process of having his respect restored, is urged not to take too literally the accompanying panel strip of "Bloom County."

For the foregoing reasons, I approve, affirm and adopt the Magistrate's order of dismissal.

IT IS SO ORDERED.

APPENDIX "A"

Your Honor:

Since it is neither reasonable nor practical to appear in court, I am writing this letter of explanation. I don't like to use the courts time on such matters but $50 represents a lot of time and hard work to

---

4. Judge Hogan had no need, in view of the government's motion, to look more closely at the citation. The Park Ranger may have been on shaky legal as well as entomological grounds. The description of the violation alleged was "Preservation of Natural, Cultural & Archeological Resources." The Ranger filled in, as the regulation he felt had been trampled upon, 36 C.F.R. 2.1(a)(1). That section provides as follows:

2.1 Preservation of Natural, Cultural and Archeological Resources:

(a) Except as otherwise provided in this chapter, the following is prohibited:

(1) Possessing, destroying, injuring, removing, digging, or disturbing its natural state:

(i) Living or dead wildlife or fish, or the parts of products thereof, such as antlers or nests.

(ii) Plants or the parts of products thereof.

(iii) Nonfossilized and fossilized paleontological specimens, cultural or archeological resources, or the parts thereof.

Wildlife is defined by 36 C.F.R. § 1.5 to mean:

"any member of the animal kingdom and includes a part, product, egg of offspring thereof, or the dead body or part thereof, except fish."

Actually, one could read Mr. Sproed's second paragraph as the functional equivalent of a Rule 12 Motion to Dismiss on the ground that the citation fails to state a claim. Under well settled constitutional principles, a criminal charge, under the Fifth Amendment must be specific enough in its charging language to notify the accused of the nature of his alleged offense so he may prepare a defense, and plead double jeopardy in the event of conviction or acquittal. Under these circumstances, however, I doubt that the Park Ranger would want to pursue the charge. He would, presumably, take to heart Wordsworth's dictum in his poem "To A Butterfly", which may not be entirely inapplicable here:

Much converse do I find in thee,
Historian of my infancy!
Float near me; do not yet depart!
Dead times revive in thee:
Thou bring'st, gay creature as thou art!
a solemn image to my heart.

UNITED STATES v. SPROED
Cite as 628 F.Supp. 1234 (D.Or. 1986)

This case charges defendant Sproed with catching butterflies in a National Park.

Sproed and his son were at Rim Village of Crater Lake National Park on the afternoon of August 23, 1985 apparently doing just that—namely, catching butterflies! Along came a Park Ranger who had apparently taken keenly to heart the "Law and Order" rhetoric which some say has been a hallmark of the current administration. Responding to this Petty Offense [2] the Ranger issued to Sproed what became enshrined in judicial records as Citation P127482.

It would not be surprising to find that most of our citizens would be embittered if accused of such a heinous crime. Sproed is no exception. For reasons which appear below, I do not have to decide whether Sproed was, in fact, guilty of a crime. If his letter is to be believed, he and his young son may well have been moved by somewhat the same poetic spirit as the "aged, aged man" invented and immortalized by Lewis Carroll:

I saw an aged, aged man,
  A-sitting on a gate.
'Who are you, aged man?' I said,
  'And how is it you live?'
And his answer tickled through my head
  Like water through a sieve.
He said, 'I look for butterflies
That sleep among the wheat:
I make them into mutton-pies,
And sell them in the street.'

"Through the Looking Glass", Ch. 8.

Or Mr. Sproed may have believed, along with the German poet Heine that:

With the rose the butterfly's deep in love,
  A thousand times hovering round;
But round himself, all tender like gold,
  The sun's sweet ray is hovering found.

Mr. Sproed may even have been mulling over the lines written by Oregon's own "poet", Joaquin Miller:

The gold-barr'd butterflies to and fro
  And over the waterside wander'd and wove
  As heedless and idle as clouds that rove
And drift by the peaks of perpetual snow.

In any event, alas, no trial will ever occur to sort these things out. The reader should be made aware of why the judicial machinery never geared up for a full trial of this case. When Sproed's letter [3] arrived at the Clerk's office, it was referred to Magistrate Hogan, along with a touching note suggesting this might be a case in which Judge Hogan would want to exercise his judicial discretion. Shortly thereafter, Assistant U.S. Attorney Kent filed a motion to dismiss pursuant to Rule 48(a) of the Federal Rules of Criminal Procedure. Judge Hogan dismissed the case. Fortunately (or otherwise), I became aware, shortly afterward, of this case of lepidopteral *lese majeste*. I chose to exercise my

---

2. Petty offenses, a species of criminal offense established by the Congress (18 U.S.C. § 1) used to carry a maximum penalty of six months in jail or a $500 fine or both. (Actually, the maximum fine for the offense charged here would have been $5,000; last year in the Comprehensive Crime Control Act of 1984, Congress "upped the ante" for petty offense fines to $5,000.) Under applicable statutes, regulations are promulgated by the various federal agencies—Department of Interior and so forth; violation of such regulations—after they are published in the Code of Federal Regulations is a petty offense. When a Park Ranger—or other agency enforcement officer comes across a violation, a citation is issued. The citation normally provides a specified sum as collateral, i.e. bail. If the ac-

cused does not wish to contest the matter, he or she sends in the bail amount and the matter is closed. The accused may demand a trial, usually before a U.S. Magistrate; the accused, however, as a matter of right, can have the case heard by a District Judge. Occasionally a sort of third option is chosen by the accused, as happened here. He will send in a letter of explanation with a request, usually explicit, that the matter be dismissed, or otherwise be disposed of.

3. I have reproduced, in typewritten form, Mr. Sproed's handwritten letter received by the Clerk's office on September 9, 1985, and it is attached as Appendix A to this opinion.

SEVEN STAR SHOE CO. v. STRICTLY GOODIES, INC.
Cite as 628 F.Supp. 1237 (S.D.N.Y. 1986)

APPENDIX A—Continued

me and more important is this decision in my boys mind.

I plead not guilty to the charge of "Destruction of Natural Cultural & Archeological Resources." The park ranger spent about 30 minutes on his C.B. and looking through his book but never did find anything against collecting insects. So he just included it in the above class.

My boy and I have always loved and enjoyed the out-of-doors and never knowingly disregard laws. In this case we were out catching butterflies. We have a collection and wherever we go we try to add to it. It never entered my mind that it was unlawful to catch a butterfly in the park. We saw no signs and there was nothing even hinting at such a thing in the paper given to us when we entered the park

(which I have enclosed). It does state that it is o.k. to catch fish.

It is this kind of incident that destroys young peoples respect for the law. I feel that a friendly explanation and a warning was all that was necessary—it would have made this a learning experience instead of a bitter remembrance. We do not have the opportunity to travel a lot and I am afraid this "special occasion" may be remembered only by the outcome of this incident.

It will take some time for me to restore my boys previous respect for park rangers. I trust that your decision will make that job easier for me.

Very Sincerely
(s) David Sproed
(208)

APPENDIX B

BLOOM COUNTY   **by Berke Breathed**

* ... And No butterfly collecting ...

SEVEN STAR SHOE COMPANY, INC., Plaintiff,

v.

STRICTLY GOODIES, INC., Good Times Industries, Inc., Ronald W. Gootkin, Robert Y. Greenberg and Ernest Williams, Defendants.

No. 83 Civ. 2904 (RWS).

United States District Court,
S.D. New York.

Jan. 9, 1986.

Footwear manufacturer and distributor brought action against another manu-

APPENDIX B

EXCERPT FROM A.L.R.5TH

2 ALR5th 966

DUTY OF RETAIL ESTABLISHMENT, OR ITS EMPLOYEES, TO ASSIST PATRON CHOKING ON FOOD

by
Frank J. Wozniak, J.D.

Each year in the United States more than 3900 people strangle because food becomes stuck in their throats. When incidents such as this occur in restaurants or in other retail establishments, a question is raised concerning the duty of the establishment or its employees to assist the patron who is choking on food. In the recent case of Drew v LeJay's Sportsmen's Cafe, Inc. (1991, Wyo) 806 P2d 301, 2 ALR5th 1172, the court stated that although there was no duty to render first aid to a choking patron, there was a duty to exercise reasonable care and that this duty could be satisfied by the summoning of medical assistance within a reasonable time. This annotation collects and discusses the cases in which the courts have considered the duty of a retail establishment, or its employees, to assist a patron who eats food on the establishment's premises, chokes on it, and is either injured or killed.

Drew v LeJay's Sportsmen's Cafe, Inc., is fully reported at page 1172, infra.

2 ALR5th   DUTY TO ASSIST CHOKING PATRON
                      2 ALR5th 966

Table of Contents

Research References
Index
Jurisdictional Table of Cited Statutes and Cases

ARTICLE OUTLINE

Research References

TOTAL CLIENT-SERVICE LIBRARY® REFERENCES

The following references may be of related or collateral interest to a user of this annotation:

Annotations

See the related annotations listed in § 1[b].

Encyclopedias and Texts

40 Am Jur 2d, Hotels, Motels, and Restaurants §§ 81, 82, 107; 57A Am Jur 2d, Negligence §§ 89-99

Am Law Prod Liab 3d, Basic Elements of Negligence Case § 10:25

DUTY TO ASSIST CHOKING PATRON   2 ALR5th
2 ALR5th 966

Practice Aids

18A Am Jur Pl & Pr Forms (Rev), Negligence, Forms 161, 163-168

2 Am Jur Proof of Facts 2d 49, Accidental Death—Food Asphyxiation

2 Am Jur Trials 1, Investigating Particular Civil Actions § 37

Digests and Indexes

L Ed Digest, Negligence § 1; Torts § 1

ALR Digests, Food § 1; Torts §§ 1, 4

Index to Annotations, Food and Food Processing; Good Samaritan Doctrine; Guests, Invitees, or Licensees; Negligence; Premises Liability; Rescue; Restaurants and Other Eating Places; Torts

Auto-Cite®

Cases and annotations referred to herein can be further researched through the Auto-Cite® computer-assisted research service. Use Auto-Cite to check citations for form, parallel references, prior and later history, and annotation references.

RESEARCH SOURCES

The following are the research sources that were found to be helpful in compiling this annotation:

Texts

Am Law Prod Liab 3d, Basic Elements of Negligence Case § 10:25.

Encyclopedias

35 Am Jur 2d, Food §§ 89 et seq.

40 Am Jur 2d, Hotels, Motels, and Restaurants §§ 81, 82, 107.

57A Am Jur 2d, Negligence §§ 89-99.

62 Am Jur 2d, Premises Liability §§ 87-107, 136-138, 441-445.

43A CJS Inns, Hotels, and Eating Places § 20 n 62.

Law Reviews

Elier, W.C., and Haugen, R.K., Food Asphyxiation—Restaurant Rescue, 289 New Eng J M 81 (1973).

Electronic Search Query

food or meal or eat! w/25 chok! or gag! or asphyxia! w/25 store or retail or restaurant or cafe or diner

West Digest Key Numbers

Food 25

Innkeeper 10, 10.1, 10.2

Negligence 29, 32(1), 32(2.8), 74, 111(1)

2 ALR5th   DUTY TO ASSIST CHOKING PATRON
2 ALR5th 966

INDEX

Jurisdictional Table of Cited Statutes and Cases*

CALIFORNIA

Health & Safety Code § 28689. See §§ 4[a], 5

Breaux v Gino's, Inc. (1984, 1st Dist) 153 **Cal** App 3d 379, 200 Cal Rptr 260—§§ 3, 4[a]

FLORIDA

Coccarello v Round Table of Coral Gables, Inc. (1982, **Fla** App D3) 421 So 2d 194—§§ 4[b], 5

---

* Statutes, rules, regulations, and constitutional provisions bearing on the subject of the annotation are included in this table only to the extent, and in the form, that they are reflected in the court opinions discussed in this annotation. The reader should consult the appropriate statutory or regulatory compilations to ascertain the current status of relevant statutes, rules, regulations, and constitutional provisions.

For federal cases involving state law, see state headings.

§ 1[a]   DUTY TO ASSIST CHOKING PATRON   2 ALR5th
2 ALR5th 966

NEW YORK

Public Health Law § 1352-b. See § 4[a]

Acosta v Fuentes (1991, Sup) 571 NYS2d 666—§§ 2[b], 4[a]

WYOMING

Drew v LeJay's Sportsmen's Cafe, Inc. (1991, **Wyo**) 806 P2d 301, 2 ALR5th 1172 §§ 2[b], 3, 4[a]

I. Preliminary Matters

§ 1. Introduction

[a] Scope

This annotation collects and discusses the cases in which the courts have considered the duty of a retail establishment, or its employees, to assist[1] a patron who eats food on the establishment's premises, chokes on it, and is either injured or killed.

A number of jurisdictions may have rules, regulations, constitutional provisions, or legislative enactments bearing upon this subject. Since these are discussed herein only to the extent that they are reflected in the reported cases within the scope of this annotation, the reader is advised to consult the appropriate statutory or regulatory compilations to ascertain the current status of all statutes discussed herein, including those listed in the Jurisdictional Table of Cited Statutes and Cases.

[b] Related annotations

Liability for injury or death allegedly caused by spoilage or contamination of beverage. 87 ALR4th 804.

Liability of proprietor of private gymnasium, reducing salon, or similar health club for injury to patron. 79 ALR4th 127.

Rescue Doctrine: applicability and application of comparative negligence principles. 75 ALR4th 875.

Construction and application of "Good Samaritan" statutes. 68 ALR4th 294.

Accident insurance: death or disability incident to partaking of food or drink as within provision as to external, violent, and accidental means. 29 ALR4th 1230.

Liability of packer, foodstore, or restaurant for causing trichinosis. 96 ALR3d 451.

Master and servant: employer's liability for injury caused by food or drink purchased by employee in plant facilities. 50 ALR3d 505.

Liability of owner or operator of drive-in restaurant for injury or death to patron. 45 ALR3d 1428.

---

1. The term "assist" includes both direct assistance and efforts to obtain assistance.

Duty of one other than carrier or employer to render assistance to one for whose initial injury he is not liable. 33 ALR3d 301.

Liability of owner or operator of drive-in movie theater for injury or death to patron or frequenter. 26 ALR3d 1314.

Liability of owner or operator of skating rink for injury to patron. 24 ALR3d 911.

Liability of hotel, motel, summer resort, or private membership club or association operating swimming pool, for injury or death of guest or member, or of member's guest. 1 ALR3d 963.

Liability of manufacturer or seller for injury caused by food or food product sold. 77 ALR2d 7.

Liability of innkeeper, restaurateur, or tavern keeper for injury occurring on or about premises to guest or patron by person other than proprietor or his servant. 70 ALR2d 628.

Duty and liability of one who voluntarily undertakes to care for injured person. 64 ALR2d 1179.

Implied warranty of fitness by one serving food. 7 ALR2d 1027.

§ 2. Summary and comment

[a] Generally

Each year in the United States more than 3900 healthy individuals strangle because food becomes stuck in their throats.[2] When incidents such as this occur in restaurants or other retail establishments, a question is raised concerning the duty of the establishment or its employees to assist the patron who is choking on food.

The courts have generally held that a retail establishment, or its employees, has a duty to assist a patron choking on food (§ 3). One court has defined this duty in general terms, stating that it creates an obligation to assist a customer who becomes ill or who is in need of medical attention. Another court has defined the duty more narrowly, holding that it requires the summoning of medical assistance within a reasonable time.

The cases in which the issue of a retail establishment's liability to a patron choking on food has been discussed make it clear that the rendering of first aid is not necessarily part of the duty to assist a choking patron. Although one court defined the duty to assist as the giving or securing of first aid (§ 4[b]), other courts have specifically stated that there was no duty to render first aid (§ 4[a]). Courts adopting the later position have often reached that conclusion after considering local statutes which specifically proscribe a duty to render first aid or grant immunity to those who attempt to administer it, or have cited public policy concerns, such as placing an undue financial burden upon food servers, in support of their position.

In cases where the courts defined the duty of an establishment, or its employees, to assist a patron choking on food as coming to the patron's aid or as giving or secur-

---

2. 2 Am Jur Proof of Facts 2d 49, Accidental Death—Food Asphyxiation (Supp).

ing first aid, they have held that the prompt summoning of medical assistance—the telephoning of an ambulance or other medical aid—fulfilled the establishment's, or its employees', duty to the patron (§ 5).

[b] Practice pointers

Whether a court specifically adopts a first aid requirement as part of the duty to assist may depend upon its finding that the imposition of such a requirement would create an undue burden upon food servers.[3] In reaching the latter conclusion, courts have relied upon statistics comparing the number of choking incidents with the number of meals served and expert testimony emphasizing the great and widespread costs that would be incurred by the food industry, the slim chance of helping a choking victim on a particular premises, and the fact that, even if trained, the decision of an employee to help a choking patron is discretionary.[4]

When plaintiffs have relied upon statutory enactments which contained provisions requiring the posting of first aid information on how to assist choking victims, the argument that an establishment's compliance subjected it to liability because the posting of instructions made a choking incident foreseeable has not been successful in cases where the enactments also contained provisions that there was

no duty to remove, to attempt to remove, or to assist in removing food from a choking victim's throat.[5]

II. Existence of Duty

§ 3. Duty to assist—generally

The courts in the following cases have held or recognized that a retail establishment, or its employees, has a duty to assist a patron choking on food.

In Breaux v Gino's, Inc. (1984, 1st Dist) 153 **Cal** App 3d 379, 200 Cal Rptr 260, a wrongful death action brought by the husband of a restaurant patron who died after choking on food at the restaurant, the court, recognizing a restaurant owner's duty to assist a patron choking on food, affirmed summary judgment in the restaurant owner's favor. Although no one attempted to give the choking customer first aid, the assistant manager did telephone for an ambulance as soon as he became aware of the need, and the customer was alive when the ambulance arrived. After stating that it was well established that restaurants had a duty to assist customers who were ill or needed medical attention, the court, relying on a local statute which proscribed any obligation on any person to remove, assist in removing, or attempt to remove food which had become stuck in another person's throat, held that

---

3. Acosta v Fuentes (1991, Sup) 571 NYS2d 666; Drew v LeJay's Sportsmen's Cafe, Inc. (1991, Wyo) 806 P2d 301, 2 ALR5th 1172.

4. Acosta v Fuentes (1991, Sup) 571 NYS2d 666; Drew v LeJay's Sports-

men's Cafe, Inc. (1991, **Wyo**) 806 P2d 301, 2 ALR5th 1172.

5. Acosta v Fuentes (1991, Sup) 571 NYS2d 666; Drew v LeJay's Sportsmen's Cafe, Inc. (1991, **Wyo**) 806 P2d 301, 2 ALR5th 1172.

the well-established duty was met by a restaurant owner or his employees when they summoned medical help within a reasonable time. In this case the court found that the prompt action taken by the assistant manager was sufficient to fulfill the establishment's duty to assist.

In Drew v LeJay's Sportsmen's Cafe, Inc. (1991, **Wyo**) 806 P2d 301, 2 ALR5th 1172, a wrongful death action, the court affirmed a decision in favor of a restaurant owner whose employees were alleged to be negligent in having failed to summon emergency help for a customer, choking on a 2-inch by 2-inch piece of meat, after the employees knew or had reason to know that the customer was in imminent need of medical assistance, since the court found that the employees did not violate a duty to assist the patron. A companion to the victim testified that he had trouble getting help from restaurant employees despite his stating several times that his friend was dying and his attempting, more than once, to solicit assistance from the waitress, the cashier, and the cook. The court, however, pointed out that the companion's testimony regarding the sequence of events was confusing, noting that even he was slow to recognize the seriousness of the victim's condition. During the time the customer was in the restaurant, someone telephoned for assistance, and mouth-to-mouth resuscitation was given by other customers and by police officers. Medical help—an ambulance—arrived after an undetermined amount of time, but efforts to resuscitate the customer during the ride to the hospital, at

the hospital, and following a flight for life were futile. The customer died of cardiorespiratory arrest. The court identified the duty owed by a restaurant owner to a customer who was choking and in imminent need of medical assistance as being to summon medical assistance within a reasonable time after having notice of the customer's illness or injury. In formulating this duty statement, the court rejected the plaintiff's position, based upon Restatement (Second) of Torts § 314A (1965), that the restaurant owner, by virtue of its business-invitor status, had a duty to render first aid to its invitee-customer. The court also rejected the plaintiff's attempt to justify implementation of a first aid requirement by reliance on cases that dealt only with a general duty to render aid.

§ 4. —Duty to render first aid

[a] View that there is no duty to provide first aid

It has been held or recognized in the following cases that a retail establishment, or its employees, has no duty to render first aid to a patron choking on food.

In Breaux v Gino's, Inc. (1984, 1st Dist) 153 **Cal** App 3d 379, 200 Cal Rptr 260, a wrongful death action brought by the husband of a restaurant patron who died after choking on food at the restaurant, the court affirmed summary judgment in the restaurant owner's favor, holding that the restaurant had no duty to render first aid to the victim. Although no one attempted to give the choking customer first aid, the assistant manager did telephone for an ambulance as soon as he became aware of the need, and the customer was alive when the ambulance arrived. After stating that it was well established that restaurants had a duty to assist customers who were ill or needed medical attention, the court, citing Health & Safety Code § 28689, held that there was no obligation on any person to remove, assist in removing, or attempt to remove food which had become stuck in another person's throat.

In the wrongful death action of Acosta v Fuentes (1991, Sup) 571 NYS2d 666, the court affirmed summary judgment in favor of restaurant owners whose employees were alleged to have been negligent in that they failed to assist a choking customer, holding that the restaurant had no duty to attempt to remove food from the throat of the choking victim. In this case, the customer, who was eating a meal at the defendants' restaurant, began choking on food, lost his ability to speak, and was carried outside and placed on the sidewalk by restaurant employees. After lying on the sidewalk for one-half hour, an ambulance, summoned by a restaurant employee, arrived. The customer never regained consciousness and died approximately 2 weeks later. Relying upon Public Health Law § 1352-b, a local statute which proscribed the imposition of any duty or obligation on any proprietor, employee, or other person to remove, assist in removing, or attempt to remove food from the throat of a choking victim and which granted immunity to those who voluntarily assisted choking victims according to officially adopted instructions on first aid,

the court found that the defendants, as a matter of statutory law, incurred no liability based on a failure to administer the Heimlich maneuver or to render assistance to the victim. The court found that the employees' carrying of the victim to the sidewalk was outside actions covered by the statutorily granted immunity, but also found that no evidence was presented to show that the customer's condition was exacerbated by the employees' actions.

In Drew v LeJay's Sportsmen's Cafe, Inc. (1991, **Wyo**) 806 P2d 301, 2 ALR5th 1172, the facts of which are more fully discussed in § 3, the court affirmed a decision in favor of a restaurant owner whose employees were alleged to be negligent in failing to summon emergency help for a customer after the employees knew or had reason to know that the customer was in imminent need of medical assistance, holding that neither the restaurant nor its employees had a duty to render first aid for the choking victim. After defining the duty to assist a choking patron as being to summon medical assistance within a reasonable time, the court rejected the plaintiff's position, based upon Restatement (Second) of Torts § 314A (1965), that the restaurant owner, by virtue of its business-invitor status, had a duty to render first aid to its invitee-customer. The court also rejected the plaintiff's attempt to justify implementation of a first aid requirement by reliance on cases which dealt only with a general duty to render aid. To hold otherwise, said the court, would place upon all food servers the undue burden of providing resources to train employees, in an industry with high employee turnover, for the remote possibility that they would be able to provide effective assistance to a choking customer. The court's decision not to impose a first aid requirement was also influenced by expert testimony that the rendering of first aid by a lay person, such as a restaurant employee, was discretionary.

[b] View that there may be a duty to provide first aid

The court in the following case held or recognized that a retail establishment, or its employees, may have a duty, in some circumstances, to provide first aid to a patron choking on food.

In a wrongful death action brought by the wife of a restaurant patron who died after choking on food at the restaurant, the court in Coccarello v Round Table of Coral Gables, Inc. (1982, **Fla** App D3) 421 So 2d 194, affirmed summary judgment in favor of the restaurant, notwithstanding its recognition of a duty on behalf of the restaurant to render first aid for a choking patron under some circumstances. The patron was assisted by a medical doctor, who was also a customer, and by a rescue team that arrived within 5 minutes after being summoned by employees. The court, relying indirectly upon the Restatement (Second) of Torts § 314A, stated that a proprietor of a public place has a duty only to take reasonable action to give or secure first aid after he knows that a patron is ill or injured, but added that there was no requirement to take any action beyond that which is reasonable. The court found that the action taken by the employees—the summoning of a rescue team—was reasonable under the circumstances and fulfilled the duty owed to the patron.

III. Satisfaction of Duty in Particular Circumstances

§ 5. Telephone calls to summon medical assistance

The courts in the following cases found that a retail establishment, or its employees, fulfilled the duty to assist a patron choking on food where a telephone call was made for assistance within a reasonable time.

In Breaux v Gino's, Inc. (1984, 1st Dist) 153 **Cal** App 3d 379, 200 Cal Rptr 260, a wrongful death action brought by the husband of a restaurant patron who died after choking on food at the restaurant, the court affirmed summary judgment in the restaurant owner's favor, since the owner had fulfilled his duty to the choking patron by telephoning for help. The facts showed that although no one attempted to give the choking customer first aid, the assistant manager did telephone for an ambulance as soon as he became aware of the need and that the customer was alive when the ambulance arrived. After stating that it was well established that restaurants have a duty to assist a customer who was ill or needed medical attention, the court, citing Health & Safety Code § 28689—a statute which proscribed any obligation on any person to remove, assist in removing, or attempt to remove food which had become stuck in another person's throat, held that this well-established duty was met by a restaurant owner or his employees when medical help was summoned within a reasonable time. The court found that the action taken by the assistant manager in promptly summoning an ambulance was sufficient to fulfill the establishment's duty to assist.

In a wrongful death action brought by the wife of a restaurant patron who died after choking on food at the restaurant, the court in Coccarello v Round Table of Coral Gables, Inc. (1982, **Fla** App D3) 421 So 2d 194, the facts of which are more fully set out in § 4[b], affirmed summary judgment in favor of the restaurant, noting that the restaurant had fulfilled its duty to the patron when its employees telephoned for an ambulance. The patron was assisted by a medical doctor, who was also a customer, and by a rescue team that arrived within 5 minutes after being summoned by employees.

Consult POCKET PART in this volume for later cases

APPENDIX C

INDIANA ORDER AMENDING RULES OF PROFESSIONAL CONDUCT

IN THE

SUPREME COURT OF INDIANA

<u>ORDER AMENDING RULES OF PROFESSIONAL CONDUCT</u>

Pursuant to the authority vested in this Court in matters involving the discipline and disbarment of attorneys admitted to the practice of law, the following guidelines for the use of legal assistants is [sic] adopted as part of the *Rules of Professional Conduct:*

USE OF LEGAL ASSISTANTS

GUIDELINE 9.1   SUPERVISION

A legal assistant shall perform services only under the direct supervision of a lawyer authorized to practice in the State of Indiana and in the employ of the lawyer or the lawyer's employer. Independent legal assistants, to-wit, those not employed by a specific firm or by specific lawyers are prohibited. A lawyer is responsible for all of the professional actions of a legal assistant performing legal assistant services at the lawyer's direction and should take reasonable measures to insure that the legal assistant's conduct is consistent with the lawyer's obligations under the *Rules of Professional Conduct.*

GUIDELINE 9.2   PERMISSIBLE DELEGATION

Provided the lawyer maintains responsibility for the work product, a lawyer may delegate to a legal assistant any task normally performed by the lawyer; however, any task prohibited by statute, court rule, administrative rule or regulation, controlling authority, *Indiana Rules of Professional Conduct* may not be assigned to a non-lawyer.

GUIDELINE 9.3   PROHIBITED DELEGATION

A lawyer may not delegate to a legal assistant:

(a) responsibility for establishing an attorney-client relationship;
(b) responsibility for establishing the amount of a fee to be charged for a legal service; or
(c) responsibility for a legal opinion rendered to a client.

GUIDELINE 9.4   DUTY TO INFORM

It is the lawyer's responsibility to take reasonable measures to ensure that clients, courts, and other lawyers are aware that a legal assistant, whose services are utilized by the lawyer in performing legal services, is not licensed to practice law.

GUIDELINE 9.5   IDENTIFICATION ON LETTERHEAD

A lawyer may identify legal assistants by name and title on the lawyer's letterhead and on business cards identifying the lawyer's firm.

GUIDELINE 9.6   CLIENT CONFIDENCES

It is the responsibility of a lawyer to take reasonable measures to ensure that all client confidences are preserved by a legal assistant.

GUIDELINE 9.7   CHARGE FOR SERVICES

A lawyer may charge for the work performed by a legal assistant.

GUIDELINE 9.8   COMPENSATION

A lawyer may not split legal fees with a legal assistant nor pay a legal assistant for the referral of legal business. A lawyer may compensate a legal assistant based on the quantity and quality of the legal assistant's work and the value of that work to a law practice, but the legal assistant's compensation may not be contingent, by advance agreement, upon the profitability of the lawyer's practice.

GUIDELINE 9.9   CONTINUING LEGAL EDUCATION

A lawyer who employs a legal assistant should facilitate the legal assistant's participation in appropriate continuing education and *pro bono publico* activities.

GUIDELINE 9.10   LEGAL ASSISTANT ETHICS

All lawyers who employ legal assistants in the State of Indiana shall assure that such legal assistants conform their conduct to be consistent with the following ethical standards:

(a) A legal assistant may perform any task delegated and supervised by a lawyer so long as the lawyer is responsible to the client, maintains a direct relationship with the client, and assumes full professional responsibility for the work product.

(b) A legal assistant shall not engage in the unauthorized practice of law.

(c) A legal assistant shall serve the public interest by contributing to the delivery of quality legal services and the improvement of the legal system.

(d) A legal assistant shall achieve and maintain a high level of competence, as well as a high level of personal and professional integrity and conduct.

(e) A legal assistant's title shall be fully disclosed in all business and professional communications.

(f) A legal assistant shall preserve all confidential information provided by the client or acquired from other sources before, during, and after the course of the professional relationship.

(g) A legal assistant shall avoid conflicts of interest and shall disclose any possible conflict to the employer or client, as well as to the prospective employers or clients.

(h) A legal assistant shall act within the bounds of the law, uncompromisingly for the benefit of the client.

(i) A legal assistant shall do all things incidental, necessary, or expedient for the attainment of the ethics and responsibilities imposed by statute or rule of court.

(j) A legal assistant shall be governed by the American Bar Association Model Code of Professional Responsibility and the American Bar Association Model Rules of Profession [sic] Conduct.

This amendment shall be effective January 1, 1994.

The Clerk of this Court is directed to forward a copy of this Order to the Clerk of each Circuit Court in the State of Indiana, to the Indiana State Bar Association, to the Legislative Services Agency of this state, to the Office of Code Revision of the Legislative Services Agency, to the Attorney General of Indiana, to the Indiana Judicial Center, to the Michie Company, and to West Publishing Company for publication in the advance sheets of this Court.

The Clerks of the Circuit Court are directed to bring this Order to the attention of all judges within their respective counties and to post this Order for examination by the Bar and general public.

Done at Indianapolis, Indiana, this 29th day of October, 1993.

_____
Acting Chief Justice of Indiana

APPENDIX D

THE CONSTITUTION OF THE UNITED STATES OF AMERICA

We the People of the United States, in Order to form a more perfect Union, establish Justice, insure domestic Tranquility, provide for the common defence, promote the general Welfare, and secure the Blessings of Liberty to ourselves and our Posterity, do ordain and establish this Constitution for the United States of America.

ARTICLE I

Section 1

All legislative Powers herein granted shall be vested in a Congress of the United States, which shall consist of a Senate and House of Representatives.

Section 2

(1) The House of Representatives shall be composed of Members chosen every second Year by the People of the several States, and the Electors in each State shall have the Qualifications requisite for Electors of the most numerous Branch of the State Legislature.

(2) No Person shall be a Representative who shall not have attained to the age of twenty-five Years, and been seven Years a Citizen of the United States, and who shall not, when elected, be an Inhabitant of that State in which he shall be chosen.

(3) Representatives and direct Taxes shall be apportioned among the several States which may be included within this Union, according to their respective Numbers, which shall be determined by adding to the whole Number of free Persons, including those bound to Service for a Term of Years, and excluding Indians not taxed, three fifths of all other Persons. The actual Enumeration shall be made within three Years after the first Meeting of the Congress of the United States, and within every subsequent Term of ten Years, in such Manner as they shall by Law direct. The Number of Representatives shall not exceed one for every thirty Thousand, but each State shall have at Least one Representative; and until such enumeration shall be made, the State of New Hampshire shall be entitled to chuse three, Massachusetts eight, Rhode Island and Providence Plantations one, Connecticut five, New York six, New Jersey four, Pennsylvania eight, Delaware one, Maryland six, Virginia ten, North Carolina five, South Carolina five, and Georgia three.

(4)   When vacancies happen in the Representation from any State, the Executive Authority thereof shall issue Writs of Election to fill such Vacancies.

(5)   The House of Representatives shall chuse their Speaker and other Officers; and shall have the sole Power of Impeachment.

Section 3

(1)   The Senate of the United States shall be composed of two Senators from each State, chosen by the Legislature thereof, for six Years; and each Senator shall have one Vote.

(2)   Immediately after they shall be assembled in Consequence of the first Election, they shall be divided as equally as may be into three Classes. The Seats of the Senators of the first Class shall be vacated at the Expiration of the second Year, of the second Class at the Expiration of the fourth Year, and of the third Class at the Expiration of the sixth Year, so that one third may be chosen every second Year; and if Vacancies happen by Resignation, or otherwise, during the Recess of the Legislature of any State, the Executive thereof may make temporary Appointments until the next Meeting of the Legislature, which shall then fill such Vacancies.

(3)   No Person shall be a Senator who shall not have attained to the Age of thirty Years, and been nine Years a Citizen of the United States, and who shall not, when elected, be an Inhabitant of that State for which he shall be chosen.

(4)   The Vice President of the United States shall be President of the Senate, but shall have no Vote, unless they be equally divided.

(5)   The Senate shall chuse their other Officers, and also a President pro tempore, in the Absence of the Vice President, or when he shall exercise the Office of the President of the United States.

(6)   The Senate shall have the sole Power to try all Impeachments. When sitting for that Purpose, they shall be on Oath or Affirmation. When the President of the United States is tried, the Chief Justice shall preside: And no Person shall be convicted without the Concurrence of two thirds of the Members present.

(7)   Judgment in Cases of Impeachment shall not extend further than to removal from Office, and disqualification to hold and enjoy any Office of honor, Trust or Profit under the United States: but the Party convicted shall nevertheless be liable and subject to Indictment, Trial, Judgment and Punishment, according to Law.

Section 4

(1)   The Times, Places and Manner of holding Elections for Senators and Representatives, shall be prescribed in each State by the Legislature thereof; but the Congress may at any time by Law make or alter such Regulations, except as to the Places of chusing Senators.

(2)   The Congress shall assemble at least once in every Year, and such Meeting shall be on the first Monday in December, unless they shall by Law appoint a different Day.

Section 5

(1)   Each House shall be the Judge of the Elections, Returns and Qualifications of its own Members, and a Majority of each shall constitute a Quorum to do Business; but a smaller Number may adjourn from day to day, and may be authorized to compel the Attendance of absent Members, in such Manner, and under such Penalties as each House may provide.

(2)   Each House may determine the Rules of its Proceedings, punish its Members for disorderly Behaviour, and, with the Concurrence of two thirds, expel a Member.

(3)   Each House shall keep a Journal of its Proceedings, and from time to time publish the same, excepting such Parts as may in their Judgment require Secrecy; and the Yeas and Nays of the Members of either House on any question shall, at the Desire of one fifth of those Present, be entered on the Journal.

(4)   Neither House, during the Session of Congress, shall, without the Consent of the other, adjourn for more than three days, nor to any other Place than that in which the two Houses shall be sitting.

Section 6

(1)   The Senators and Representatives shall receive a Compensation for their Services, to be ascertained by Law, and paid out of the Treasury of the United States. They shall in all Cases, except Treason, Felony and Breach of the Peace, be privileged from Arrest during their Attendance at the Session of their respective Houses, and in going to and returning from the same; and for any Speech or Debate in either House, they shall not be questioned in any other Place.

(2)   No Senator or Representative shall, during the Time for which he was elected, be appointed to any civil Office under the Authority of the United States, which shall have been created, or the Emoluments whereof shall have been encreased during such time; and no Person holding any Office under the United States, shall be a Member of either House during his Continuance in Office.

Section 7

(1)   All Bills for raising Revenue shall originate in the House of Representatives; but the Senate may propose or concur with Amendments as on other Bills.

(2)   Every Bill which shall have passed the House of Representatives and the Senate, shall, before it become a Law, be presented to the President of the United States; If he approve he shall sign it, but if not he shall return it, with his Objections to that House in which it shall have originated, who shall enter the Objections at large on their Journal, and proceed to reconsider it. If after such Reconsideration two thirds of that House shall agree to pass the Bill, it shall be sent, together with the Objections, to the other House, by which it shall likewise be reconsidered, and if approved by two thirds of that House, it shall become a law. But in all such Cases the Votes of both Houses shall be determined by Yeas and Nays, and the Names of the Persons voting for and against the Bill shall be entered on the Journal of each

House respectively. If any Bill shall not be returned by the President within ten Days (Sunday excepted) after it shall have been presented to him, the Same shall be a Law, in like Manner as if he had signed it, unless the Congress by their Adjournment prevent its Return, in which Case it shall not be a Law.

(3)   Every Order, Resolution, or Vote to which the Concurrence of the Senate and House of Representatives may be necessary (except on a question of Adjournment) shall be presented to the President of the United States; and before the Same shall take Effect, shall be approved by him, or being disapproved by him, shall be repassed by two thirds of the Senate and House of Representatives, according to the Rules and Limitations prescribed in the Case of a Bill.

Section 8

(1)   The Congress shall have Power To lay and collect Taxes, Duties, Imposts and Excises, to pay the Debts and provide for the common Defence and general Welfare of the United States; but all Duties, Imposts and Excises shall be uniform throughout the United States;

(2)   To borrow Money on the credit of the United States;

(3)   To regulate Commerce with foreign Nations, and among the several States, and with the Indian Tribes;

(4)   To establish an uniform Rule of Naturalization, and uniform Laws on the subject of Bankruptcies throughout the United States;

(5)   To coin Money, regulate the Value thereof, and of foreign Coin, and to fix the Standard of Weights and Measures;

(6)   To provide for the Punishment of counterfeiting the Securities and current Coin of the United States;

(7)   To establish Post Offices and post Roads;

(8)   To promote the Progress of Science and useful Arts, by securing for limited Times to Authors and Inventors the exclusive Right to their respective Writings and Discoveries;

(9)   To constitute Tribunals inferior to the supreme Court;

(10) To define and punish Piracies and Felonies committed on the high Seas, and Offenses against the Law of Nations;

(11) To declare War, grant Letters of Marque and Reprisal, and make Rules concerning Captures on Land and Water;

(12) To raise and support Armies, but no Appropriation of Money to that Use shall be for a longer Term than two Years;

(13) To provide and maintain a Navy;

(14) To make Rules for the Government and Regulation of the land and naval Forces;

(15) To provide for calling forth the Militia to execute the Laws of the Union, suppress Insurrections and repel Invasions;

(16) To provide for organizing, arming, and disciplining, the Militia, and for governing such Part of them as may be employed in the Service of the United States, reserving to the States respectively, the Appointment of the Officers, and the Authority of training the Militia according to the discipline prescribed by Congress;

(17) To exercise exclusive Legislation in all Cases whatsoever, over such District (not exceeding ten Miles square) as may, by Cession of particular States, and the Acceptance of Congress, become the Seat of the Government of the United States, and to exercise like Authority over all Places purchased by the Consent of the Legislature of the State in which the Same shall be, for the Erection of Forts, Magazines, Arsenals, dock-Yards, and other needful Buildings;—And

(18) To make all Laws which shall be necessary and proper for carrying into Execution the foregoing Powers, and all other Powers vested by this Constitution in the Government of the United States, or in any Department or Officer thereof.

Section 9

(1) The Migration or Importation of such Persons as any of the States now existing shall think proper to admit, shall not be prohibited by the Congress prior to the Year one thousand eight hundred and eight, but a Tax or Duty may be imposed on such Importation, not exceeding ten dollars for each Person.

(2) The Privilege of the Writ of Habeas Corpus shall not be suspended unless when in Cases of Rebellion or Invasion the public Safety may require it.

(3) No Bill of Attainder or ex post facto Law shall be passed.

(4) No Capitation, or other direct, Tax shall be laid, unless in Proportion to the Census or Enumeration herein before directed to be taken.

(5) No Tax or Duty shall be laid on Articles exported from any State.

(6) No Preference shall be given by any Regulation of Commerce or Revenue to the Ports of one State over those of another; nor shall Vessels bound to, or from, one State, be obliged to enter, clear or pay Duties in another.

(7) No Money shall be drawn from the Treasury, but in Consequence of Appropriations made by Law; and a regular Statement and Account of the Receipts and Expenditures of all public Money shall be published from time to time.

(8) No Title of Nobility shall be granted by the United States: And no Person holding any Office of Profit or Trust under them, shall, without the Consent of the Congress, accept of any present, Emolument, Office, or Title, of any kind whatever, from any King, Prince or foreign State.

Section 10

(1) No State shall enter into any Treaty, Alliance, or Confederation; grant Letters of Marque and Reprisal; coin Money; emit Bills of Credit; make any Thing but gold and silver Coin a Tender in Payment of Debts; pass any Bill of Attainder, ex post

facto Law, or Law impairing the Obligation of Contracts, or grant any Title of Nobility.

(2) No State shall, without the Consent of Congress, lay any Imposts or Duties on Imports or Exports, except what may be absolutely necessary for executing its inspection Laws: and the net Produce of all Duties and Imposts, laid by any State on Imports or Exports, shall be for the Use of the Treasury of the United States; and all such Laws shall be subject to the Revision and Controul of the Congress.

(3) No State shall, without the Consent of Congress, lay any Duty of Tonnage, keep Troops, or Ships of War in time of Peace, enter into any Agreement or Compact with another State, or with a foreign Power, or engage in War, unless actually invaded, or in such imminent Danger as will not admit of Delay.

ARTICLE II

Section 1

(1) The executive Power shall be vested in a President of the United States of America. He shall hold his Office during the Term of four Years, and, together with the Vice President, chosen for the same Term, be elected, as follows:

(2) Each State shall appoint, in such Manner as the Legislature thereof may direct, a Number of Electors, equal to the whole Number of Senators and Representatives to which the State may be entitled in the Congress: but no Senator or Representative, or Person holding an Office of Trust or Profit under the United States, shall be appointed an Elector.

The Electors shall meet in their respective States, and vote by Ballot for two Persons, of whom one at least shall not be an Inhabitant of the same State with themselves. And they shall make a List of all the Persons voted for, and of the Number of Votes for each; which List they shall sign and certify, and transmit sealed to the Seat of the Government of the United States, directed to the President of the Senate. The President of the Senate shall, in the presence of the Senate and House of Representatives, open all the Certificates, and the Votes shall then be counted. The Person having the greatest Number of Votes shall be the President, if such Number be a Majority of the whole Number of Electors appointed; and if there be more than one who have such Majority, and have an equal Number of Votes, then the House of Representatives shall immediately chuse by Ballot one of them for President; and if no Person have a Majority, then from the five highest on the List the said House shall in like Manner chuse the President. But in chusing the President, the Votes shall be taken by States, the Representation from each State having one Vote; a quorum for this Purpose shall consist of a Member or Members from two thirds of the States, and a Majority of all the States shall be necessary to a Choice. In every Case, after the Choice of the President, the Person having the greatest Number of Votes of the Electors shall be the Vice President. But if there should remain two or more who have equal Votes, the Senate shall chose from them by Ballot the Vice President.

(3)   The Congress may determine the Time of chusing the Electors, and the Day on which they shall give their Votes; which Day shall be the same throughout the United States.

(4)   No Person except a natural born Citizen, or a Citizen of the United States, at the time of the Adoption of this Constitution, shall be eligible to the Office of President; neither shall any Person be eligible to that Office who shall not have attained to the Age of thirty five Years, and been fourteen Years a Resident within the United States.

(5)   In Case of the Removal of the President from Office, or of his Death, Resignation, or Inability to discharge the Powers and Duties of the said Office, the Same shall devolve on the Vice President, and the Congress may by Law provide for the Case of Removal, Death, Resignation or Inability, both of the President and Vice President, declaring what Officer shall then act as President, and such Officer shall act accordingly, until the Disability be removed, or a President shall be elected.

(6)   The President shall, at stated Times, receive for his Services, a Compensation, which shall neither be increased nor diminished during the Period for which he shall have been elected, and he shall not receive within that Period any other Emolument from the United States, or any of them.

(7)   Before he enter on the Execution of his Office, he shall take the following Oath or Affirmation:—"I do solemnly swear (or affirm) that I will faithfully execute the Office of President of the United States, and will to the best of my Ability, preserve, protect and defend the Constitution of the United States."

Section 2

(1)   The President shall be Commander in Chief of the Army and Navy of the United States, and of the Militia of the several States, when called into the actual Service of the United States; he may require the Opinion, in writing, of the principal Officer in each of the executive Departments, upon any Subject relating to the Duties of their respective Offices, and he shall have Power to grant Reprieves and Pardons for Offenses against the United States, except in Cases of Impeachment.

(2)   He shall have Power, by and with the Advice and Consent of the Senate, to make Treaties, provided two thirds of the Senators present concur; and he shall nominate, and by and with the Advice and Consent of the Senate, shall appoint Ambassadors, other public Ministers and Consuls, Judges of the supreme Court, and all other Officers of the United States, whose Appointments are not herein otherwise provided for, and which shall be established by Law: but the Congress may by Law vest the Appointment of such inferior Officers, as they think proper, in the President alone, in the Courts of Law, or in the Heads of Departments.

(3)   The President shall have Power to fill up all Vacancies that may happen during the Recess of the Senate, by granting Commissions which shall expire at the End of their next Session.

Section 3

He shall from time to time give to the Congress Information of the State of the Union, and recommend to their Consideration such Measures as he shall judge necessary and expedient; he may, on extraordinary Occasions, convene both Houses, or either of them, and in Case of Disagreement between them, with Respect to the Time of Adjournment, he may adjourn them to such Time as he shall think proper; he shall receive Ambassadors and other public Ministers; he shall take Care that the Laws be faithfully executed, and shall Commission all the Officers of the United States.

Section 4

The President, Vice President and all Civil Officers of the United States, shall be removed from Office on Impeachment for, and Conviction of, Treason, Bribery, or other high Crimes and Misdemeanors.

ARTICLE III

Section 1

The judicial Power of the United States, shall be vested in one supreme Court, and in such inferior Courts as the Congress may from time to time ordain and establish. The Judges, both of the supreme and inferior Courts, shall hold their Offices during good Behaviour, and shall, at stated Times, receive for their Services, a Compensation, which shall not be diminished during their Continuance in Office.

Section 2

(1)   The judicial Power shall extend to all Cases, in Law and Equity, arising under this Constitution, the Laws of the United States, and Treaties made, or which shall be made, under their Authority;—to all Cases affecting Ambassadors, other public Ministers and Consuls;—to all Cases of admiralty and maritime Jurisdiction;—to Controversies to which the United States shall be a party;—to Controversies between two or more States;—between a State and Citizens of another State;—between Citizens of different States;—between Citizens of the same State claiming Lands under Grants of different States, and between a State, or the Citizens thereof, and foreign States, Citizens or Subjects.

(2)   In all Cases affecting Ambassadors, other public Ministers and Consuls, and those in which a State shall be Party, the supreme Court shall have original Jurisdiction. In all the other Cases before mentioned, the supreme Court shall have appellate Jurisdiction, both as to Law and Fact, with such Exceptions, and under such Regulations as the Congress shall make.

(3)   The Trial of all Crimes, except in Cases of Impeachment, shall be by Jury; and such Trial shall be held in the State where the said Crimes shall have been committed; but when not committed within any State, the Trial shall be at such Place or Places as the Congress may by Law have directed.

Section 3

(1)   Treason against the United States, shall consist only in levying War against them, or in adhering to their Enemies, giving them Aid and Comfort. No Person shall be convicted of Treason unless on the Testimony of two Witnesses to the same overt Act, or on Confession in open Court.

(2)   The Congress shall have Power to declare the Punishment of Treason, but no Attainder of Treason shall work Corruption of Blood, or Forfeiture except during the Life of the Person attainted.

ARTICLE IV

Section 1

Full Faith and Credit shall be given in each State to the public Acts, Records, and judicial Proceedings of every other State. And the Congress may by general Laws prescribe the Manner in which such Acts, Records and Proceedings shall be proved, and the Effect thereof.

Section 2

(1)   The Citizens of each State shall be entitled to all privileges and Immunities of Citizens in the several States.

(2)   A Person charged in any State with Treason, Felony, or other Crime, who shall flee from Justice, and be found in another State, shall on Demand of the executive Authority of the State from which he fled, be delivered up, to be removed to the State having Jurisdiction of the Crime.

(3)   No Person held to Service of Labour in one State, under the Laws thereof, escaping into another, shall, in Consequence of any Law or Regulation therein, be discharged from such Service or Labour, but shall be delivered up on Claim of the Party to whom such Service or Labour may be due.

Section 3

(1)   New States may be admitted by the Congress into this Union; but no new State shall be formed or erected within the Jurisdiction of any other State; nor any State be formed by the Junction of two or more States, or Parts of States, without the Consent of the Legislatures of the States concerned as well as of the Congress.

(2)   The Congress shall have power to dispose of and make all needful Rules and Regulations respecting the Territory or other Property belonging to the United States; and nothing in this Constitution shall be so construed as to Prejudice any Claims of the United States, or of any particular State.

Section 4

The United States shall guarantee to every State in this Union a Republican Form of Government, and shall protect each of them against Invasion; and on Application of the Legislature, or of the Executive (when the Legislature cannot be convened) against domestic Violence.

ARTICLE V

The Congress, whenever two thirds of both Houses shall deem it necessary, shall propose Amendments to this Constitution, or, on the Application of the Legislatures of two thirds of the several States, shall call a Convention for proposing Amendments, which, in either Case, shall be valid to all Intents and Purposes, as Part of this Constitution, when ratified by the Legislatures of three fourths of the several States, or by Conventions in three fourths thereof, as the one or the other Mode of Ratification may be proposed by the Congress; Provided that no Amendment which may be made prior to the Year One thousand eight hundred and eight shall in any Manner affect the first and fourth Clauses in the Ninth Section of the first Article; and that no State, without its Consent, shall be deprived of its equal Suffrage in the Senate.

ARTICLE VI

(1)   All Debts contracted and Engagements entered into, before the Adoption of this Constitution, shall be as valid against the United States under this Constitution, as under the Confederation.

(2)   This Constitution, and the Laws of the United States which shall be made in Pursuance thereof; and all Treaties made, or which shall be made, under the Authority of the United States, shall be the supreme Law of the Land; and the Judges in every State shall be bound thereby, any Thing in the Constitution or Laws of any State to the Contrary notwithstanding.

(3)   The Senators and Representatives before mentioned, and the Members of the several State Legislatures, and all executive and judicial Officers, both of the United States and of the several States, shall be bound by Oath or Affirmation, to support this Constitution; but no religious Test shall ever be required as a Qualification to any Office or public Trust under the United States.

ARTICLE VII

The Ratification of the Conventions of nine States, shall be sufficient for the Establishment of this Constitution between the States so ratifying the Same.

ARTICLES IN ADDITION TO, AND AMENDMENT OF, THE CONSTITUTION OF THE UNITED STATES OF AMERICA, PROPOSED BY CONGRESS, AND RATIFIED BY THE SEVERAL STATES, PURSUANT TO THE FIFTH ARTICLE OF THE ORIGINAL CONSTITUTION

AMENDMENT I (1791)

Congress shall make no law respecting an establishment of religion, or prohibiting the free exercise thereof; or abridging the freedom of speech, or of the press; or the right of the people peaceably to assemble, and to petition the Government for a redress of grievances.

AMENDMENT II (1791)

A well regulated Militia, being necessary to the security of a free state, the right of the people to keep and bear Arms, shall not be infringed.

AMENDMENT III (1791)

No Soldier shall, in time of peace be quartered in any house, without the consent of the Owner, nor in time of war, but in a manner to be prescribed by law.

AMENDMENT IV (1791)

The right of the people to be secure in their persons, houses, papers, and effects, against unreasonable searches and seizures, shall not be violated, and no Warrants shall issue, but upon probable cause, supported by Oath or affirmation, and particularly describing the place to be searched, and the persons or things to be seized.

AMENDMENT V (1791)

No person shall be held to answer for a capital, or otherwise infamous crime, unless on a presentment or indictment of a Grand Jury, except in cases arising in the land or naval forces, or in the Militia, when in actual service in time of War or public danger; nor shall any person be subject for the same offence to be twice put in jeopardy of life or limb; nor shall be compelled in any criminal case to be a witness against himself, nor be deprived of life, liberty, or property, without due process of law; nor shall private property be taken for public use, without just compensation.

AMENDMENT VI (1791)

In all criminal prosecutions, the accused shall enjoy the right to a speedy and public trial, by an impartial jury of the State and district wherein the crime shall have been committed, which district shall have been previously ascertained by law, and to be informed of the nature and cause of the accusation; to be confronted with the witnesses against him; to have compulsory process for obtaining witnesses in his favor, and to have the Assistance of Counsel for his defence.

AMENDMENT VII (1791)

In Suits at common law, where the value in controversy shall exceed twenty dollars, the right of trial by jury shall be preserved, and no fact tried by a jury, shall be otherwise re-examined in any Court of the United States, than according to the rules of the common law.

AMENDMENT VIII (1791)

Excessive bail shall not be required, nor excessive fines imposed, nor cruel and unusual punishments inflicted.

AMENDMENT IX (1791)

The enumeration in the Constitution, of certain rights, shall not be construed to deny or disparage others retained by the people.

AMENDMENT X (1791)

The powers not delegated to the United States by the Constitution, nor prohibited by it to the States, are reserved to the States respectively, or to the people.

AMENDMENT XI (1798)

The Judicial power of the United States shall not be construed to extend to any suit in law or equity, commenced or prosecuted against one of the United States by Citizens of another State, or by Citizens or Subjects of any Foreign State.

AMENDMENT XII (1804)

The Electors shall meet in their respective states and vote by ballot for President and Vice-President, one of whom, at least, shall not be an inhabitant of the same state with themselves; they shall name in their ballots the person voted for as President, and in distinct ballots the person voted for as Vice-President, and they shall make distinct lists of all persons voted for as President, and of all persons voted for as Vice-President, and of the number of votes for each, which lists they shall sign and certify, and transmit sealed to the seat of the government of the United States, directed to the President of the Senate;—The President of the Senate shall, in the presence of the Senate and House of Representatives, open all the certificates and the votes shall then be counted;—The person having the greatest number of votes for President, shall be the President, if such number be a majority of the whole number of Electors appointed; and if no person have such majority, then from the persons having the highest numbers not exceeding three on the list of those voted for as President, the House of Representatives shall choose immediately, by ballot, the President. But in choosing the President, the votes shall be taken by states, the representation from each state having one vote; a quorum for this purpose shall consist of a member or members from two-thirds of the states, and a majority of all the states shall be necessary to a choice. And if the House of Representatives shall not choose a President whenever the right of choice shall devolve upon them, before the fourth day of March next following, then the Vice-President shall act as President, as in the case of the death or other constitutional disability of the President—The person having the greatest number of votes as Vice-President, shall be the Vice-President, if such number be a majority of the whole number of Electors appointed, and if no person have a majority, then from the two highest numbers on the list, the Senate shall choose the Vice-President; A quorum for the purpose shall consist of two-thirds of the whole number of Senators, and a majority of the whole number shall be necessary to a choice. But no person constitutionally ineligible to the office of President shall be eligible to that of Vice-President of the United States.

AMENDMENT XIII (1865)

Section 1

Neither slavery nor involuntary servitude, except as a punishment for crime whereof the party shall have been duly convicted, shall exist within the United States, or any place subject to their jurisdiction.

Section 2

Congress shall have power to enforce this article by appropriate legislation.

AMENDMENT XIV (1868)

Section 1

All persons born or naturalized in the United States and subject to the jurisdiction thereof, are citizens of the United States and of the State wherein they reside. No State shall make or enforce any law which shall abridge the privileges or immunities of citizens of the United States; nor shall any State deprive any person of life, liberty, or property, without due process of law; nor deny to any person within its jurisdiction the equal protection of the laws.

Section 2

Representatives shall be apportioned among the several States according to their respective numbers, counting the whole number of persons in each State, excluding Indians not taxed. But when the right to vote at any election for the choice of electors for President and Vice-President of the United States, Representatives in Congress, the Executive and Judicial officers of a State, or the members of the Legislature thereof, is denied to any of the male inhabitants of such State, being twenty-one years of age, and citizens of the United States, or in any way abridged, except for participation in rebellion, or other crime, the basis of representation therein shall be reduced in the proportion which the number of such male citizens shall bear to the whole number of male citizens twenty-one years of age in such State.

Section 3

No person shall be a Senator or Representative in Congress, or elector of President and Vice-President, or hold any office, civil or military, under the United States, or under any State, who, having previously taken an oath, as a member of Congress, or as an officer of the United States, or as a member of any State legislature, or as an executive or judicial officer of any State, to support the Constitution of the United States, shall have engaged in insurrection or rebellion against the same, or given aid or comfort to the enemies thereof. But Congress may by a vote of two-thirds of each House, remove such disability.

Section 4

The validity of the public debt of the United States, authorized by law, including debts incurred for payment of pensions and bounties for services in suppressing insurrection or rebellion, shall not be questioned. But neither the United States nor any State shall assume or pay any debt or obligation incurred in aid of insurrection or rebellion against the United States, or any claim for the loss or emancipation of any slave; but all such debts, obligations and claims shall be held illegal and void.

Section 5

The Congress shall have power to enforce, by appropriate legislation, the provisions of this article.

AMENDMENT XV (1870)

Section 1

The right of citizens of the United States to vote shall not be denied or abridged by the United States or by any State on account of race, color, or previous condition of servitude.

Section 2

The Congress shall have power to enforce this article by appropriate legislation.

AMENDMENT XVI (1913)

The Congress shall have power to lay and collect taxes on incomes, from whatever source derived, without apportionment among the several States, and without regard to any census or enumeration.

AMENDMENT XVII (1913)

The Senate of the United States shall be composed of two Senators from each State, elected by the people thereof, for six years; and each Senator shall have one vote. The electors in each State shall have the qualifications requisite for electors of the most numerous branch of the State legislatures.

When vacancies happen in the representation of any State in the Senate, the executive authority of such State shall issue writs of election to fill such vacancies: *Provided,* That the legislature of any State may empower the executive thereof to make temporary appointments until the people fill the vacancies by election as the legislature may direct.

This amendment shall not be so construed as to affect the election or term of any Senator chosen before it becomes valid as part of the Constitution.

AMENDMENT XVIII (1919)

Section 1

After one year from the ratification of this article the manufacture, sale, or transportation of intoxicating liquors within, the importation thereof into, or the exportation thereof from the United States and all territory subject to the jurisdiction thereof for beverage purposes is hereby prohibited.

Section 2

The Congress and the several States shall have concurrent power to enforce this article by appropriate legislation.

Section 3

This article shall be inoperative unless it shall have been ratified as an amendment to the Constitution by the legislatures of the several States, as provided in the Constitution, within seven years from the date of the submission hereof to the States by the Congress.

AMENDMENT XIX (1920)

The right of citizens of the United States to vote shall not be denied or abridged by the United States or by any State on account of sex.

Congress shall have power to enforce this article by appropriate legislation.

AMENDMENT XX (1933)

Section 1

The terms of the President and Vice President shall end at noon on the 20th day of January, and the terms of Senators and Representatives at noon on the 3d day of January, of the years in which such terms would have ended if this article had not been ratified; and the terms of their successors shall then begin.

Section 2

The Congress shall assemble at least once in every year, and such meeting shall begin at noon on the 3d day of January, unless they shall by law appoint a different day.

Section 3

If, at the time fixed for the beginning of the term of the President, the President elect shall have died, the Vice President elect shall become President. If a President shall not have been chosen before the time fixed for the beginning of his term, or if the President elect shall have failed to qualify, then the Vice President elect shall act as President until a President shall have qualified; and the Congress may by law provide for the case wherein neither a President elect nor a Vice President elect shall have qualified, declaring who shall then act as President, or the manner in which one who is to act shall be selected, and such person shall act accordingly until a President or Vice President shall have qualified.

Section 4

The Congress may by law provide for the case of the death of any of the persons from whom the House of Representatives may choose a President whenever the right of choice shall have devolved upon them, and for the case of the death of any of the persons from whom the Senate may choose a Vice President whenever the right of choice shall have devolved upon them.

Section 5

Sections 1 and 2 shall take effect on the 15th day of October following the ratification of this article.

Section 6

This article shall be inoperative unless it shall have been ratified as an amendment to the Constitution by the legislatures of three-fourths of the several States within seven years from the date of its submission.

AMENDMENT XXI (1933)

Section 1

The eighteenth article of amendment to the Constitution of the United States is hereby repealed.

Section 2

The transportation or importation into any State, Territory or possession of the United States for delivery or use therein of intoxicating liquors, in violation of the laws thereof, is hereby prohibited.

Section 3

This article shall be inoperative unless it shall have been ratified as an amendment to the Constitution by conventions in the several States, as provided in the Constitution, within seven years from the date of the submission hereof to the States by the Congress.

AMENDMENT XXII (1951)

Section 1

No person shall be elected to the office of the President more than twice, and no person who has held the office of President, or acted as President, for more than two years of a term to which some other person was elected President shall be elected to the office of the President more than once. But this Article shall not apply to any person holding the office of President when this Article was proposed by the Congress, and shall not prevent any person who may be holding the office of President, or acting as President, during the term within which this Article becomes operative from holding the office of President or acting as President during the remainder of such term.

Section 2

This Article shall be inoperative unless it shall have been ratified as an amendment to the Constitution by the legislatures of three-fourths of the several States within seven years from the date of its submission to the States by the Congress.

AMENDMENT XXIII (1961)

Section 1

The District constituting the seat of Government of the United States shall appoint in such manner as the Congress may direct:

A number of electors of President and Vice President equal to the whole number of Senators and Representatives in Congress to which the District would be entitled if it were a State, but in no event more than the least populous State; they shall be in addition to those appointed by the States, but they shall be considered, for the purposes of the election of President and Vice President, to be electors appointed by a State; and they shall meet in the District and perform such duties as provided by the twelfth article of amendment.

Section 2

The Congress shall have power to enforce this article by appropriate legislation.

AMENDMENT XXIV (1964)

Section 1

The right of citizens of the United States to vote in any primary or other election for President or Vice President, for electors for President or Vice President, or for Senator or Representative in Congress, shall not be denied or abridged by the United States or any State by reason of failure to pay any poll tax or other tax.

Section 2

The Congress shall have power to enforce this article by appropriate legislation.

AMENDMENT XXV (1967)

Section 1

In case of the removal of the President from office or of his death or resignation, the Vice President shall become President.

Section 2

Whenever there is a vacancy in the office of the Vice President, the President shall nominate a Vice President who shall take office upon confirmation by a majority vote of both Houses of Congress.

Section 3

Whenever the President transmits to the President pro tempore of the Senate and the Speaker of the House of Representatives his written declaration that he is unable to discharge the powers and duties of his office, and until he transmits to them a written declaration to the contrary, such powers and duties shall be discharged by the Vice President as Acting President.

Section 4

Whenever the Vice President and a majority of either the principal officers of the executive departments or of such other body as Congress may by law provide, transmit to the President pro tempore of the Senate and the Speaker of the House of Representatives their written declaration that the President is unable to discharge the powers and duties of his office, the Vice President shall immediately assume the powers and duties of the office as Acting President.

Thereafter, when the President transmits to the President pro tempore of the Senate and the Speaker of the House of Representatives his written declaration that no inability exists, he shall resume the powers and duties of his office unless the Vice President and a majority of either the principal officers of the executive department or of such other body as Congress may by law provide, transmit within four days to the President pro tempore of the

Senate and the Speaker of the House of Representatives their written declaration that the President is unable to discharge the powers and duties of his office. Thereupon Congress shall decide the issue, assembling within forty-eight hours for that purpose if not in session. If the Congress, within twenty-one days after receipt of the latter written declaration, or, if Congress is not in session, within twenty-one days after Congress is required to assemble, determines by two-thirds vote of both Houses that the President is unable to discharge the powers and duties of his office, the Vice President shall continue to discharge the same as Acting President; otherwise, the President shall resume the powers and duties of his office.

AMENDMENT XXVI (1971)

Section 1

The right of citizens of the United States, who are eighteen years of age or older, to vote shall not be denied or abridged by the United States or by any State on account of age.

Section 2

The Congress shall have power to enforce this article by appropriate legislation.

AMENDMENT XXVII (1992)

No law varying the compensation for the services of the senators and representatives shall take effect, until an election of representatives shall have intervened.

APPENDIX E

RESOURCE MANUAL

This Resource Manual is the paralegal student's primary tool for reinforcing the material presented in *Legal Research* and for putting into practice the skills required in the use of the various legal source materials discussed in the text. Its purpose is to help students learn to perform legal research. For each chapter there are three sections to aid students in their review of the important concepts and skills presented in text.

The first of these sections is a set of Test Your Knowledge Questions that consists of various types of objective questions—true/false, completion, multiple choice, short answer—designed to help students evaluate how much they have learned. Answers to these questions appear in the third section, after the Legal Research Exercises for each chapter, enabling students to review on their own.

The second and most important section is called Legal Research Exercises. As its name implies, this section provides opportunity for students to practice their newly acquired skills and familiarize themselves with the range of legal source materials they will be required to consult as paralegals. The exercises are divided into five distinct groups so that students may photocopy and complete one or more sets to be turned in to the instructor. None of the exercises is designed to be overly time-consuming. If you find you are unable to complete an exercise, ask your instructor for assistance.

The citation rules that follow are this introduction are basic rules drawn from *The Bluebook: A Uniform System of Citation* and should be used in citing all legal sources when answering the Legal Research Exercises for each chapter unless you are otherwise instructed.

Your progress as a legal researcher depends on your learning and using the right techniques and refining your skills through practice. *Legal Research* presents those techniques, and this Resource Manual starts you along the road to their implementation. Remember that your legal research skills must be practiced. The more you perform legal research, the better a legal researcher you will become.

CITATION RULES

(Based on *The Bluebook: A Uniform System of Citation*)

CASES

A standard case citation contains:

(1) Name of the case;

(2) Reference(s) to the published source(s) in which you can find the case;

(3) Date (year) decision was issued and, if not apparent from the reporter(s), the court; and (sometimes)

(4) Subsequent case history, if any.

Example: Smith v. Jones, 369 Pa. 13, 85 A.2d 23 (1951).

Name of case	Parallel citations	Date

Instructions:

- The name of the case is always italicized or underlined continuously (*i.e.,* no gaps).

- Cite only the first party on each side:

    —if the party is a person, use only the last name (no first name, middle initial, or title)

    —if the party is a business, use the full business name (but stop after the first business indicator term such as "Co." or "Inc.")

    —omit "The"

    —abbreviate only the following: Association to "Ass'n," Brothers to "Bros.," Company to "Co.," Corporation to "Corp.," Incorporated to "Inc.," Limited to "Ltd.," Number to "No.," *and* to "&," and any widely recognized acronym (*e.g.,* National Aeronautics and Space Administration to "NASA"—do not use periods)

- Cite an "in rem" action (involving real or personal property) by the name in full as it appears in the caption of the case.

- Cite volume number followed by reporter abbreviation followed by beginning page number.

- Cite the official reporter first and the unofficial reporter, if any, second. [*Note:* The official reporter generally has a state abbreviation in it.] The A.L.R. citation, if any, goes last.

- Put no space between single-letter abbreviations, including "2d" and "3d" (*e.g.,* U.S. and A.2d) and one space between multiple-letter abbreviations (*e.g.,* S. Ct., Pa. Super., and W.E.B. DuBois Co.).

CONSTITUTIONS

A standard constitutional citation contains:

(1) Abbreviation of the jurisdiction;

(2) Abbreviation for "Constitution" ("Const.");

(3) Abbreviation for "Article" ("art.") followed by its number (in Roman numeral);

(4) Section symbol (§) followed by its number (and abbreviation for "clause"—"cl."—followed by its number, if any); and

(5) Date (year) only if jurisdiction has more than one.

Examples: U.S. Const. art. I, § 9, cl. 2.
Pa. Const. art. I, § 28 (1968).

STATUTES

A standard statutory citation contains:

(1) Title number;

(2) Code abbreviation;

(3) Section (§) number, including any subsection(s) in parentheses; and

(4) Date (year).

Note: For federal statutes, use date of latest codification (1994) or amendment, whichever is later; for state statutes, use date of enactment or latest amendment, if any.

Examples: 22 U.S.C. § 2567(a)(1) (1994).
20 Pa. Cons. Stat. Ann. § 201(c) (1985).

REGULATIONS

A standard federal regulatory citation contains:

(1) Volume number;

(2) Abbreviation of set of regulations cited (generally, C.F.R.);

(3) Section (§) number, including any subsection(s); and

(4) Date (year) of volume cited.

Example: 7 C.F.R. § 319.76 (1990).

COURT RULES

A standard citation to a court rule contains:

(1) Abbreviation for the set of rules; and

(2) Number of the rule, including any subpart(s).

Example: Fed. R. Civ. P. 12(b)(6).

CHAPTER 1

TEST YOUR KNOWLEDGE QUESTIONS

1. A legal researcher can access all legal source materials by computer. T ___ /F ___

2. A binding authority is a law that the court must follow. T ___ /F ___

3. Circuit courts are the trial courts in the federal court system. T ___ /F ___

4. Federal law is an "official" source, and state law is an "unofficial" source. T ___ /F ___

5. If a statute conflicts with a constitutional provision, it is invalid. T ___ /F ___

6. If a regulation conflicts with a statute, it is invalid. T ___ /F ___

7. Cases involving constitutional issues may begin in an appellate court. T ___ /F ___

8. There is no generally accepted system for citation to legal authority. T ___ /F ___

9. Federal and state courts are independent of one another, and neither has authority over the other. T ___ /F ___

10. Statutes are written laws enacted by a legislature. T ___ /F ___

11. Define "ordinance."

12. Name the two kinds of administrative agencies.

13. What are the two threshold questions every legal researcher should answer before proceeding with research?

14. What does "TAPP" stand for?

15. When does a legal researcher use the TAPP rule?

16. Law in the United States is made by:

    a. legislatures
    b. courts
    c. administrative agencies
    d. local governments
    e. all of the above

17. Which of the following is *never* a primary authority?

    a. constitutions
    b. statutes
    c. digests
    d. regulations
    e. cases

18. Legal publishers update their law sources in the following manner:

    a. pocket parts
    b. replacement volumes
    c. looseleaf system
    d. any of the above
    e. none of the above

19. Which of the following statements is false?

    a. Court rules can be used to find statutes.
    b. Court rules can be considered primary authority in some circumstances.
    c. Court rules can govern practice and procedure for the parties who come before the courts.
    d. There are general court rules that apply across the board to similar courts.
    e. Some courts have particular rules just for those practicing before a particular court.

20. According to *Bluebook* rules, in citing case names, which of these words may *not* be abbreviated:

    a. Association
    b. Brotherhood
    c. Company
    d. Corporation
    e. Incorporated

21. Law is classified as substantive or _____, binding or _____, and _____ or secondary.

22. Persuasive authority is law that is not _____ on the resolution of a problem.

23. Works that write about or explain primary sources are called _____ sources.

24. _____ place statutes in chronological order, and _____ put them in subject categories by title.

25. Courts are organized in a(n) _____ manner.

LEGAL RESEARCH EXERCISES

Group A

Look up each cited case and provide the correct complete citation:

1. 64 S. Ct. 548

2. 105 S. Ct. 1676

3. 782 F.2d 547

4. 920 F.2d 900

5. 647 F. Supp. 1064

6. 784 F. Supp. 1471

For each of the following questions, supply a correct citation from the information supplied:

7. John V. Smith, Mary T. Smith, and James Smith-Jones versus The Antoinette E. Smith-Jones Company, Incorporated.

8. Bailey and Bailey, Attorneys at Law against Marcy Weingrad, *et al.*

9. Anita Steptoe by her mother, Wanda Steptoe, against The Martha and George Washington Corporation, Incorporated, as reported in volume 1001 of the *Federal Reporter, Second Series* on pages 1,234 through 1,245, and decided on February 9, 1995, by the Eleventh Circuit Court of Appeals.

10. The United States of America versus The Honorable Jeremiah Fish, Jordan R. Conston, and Zachary M. Holtzman, as reported in volume 899 of the *Federal Supplement* on pages 212 through 300 by Judge Juanita Berger of the United States District Court for the Eastern District of New York. Argued 12/5/94. Submitted 3/15/95. Rehearing denied 1/5/96.

Group B

Look up each cited case and provide the correct complete citation:

1. 70 S. Ct. 123

2. 94 S. Ct. 2449

3. 530 F.2d 515

4. 772 F.2d 602

5. 663 F. Supp. 1

6. 802 F. Supp. 752

For each of the following questions, supply a correct citation from the information supplied:

7. Herbert Johnson, Keisha Johnson, and Jonathan Johnson-Jones versus The Aloysius B. Johnson-Jones Company, Incorporated.

8. Versituk and Versituk, Attorneys at Law against Roberta Reno, *et al.*

9. Rebecca Pottersburg by her father, Pietro Pottersburg, against The Mack and Mickey Moose Manufacturing Company, Incorporated, as reported in volume 1002 of the *Federal Reporter, Second Series* on pages 1,111 through 1,119, and decided on May 15, 1995, by the Tenth Circuit Court of Appeals.

10. The United States of America versus The Reverend Doctor Hannibal I. Lechtor, Sarah S. Kirk, and Karen R. Kirk, as reported in volume 898 of *Federal Supplement* on pages 257 through 290 by Judge Roberta P. Shoefly of the United States District Court for the Eastern District of Pennsylvania. Argued 11/14/94. Submitted 2/14/95. Rehearing denied 1/8/96.

Group C

Look up each cited case and provide the correct complete citation:

1. 68 S. Ct. 682

2. 82 S. Ct. 1261

3. 552 F.2d 1036

4. 957 F.2d 1513

5. 611 F. Supp. 1223

6. 759 F. Supp. 612

For each of the following questions, supply a correct citation from the information supplied:

7. Ramona Alvarez, Lucinda Alvarez, and Jaime Alvarez-Jones versus The Juanita Q. Alvarez-Jones Company, Incorporated.

8. Guzman and Guzman, Attorneys at Law against Richard Steinmetz, *et al.*

9. Wilhelmina Bramblesby by her guardian, Waldo Bramblesby, against The Parker and Piper Piano Tuning Association, Limited, as reported in volume 1003 of the *Federal Reporter, Second Series* on pages 1,088 through 1,099, and decided by the Ninth Circuit Court of Appeals on April 19, 1995.

10. The United States of America versus Gerald Garibaldi, Jr., Esquire, Lori A. Seger, and Kimberly D. Seger, as reported in volume 897 of the *Federal Supplement* on pages 307 through 389, by Judge Antonia Baynton-Baskin of the United States District Court for the Eastern District of Michigan. Argued 10/7/94. Submitted 3/29/95. Rehearing denied 2/2/96.

Group D

Look up each cited case and provide the correct complete citation:

1. 77 S. Ct. 1269

2. 93 S. Ct. 1241

3. 617 F.2d 875

4. 927 F.2d 39

5. 501 F. Supp. 452

6. 741 F. Supp. 395

For each of the following questions, supply a correct citation from the information supplied:

7. Dominic Chang, Kristine Chang, and Winston Chang-Jones versus The Michael F. Chang-Jones Company, Incorporated.

8. Chun and Chun, Attorneys at Law against B.D. Stokowski, et *al.*

9. Patrice Delacorte by her husband, Peter-Paul Delacorte, against The Delia and David Vanderhoven Vegetable Vendors Corporation, Incorporated, as reported in volume 1004 of the *Federal Reporter, Second Series* on pages 1,345 through 1,357, and decided by the Eighth Circuit Court of Appeals on July 12, 1995.

10. The United States of America versus Lt. Major Jane Eyre, Michael Hensley, and Melinda D. McCormick, as reported in volume 892 of the *Federal Supplement* on pages 368 through 399, by Judge Ruthellen Lockjaw of the United States District Court for the Eastern District of Washington. Argued 10/20/94. Submitted 8/16/95. Rehearing denied 3/5/96.

Group E

Look up each cited case and provide the correct complete citation:

1. 84 S. Ct. 1561

2. 107 S. Ct. 2607

3. 669 F.2d 1364

4. 881 F.2d 1006

5. 690 F. Supp. 1261

6. 810 F. Supp. 277

For each of the following questions, supply a correct citation from the information supplied:

7. James Peterson, Maria Peterson, and Wiley Peterson-Jones versus The Talullah S. Peterson-Jones Company, Incorporated.

8. Brock and Brock, Attorneys at Law against Carolann McCowan, *et al.*

9. Veronica Venus, by her sister, Vanessa Venus, against The Christine and Christopher Columbia Coeducational Camps Company Corporation, as reported in volume 1005 of the *Federal Reporter, Second Series* on pages 1,001 through 1,011, and decided by the Seventh Circuit Court of Appeals on April 24, 1995.

10. The United States of America versus Mrs. Maria Madonna, Ph.D., Andrew L. Gangolf III, and C.C. Carter, as reported in volume 895 of the *Federal Supplement* on pages 446 through 489, by Judge Keolani Kukura of the United States District Court for the Eastern District of Virginia. Argued 12/30/94. Submitted 11/20/95. Rehearing denied 6/5/96.

ANSWERS TO TEST YOUR KNOWLEDGE QUESTIONS

1. False
2. True
3. False
4. False
5. True
6. True
7. False
8. False
9. False
10. True
11. law passed by a local governmental entity
12. administrative and executive
13. a. What is the source authority?
    b. What jurisdiction's law will determine the outcome of the case?
14. Things
    Actions
    Persons
    Places
15. to select words that will provide access to the indexes found in the various research tools
16. e
17. c
18. d
19. a
20. b
21. procedural, persuasive, primary
22. binding
23. secondary
24. session laws, codes
25. hierarchical

CHAPTER 2

TEST YOUR KNOWLEDGE QUESTIONS

1. Federal session laws are called *Statutes at Large*. T ___ /F ___

2. The *United States Code* is revised every six years. T ___ /F ___

3. The federal Constitution is the law over federal matters only. T ___ /F ___

4. Unlike federal agencies, state agencies cannot issue rules. T ___ /F ___

5. Agency actions must be consistent with the statute(s) Congress passed to set up that agency. T ___ /F ___

6. Constitutions are usually researched by using an annotated code. T ___ /F ___

7. An annotated code is the official version of statutes published by the legislature. T ___ /F ___

8. Identify the various stages in the publication of enacted statutes.

9. How is the *United States Code* kept current between revisions?

10. Describe the steps in researching an annotated code.

11. An administrative agency makes laws by:

    a. rules
    b. regulations
    c. decisions
    d. all of the above
    e. none of the above

12. Every state has:

    a. a constitution
    b. a code
    c. administrative agencies
    d. a and b only
    e. a, b, and c

13. Federal regulations are kept chronologically in the _____ and by subject matter in the _____.

14. The *United States Code* is divided into _____ titles.

15. Cities and counties make laws called _____.

LEGAL RESEARCH EXERCISES

Group A

Answer the following question and cite the appropriate section of the United States Constitution:

1. Which house of Congress has the sole power to try all impeachments—the Senate or the House of Representatives?

Answer the following questions and cite the appropriate title and section of the United States Code:

2. Which title and section of the *United States Code* deal with the maintenance of records of persons dealing in credit in foreign currency? What is the date and *Statutes at Large* reference for the most recent amendment to that section?

3. Which law which establishes the National Sea Grant College Program? Give the citation to that law.

Using the case annotations in the U.S.C.A. or the U.S.C.S., answer the following question and cite a case supporting that answer:

4. Does the sale of disassembled elements together with the intention that they be put in operable relationship only once abroad constitute contributory infringement of a patented device under 35 U.S.C. § 271? Provide a case citation.

Use the most recent edition of the Code of Federal Regulations *to answer the following questions:*

5. Find Executive Order 12826 issued on December 30, 1992. What is its title?

6. What did the President proclaim with Proclamation 6487 on October 8, 1992?

7. Using the Index and Finding Aids volume, find the regulation for permits to take golden eagle nests.

Group B

Answer the following question and cite the appropriate section of the United States Constitution:

1. List the main federal officials for which the President must have the advice and consent of the United States Senate in the confirmation of their appointment to office.

Answer the following questions and cite the appropriate title and section of the United States Code:

2. Which title and section of the *United States Code* deal with resolutions approving commercial agreements for international trade with communist countries? What is the date and *Statutes at Large* reference for the most recent amendment to that section?

3. Which law establishes the National Foundation for the Arts and Humanities? Give the citation to that law.

Using the case annotations in the U.S.C.A. or the U.S.C.S., answer the following question and cite a case supporting that answer:

4. Would 18 U.S.C. § 1341, which outlaws the use of the mails to execute a scheme to defraud, include premarital promises? Provide a case citation.

Use the most recent edition of the Code of Federal Regulations *to answer the following questions:*

5. Find Executive Order 12819 issued on October 28, 1992. What is its title?

6. What did the President proclaim with Proclamation 6496 on October 20, 1992?

7. Using the Index and Finding Aids volume, find the regulation concerning the issuance of peddlers' permits on Zuni Indian Reservations in New Mexico.

Group C

Answer the following question and cite the appropriate section of the United States Constitution:

1. What limitations, if any, does the Constitution provide in regard to the formation of new states?

Answer the following questions and cite the appropriate title and section of the United States Code:

2. Which title and section of the *United States Code* deal with rehearings of courts-martial under the *Uniform Code of Military Justice?* What is the date and *Statutes at Large* reference for the most recent amendment to that section?

3. Which law grants natives of the Pribilof Islands free dental care from the United States government? Give the citation to that law.

Using the case annotations in the U.S.C.A. or the U.S.C.S., answer the following question and cite a case supporting that answer:

4. Is laches likely to be a good defense to a charge of conspiracy under 18 U.S.C. § 371? Provide a case citation.

Use the most recent edition of the Code of Federal Regulations *to answer the following questions:*

5. Find Executive Order 12816 issued on October 14, 1992. What is its title?

6. What did the President proclaim with Proclamation 6448 on June 17, 1992?

7. Using the Index and Finding Aids volume, find the regulation concerning requirements for disclosure in print advertising of smokeless tobacco products.

Group D

Answer the following question and cite the appropriate section of the United States Constitution:

1. Are treaties the supreme law of the land?

Answer the following questions and cite the appropriate title and section of the United States Code:

2. Which title and section of the *United States Code* deal with the application of tax law to distilled spirits in Puerto Rico? What is the date and *Statutes at Large* reference for the most recent amendment to that section?

3. Which law prohibits the publishing of counterfeit weather reports? Give the citation to that law.

Using the case annotations in the U.S.C.A. or the U.S.C.S., answer the following question and cite a case supporting that answer:

4. Under 20 U.S.C. § 1082, what law have the courts determined governs the rights and liabilities of the government and student borrower under federally insured student loan programs—federal, state, or local? Provide a case citation.

Use the most recent edition of the Code of Federal Regulations *to answer the following questions:*

5. Find Executive Order 12805 issued on May 11, 1992. What is its title?

6. What did the President proclaim with Proclamation 6441 on May 20, 1992?

7. Using the Index and Finding Aids volume, find the regulation concerning the requirements for labeling and packaging of goat's milk ice cream.

Group E

Answer the following question and cite the appropriate section of the United States Constitution:

1. List the types of cases for which the United States Supreme Court has original jurisdiction.

Answer the following questions and cite the appropriate title and section of the United States Code:

2. Which title and section of the *United States Code* deal with the periodic issuance of guarantees by the Small Business Administration? What is the date and *Statutes at Large* reference for the most recent amendment to that section?

3. Which law makes it unlawful to transport refrigerators without safety devices enabling the door to be opened from the inside? Give the citation to that law.

Using the case annotations in the U.S.C.A. or the U.S.C.S., answer the following question and cite a case supporting that answer:

4. Discrimination and segregation in public places are prohibited by 42 U.S.C. § 2000a. Would this prohibition apply to a roller skating rink? Provide a case citation.

Use the most recent edition of the Code of Federal Regulations *to answer the following questions:*

5. Find Executive Order 12803 issued on April 30, 1992. What is its title?

6. What did the President proclaim with Proclamation 6439 on May 18, 1992?

7. Using the Index and Finding Aids volume, find the regulation regarding standard time zone boundaries for the Alaska Time Zone.

ANSWERS TO TEST YOUR KNOWLEDGE QUESTIONS

1. True
2. True
3. False
4. False
5. True
6. True
7. False
8. slip law, session law, code, and annotated code
9. cumulative supplements
10. 1. Identify the applicable annotated code.
    2. Locate the appropriate statute by using an index/table.
    3. Read the statute.
    4. Scan the annotated materials.
    5. Examine the updating sources.
11. d
12. e
13. *Federal Register*
    Code of Federal Regulations
14. fifty
15. ordinances

CHAPTER 3

TEST YOUR KNOWLEDGE QUESTIONS

1. The doctrine of stare decisis requires that a precedent once decided never can be changed. T___ /F___

2. Courts interpret and apply only the common law. T___ /F___

3. A slip opinion is the first published form of a court decision. T___ /F___

4. All courts publish their decisions. T___ /F___

5. A decision by a federal district court is not binding on other district courts. T___ /F___

6. Early United States Supreme Court cases were published by private publishers in reporters that used the name of the publisher. T___ /F___

7. A citation to a United States Supreme Court decision is usually made only to *United States Reports*. T___ /F___

8. The final court of appeals for all state courts is called "Supreme Court." T___ /F___

9. Describe the general format of most court opinions.

10. List the seven West regional reporters.

11. The federal district courts currently report their decisions in _____.

12. The federal circuit courts of appeals currently report their decisions in _____.

13. Which of the following does *not* report United States Supreme Court cases?

    a. *United States Reports*
    b. *Supreme Court Reporter*
    c. *United States Supreme Court Reports—Lawyers' Edition*
    d. *United States Law Week*
    e. *Federal Reporter*

14. Which of the following is *not* an example of a specialized reporter?

    a. *American Law Reports*
    b. *Bankruptcy Reporter*
    c. *Education Reporter*
    d. *Military Justice Reporter*
    e. *Social Security Reporter*

15. Which of the following is *not* a component editorial feature of most reported court decisions?

    a. caption
    b. syllabus
    c. headnotes
    d. briefs of counsel
    e. names of judges

LEGAL RESEARCH EXERCISES

Group A

1. Using volume 65 of the *Supreme Court Reporter*, look up the case that begins on page 193 and complete this citation: *Korematsu v. United States*.

2. What is the topic and key number of headnote 3 in *Korematsu*?

3. Discussion of headnote 3 begins in the opinion on what page number in the *Supreme Court Reporter?*

4. Using the star pagination system in *Korematsu* as it appears in the *Supreme Court Reporter*, determine the first word on page 220 in the *United States Reports*.

5. Which Justice delivered the (majority) opinion of the Court?

6. Using volume 800 of the *Federal Reporter, Second Series*, give the complete citation for the case beginning on page 1558.

7. How many cases were decided by the First Circuit Court of Appeals in that same volume?

8. Using volume 700 of the *Federal Supplement*, give the complete citation for the case in which the defendant is named "Fielitz."

9. Using that same volume, on what page is there a case that construes Rule 17(c) of the Federal Rules of Criminal Procedure?

10. Using volume 989 of the *Federal Reporter, Second Series*, how many judges heard the case beginning on page 1211? _____

11. What was the disposition of the court in that case?

12. Was the decision unanimous?

Group B

1. Using volume 94 of the *Supreme Court Reporter*, look up the case that begins on page 3090 and complete this citation: *United States v. Nixon*.

2. What is the topic and key number of headnote 9 in *Nixon*?

3. Discussion of headnote 9 begins in the opinion on what page number in the *Supreme Court Reporter?*

4. Using the star pagination system in *Nixon* as it appears in the *Supreme Court Reporter*, determine the first word on page 692 in the *United States Reports*.

5. Which Justice delivered the (majority) opinion of the Court?

6. Using volume 400 of the *Federal Reporter, Second Series*, give the complete citation for the case beginning on page 194.

7. How many cases were decided by the Seventh Circuit Court of Appeals in that same volume?

8. Using volume 400 of the *Federal Supplement*, give the complete citation for the case in which the defendant is named "Bruch."

9. Using that same volume, on what page is there a case that construes Rule 16 of the Federal Rules of Criminal Procedure?

10. Using volume 915 of the *Federal Reporter, Second Series*, how many judges heard the case beginning on page 1435?

11. What was the disposition of the court in that case?

12. Was the decision unanimous?

Group C

1. Using volume 83 of the *Supreme Court Reporter*, look up the case that begins on page 792 and complete this citation: *Gideon v. Wainwright*.

2. What is the topic and key number of headnote 2 in *Gideon*?

3. Discussion of headnote 2 begins in the opinion on what page number in the *Supreme Court Reporter*?

4. Using the star pagination system in *Gideon* as it appears in the *Supreme Court Reporter*, determine the first word on page 344 in the *United States Reports*.

5. Which Justice delivered the (majority) opinion of the Court?

6. Using volume 500 of the *Federal Reporter, Second Series*, give the complete citation for the case beginning on page 960.

7. How many cases were decided by the District of Columbia Circuit Court of Appeals in that same volume?

8. Using volume 300 of the *Federal Supplement*, give the complete citation for the case in which the defendant is named "Heim."

9. Using that same volume, on what page is there a case that construes Rule 39 of the Federal Rules of Civil Procedure?

10. Using volume 841 of the *Federal Reporter, Second Series*, how many judges heard the case beginning on page 1358?

11. What was the disposition of the court in that case?

12. Was the decision unanimous?

Group D

1. Using volume 93 of the *Supreme Court Reporter*, look up the case that begins on page 705 and complete this citation: *Roe v. Wade*.

2. What is the topic and key number of headnote 4 in *Roe*?

3. Discussion of headnote 4 begins in the opinion on what page number in the *Supreme Court Reporter*?

4. Using the star pagination system in *Roe* as it appears in the *Supreme Court Reporter*, determine the first word on page 149 in the *United States Reports*.

5. Which Justice delivered the (majority) opinion of the Court?

6. Using volume 600 of the *Federal Reporter, Second Series*, give the complete citation for the case beginning on page 452.

7. How many cases were decided by the Tenth Circuit Court of Appeals in that same volume?

8. Using volume 500 of the *Federal Supplement*, give the complete citation for the case in which the defendant is named "Lamb."

9. Using that same volume, on what page is there a case that construes Rule 201 of the Federal Rules of Evidence?

10. Using volume 729 of the *Federal Reporter, Second Series*, how many judges heard the case beginning on page 1270?

11. What was the disposition of the court in that case?

12. Was the decision unanimous?

Group E

1. Using volume 86 of the *Supreme Court Reporter*, look up the case that begins on page 1602 and complete this citation: *Miranda v. Arizona*.

2. What is the topic and key number of headnote 17 in *Miranda*?

3. Discussion of headnote 17 begins in the opinion on what page number in the *Supreme Court Reporter*?

4. Using the star pagination system in *Miranda* as it appears in the *Supreme Court Reporter*, determine the first word on page 468 in the *United States Reports*.

5. Which Justice delivered the (majority) opinion of the Court?

6. Using volume 700 of the *Federal Reporter, Second Series*, give the complete citation for the case beginning on page 1033.

7. How many cases were decided by the Fourth Circuit Court of Appeals in that same volume?

8. Using volume 600 of the *Federal Supplement*, give the complete citation for the case in which the defendant is named "Hutson."

9. Using that same volume, on what page is there a case that construes Rule 39 of the Federal Rules of Appellate Procedure?

10. Using volume 673 of the *Federal Reporter, Second Series*, how many judges heard the case beginning on page 984?

11. What was the disposition of the court in that case?

12. Was the decision unanimous?

ANSWERS TO TEST YOUR KNOWLEDGE QUESTIONS

1. False
2. False
3. True
4. False
5. True
6. True
7. True
8. False
9. Procedural posture, statement of facts, statement of issue(s), holding, legal reasoning for each holding, and disposition.
10. Atlantic, Northeastern, Northwestern, Pacific, Southern, Southeastern, and Southwestern.
11. *Federal Supplement*
12. *Federal Reporter*
13. e
14. a
15. d

CHAPTER 4

TEST YOUR KNOWLEDGE QUESTIONS

1. All digests follow West's topic and key number system. T ___ /F ___

2. The most commonly used method for locating a particular topic and key number is the descriptive-word index. T ___ /F ___

3. The most current volumes of the American Digest system are always called the "General Digest." T ___ /F ___

4. Few states have their own state-specific digest. T ___ /F ___

5. All seven regional reporters have a regional digest. T ___ /F ___

6. For states that do not have a state-specific digest, the legal researcher must use a regional digest or the American Digest system to find state cases. T ___ /F ___

7. The American Law Reports series covers only state cases. T ___ /F ___

8. A.L.R. annotations constitute primary authority. T ___ /F ___

9. The only method of locating A.L.R. annotations is through *A.L.R. Digest*. T ___ /F ___

10. *Words and Phrases* is consulted mainly for case authority in which a word or phrase is interpreted or defined. T ___ /F ___

11. Digests may be updated by:

    a. pocket parts
    b. separate pamphlets
    c. volume replacement
    d. a combination of any of the above
    e. none of the above

12. United States Supreme Court cases *cannot* be found in which of the following digests?

    a. *United States Supreme Court Digest, West*
    b. *United States Supreme Court Digest, Lawyers Cooperative*
    c. any federal digest
    d. *A.L.R. Digest*
    e. any state digest

13. Which of the following is *not* a standard component volume in a West digest set?

    a. Popular Names Table
    b. Table of Cases
    c. Defendant/Plaintiff Table
    d. Words and Phrases
    e. Descriptive-Word Index

14. Annotations in the current A.L.R. series contain all but which of the following components:

    a. Total Client-Service Library References
    b. Table of Jurisdictions Reported
    c. Table of Cases Arranged Chronologically
    d. An index
    e. A scope note

15. A.L.R. series are updated by:

    a. separate pamphlets
    b. pocket parts
    c. volume replacement
    d. all of the above
    e. none of the above

16. West reporters are more _____ in their reporting of cases, and Lawyers Cooperative's A.L.R. series is more _____ in its coverage.

17. *Bankruptcy Digest* and *Social Security Digest* are examples of _____ digests.

18. The American Digest system begins with the _____.

19. A.L.R. _____ are extensively footnoted articles written by experts on particular legal issues of current interest.

20. _____ is a series of books that helps locate cases that have defined or interpreted particular words or phrases.

LEGAL RESEARCH EXERCISES

Group A

Citation Instructions: Cite all cases as if they were to appear in a document to be submitted to a court in the state in which the case was decided. (Consult The Bluebook.)

1. Using the Words and Phrases volume for *F.P.D.3d*, cite the first case listed that defines "compete."

2. Using the appropriate volume(s) of *F.P.D.3d*, cite the cases below and give the topic and key number listed first in the Table of Cases volume.

    a. *Yabsley v. Conover*
    b. Defendant is named "Dile"

3. Is the use of a flashlight from outside to look into the interior of an automobile an unlawful search under the Fourth Amendment? Use the *Tenth Decennial Digest* to find an Alabama case. Provide the topic and key number and the case citation for that case.

4. Our client claims she was mistaken about whether her shotgun was capable of causing death. Is this a good defense based upon mistake of fact? Use the *Tenth Decennial Digest* to find a Texas case. Provide the topic and key number and the case citation for that case.

5. Our client was personally served with a summons in a divorce while he was present in the state only to attend his parents' fiftieth wedding anniversary celebration. Does personal service under such circumstances grant the court personal jurisdiction over him in this matter? Use the *Tenth Decennial Digest* to find an Illinois case. Provide the topic and key number and the case citation for that case.

6. Our client retained an attorney whose fee is contingent upon success in the lawsuit. The attorney will receive fifty percent of anything that is recovered plus costs. Does the court have the authority to monitor such a fee arrangement? Find a case using *F.P.D.3d*. Provide the topic and key number and the case citation for that case.

7. Is a regional telephone company's decision to exclude adult entertainment companies from its 976 network discrimination in telecommunications? Find a case using *F.P.D. 4th*. Provide the topic and key number and the case citation for that case.

8. Provide the complete citation for the annotation in volume 4 of *A.L.R. 4th* that begins on page 380.

9. Cite the case whose text is printed in full immediately preceding the annotation.

10. To which section(s) of the *Am. Jur. 2d* article *Public Officers & Employees* could you turn to find related material?

11. Are any Texas cases cited in this annotation? If so, state the name of the first one found in the annotation.

12. State the name of the case, other than *Doris*, that involved a ten-mile residency limitation.

13. Is there a New York case cited in the pocket part concerning any section of the annotation? If so, state the name of the case.

14. In section 1(b), find a related A.L.R. annotation regarding mandatory retirement.

15. In section 2, determine whether residency requirements generally have been upheld by courts.

16. Using the *A.L.R. Index*, find the citation of an article in *A.L.R. 4th* concerning waterfront property owners who share a cove.

17. Using the *A.L.R. Index*, find the citation (including the section number, if any) of an article in any A.L.R. series relating to whether engravings can be copyrighted.

18. Using *Words and Phrases*, cite the case that defines or interprets "last in time."

Group B

Citation Instructions: Cite all cases as if they were to appear in a document to be submitted to a court in the state in which the case was decided. (Consult The Bluebook.*)*

1. Using the Words and Phrases volume for *F.P.D.3d*, cite the first case listed that defines "rifle."

2. Using the appropriate volume(s) of *F.P.D.3d*, cite the cases below and give the topic and key number listed first in the Table of Cases volume.

    a. *Buddle v. Heublein, Inc.*
    b. Defendant is named "Trepel"

3. Is there an alternate method for calculation of arbitrators' fees other than by the basis of actual time worked? Use the *Tenth Decennial Digest* to find a Rhode Island case. Provide the topic and key number and the case citation for that case.

4. Our client is a spectator at a high school football game who was injured when a player ran into him on the sidelines. Can he recover against the school board on the theory of public nuisance? Use the *Atlantic Digest 2d* to find a Connecticut case decided after 1985. Provide the topic and key number and the case citation for that case.

5. Our client purchased a baseball jacket from a reputable sportswear company. He put it on, doused it with gasoline, and set it on fire. Will he win if he sues the manufacturer of the jacket for his injuries on a product liability claim? Find a Pennsylvania case decided after 1985 using the *Atlantic Digest 2d*. Provide the topic and key number and the case citation for that case.

6. Our client works for a company whose allowable retirement age is fifty-seven. Will she receive higher pension funds if she waits until she is sixty to apply? Find a case using *F.P.D.3d*. Provide the topic and key number and the case citation for that case.

7. Is medical necessity a valid defense to conviction of possession of marijuana or other drugs on the ground that it alleviated our client's glaucoma condition? Find a case using *F.P.D. 4th*. Provide the topic and key number and the case citation for that case.

8. Provide the complete citation for the A.L.R. annotation in volume 5 of *A.L.R. 4th* that begins on page 311.

9. Cite the case whose text is printed in full immediately preceding the annotation.

10. To which section(s) of the *Am. Jur. 2d* article *Restitution & Implied Contracts* could you turn to find related material?

11. Are any New Jersey cases cited in this annotation? If so, state the name of the first one found in the annotation.

12. State the name of the case involving an advertised special cited in this annotation.

13. Is there a New Hampshire case cited in the pocket part concerning any section of the annotation? If so, state the name of the case.

14. In section 2(a), determine whether the owner of a vehicle generally has been held liable where work on the vehicle was found to be authorized without any express agreement respecting the price.

15. In section 2(b), what does the author suggest that counsel for the owner of a motor vehicle on which allegedly unauthorized repairs were performed should consider whether or not to seek?

16. Using the *A.L.R. Index*, find the citation of an article in *A.L.R. 4th* concerning the liability of livestock sellers for the sale of animals infected with brucellosis.

17. Using the *A.L.R. Index*, find the citation (including the section number, if any) of an article in any A.L.R. series relating to National Flood Insurance risks for balconies.

18. Using *Words and Phrases*, find a case that defines or interprets "public bathing or swimming place."

Group C

Citation Instructions: Cite all cases as if they were to appear in a document to be submitted to a court in the state in which the case was decided. (Consult The Bluebook.)

1. Using the Words and Phrases volume for *F.P.D.3d*, cite the first case listed that defines "pirated."

2. Using the appropriate volume(s) of *F.P.D.3d*, cite the cases below and give the topic and key number listed first in the Table of Cases volume.

   a. *Culbreth v. Simone,*
   b. Defendant is named "Yockey"

3. Is "spot zoning" illegal where it is in the public interest and not solely for the benefit of the petitioning property owner? Use the *Tenth Decennial Digest* to find a Wisconsin case. Provide the topic and key number and the case citation for that case.

4. Our client did not notice a police squad car parked on the shoulder of the road. Is his failure evidence of unsafe operation of a vehicle for failure to maintain a proper lookout? Use the *Northwestern Digest 2d* to find a Minnesota case decided after 1981. Provide the topic and key number and the case citation for that case.

5. Our client is the mother of a healthy, able-bodied nineteen-year-old. Is she generally obligated to pay support for this child? Use the *Northwestern Digest 2d* to find an Iowa case decided after 1985. Provide the topic and key number and the case citation for that case.

6. Our client is a prisoner in a county jail. She complains that the food is often served cold and sometimes has foreign objects in it. Does this amount to constitutional deprivation? Find a case using *F.P.D.3d*. Provide the topic and key number and the case citation for that case.

7. Is it a good defense that a defendant witness was not warned of consequences of perjury before a grand jury? Find a case using *F.P.D. 4th*. Provide the topic and key number and the case citation for that case.

8. Provide the compete citation for the A.L.R. annotation in volume 1 of *A.L.R. 4th* that begins on page 251.

9. Cite the case whose text is printed in full immediately preceding the annotation.

10. To which section(s) of the *Am. Jur. 2d* article *Products Liability* could you turn to find related material?

11. Are there any Nebraska cases cited in this annotation? If so, state the name of the first one found in the annotation.

12. State the name of the case involving a hula skirt cited in this annotation.

13. Is there a Minnesota case cited in the pocket part concerning any section of the annotation? If so, state the name of the case.

14. In section 2(a), find the name of a federal statute or act.

15. In section 2(b), find another A.L.R. reference regarding a question of jurisdiction over a defendant.

16. Using the *A.L.R. Index*, find the cite of an article in *A.L.R. 4th* concerning the applicability of sales taxes to videotapes and videocassette recorders (VCRs).

17. Using the *A.L.R. Index*, find the citation (including the section number, if any) of an article in any A.L.R. series relating to vermin and prisoners' rights.

18. Using *Words and Phrases*, cite a case that defines or interprets "termination of benefits."

Group D

Citation Instructions: Cite all cases as if they were to appear in a document to be submitted to a court in the state in which the case was decided. (Consult The Bluebook.*)*

1. Using the Words and Phrases volume for *F.P.D.3d*, cite the first case listed that defines "jack."

2. Using the appropriate volume(s) of *F.P.D.3d*, cite the cases below and give the topic and key number listed first in the Table of Cases volume.

   a. *Gorelick v. State of Texas*
   b. Defendant is named "Meagan"

3. Can a child of tender years be guilty of contributory negligence? Use the *Tenth Decennial Digest* to find an Oklahoma case. Provide the topic and key number and the case citation for that case.

4. Our client is the father of a child who was born out of wedlock but was later legitimated. Does he have an obligation to support that child? Find a California case decided after 1971 using *Pacific Digest*. Provide the topic and key number and the case citation for that case.

5. Our client is an employee who was injured on her lunch hour while in the company parking lot. Can her employer properly deny her workers' compensation benefits on the basis that she was away from the workplace? Find a case from Oregon decided after 1981 using *Pacific Digest*. Provide the topic and key number and the case citation for that case.

6. Our client is the lessor of property seized temporarily under eminent domain. Is he a person entitled to compensation where the taking ended before the leasehold expired? Find a case using *F.P.D.3d*. Provide the topic and key number and the case citation for that case.

7. Should inmates confined for more than ninety days be allowed recreation and exercise outside their cells for at least five hours per week? Find a case using *F.P.D. 4th*. Provide the topic and key number and the case citation for that case.

8. Provide the complete citation for the A.L.R. annotation in volume 2 of *A.L.R. 4th* that begins on page 704.

9. Cite the case whose text is printed in full immediately preceding the annotation.

10. To which section(s) of the *Am. Jur. 2d* article *Criminal Law* could you turn to find related material?

11. Are there any Colorado cases cited in this annotation? If so, state the name of the first one found in the annotation.

12. State the name of the case involving driving without a license cited in this annotation.

13. Is there an Arizona case cited in the pocket part concerning any section of the annotation? If so, state the name of the case.

14. In section 2(a), determine whether a person accused of a crime traditionally has been held to be entitled to take pretrial depositions of witnesses.

15. In section 2(b), find another A.L.R. reference regarding the right of an accused to discovery.

16. Using the *A.L.R. Index*, find the citation of an article in *A.L.R. 4th* concerning the property tax exemption of nursery schools.

17. Using the *A.L.R. Index*, find the citation (including the section number, if any) of an article in any A.L.R. series relating to the voting eligibility of employees absent due to malaria.

18. Using *Words and Phrases*, cite the case that defines or interprets "forcible restraint."

Group E

Citation Instructions: Cite all cases as if they were to appear in a document to be submitted to a court in the state in which the case was decided. (Consult The Bluebook.*)*

1. Using the Words and Phrases volume for *F.P.D.3d*, cite the first case listed that defines "film."

2. Using the appropriate volume(s) of *F.P.D.3d*, cite the case indicated and give the topic and key number listed first in the Table of Cases volume.

   a. *Peth v. Breitzmann*
   b. Defendant is named "Ink"

3. Would particular immoral conduct by itself be sufficient grounds to deny a parent custody of a minor child? Use the *Tenth Decennial Digest* to find a South Carolina case. Provide the topic and key number and the case citation for that case.

4. Our client is the mother of an illegitimate child whose brother was awarded guardianship of her minor child by the court. Can the mother remain as natural guardian under such circumstances? Find a Georgia case decided after 1985 using the *Southeastern Digest 2d*. Provide the topic and key number and the case citation for that case.

5. Under common law do defamatory words that are actionable per se include those which impute that a person is infected with some contagious disease, which if true would exclude that person from society? Find a Virginia case decided after 1981 using the *Southeastern Digest 2d*. Provide the topic and key number and the case citation for that case.

6. Our client is a corporation that has failed to hold an annual meeting of its shareholders for well over a year. Does such failure deprive the corporation's management of its authority to run the corporation? Find a circuit court case using *F.P.D.3d*. Provide the topic and key number and the case citation for that case.

7. Do video games qualify as "audiovisual work" for copyright protection? Find a case using *F.P.D. 4th*. Provide the topic and key number and the case citation for that case.

8. Provide the complete citation for the A.L.R. annotation in volume 3 of *A.L.R. 4th* that begins on page 13.

9. Cite the case whose text is printed in full immediately preceding the annotation.

10. To which section(s) of the *Am. Jur. 2d* article *Marriage* could you turn to find related material?

11. Are there any North Carolina cases cited in this annotation? If so, state the name of the first one found in the annotation.

12. State the name of the case involving the division of a grocery business cited in this annotation.

13. Is there a West Virginia case cited in the pocket part concerning any section of the annotation? If so, state the name of the case.

14. In section 2(a), determine whether the rights of cohabitants to share property have ever been decided by statute.

15. In section 2(b), determine whether it is advisable to draw up a property agreement to determine the rights of nonmarital cohabitants?

16. Using the *A.L.R. Index*, find the citation of an article in *A.L.R. 4th* concerning the courts' power to order withdrawal of life support.

17. Using the *A.L.R. Index*, find the citation (including the section number, if any) of an article in any A.L.R. series relating to kitchen privileges and prisoners' rights.

18. Using *Words and Phrases*, cite the case that defines or interprets "de jure functional."

ANSWERS TO TEST YOUR KNOWLEDGE QUESTIONS

1. False
2. True
3. True
4. False
5. False
6. True
7. False
8. False
9. False
10. True
11. d
12. e
13. a
14. c
15. b
16. comprehensive, selective
17. specialty
18. *Century Digest*
19. annotations
20. *Words and Phrases*

CHAPTER 5

TEST YOUR KNOWLEDGE QUESTIONS

1. All legal source materials are easily categorized as either purely primary or secondary in nature. T___ /F___

2. Most legal encyclopedias have both a general index and more specific volume indexes. T___ /F___

3. Legal encyclopedias are not law but rather merely a discussion of the law. T___ /F___

4. Treatises are texts written by legal experts on particular legal topics. T___ /F___

5. Some treatises are considered primary authority. T___ /F___

6. The Restatements of the Law are written by committees. T___ /F___

7. In the most recent series, Restatement principles are simply summaries of existing rules of law. T___ /F___

8. Continuing legal education materials are never appropriate for use in legal research. T___ /F___

9. All treatises are updated by pocket parts. T___ /F___

10. *Corpus Juris* has been superseded by *Corpus Juris Secundum* as West's national legal encyclopedia. T___ /F___

11. Which of the following types of articles may be found in legal periodicals?

    a. articles written by legal experts

    b. comments or notes written by law students

    c. case notes written by law students

    d. book reviews written by law professors

    e. all of the above

12. Which of the following is *not* a usual method for accessing information in a legal encyclopedia?

    a. volume index
    b. general index
    c. Table of Cases
    d. Table of Statutes, Rules, and Regulations Cited
    e. topic outline

13. Which of the following statements about the *Restatements of the Law* is *not* true?

   a. Restatements are considered primary authority in some courts.
   b. Restatements contain citations to cases that have cited the Restatements.
   c. The comments in the Restatements explain the rationale for the rule.
   d. The illustrations in the Restatements show examples of how the principle works.
   e. Each chapter in a Restatement is divided into topics and subtopics.

14. Legal encyclopedias can be classified as national, state, or _____.

15. West Publishing Company publishes single-volume treatises called _____.

LEGAL RESEARCH EXERCISES

Group A

1. Does a college have the legal authority to forbid membership in Greek-letter fraternities or other secret societies? Use *Am. Jur. 2d* to find an answer and provide the citation to *Am. Jur. 2d*.

2. Is it possible in a community property state for one spouse to be held entitled to a share of community property acquired in a community property state by the other spouse without ever having entered the state? Use *Am. Jur. 2d* to find an answer and provide the citation to *Am. Jur. 2d*.

3. Does the mere inability to read or write raise a presumption of undue influence in a signed contract? Use *C.J.S.* to find an answer and provide the citation to *C.J.S.*

4. Can a state under its police power require the owner or operator of a motor vehicle to obtain a special permit before operating the vehicle as a private carrier? Use *C.J.S.* to find an answer and provide the citation to *C.J.S.*

5. May a bank generally certify and accept for payment a postdated check? Use either *Am. Jur. 2d* or *C.J.S.* to find an answer and provide the encyclopedic citation.

6. Can a state legislature enact a law requiring prospective veterinarians to pass an examination? Consult the topical outline for the topic "Veterinarians" in *Am. Jur. 2d* to find an answer and provide the citation to *Am. Jur. 2d*.

7. Consult the volume index for the topic "Accord & Satisfaction" in *C.J.S.* and find the section that discusses the admissibility of evidence of fraud. Give that section citation.

8. According to the black letter rule in that section, where accord and satisfaction is an issue, is evidence of fraud admissible if it tends to prove the point?

9. Does this section refer to a related West topic and key number? If so, provide them.

10. Using the *Am. Jur. 2d Deskbook*, find what the closing date is for voter registration before the general election in Florida and provide the item in which the answer was found.

Group B

1. Under the common law, are communications between a client and her accountant privileged? Use *Am. Jur. 2d* to find an answer and provide the citation to *Am. Jur. 2d*.

2. Can a public officer claim a reward for the performance of a service that it was the officer's duty to discharge? Use *Am. Jur. 2d* to find an answer and provide the citation to *Am. Jur. 2d*.

3. Is a shipper of goods by water liable for damages to cargo resulting from unreasonable delay in either the commencement or completion of the voyage? Use *C.J.S.* to find an answer and provide the citation to *C.J.S.*

4. Is it an offense to mail obscene matter via the United States Postal Service? Use *C.J.S.* to find an answer and provide the citation to *C.J.S.*

5. May a will executed by an insane person (lunatic) be considered valid if made during a "lucid interval"? Use either *Am. Jur. 2d* or *C.J.S.* to find an answer and provide the encyclopedic citation.

6. May a right to the use of water for irrigation purposes be lost by disuse or abandonment? Consult the topical outline for the topic "Irrigation" in *Am. Jur. 2d* for an answer and provide the citation to *Am. Jur. 2d*.

7. Consult the volume index for the topic "Officers & Public Employees" in *C.J.S.* and find the section that discusses grounds for impeachment. Give that section citation.

8. According to the black letter rule in that section, is proper cause for impeachment restricted solely to something of a substantial nature directly affecting the rights and interests of the public?

9. Does this section refer to a related West topic and key number? If so, provide them.

10. Using the *Am. Jur. 2d Deskbook*, determine the maximum first-party funeral benefits available under New Jersey's no-fault motor vehicle law. Provide the amount of benefits and the item in which the answer was found.

Group C

1. In order to name a beneficiary under a policy of life insurance through a fraternal order, is it necessary that the beneficiary have an "insurable interest" in the life of the insured? Use *Am. Jur. 2d* to find an answer and provide the citation to *Am. Jur. 2d*.

2. Does the fact that parties to an alleged common law marriage later go through a marriage ceremony automatically mean that the parties were not considered lawfully married before the ceremonial marriage? Use *Am. Jur. 2d* to find an answer and provide the citation to *Am. Jur. 2d*.

3. Must zoning regulations restricting where gasoline filling stations may be located be reasonable and not arbitrary? Use *C.J.S.* to find an answer and provide the citation to *C.J.S.*

4. Does a state legislature generally have the power to regulate bakeries? Use *C.J.S.* to find an answer and provide the citation to *C.J.S.*

5. Can a person have a property right, subject to the police power of the state, in an animal such as a cat? Use either *Am. Jur. 2d* or *C.J.S.* to find an answer and provide the encyclopedic citation.

6. Is it generally essential to the validity of an arrest warrant that the person to be arrested be identified clearly? Consult the topical outline for the topic "Arrest" in *Am. Jur. 2d* to find an answer and provide the citation to *Am. Jur. 2d.*

7. Consult the volume index to the topic "Justices of the Peace" in *C.J.S.* and find the section that discusses resignation. Give that section citation.

8. According to the black letter rule in that section, can the resignation of a justice of the peace be withdrawn once it has been accepted by the proper official?

9. Does this section refer to a related West topic and key number? If so, provide them.

10. Using the *Am. Jur. 2d Deskbook*, find the statute of limitations for libel in Nebraska. Provide the number of year(s) and the item in which the answer was found.

Group D

1. Will ignorance of the contents of a written contract ordinarily affect the liability of the party who signs it? Use *Am. Jur. 2d* to find an answer and provide the citation to *Am. Jur. 2d.*

2. Does a convict have a right to be represented by counsel at the hearings of a parole board for the purpose of determining the convict's eligibility for parole? Use *Am. Jur. 2d* to find an answer and provide the citation to *Am. Jur. 2d.*

3. Is a carrier liable for injuries occurring where a passenger steps on a foreign object as long as the carrier is neither negligent nor made aware of the object? Use *C.J.S.* to find an answer and provide the citation to *C.J.S.*

4. Is a note payable on the happening of an uncertain event, without other consideration, valid as a wager? Use *C.J.S.* to find an answer and provide the citation to *C.J.S.*

5. If a state statute concerning adoption provides only for the adoption of "minors," may one adult adopt another adult? Use either *Am. Jur. 2d* or *C.J.S.* to find an answer and provide the encyclopedic citation.

6. Under the common law rule, could burglary be committed only at night? Consult the topical outline for the topic "Burglary" in *Am. Jur. 2d* to find an answer and provide the citation to *Am. Jur. 2d.*

7. Consult the volume index to the topic "International Law" in *C.J.S.* and find the section that discusses fish and game on the high seas. Give that section citation.

8. According to the black letter rule in that section, may a nation assert jurisdiction beyond its international waters for the purposes of fisheries management?

9. Does this section refer to a West related topic and key number? If so, provide them.

10. Using the *Am. Jur. 2d Deskbook*, find out for what age children child restraints are mandatory in California. Provide that age and the item in which the answer was found.

Group E

1. Do persons who enter the military service thereby lose the domicile they had before entering the service? Use *Am. Jur. 2d* to find an answer and provide the citation to *Am. Jur. 2d.*

2. Is a minor generally held to be liable for injuries caused by his own negligence? Use *Am. Jur. 2d* to find an answer and provide the citation to *Am. Jur. 2d.*

3. Is a gift for the maintenance of a burial ground considered to be for a charitable use? Use *C.J.S.* to find an answer and provide the citation to *C.J.S.*

4. Is the federal government obligated to provide its indigent prisoners with paper and pen to draft legal documents and stamps to mail them? Use *C.J.S.* to find an answer and provide the citation to *C.J.S.*

5. Can an alien be excluded from the United States (i.e., denied admission) after committing a crime involving "moral turpitude"? Use either *Am. Jur. 2d* or *C.J.S.* to find an answer and provide the encyclopedic citation.

6. Is it a crime under federal law to alter, counterfeit, or forge a patent? Consult the topical outline for the topic "Patents" in *Am. Jur. 2d* to find an answer and provide the citation to *Am. Jur. 2d.*

7. Consult the volume index for the topic "Canals" in *C.J.S.* and find the section that discusses state tort liability for negligence in the maintenance or construction of culverts. Give that section citation.

8. According to the black letter rule in that section, are states liable for damages resulting from construction and maintenance of canals if they do not expressly assume such liability?

9. Does this section refer to a related West topic and key number? If so, provide them.

10. Using the *Am. Jur. 2d Deskbook*, determine the minimum age a person must be in Virginia before the death penalty can be imposed. Provide that age and the item in which the answer was found.

ANSWERS TO TEST YOUR KNOWLEDGE QUESTIONS

1. False
2. True
3. True
4. True
5. False
6. True
7. False
8. False
9. False
10. True
11. e
12. c
13. a
14. specialty
15. hornbooks

CHAPTER 6

TEST YOUR KNOWLEDGE QUESTIONS

1. Treatises and looseleaf services are basically the same except that looseleaf services are updated more frequently. T___ /F___

2. Looseleaf services do not use page references. T___ /F___

3. Looseleaf services often have more than one index. T___ /F___

4. Both uniform and model codes are secondary authority. T___ /F___

5. Opinions of the United States Attorney General are primary authority in federal court. T___ /F___

6. Federal legislation is usually begun with the introduction of a _____ in the House or Senate.

7. Preliminary action on federal legislation takes place in _____.

8. A congressional committee may commission a study about proposed legislation called a _____.

9. The original text of a federal bill or resolution can be located at a United States _____ library.

10. A congressional committee studying a bill may hold a _____ on it, inviting testimony from government officials, experts, scholars, and concerned citizens on the merits of the proposed legislation.

11. Which of the following would a typical looseleaf service *not* include?

    a. actual text of any statutes or regulations relevant to the subject covered by the looseleaf service
    b. legislative history for each statute covered
    c. actual text of relevant cases and administrative decisions
    d. explanatory text that helps the reader understand the area of law
    e. extensive and varied indexes

12. Which of the following sources would *not* be useful in constructing a federal legislative history?

    a. *CIS/Index*
    b. *United States Code Congressional and Administrative News*
    c. *Congressional Record*
    d. *CCH Congressional Index*
    e. *Uniform Laws Annotated*

13. Which of the following is *not* a section in each issue of the *Congressional Record*?

    a. Proclamations of the President
    b. Proceedings of the House
    c. Proceedings of the Senate
    d. Extensions of Remarks
    e. Daily Digest

14. Which of the following materials generally contain some primary authority sources?

    a. model codes
    b. uniform codes
    c. United States Attorney General opinions
    d. state attorney general opinions
    e. looseleaf services

15. Which of the following is *not* an acceptable method for introducing federal legislation?

    a. bill
    b. committee report
    c. joint resolution
    d. concurrent resolution
    e. simple resolution

LEGAL RESEARCH EXERCISES

Group A

1. Using the *Uniform Laws Annotated*, determine when a gift of all or part of the body under the Uniform Anatomical Gifts Act when made by will is effective. Provide a citation.

2. Has New York state adopted the Uniform Anatomical Gifts Act? If so, indicate the statutory citation and effective date.

3. Using the *Opinions of the Office of Legal Counsel* for 1992, find an opinion of the United States Attorney General concerning whether the Federal Bureau of Prisons has statutory authority to contract with the private sector for secure facilities. What was the conclusion of the Office of Legal Counsel? Does the Bureau of Prisons have such authority? Provide a citation and the date of the opinion.

4. Using the BNA *Environment Reporter*, find a 1988 case concerning whether environmental groups and humane societies have standing to challenge Department of the Interior rules under the Endangered Species Act. Provide a case citation.

5. Using the CCH *Labor Law Reporter* Topical Index, find a paragraph (¶) reference concerning a union's demand for arbitration of certain claims by employees for vacation pay allegedly owed to them under a collective bargaining agreement.

6. Using the 1993–94 CCH *Congressional Index*, determine which representative(s) sponsored House Bill 3471. On what date was H.3471 introduced? When did it pass the Senate?

7. Using the 1993–94 CCH *Congressional Index*, determine which Senate Bill concerned assistance grants to Native Americans (Indians) for the protection of the environment. Which senator(s) sponsored the bill? Was the bill enacted into law? If so, when?

8. Using the *CIS 1992 Annual: Legislative Histories*, find the legislative history for Public Law 102-274. What is the name of the act? What is its citation in the *Statutes at Large*? What was the date of its enactment? Were there any reports on this statute? Was there any debate on it? Were any hearings held on it? If so, what was the date of the first hearing?

9. Using the *CIS 1992 Annual: Index*, find the *CIS* abstract number for a government publication concerning the extension and review of a program for the temporary care of handicapped children.

10. Locate that abstract in *CIS 1992 Annual: Abstracts*. What is the title of the document abstracted? What committee or subcommittee held the hearing? On what date was the hearing held?

11. Using the *United States Code Congressional and Administrative News* volumes for 1992, find the legislative history for the Fertility Clinics Success Rate and Certification Act of 1992. What are the date and number of the Senate report on that statute?

12. Using the Tables in *USCCAN* volumes for 1992, find the date of enactment and public law number for the Education of the Deaf Act Amendments of 1992.

Group B

1. Using the *Uniform Laws Annotated*, determine the maximum amount of security deposit a landlord may demand from a tenant under the Uniform Residential Landlord and Tenant Act. Provide a citation.

2. Has Rhode Island adopted the Uniform Residential Landlord and Tenant Act? If so, indicate the statutory citation and effective date.

3. Using the *Opinions of the Office of Legal Counsel* for 1992, find an opinion of the United States Attorney General concerning whether federal law prevents a state or local law enforcement agency from transferring to other state or local agencies forfeited property that has been transferred from the federal government, where the other agency intends to use the property for purposes not directly related to law enforcement. What was the conclusion of the Office of Legal Counsel? Is such a transfer authorized? Provide a citation and the date of the opinion.

4. Using the BNA *Media Law Reporter*, find a 1976 case concerning whether the Federal Bureau of Prisons' policy prohibiting interviews by news media of specifically named inmates of a maximum-security prison violated the First Amendment. Provide a case citation.

5. Using the CCH *Medicare and Medicaid Guide* Topical Index, find a paragraph (¶) reference to provisions of the Indian Health Care Improvement Act of 1976 that affect Medicare and Medicaid.

6. Using the 1993–94 CCH *Congressional Index*, determine which representative(s) sponsored House Bill 3514. When was H.3514 introduced? When did it pass the Senate?

7. Using the 1993–94 CCH *Congressional Index*, determine which Senate Bill concerned the exchange of lands for schools within Utah. Which senator(s) sponsored the bill? Was the bill enacted into law? If so, when?

8. Using the *CIS 1992 Annual: Legislative Histories*, find the legislative history for Public Law 102-346. What is the name of the act? What is its citation in the *Statutes at Large*? What was the date of its enactment? Were there any reports on this statute? Was there any debate on it? Were any hearings held on it? If so, what was the date of the first hearing?

9. Using the *CIS 1992 Annual: Index*, find the *CIS* abstract number for a government publication concerning regulatory proposals for political advertising on television and radio.

10. Locate that abstract number in *CIS 1992 Annual: Abstracts*. What is the title of the document abstracted? What committee or subcommittee held the hearing? On what date was the hearing held?

11. Using the *United States Code Congressional and Administrative News* volumes for 1992, find the legislative history for the Alzheimer's Disease Research, Training, and Education Amendment of 1992. What are the date and number of the Senate report on that statute?

12. Using the Tables in the *USCCAN* volumes for 1992, find the date of enactment and public law number for the Veterans Health Care Act of 1992.

Group C

1. Using the *Uniform Laws Annotated*, determine the time limit for application to modify or correct an award under the Uniform Arbitration Act. Provide a citation.

2. Has Nebraska adopted the Uniform Arbitration Act? If so, indicate the statutory citation and effective date.

3. Using the *Opinions of the Office of Legal Counsel* for 1992, find an opinion of the United States Attorney General concerning whether the Department of Defense may make $5 million available to the Director of the National Science Foundation to support the activities of the Continuing Technologies Institute. What was the conclusion of the Office of Legal Counsel? May the Department of Defense make those monies available for funding the activities of the Institute? Provide a citation and the date of the opinion.

4. Using the BNA *Criminal Law Reporter*, find a 1991 case concerning whether treatment-by-prayer is a valid defense to child abuse. Provide a case citation.

5. Using the CCH *Bankruptcy Law Reporter* Topical Index, find a paragraph (¶) reference concerning whether usurious loans are considered fraudulent conveyances.

6. Using the 1993–94 CCH *Congressional Index*, determine which representative(s) sponsored House Joint Resolution 159. When was H.J.R. 159 introduced? When did it pass the Senate?

7. Using the 1993–94 CCH *Congressional Index*, determine which Senate Bill concerned the amendment of the National Trails System Act to provide for a study of El Camino Real de Tierra Adentro. Which senator(s) sponsored that bill? Was the bill enacted into law? If so, when?

8. Using the *CIS 1992 Annual: Legislative Histories*, find the legislative history for Public Law 102-366. What is the name of the act? What is its citation in the *Statutes at Large*? What was its date of enactment? Were there any reports on the statute? Was there any debate on it? Were there any hearings held on it? If so, when was the first hearing?

9. Using the *CIS 1992 Annual: Index*, find the *CIS* abstract number for a government publication concerning the review of the pricing and marketing process for lamb in the United States.

10. Locate that abstract in the *CIS 1992 Annual: Abstracts*. What is the title of the document abstracted? What committee or subcommittee held the hearing? On what date was the hearing held?

11. Using the *United States Code Congressional and Administrative News* volumes for 1992, find the legislative history for the Veterans Home Loan Program Amendments of 1992. What are the date and number of the Senate report on that statute?

12. Using the *USCCAN* volumes for 1992, find the date of enactment and public law number for the Patent and Plant Variety Protection Remedy Clarification Act.

Group D

1. Using the *Uniform Laws Annotated*, determine who has first priority in authority to consent to withhold or withdraw life-sustaining treatment under the Uniform Rights of the Terminally Ill Act (as revised in 1989). Provide a citation.

2. Has California adopted the Uniform Rights of the Terminally Ill Act (as revised in 1989)? If so, indicate the statutory citation and effective date.

3. Using the *Opinions of the Office of Legal Counsel* for 1992, find an opinion of the United States Attorney General concerning whether the Immigration and Naturalization Service (INS) has legal authority to participate in a computer matching program with the Department of Education involving alien applicants for federal student aid under Title IV of the Higher Education Act of 1965. What was the conclusion of the Office of Legal Counsel? Does the INS have legal authority to participate in the matching program? Provide a citation and the date of the opinion.

4. Using the BNA *Occupational Safety and Health Cases*, find a 1989 case concerning whether the lack of a no-smoking sign and testimony that current employees were smoking in a battery changing area established a violation of a regulation prohibiting smoking in a battery changing area.

5. Using the CCH *Employment Practices Guide* Topical Index, find a paragraph (¶) reference concerning a case involving a woman television news anchor's sex discrimination claim based on a dress code.

6. Using the 1993–94 CCH *Congressional Index*, determine which representative(s) House Joint Resolution 272. When was H.J.R. 272 introduced? When did it pass the Senate?

7. Using the 1993–94 CCH *Congressional Index*, determine which Senate Bill concerned the amendment of the National Wool Act of 1954 to eliminate and eventually reduce government subsidies for wool and mohair producers. Which senator(s) sponsored that bill? Was the bill enacted into law? If so, when?

8. Using the *CIS 1992 Annual: Legislative Histories*, find the legislative history for Public Law 102-524. What is the name of the act? What is its citation in the *Statutes at Large*? When was its date of enactment? Were there any reports on this statute? Was there any debate on it? Were there any hearings held on it? If so, when was the first hearing?

9. Using the *CIS 1992 Annual: Index*, find the *CIS* abstract number for a government publication concerning the management and royalty valuation issues of coal leasing on federal lands.

10. Locate that abstract in *CIS 1992 Annual: Abstracts*. What is the title of the document abstracted? What committee or subcommittee held the hearing? On what date was the hearing held?

11. Using the *United States Code Congressional and Administrative News* volumes for 1992, find the legislative history for the Child Abuse, Domestic Violence, Adoption and Family Services Act of 1992. What are the date and number of the Senate report on that act?

12. Using the Tables of the *USCCAN* volumes for 1992, find the date of enactment and the public law number for the Housing and Community Development Act of 1992.

Group E

1. Using the *Uniform Laws Annotated*, determine the maximum number of months that a child may be absent from a state for that state to still be able to assume jurisdiction in child custody matters under the Uniform Child Custody Jurisdiction Act. Provide a citation.

2. Has South Carolina adopted the Uniform Child Custody Jurisdiction Act? If so, indicate the statutory citation and effective date.

3. Using the *Opinions of the Office of Legal Counsel* for 1992, find an opinion of the United States Attorney General concerning whether the Congressional Pay Amendment has been duly adopted in accordance with the formal requirements of Article V of the Constitution. What was the conclusion of the Office of Legal Counsel? Was the amendment properly adopted? Provide a citation and the date of the opinion.

4. Using the BNA *Fair Employment Practices*, find a 1990 case concerning whether a man was wrongfully discharged for wearing jewelry on the job where the employer maintained different standards of grooming and appearance for men and women. Provide a case citation.

5. Using the CCH *Aviation Law Reporter* Topical Index, find a paragraph (¶) reference concerning limitations on advertising by pilot schools.

6. Using the 1993–94 CCH *Congressional Index*, determine which representative(s) sponsored House Concurrent Resolution 34. When was H.C.R. 34 introduced? When did it pass the Senate?

7. Using the 1993–94 CCH *Congressional Index*, determine which Senate Joint Resolution concerned the designation of National Historically Black Colleges and Universities Week. Which senator(s) sponsored the resolution? Was the resolution enacted into law? If so, when?

8. Using the *CIS 1992 Annual: Legislative Histories*, find the legislative history for Public Law 102-556. What is the name of the act? What is its citation in the *Statutes at Large*? What was its date of enactment? Were there any reports on this statute? Was there any debate on it? Were there any hearings held on it? If so, when was the first hearing?

9. Using the *CIS 1992 Annual: Index*, find the *CIS* abstract number for a government publication concerning the revision of alien nonimmigrant admission categories for athletes.

10. Locate that abstract in *CIS 1992 Annual: Abstracts*. What is the title of the document abstracted? What committee or subcommittee held the hearing? On what date was the hearing held?

11. Using the *United States Code Congressional and Administrative News* volumes for 1992, find the legislative history for the Cable Television Consumer Protection and Competition Act of 1992. What are the date and number of the Senate report on that act?

12. Using the *USCCAN* volumes for 1992, find the date of enactment and public law number for the Energy Policy Act of 1992.

ANSWERS TO TEST YOUR KNOWLEDGE QUESTIONS

1. False
2. True
3. True
4. True
5. False
6. bill
7. committee
8. committee print
9. depository
10. hearing
11. b
12. e
13. a
14. e
15. b

CHAPTER 7

TEST YOUR KNOWLEDGE QUESTIONS

1. A computer is always the fastest way to perform legal research. T___ /F___

2. The legal researcher should prepare a search query before going on-line. T___ /F___

3. A case can be located by name or title in a database. T___ /F___

4. WESTLAW and LEXIS are identical in their access to secondary authority materials. T___ /F___

5. CD-ROM "libraries" typically include primary and secondary sources on a particular topic. T___ /F___

6. In devising a query or search request for a legal database, the legal researcher should consider which of the following:

   a. synonyms
   b. numerical connectors
   c. grammatical connectors
   d. expanders
   e. all of the above

7. Which of the following is *not* a typical field in WESTLAW or segment in LEXIS?

   a. attorney
   b. citation
   c. court
   d. case history
   e. judge

8. The so-called _____ approach allows the computer to search without connectors or expanders and avoids the necessity to phrase queries according to Boolean logic.

9. If a search turns up either too few or too many documents, the legal researcher may _____ it.

10. What does CD-ROM stand for?

LEXIS TUTORIAL

1. Before going on-line always complete a search strategy of possible queries to use and libraries to consult.

2. Log onto LEXIS. Be sure to follow your school's particular instructions.

3. Decide what library to consult first. In this example, you will be looking for federal cases involving the application of the death penalty to minors; therefore, a logical library to search would be GENFED, which covers all the federal courts. Type in "GENFED" and press <enter>.

4. Next enter your search query and press <enter>. If you retrieve more than a dozen or so cases, try to edit your search query by pressing <M> and <enter> and modifying the original search query.

5. Type "CITE" and press <enter> to display a list of the cases retrieved by your search.

6. Find the United States Supreme Court case from Kentucky and press the number for that case and <enter>.

7. You can read the entire case or review it in KWIC mode by typing ".KW" and pressing <enter>. In this mode, you will see only the pages from the case that contain your search terms surrounded by twenty-five words on either side of the terms.

8. While reading the case, you also may shepardize it by typing ".SH" and pressing <enter>. This will provide you with a list of entries for that case as it would appear in Shepard's.

9. You may change libraries and conduct your search in your own state by typing ".CL" and pressing <enter> and then typing in the two-letter abbreviation for your state and pressing <enter>. You will need to choose a file (such as your state's supreme court cases), then type in that abbreviation and press <enter> again. See how many cases, if any, from your state deal with this same issue.

10. When you have completed your search, sign off by typing ".SO" and pressing <enter>. If you do not wish LEXIS to save your last search query, type <N> and press <enter>.

WESTLAW TUTORIAL

1. Before going on-line always complete a search strategy of possible queries to use and databases to consult.

2. Log onto WESTLAW. Be sure to follow your school's particular instructions.

3. Decide what database to consult first. In this example, you will be looking for cases from all fifty states dealing with the liability of ski resort operators for injuries incurred by skiers at the resort; therefore, a logical database to search would be ALLSTATES, which covers all fifty states. Type in "ALLSTATES" and press <enter>.

4. Next enter your search query and press <enter>. If you retrieve more than a dozen or so cases, try to edit your search query by pressing <Q> and <enter> and modifying the original search query.

5. Press <L> and <enter> to display a list of the cases retrieved by your search.

6. Find the 1985 case from the Colorado Supreme Court and press that number and <enter>.

7. You can read the entire case or review it in TERM mode, which you are in by default. In this mode, you will see only the pages from the case that contain your search terms.

8. While reading the case, you also may shepardize it by typing "SH" and pressing <enter>. This will provide you with a list of entries for that case as it would appear in Shepard's.

9. You may limit your search to your own state by typing in "DB" and pressing <enter> and then typing in the two-letter abbreviation for your state and pressing <enter>. See how many cases, if any, from your state deal with this issue.

10. When you have completed your search, you should sign off by typing "OFF" and pressing <enter>. If you do not wish WESTLAW to save your last search query, type and press <enter>.

LEGAL RESEARCH EXERCISES

Group A

Use either LEXIS or WESTLAW to answer all questions.

1. Could a gay man successfully claim under a domestic partnership ordinance that he was illegally denied funeral leave benefits available to married employees when his long-term same-sex partner died? Find a federal case. What query did you use? Give the citation of the case in proper format.

2. Find a Pennsylvania case entitled *Blue v. Blue* involving a noncustodial parent's obligation to pay for the college expenses of a child who has reached the age of majority. Where did the son work in the summer and fall of 1988? Answer the question by using the LEXSEE command on LEXIS or EZ ACCESS on WESTLAW. Give the citation of the case in proper format.

3. Retrieve *Stanford v. Kentucky* by its official citation: 492 U.S. 361. What are its parallel citations in *Supreme Court Reporter*, in *Lawyers' Edition*, and in *United States Law Week*? What is the title of the companion suit?

4. Browse through that case and complete the following quotation: "And it appears that actual executions for crimes committed under age 18 accounted for only about _____ percent of the total number of executions that occurred between _____ and 1986."

5. Retrieve a 1985 Colorado Supreme Court case entitled *Pizza v. Wolf Creek Ski Development Corp.* Give the citation of that case in proper format.

6. What is the West topic and key number assigned to the first headnote?

7. Browse through that case and complete the following quotation: "On December 5, _____, Pizza suffered severe injuries while skiing down _____, a slope marked 'more difficult' at Wolf Creek Ski area."

8. Find a 1989 United States Supreme Court case concerning the constitutionality of drug testing in the workplace. Give the citation of that case in proper format.

9. Shepardize a 1991 Pennsylvania case entitled *Commonwealth of Pennsylvania v. Chester*, which is reported at 587 A.2d 1367. What is the *Supreme Court Reporter* citation of the denial of certiorari by the United States Supreme Court? What is the *Pennsylvania Reports* citation to a later Pennsylvania Supreme Court case which followed that decision?

Group B

Use either LEXIS or WESTLAW to answer all questions.

1. Would a seminary student for the ministry be entitled to damages if a dorm mascot dog bit her on the nose? Find a federal case. What query did you use? Give the citation of the case in proper format.

2. Find a Pennsylvania case entitled *Blue v. Blue* involving a noncustodial parent's obligation to pay for the college expenses of a child who has reached the age of majority. Where did the son work in the summer and fall of 1988? Answer the question by using the LEXSEE command on LEXIS or EZ ACCESS on WESTLAW. Give the citation of the case in proper format.

3. Retrieve *Stanford v. Kentucky* by its official citation: 492 U.S. 361. What are its parallel citations in *Supreme Court Reporter*, in *Lawyers' Edition*, and in *United States Law Week*? What is the title of the companion suit?

4. Browse through that case and complete the following quotation: "In accordance with the standards of this common-law tradition, at least _____ offenders under the age of 18 have been executed in this country, and at least _____ under the age of 17."

5. Retrieve a 1985 Colorado Supreme Court case entitled *Pizza v. Wolf Creek Ski Development Corp.* Give the citation of that case in proper format.

6. What is the West topic and key number assigned to the first headnote?

7. Browse through that case and complete the following quotation: "Shortly after the accident, Pizza's _____ and _____ were found 20 to 25 feet from the downhill side of the service road."

8. Find a 1993 United States Supreme Court case involving the application of the death penalty on mentally retarded individuals. Give the citation of that case in proper format.

9. Shepardize a 1991 Pennsylvania case entitled *Commonwealth of Pennsylvania v. Chester*, which is reported at 587 A.2d 1367. What is the *Supreme Court Reporter* citation of the denial of certiorari by the United States Supreme Court? What is the *Pennsylvania Reports* citation to a later Pennsylvania Supreme Court case which followed that decision?

Group C

Use either LEXIS or WESTLAW to answer all questions.

1. Does the brother of a quadriplegic (sometimes spelled "quadraplegic") have the right to sue for loss of consortium due to his injured brother's injuries? Find a federal case. What query did you use? Give the citation of the case in proper format.

2. Find a Pennsylvania case entitled *Blue v. Blue* involving a noncustodial parent's obligation to pay for the college expenses of a child who has reached the age of majority. Where did the son work in the summer and fall of 1988? Answer the question by using the LEXSEE command on LEXIS or EZ ACCESS on WESTLAW. Give the citation of the case in proper format.

3. Retrieve *Stanford v. Kentucky* by its official citation: 492 U.S. 361. What are its parallel citations in *Supreme Court Reporter*, in *Lawyers' Edition*, and in *United States Law Week*? What is the title of the companion suit?

4. Browse through that case and complete the following quotation: "Wilkins would have us define juveniles as individuals _____ years of age and under; Stafford would draw the line at _____."

5. Retrieve a 1985 Colorado Supreme Court case entitled *Pizza v. Wolf Creek Ski Development Corp.* Give the citation of that case in proper format.

6. What is the West topic and key number assigned to the first headnote?

7. Browse through that case and complete the following quotation: "Here, it is uncontested that Pizza's injuries occurred upon _____ with the slope after he became _____."

8. Find a 1991 Ninth Circuit Court of Appeals case against the United States Attorney General discussing whether AIDS can be considered a handicap. Give the citation of that case in proper format.

9. Shepardize a 1991 Pennsylvania case entitled *Commonwealth of Pennsylvania v. Chester*, which is reported at 587 A.2d 1367. What is the *Supreme Court Reporter* citation of the denial of certiorari by the United States Supreme Court? What is the *Pennsylvania Reports* citation to a later Pennsylvania Supreme Court case which followed that decision?

Group D

Use either LEXIS or WESTLAW to answer all questions.

1. Was former Beatle George Harrison held liable for copyright infringement for his song "My Sweet Lord"? Find the most recent federal case. What query did you use? Give the citation of the case in proper format.

2. Find a Pennsylvania case entitled *Blue v. Blue* involving a noncustodial parent's obligation to pay for the college expenses of a child who has reached the age of majority. Where did the son work in the summer and fall of 1988? Answer the question by using the LEXSEE command on LEXIS or EZ ACCESS on WESTLAW. Give the citation of the case in proper format.

3. Retrieve *Stanford v. Kentucky* by its official citation: 492 U.S. 361. What are its parallel citations in *Supreme Court Reporter*, in *Lawyers' Edition*, and in *United States Law Week*? What is the title of the companion suit?

4. Browse through that case and complete the following quotation: "Three more States preclude the death penalty for offenders under 17: _____; _____; _____."

5. Retrieve a 1985 Colorado Supreme Court case entitled *Pizza v. Wolf Creek Ski Development Corp.* Give the citation of that case in proper format.

6. What is the West topic and key number assigned to the first headnote?

7. Browse through that case and complete the following quotation: "However, when a skier's injury is unrelated to an operator's _____ of a specific duty, as in this case where the injury involved a variation in _____, the legislature has chosen to create a rebuttable presumption that the skier is solely responsible for the collision."

8. Find a 1992 New Jersey Supreme Court case concerning independent paralegals and the unauthorized practice of law. Give the citation of that case in proper format.

9. Shepardize a 1991 Pennsylvania case entitled *Commonwealth of Pennsylvania v. Chester,* which is reported at 587 A.2d 1367. What is the *Supreme Court Reporter* citation of the denial of certiorari by the United States Supreme Court? What is the *Pennsylvania Reports* citation to a later Pennsylvania Supreme Court case which followed that decision?

Group E

Use either LEXIS or WESTLAW to answer all questions.

1. Can an inmate successfully allege a products liability claim for canned tuna that contained cat food? Find a federal case. What query did you use? Give the citation of the case in proper format.

2. Find a Pennsylvania case entitled *Blue v. Blue* involving a noncustodial parent's obligation to pay for the college expenses of a child who has reached the age of majority. Where did the son work in the summer and fall of 1988? Answer the question by using the LEXSEE command on LEXIS or EZ ACCESS on WESTLAW. Give the citation of the case in proper format.

3. Retrieve *Stanford v. Kentucky* by its official citation: 492 U.S. 361. What are its parallel citations in *Supreme Court Reporter*, in *Lawyers' Edition*, and in *United States Law Week*? What is the title of the companion suit?

4. Browse through that case and complete the following quotation: "It is not the burden of _____ and _____, however, to establish a national consensus approving what their citizens have voted to do."

5. Retrieve a 1985 Colorado Supreme Court case entitled *Pizza v. Wolf Creek Ski Development Corp.* Give the citation of that case in proper format.

6. What is the West topic and key number assigned to the first headnote?

7. Browse through that case and complete the following quotation: "He argues that, by creating a presumption that the skier is responsible for a collision on the slopes, skiers have been arbitrarily and unreasonably treated differently from other individuals such as _____, _____, or _____."

8. Find a 1992 Third Circuit Court of Appeals case from the Virgin Islands concerning the admissibility of videotaped testimony of a minor child at trial. Give the citation of that case in proper format.

9. Shepardize a 1991 Pennsylvania case entitled *Commonwealth of Pennsylvania v. Chester,* which is reported at 587 A.2d 1367. What is the *Supreme Court Reporter* citation of the denial of certiorari by the United States Supreme Court? What is the *Pennsylvania Reports* citation to a later Pennsylvania Supreme Court case which followed that decision?

ANSWERS TO TEST YOUR KNOWLEDGE QUESTIONS

1. False
2. True
3. True
4. False
5. True
6. e
7. d
8. natural language
9. modify
10. Compact Disc with Read Only Memory

CHAPTER 8

TEST YOUR KNOWLEDGE QUESTIONS

1. Shepard's citators usually combine cases and statutes in the same volume. T___ /F___

2. One use of a case citator is to find the direct history of the case. T___ /F___

3. Citators are not cumulative. T___ /F___

4. The superscript number in the citing source refers to the headnote number from the cited source which the citing source mentions. T___ /F___

5. All statutes citators include tables of statutes that have been referred to by a popular name or by a short title. T___ /F___

6. Describe the step-by-step process for using a citator.

7. What are the three main uses of a case citator?

8. When a researcher only needs a parallel citation, one of the quickest methods is to consult the _____.

9. WESTLAW's _____ and LEXIS's _____ are on-line systems that allow the legal researcher to verify a citation or the case history for a case or statute.

10. The process of consulting Shepard's citators has been nicknamed _____.

LEGAL RESEARCH EXERCISES

Group A

Using Shepard's United States Citations: *Case Edition, answer the following questions:*

1. Give the parallel citations for 68 S. Ct. 1148.

2. Has this case ever been cited by a Tenth Circuit Court of Appeals?

3. What headnote from the cited case did the Tenth Circuit court refer to in its opinion?

4. Using *Shepard's United States Supreme Court Case Names Citator*, give the complete citation (i.e., both official *and* unofficial citations) for *Caban v. Mohammed*.

Using Shepard's Federal Citations, *answer the following questions:*

5. State the citation of the A.L.R. annotation that cited 169 F.2d 583.

6. Trace the direct history of 122 F.R.D. 344 and indicate the higher court's decision on appeal.

7. Was that case cited by the Second Circuit Court of Appeals?

8. Was that case cited by a text or periodical? If so, give the title.

9.   What was the higher court's treatment of 800 F. Supp. 1405 on appeal? Give the citation of the citing case.

10. What was the higher court's treatment of 801 F. Supp. 1134 on appeal? Give the citation of the citing case.

11. What was the higher court's treatment of 794 F. Supp. 55 on appeal? Give the citation of the citing case.

12. What was the higher court's treatment of 803 F. Supp. 1215 on appeal? Give the citation of the citing case.

13. Shepardize 725 F. Supp. 936. A connected case is from which state? Give the regional citation for that case.

Using Shepard's United States Citations: Statute Edition, *answer the following questions:*

14. State the citation of the citing opinion that decided whether 18 U.S.C. § 1714 was constitutional.

15. Did the court hold that section to be constitutional, unconstitutional, or unconstitutional in part?

16. State the citation for the A.L.R. annotation that cited 18 U.S.C. § 201(3)(f).

17. How did Congress affect 16 U.S.C. § 659?

18. Cite the session law (*Statutes at Large* reference) that amended 15 U.S.C. § 1703.

Using Shepard's Federal Citations, *answer the following questions:*

19. Shepardize 594 F. Supp. 226. Cite that case in proper citation format (including the parallel citation).

20. What happened to that case on appeal?

21. What is the citation in *Shepard's* to the appeals case?

22. Has the cited case been cited in any dissenting opinion?

23. What is the citation in *Shepard's* to that case?

24. The citing case at 637 F. Supp. 564 referred to what headnote in the cited case? What West topic and key number are assigned to that headnote in the cited case?

25. Give the citation in proper format for the citing case.

Group B

Using Shepard's United States Citations: Case Edition, *answer the following questions:*

1.   Give the parallel citations for 81 S. Ct. 1122.

2.   Has this case ever been cited by a Seventh Circuit District Court?

3.   What headnote from the cited case did the Seventh Circuit court refer to in its opinion?

4. Using *Shepard's United States Supreme Court Case Names Citator*, give the complete citation (i.e., both official *and* unofficial citations) for *Mapp v. Ohio*.

Using Shepard's Federal Citations, *answer the following questions:*

5. State the citation of the A.L.R. annotation that cited 328 F.2d 844.

6. Trace the direct history of 71 F.R.D. 357 and indicate the higher court's decision on appeal.

7. Was that case cited by the First Circuit Court of Appeals?

8. Was that case cited by a text or periodical? If so, give the title.

9. What was the higher court's treatment of 799 F. Supp. 1364 on appeal? Give the citation of the citing case.

10. What was the higher court's treatment of 798 F. Supp. 762 on appeal? Give the citation of the citing case.

11. What was the higher court's treatment of 792 F. Supp. 161 on appeal? Give the citation of the citing case.

12. What was the higher court's treatment of 798 F. Supp. 904 on appeal? Give the citation of the citing case.

13. Sheperdize 767 F. Supp. 17. A connected case is from which state? Give the regional citation for that case.

Using Shepard's United States Citations: Statute Edition, *answer the following questions:*

14. State the citation of the citing opinion that decided whether 17 U.S.C. § 601 was constitutional.

15. Did the court hold that section to be constitutional, unconstitutional, or unconstitutional in part?

16. State the citation for the A.L.R. annotation that cited 21 U.S.C. § 849.

17. How did Congress affect 11 U.S.C. § 15704?

18. Cite the session law (*Statutes at Large* reference) that amended 11 U.S.C. § 15704.

Using Shepard's Atlantic Reporter Citations, *answer the following questions:*

19. Sheperdize 419 A.2d 18. Cite that case in proper citation format (including the parallel citation).

20. What happened to that case on appeal?

21. What is the citation in *Shepard's* to the appeals case?

22. Has the cited case been cited in any dissenting opinion?

23. What is the citation in *Shepard's* to that case?

24. The citing case at 451 A.2d 680 referred to what headnote in the cited case? What West topic and key number are assigned to that headnote in the cited case?

25. Give the citation in proper format for the citing case.

Group C

Using Shepard's United States Citations: Case Edition, *answer the following questions:*

1. Give the parallel citations for 88 S. Ct. 2084.

2. Has this case ever been cited by a Sixth Circuit District Court?

3. What headnote from the cited case did the Sixth Circuit court refer to in its opinion?

4. Using *Shepard's United States Supreme Court Names Citator*, give the complete citation (i.e., official *and* unofficial citations) for *Erie Railway Co. v. Tompkins*.

Using Shepard's Federal Citations, *answer the following questions:*

5. State the citation of the A.L.R. annotation that cited 258 F.2d 918.

6. Trace the direct history of 141 F.R.D. 107 and indicate the higher court's decision on appeal.

7. Was that case cited by the Eighth Circuit Court of Appeals?

8. Was that case cited by a text or periodical? If so, give its title.

9. What was the higher court's treatment of 799 F. Supp. 39 on appeal? Give the citation of the citing case.

10. What was the higher court's treatment of 791 F. Supp. 238 on appeal? Give the citation of the citing case.

11. What was the higher court's treatment of 789 F. Supp. 856 on appeal? Give the citation of the citing case.

12. What was the higher court's treatment of 794 F. Supp. 321 on appeal? Give the citation of the citing case.

13. Shepardize 740 F. Supp. 694. A connected case is from which state? Give the regional citation for that case.

Using Shepard's United States Citations: Statute Edition, *answer the following questions:*

14. State the citation of the citing opinion that decided whether 5 U.S.C. § 8312 was constitutional.

15. Did the court hold that section to be constitutional, unconstitutional, or unconstitutional in part?

16. State the citation for the A.L.R. annotation that cited 1 U.S.C. § 113.

17. How did Congress affect 5 U.S.C. § 906(a)?

18. Cite the session law (*Statutes at Large* reference) that amended 7 U.S.C. § 13c(a).

Using Shepard's Northwestern Reporter Citations, *answer the following questions:*

19. Shepardize 445 N.W.2d 428. Cite that case in proper citation format (including the parallel citation).

20. What happened to that case on appeal?

21. What is the citation in *Shepard's* to the appeals case?

22. Has the cited case been cited in any dissenting opinion?

23. What is the citation in *Shepard's* to that case?

24. The citing case at 466 N.W.2d 296 referred to what headnote in the cited case? What West topic and key number are assigned to that headnote in the cited case?

25. Give the citation in proper format for the citing case.

Group D

Using Shepard's United States Citations: Case Edition, *answer the following questions:*

1. Give the parallel citations for 96 S. Ct. 943.

2. Has this case ever been cited by a Fifth Circuit Court of Appeals?

3. What headnote from the cited case did the Fifth Circuit court refer to in its opinion?

4. Using *Shepard's United States Supreme Court Case Names Citator*, give the complete citation (i.e., both official *and* unofficial citations) for *Miranda v. Arizona*.

Using Shepard's Federal Citations, *answer the following questions:*

5. State the citation of the A.L.R. annotation that cited 42 F.2d 461.

6. Trace the direct history of 98 F.R.D. 48 and indicate the higher court's decision on appeal.

7. Was that case cited by the Ninth Circuit Court of Appeals?

8. Was that case cited by a text or periodical? If so, give the title.

9. What was the higher court's treatment of 798 F. Supp. 1019 on appeal? Give the citation of the citing case.

10. What was the higher court's treatment of 784 F. Supp. 1533 on appeal? Give the citation of the citing case.

11. What was the higher court's treatment of 788 F. Supp. 1112 on appeal? Give the citation of the citing case.

12. What was the higher court's treatment of 793 F. Supp. 894 on appeal? Give the citation of the citing case.

13. Shepardize 795 F. Supp. 953. A connected case is from which state? Give the regional citation for that case.

Using Shepard's United States Citations: Statute Edition, *answer the following questions:*

14. State the citation of the citing opinion that decided whether 33 U.S.C. § 1319(b) was constitutional.

15. Did the court hold that section to be constitutional, unconstitutional, or unconstitutional in part?

16. State the citation for the A.L.R. annotation that cited 45 U.S.C. § 159.

17. How did Congress affect 46 U.S.C. § 16?

18. Cite the session law (*Statutes at Large* reference) that amended 46 U.S.C. § 816.

Using Shepard's Pacific Reporter Citations, *answer the following questions:*

19. Shepardize 581 P.2d 1074. Cite that case in proper citation format (including the parallel citation).

20. What happened to that case on appeal?

21. What is the citation in *Shepard's* to the appeals case?

22. Has the cited case been cited in any dissenting opinion?

23. What is the citation in *Shepard's* to that case?

24. The citing case at 617 P.2d 448 referred to what headnote in the cited case? What West topic and key number are assigned to that headnote in the cited case?

25. Give the citation in proper format for the citing case.

Group E

Using Shepard's United States Citations: Case Edition, *answer the following questions:*

1. Give the parallel citations for 103 S. Ct. 281.

2. Has this case ever been cited by a Sixth Circuit Court of Appeals?

3. What headnote from the cited case did the Sixth Circuit court refer to in its opinion?

4. Using *Shepard's United States Supreme Court Case Names Citator*, give the complete citation (i.e., both official *and* unofficial citations) for *Buckley v. Valeo.*

Using Shepard's Federal Citations, *answer the following questions:*

5. State the citation of the A.L.R. annotation that cited 83 F.2d 961.

6. Trace the direct history of 125 F.R.D. 687 and indicate the higher court's decision on appeal.

7. Was that case cited by the Fourth Circuit Court of Appeals?

8. Was that case cited by a text or periodical? If so, give the title.

9. What was the higher court's treatment of 794 F. Supp. 85 on appeal? Give the citation of the citing case.

10. What was the higher court's treatment of 783 F. Supp. 1511 on appeal? Give the citation of the citing case.

11. What was the higher court's treatment of 771 F. Supp. 1520 on appeal? Give the citation of the citing case.

12. What was the higher court's treatment of 787 F. Supp. 458 on appeal? Give the citation of the citing case.

13. Shepardize 727 F. Supp. 999. A connected case is from which state? Give the regional citation for that case.

Using Shepard's United States Citations: Statute Edition, *answer the following questions:*

14. State the citation of the citing opinion that decided whether 26 U.S.C. § 3505(b) was constitutional.

15. Did the court hold that section to be constitutional, unconstitutional, or unconstitutional in part?

16. State the citation for the A.L.R. annotation that cited 26 U.S.C. § 521.

17. How did Congress affect 26 U.S.C. § 6532(c)?

18. Cite the session law (*Statutes at Large* reference) that amended 28 U.S.C. § 1541.

Using Shepard's Southeastern Reporter Citations, *answer the following questions:*

19. Shepardize 284 S.E.2d 188. Cite that case in proper citation format (including the parallel citation).

20. What happened to that case on appeal?

21. What is the citation in *Shepard's* to the appeals case?

22. Has the cited case been cited in any dissenting opinion?

23. What is the citation in *Shepard's* to that case?

24. The citing case at 318 S.E.2d 531 referred to what headnote in the cited case? What West topic and key number are assigned to that headnote in the cited case?

25. Give the citation in proper format for the citing case.

ANSWERS TO TEST YOUR KNOWLEDGE QUESTIONS

1. False
2. True
3. True
4. True
5. False
6. Step 1 - Select the appropriate citator.
   Step 2 - Check all relevant volumes of the set.
   Step 3 - Look up the citation.
   Step 4 - Check for abbreviations and superscript numbers.
   Step 5 - Repeat the process in each volume.
7. (1) To update research (ascertain current status and validity);
   (2) To find parallel case citation(s); and
   (3) To find primary and secondary authority that cites the cited source as a research tool.
8. *National Reporter Blue Book*
9. Insta-Cite and Auto-Cite
10. shepardizing

CHAPTER 9

TEST YOUR KNOWLEDGE QUESTIONS

1. Paralegals will find model forms in a _____.

2. A _____ typically deals with rules and procedure questions in a particular court or jurisdiction.

3. A _____ provides synonyms and antonyms.

4. A paralegal would consult a _____ to find information about a particular lawyer or law firm.

5. The *Martindale-Hubbell Law Directory* contains _____, which summarize the statutory law of all fifty states, the Canadian provinces, and numerous other countries.

6. A form book might prove helpful in drafting the following:

   a. a will
   b. a complaint
   c. interrogatories
   d. jury instructions
   e. all of the above

7. The researcher seeking to prepare for trial would do best to consult which of the following:

   a. a form book
   b. a practice guide
   c. a trial practice book
   d. a law directory
   e. a desk reference

8. Which of the following is *not* a primary use of *Proof of Facts*?

   a. finding sample questions to ask a client or witness
   b. reading articles offering practical and technical background information
   c. finding citations to other Lawyers Cooperative publications such as A.L.R.s
   d. finding sample forms
   e. finding citations to law review articles

9. Pattern or model jury instructions are available for all federal and state courts.
   T___ /F___

10. A form should be used only as a guide, and not necessarily copied verbatim.
    T___ /F___

LEGAL RESEARCH EXERCISES

Group A

1. Using the general index to *West's Legal Forms*, find the statutory form for a Kentucky Designation of Health Care Surrogate. Provide the citation to that form.

2. Using the general index to *Am. Jur. Legal Forms 2d*, find a sample form of agreement between a news syndicate and a newspaper for supplying the work product of a cartoonist or columnist. Provide the citation to that form.

3. Using the index to *Bender's Federal Practice Forms*, find a sample complaint under the Fair Credit Reporting Act. Provide the citation to that form.

4. Using the general index to *Am. Jur. Pleading and Practice Forms*, find a sample form vacating an adoption where a defect in the child was discovered after the adoption was finalized. Provide the citation to that form.

5. Using the general index to *Federal Procedural Forms—Lawyers' Edition*, find a sample form for trust agreement for use with one or more letters of credit in lieu of bond under the Packers and Stockyards Act. Provide the citation to that form.

6. Using the index to volume 7 of *West's Federal Forms*, find a sample motion for permission to remove equipment from a vessel. Provide the citation to that form.

7. Using the index to volumes 1–10 of *Bender's Forms of Discovery*, find sample defendant's interrogatories to plaintiff in a case involving the explosion of a beverage bottle. Provide the citation.

8. Using the general index to *Am. Jur. Trials*, find information on the procedural requirements of petitioning for certiorari in a mail fraud appeal. Provide the citation.

9. Is there a sample form available?

10. Find an article in *Proof of Facts 2d* concerning employer's discriminatory appearance codes. Provide the citation.

11. Are there any references to litigation form books in the Collateral References section of the article? If so, list the title of one of them.

12. Using the index to the article, determine who bears the initial burden of proof in a prima facie case of employer discrimination under Title VII. Cite the section of the article in which you found the answer.

13. Using the index to the article, determine whether there is any mention in the article of cases involving appearance codes proscribing facial hair. If so, cite the section of the article. Give the citation to a federal case from the District of Columbia.

14. Using the *Law Digests* volume of the *Martindale-Hubbell Law Directory*, determine the minimum age of competence under Irish law for making a valid will.

15. Using the current edition of *Black's Law Dictionary*, give the first definition and first case citation listed under "attestation of will."

Group B

1. Using the general index to *West's Legal Forms*, find a sample form for a computer software maintenance agreement. Provide the citation to that form.

2. Using the general index to *Am. Jur. Legal Forms 2d*, find a sample form of agreement for a franchisee's responsibility to provide for insurance. Provide the citation to that form.

3. Using the index to *Bender's Federal Practice Forms*, find a sample order granting dismissal for failure to prosecute. Provide the citation to that form.

4. Using the general index to *Am. Jur. Pleading and Practice Forms*, find a sample class action complaint by shareholders for failure to apportion profits fairly. Provide the citation to that form.

5. Using the general index to *Federal Procedural Forms—Lawyers' Edition*, find a sample form of psychiatrist's affidavit in support of a motion for mental examination. Provide the citation to that form.

6. Using the index to volume 6A of *West's Federal Forms*, find a sample motion to avoid a lien on and to redeem exempt property in a bankruptcy proceeding. Provide the citation to that form.

7. Using the index to volumes 1–10 of *Bender's Forms of Discovery*, find sample plaintiff's interrogatories to defendant in a case involving a train collision with a bicycle. Provide the citation.

8. Using the general index to *Am. Jur. Trials*, find information on drafting a motion for summary judgment by defense counsel in a litigation involving a pitbull dog attack. Provide the citation.

9. Is there a sample form available?

10. Find an article in *Proof of Facts 2d* concerning an award of punitive damages in an aggravated wrongful detention case. Provide the citation.

11. Are there any references to litigation form books in the Collateral References section of the article? If so, list the title of one of them.

12. Using the index to the article, determine who has the burden of proving probable cause in a jurisdiction like California. Cite the section of the article in which you found the answer.

13. Using the index to the article, determine whether rudeness on the part of the store personnel in detaining a suspect has ever been held to be a factor in determining that the manner of detention was unreasonable. If so, cite the section of the article. Give the citation of a case from Florida.

14. Using the *Law Digests* volume of the *Martindale-Hubbell Law Directory*, determine what persons under Guatemalan law have the authority to perform a ceremonial marriage.

15. Using the current edition of *Black's Law Dictionary*, give the first definition and first case citation listed under "change of circumstances."

Group C

1. Using the general index to *West's Legal Forms*, find a sample form of Articles of Incorporation for a cooperative apartment. Provide the citation to that form.

2. Using the general index to *Am. Jur. Legal Forms 2d*, find an American Medical Association model form of consent to operation for cosmetic purposes. Provide the citation to that form.

3. Using the index to *Bender's Federal Practice Forms*, find a sample writ of garnishment in an action for replevin. Provide the citation to that form.

4. Using the general index to *Am. Jur. Pleading and Practice Forms*, find a sample form of complaint against a railroad for interference with the extinguishment of fires. Provide the citation to that form.

5. Using the general index to *Federal Procedural Forms—Lawyers' Edition*, find a sample class action complaint for declaratory and injunctive relief and damages for racially discriminatory lending practices of a mortgage lender. Provide the citation to that form.

6. Using the index to volume 5A of *West's Federal Forms*, find a sample application for appointment of counsel for an indigent defendant. Provide the citation to that form.

7. Using the index to volumes 1–10 of *Bender's Forms of Discovery*, find sample plaintiff next friend's interrogatories to defendant in a case involving the sexual molestation of a child in a day care center. Provide the citation.

8. Using the general index to *Am. Jur. Trials*, find information on obtaining a gag order on publicity in defending a bribery prosecution. Provide the citation.

9. Is there a sample form available?

10. Find an article in *Proof of Facts 2d* concerning the equitable adoption of a child by its foster parent. Provide the citation.

11. Are there any references to litigation form books in the Collateral References section of the article? If so, list the title of one of them.

12. Using the index to the article, determine who bears the burden of proving that a contract to adopt was made between competent parties. Cite the section of the article in which you found the answer.

13. Using the index to the article, determine whether, when there has been an adequate part performance of the adoption contract, one of the factors considered is whether the child remains close to the foster parent after reaching adulthood. If so, cite the section of the article. Give the citation to a case from Arizona.

14. Using the *Law Digests* volume of the *Martindale-Hubbell Law Directory*, determine whether marriage by proxy is allowed under Hungarian law.

15. Using the current edition of *Black's Law Dictionary*, give the first definition and first case citation listed under "legal capacity to sue."

Group D

1. Using the general index to *West's Legal Forms*, find a sample form for an employment at will agreement. Provide the citation to that form.

2. Using the general index to *Am. Jur. Legal Forms 2d*, find a statutory mortgage form for Colorado. Provide the citation to that form.

3. Using the index to *Bender's Federal Practice Forms*, find a sample complaint for the infringement of registration of a service mark. Provide the citation to that form.

4. Using the general index to *Am. Jur. Pleading and Practice Forms*, find a sample complaint for wrongful life against a hospital and physician for failure to diagnose rubella and to inform the patient of its effects on the fetus. Provide the citation to that form.

5. Using the general index to *Federal Procedural Forms—Lawyers' Edition*, find a sample complaint for interference with a competitor's contract for the supply of raw materials. Provide the citation to that form.

6. Using the index to volume 1B of *West's Federal Forms*, find a sample notice of appeal after mandate in the United States Tax Court. Provide the citation to that form.

7. Using the index to volumes 11–16 of *Bender's Forms of Discovery*, find a sample affidavit supporting opposition to a motion to compel production on the ground of attorney-client privilege. Provide the citation.

8. Using the general index to *Am. Jur. Trials*, find information on the requisite notice and its publication in a mass disaster class action. Provide the citation.

9. Is there a sample form available?

10. Find an article in *Proof of Facts 2d* concerning the existence of grounds for an annulment of marriage. Provide the citation.

11. Are there any references to litigation form books in the Collateral References section of the article? If so, list the title of one of them.

12. Using the index to the article, determine who has the burden of proof in cases alleging the physical incapacity of the spouse. Cite the section of the article in which you found the answer.

13. Using the index to the article, determine whether it has been held in any jurisdiction that the undisclosed intent on the part of one of the parties to the marriage not to have children was sufficient fraud to warrant an annulment. If so, cite the section of the article. Give the citation to a case from the District of Columbia.

14. Using the *Law Digests* volume of the *Martindale-Hubbell Law Directory*, determine the two methods allowed under Thai law for filing for divorce.

15. Using the current edition of *Black's Law Dictionary*, give the first definition and case citation listed under "equitable assignment."

Group E

1. Using the general index to *West's Legal Forms*, find a sample form for surrender of lease. Provide the citation to that form.

2. Using the general index to *Am. Jur. Legal Forms 2d*, find a sample form of contract for maintenance of an automatic temperature control system. Provide the citation to that form.

3. Using the index to *Bender's Federal Practice Forms*, find a set of sample interrogatories to discover the name of an expert witness. Provide the citation to that form.

4. Using the general index to *Am. Jur. Pleading and Practice Forms*, find a sample form for complaint by pedestrian injured by ice and snow falling from a building. Provide the citation to that form.

5. Using the general index to *Federal Procedural Forms—Lawyers' Edition*, find a sample complaint to enjoin infringement of copyright for a motion picture. Provide the citation to that form.

6. Using the index to volume 1A of *West's Federal Forms*, find a sample motion for leave to file out-of-time or consecutive petition for rehearing in the United States Supreme Court. Provide the citation to that form.

7. Using the index to volumes 11–16 of *Bender's Forms of Discovery*, find a sample order granting leave to videotape a deposition. Provide the citation.

8. Using the general index to *Am. Jur. Trials*, find information on drafting interrogatories to be submitted in a helicopter accident case. Provide the citation.

9. Is there a sample form available?

10. Find an article in *Proof of Facts 2d* concerning whether extreme hardship exists that will warrant the suspension of deportation of an otherwise deportable alien. Provide the citation.

11. Are there any references to litigation form books in the Collateral References section of the article? If so, list the title of one of them.

12. Using the index to the article, determine who has the burden of proof of establishing eligibility for such relief. Cite the section of the article in which you found the answer.

13. Using the index to the article, determine whether an alien's dependence on public assistance can be relied on by the Immigration and Naturalization Service in denying an application for suspension of deportation. If so, cite the section of the article. Give the citation of a federal case from the Third Circuit.

14. Using the *Law Digests* volume of the *Martindale-Hubbell Law Directory*, determine at what age a South African citizen may marry without parental consent.

15. Using the current edition of *Black's Law Dictionary*, give the first definition and first case citation listed under "strict liability."

ANSWERS TO TEST YOUR KNOWLEDGE QUESTIONS

1. form book
2. practice guide
3. legal thesaurus
4. law directory
5. law digests
6. e
7. c
8. d
9. False
10. True

CHAPTER 10

TEST YOUR KNOWLEDGE QUESTIONS

1. There is only one way to perform legal research. T___ /F___

2. The first step in performing legal research is to ascertain all the relevant facts.
   T___ /F___

3. In a new area of law, usually the best approach is to consult a descriptive-word index.
   T___ /F___

4. Primary and secondary authorities are equally valuable to the legal researcher.
   T___ /F___

5. In researching an unfamiliar area of law, it is often advisable for the legal researcher to consult secondary source material first. T___ /F___

6. A(n) _____ is a legal question that is posed by the facts.

7. In order to understand specialized legal vocabulary, a legal researcher often must consult a _____ or a _____.

8. Generally the final step in any legal research project is to update and verify all sources found by consulting _____.

9. What are the two threshold questions that every legal researcher should answer before proceeding with any research?

10. Name three basic case-finding tools that can be used in legal research.

LEGAL RESEARCH EXERCISES

The following Legal Research Final Projects are designed to test your research skills. Your instructor may assign more than one of the five projects, or you may decide to try your hand at all of them to practice your new skills. A good way to keep track of your research is to maintain an ongoing list of sources consulted and results found. Be sure to update each source and verify it before handing in a report or memorandum detailing what you found. Following is a sample worksheet that can be used. Your instructor may require that you turn in a worksheet as well as a memorandum.

WORKSHEET

Sources consulted	Words used	Information found	Shepardizing completed

LEGAL RESEARCH FINAL PROJECTS

Group A

Our client is an unmarried woman who has been living with her live-in boyfriend for nearly twenty years. They do not claim to have a common law marriage; rather, they are cohabitants, and each considers the other to be a "domestic partner." They own property together and share all living expenses. Our client's boyfriend has been severely injured in an auto accident caused by the other driver. He is suing the driver for negligence (and in all likelihood will win). Our client wishes to sue the driver in a companion suit for loss of consortium due to her boyfriend's injuries. Research the law across the country, focusing primarily on the law (if any) in your state. Use all resources available to you, and draft a simple memorandum of law describing the status of the law on this subject in your state and in other states. Cite all sources in proper *Bluebook* form.

Group B

Our client is the divorced noncustodial parent of a college sophomore who is nineteen years old. The child is suing our client to force him to pay for the child's college education expenses. Our client feels his obligation to support his child financially ceased when the child reached the age of majority at eighteen. There is no written agreement with either the child or the child's mother specifying that our client would do such a thing, nor does the divorce decree require it. Research the law across the country, focusing primarily on the law (if any) in your state. Use all resources available to you, and draft a simple memorandum of law describing the status of the law on this subject in your state and in other states. Cite all sources in proper *Bluebook* form.

Group C

Our client is the owner of a healthy, lovable, two-year-old, mixed-breed family dog. During a recent operation to remove ingrown dewclaws, the veterinarian inadvertently gave the animal too much anesthesia, causing the dog to die. Our client wishes to find out whether she can recover against her vet for the loss of her companion animal due to veterinary malpractice. Research the law across the country, focusing primarily on the law (if any) in your state. Use all resources available to you, and draft a simple memorandum of law describing the status of the law on this subject in your state and in other states. Cite all sources in proper *Bluebook* form.

Group D

Our client is a gay man who has been living with his significant other for over ten years. They regard themselves as a couple and hold themselves out to the community at large as such. For a variety of reasons, the couple would like to be legally married. Our client asks us to investigate whether marriages between same-sex couples can be performed. Research the law across the country, focusing primarily on the law (if any) in your state. Use all resources available to you, and draft a simple memorandum of law describing the status of the law on this subject in your state and in other states. Cite all sources in proper *Bluebook* form.

Group E

Our client is the member of a religious sect that does not believe in blood transfusions. Her ten-year-old child, for whom she is the sole legal parent or guardian, is suffering from a disease that is not fatal but the effects of which are severe, and the disease can be treated effectively only with periodic blood transfusions. The child's grandparents have petitioned the court to require our client to allow blood transfusions to be administered to the child over our client's religious objections. Our client wants to know the likelihood of the court granting this request. Research the law across the country, focusing primarily on the law (if any) in your state. Use all resources available to you, and draft a simple memorandum of law describing the status of the law on this subject in your state and in other states. Cite all sources in proper *Bluebook* form.

ANSWERS TO TEST YOUR KNOWLEDGE QUESTIONS

1. False
2. True
3. True
4. False
5. True
6. issue
7. legal dictionary, legal thesaurus
8. *Shepard's Citators*
9. (1) What is the source authority?
   (2) What jurisdiction's law will determine the outcome of the case?
10. digests, legal encyclopedias, *American Law Reports*, treatises, C.L.E. materials, law reviews, computer services

GLOSSARY

administrative agency† A private organization or unit of government organized to provide a particular service or type of service.

administrative codes The published regulations of administrative agencies, arranged by subject matter.

administrative decision† The conclusion of a hearing officer in an administrative agency proceeding.

administrative opinion A formal or informal opinion statement made by an administrative agency to parties regarding the consequences of the parties' actions.

administrative ruling† A determination made by a hearing officer during the course of an administrative agency hearing.

advance sheets† Printed copies of judicial opinions published in looseleaf form shortly after the opinions are issued. These published opinions are later collected and published in bound form with the other reported cases which are issued over a longer period of time.

affirm† In the case of an appellate court, to uphold the decision or judgment of the lower court after an appeal.

agency regulations Regulations promulgated by an administrative agency that define the scope of that agency's discretion.

agency rules Rules established by an administrative agency that govern practice before that agency.

annotated codes† Books or volumes that contain both statutes and commentaries upon the statutes.

anonymous Ftp (file transfer protocol) A procedure by which files at universities, libraries, and businesses that are publicly available can be accessed and downloaded onto a personal computer through the Internet.

appellant† A party who appeals from a lower court to a higher court.

appellate court† A higher court to which an appeal is taken from a lower court.

appellee† A party against whom a case is appealed from a lower court to a higher court.

Bill of Rights† The first ten amendments to the United States Constitution, which set forth the fundamental rights of American citizens.

bills† Proposed laws that are presented to the legislature for enactment.

binding authority† Previous decisions of a higher court or statutes that a judge must follow in reaching a decision in a case.

black letter law† Fundamental and well-established rules of law.

brief† A written statement submitted to a court for the purpose of persuading it of the correctness of one's position. A brief argues the facts of the case and the applicable law, supported by citations of authority.

caption The heading of a case that contains information such as the parties' names, the court, and the date.

case† A contested question in a court of justice, a lawsuit; the written opinion of a judge or court deciding or commenting on a lawsuit.

case syllabus A short summary of the facts, issues, and disposition of a case that is written by the editor of the reporter in which the case appears.

CD-ROM (Compact Disc with Read-Only Memory) A technology by which information is stored on a plastic disc and a laser beam reads the information from that disc.

Circuit Court of Appeals† The former name of the intermediate federal appellate courts, now called the Court of Appeals of the United States.

citation† Reference to authority (a case, article, or other text) on a point of law, by name, volume, and page or section of the court report or other book in which it appears.

citator† A system of books, the use of which allows a person doing legal research to locate every court opinion in which a particular case is cited, and to determine the context in which it is cited as well as whether it has been affirmed, distinguished, followed, overruled, or simply mentioned.

cited source† A document that is shepardized; the document to which a Shepard's entry (a citing course) refers.

citing source† A document that is entered in Shepard's because it makes reference to another document (the cited source).

C.L.E. materials Books and pamphlets containing materials prepared by panelists for continuing legal education seminars.

code† The published statutes of a jurisdiction, arranged in systematic form.

Code of Federal Regulations (C.F.R.)† An arrangement, by subject matter, of the rules and regulations issued by federal administrative agencies.

committee print A study of proposed legislation commissioned by a committee and conducted by the committee staff or by outside consultants.

committee report A written report of a committee analyzing and discussing proposed legislation, and recommending whether or not it should be passed.

common law† Law found in the decisions of the courts rather than in statutes; judge-made law.

compilation† A collection of statutes or data.

computer-assisted legal research (CALR) Research by legal professionals that is conducted with the use of computers, computer networks, and CD-ROM.

concept ranking A feature of computer software programs by which documents are ranked according to how likely they are to be relevant to the legal issue in question.

concurrent resolution A resolution that originates and is passed by one house of Congress and is sent to the other house for its concurrence.

connector A word that tells a computer to search for documents containing multiple words or terms or a combination of words or terms.

constitution† The system of fundamental principles by which a nation, state, or corporation is governed. A nation's laws must conform to its constitution.

Constitution of the United States† The fundamental document of American government, as adopted by the people of the United States through their representatives in the Constitutional Convention of 1787, as ratified by the states, together with the amendments to that Constitution.

court rules† Rules promulgated by the court, governing procedure or practice before it.

database A compilation of searchable information found in a computer's memory.

deposition† The transcript of a witness's testimony given under oath outside of the courtroom, usually in advance of the trial or hearing, upon oral examination or in response to written interrogatories.

deskbook A booklet that contains the rules of trial and appellate procedure, the rules of evidence, ethical canons, and other pertinent rules for a particular jurisdiction.

desk reference A reference book that contains information about the court system, federal and state agencies, statistical information, medical diagrams, financial tables, and other reference materials.

digest† A series of volumes containing summaries of cases organized by legal topics, subject areas, and so on. Digists are essential for legal research.

discovery† A means for providing a party, in advance of trial, with access to facts that are within the knowledge of the other side, to enable the party to better try his or her case.

District Courts of the United States† Officially termed United States District Courts, the courts or original jurisdiction for both criminal prosecutions and civil cases arising under federal statutes, cases involving federal constitutional questions, and suits by and against citizens of different states. Each state and territory, and the District of Columbia, has at least one federal judicial district.

diversity case A federal lawsuit involving parties who live in different states.

executive agency An administrative agency that is set up as part of the executive branch of government.

expander A character or symbol that tells a computer to search for documents containing variations or derivatives of words.

federal depository library A library that has agreed to keep federal documents for use by the public.

Federal Register† An official publication, printed daily, containing regulations and proposed regulations issued by administrative agencies, as well as other rulemaking and other official business of the executive branch of government. All regulations are ultimately published in the Code of Federal Regulations.

federal statutes Laws enacted by the United States Congress that pertain to national concerns.

fields The term used to describe the subdivisions of documents in the WESTLAW computer program.

files The term used to describe subdivisions of a library (database) in the LEXIS computer program; narrower collections of documents.

grammatical connector A word that tells a computer to search for documents in which multiple words or terms appear in the same sentence or paragraph.

headnote† A summary statement that appears at the beginning of a reported case to indicate the points decided by the case.

hearing† A proceeding in which evidence is introduced and witnesses are examined so that findings of fact can be made and a determination rendered.

history (direct history) of a case† The path a particular case takes through the court system.

holding† The proposition of law for which a case stands; the "bottom line" of a judicial decision.

hornbook† A book that explains the fundamental aspects of an area or field of the law in basic terms. A hornbook is usually concise.

independent agency An administrative agency established by Congress that is given powers to act without political interference from the traditional branches of government.

injunction† A court order that commands or prohibits some act or course of conduct.

Internet A computer network linking over 30,000 computer networks together that is opening new opportunities for legal and non-legal research.

interrogatories† Written questions put by one party to another, or, in limited situations, to a witness in advance of trial; a form of discovery.

joint resolution A resolution adopted by both houses of Congress. If it has been approved by the president, it has the effect of law.

jurisdiction† The right of a court to adjudicate lawsuits of a certain kind; the right of a court to determine a particular case; the power of a court to hear cases only within a specific territorial area.

jury instructions† Directions given to the jury by the judge just before he or she sends the jurors out to deliberate and return a verdict, explaining the law that applies in the case and spelling out what must be proven and by whom.

law† The entire body of rules of conduct created by government and enforced by the authority of government.

legal issue† A question arising in a case with respect to the law to be applied or the meaning of the law.

library The name given to describe a database, or a compilation of searchable information, in the LEXIS computer program.

looseleaf services Legal books published in binder format that comprehensively cover the different aspects of a particular area of law.

looseleaf system A method used by publishers for updating looseleaf volumes by which pages with new information replace pages with outdated information.

model code Model legislation that is written from the perspective of how the law should be ideally written.

municipal charter† The basic law of a local unit of government, such as a city or town.

natural language or relevance A method by which a user can command a computer to search all the documents in a database using a sentence that is descriptive of the legal issue in question.

noise or stop words Words (such as the, one, he, she, or, it) that cannot be searched on either the LEXIS or the WESTLAW computer programs.

numerical connector A command that tells a computer to search for documents in which words or terms appear within a specified number of words of each other.

obiter dictum† Means "A comment in passing."

offical source Publications in which the government requires that the law be published.

on-line Used to describe a researcher who is using a computer, usually a personal computer (PC), to connect by a modem with the memory of another computer stored at a remote location.

ordinance† A law of a municipal corporation; a local law enacted by a city council, town council, board of supervisors, or the like.

parallel citation† A citation to a court opinion or decision that is printed in two or more reporters.

pattern or model jury instructions† In many jurisdictions, sample jury instruc- tions that trial judges are required to follow when charging a jury.

persuasive authority Authority that is neither binding authority nor precedent, but which a court may use to support its decision if it chooses.†

pocket part A pamphlet designed to fit in a pocket holder in the back of a book that enables publishers to update volumes without replacing the whole book.

positive law† Legislation, as opposed to natural law or moral law; unquestionable as evidence, as opposed to presumptive or probable evidence.

practice manual or guide A book or set of books that provides practical step-by-step information and how-to advice in a specific area of the law.

precedent† Prior decisions of the same court, or a higher court, which a judge must follow in deciding a subsequent case presenting similar facts and the same legal problem, even though different parties are involved and many years have elapsed.

presumptive evidence† Evidence that the law regards as proof unless it is rebutted; probable evidence.

primary source Actual law, such as a case, statute, ordinance, or regulation, as opposed to a secondary source that interprets or explains the law.

procedural law† The law governing the manner in which rights are enforced; the law prescribing the procedure to be followed in a case. Also called adjective law, procedural law dictates *how* rights are *presented* for interpretation and enforcement, as distinguished from substantive law, which *creates* legal rights.

procedural posture The present status (or stage) of a case.

query or search request A command that tells a computer to search for a particular word or phrase.

register† A book of records, particularly official records or public records; an official list; a registry.

regulation† A rule having the force of law, promulgated by an administrative agency; a rule of conduct established by a person or body in authority for the governance of those over whom they have authority.

remand† The return of a case by an appellate court to the trial court for further proceedings, for a new trial, or for entry of judgment in accordance with an order of the appellate court.

replacement volume A book produced by a legal publisher and sent to subscribers to replace a different version of the same book that now has outdated information.

reporters† Sets of books containing official, published reports of cases.

reverse† To overthrow, vacate, annul, nullify, transpose, disaffirm ("to reverse a prior decision").

scope note A note following a heading in a reference book that describes what is covered under that particular topic.

search word or term A method by which a user can command a computer to search all the documents in a database for a certain word or phrase.

secondary source† Publications that do not contain the law itself, but simply comment upon or summarize the law.

segments The term used to describe the subdivisions of documents in the LEXIS computer program.

session laws† The collected statutes enacted during a session of a legislature, arranged in chronological order.

shepardizing† A method of updating law using a citator.

simple resolution A motion passed by only one body of Congress that is used mainly for procedural housekeeping purposes.

slip opinion† A single judicial decision published shortly after it has been issued by the court and well before it is incorporated into a reporter.

stare decisis† Means "standing by the decision." *Stare decisis* is the doctrine that judicial decisions stand as precedents for cases arising in the future.

star pagination The placement of a star or other mark on the page of an unofficial reporter to show where text pages change in the official reporter.

state constitution The constitution of a state, as opposed to the United States Constitution, that establishes the framework for the state government.

statement of the facts A listing of the events that led to a legal dispute prompting litigation.

state statutes Laws enacted by state legislatures that pertain to state concerns.

statute† A law enacted by a legislature; an act.

Statutes at Large† An official publication of the federal government, issued after each session of Congress, which includes all statutes enacted by the Congress and all congressional resolutions and treaties, as well as presidential proclamations and proposed or ratified amendments to the Constitution.

substantive law† Area of the law that defines right conduct, as opposed to procedural law, which governs the process by which rights are adjudicated.

summary judgment† A method of disposing of an action without further proceedings.

TAPP rule A method for categorizing facts based on the acronym TAPP, which refers to Things, Actions, Persons, and Places.

transaction documents Documents that describe and memorialize business transactions that are prepared to prevent or solve later disputes about the transactions.

treatment (indirect history) of a case The manner in which different courts have treated a case, which will affect the value of the case as a precedent.

trial court† A court that hears and determines a case initially, as opposed to an appellate court; a court of general jurisdiction.

uniform code† Model legislation, the purpose of which is to promote uniformity throughout the country with respect to statutes governing significant areas of the law.

United States Code (U.S.C.)† The official codification of the statutes enacted by Congress.

United States Code Annotated (U.S.C.A.) An annotated version of the United States Code published by West Publishing Company.

United States Code Services (U.S.C.S.) An annotated version of the *United States Code* published by Lawyers Cooperative Publishing Company.

unofficial source Publications of legal material produced by private publishers.

Index

(References in bold indicate illustrations.)

C

D